ISSN 1543-2556

# THE HEALTH CARE SYSTEM

D1495644

Barbara Wexler

**INFORMATION PLUS® REFERENCE SERIES**
Formerly Published by Information Plus, Wylie, Texas

GALE
CENGAGE Learning·

Farmington Hills, Mich • San Francisco • New York • Waterville, Maine
Meriden, Conn • Mason, Ohio • Chicago

**The Health Care System**

Barbara Wexler

Kepos Media, Inc.: Steven Long and Janice Jorgensen, Series Editors

Project Editor: Laura Avery

Rights Acquisition and Management: Ashley M. Maynard, Carissa Poweleit

Composition: Evi Abou-El-Seoud, Mary Beth Trimper

Manufacturing: Rita Wimberley

© 2017 Gale, Cengage Learning

ALL RIGHTS RESERVED. No part of this work covered by the copyright herein may be reproduced or distributed in any form or by any means, except as permitted by U.S. copyright law, without the prior written permission of the copyright owner.

This publication is a creative work fully protected by all applicable copyright laws, as well as by misappropriation, trade secret, unfair competition, and other applicable laws. The authors and editors of this work have added value to the underlying factual material herein through one or more of the following: unique and original selection, coordination, expression, arrangement, and classification of the information.

For product information and technology assistance, contact us at
**Gale Customer Support, 1-800-877-4253.**
For permission to use material from this text or product,
submit all requests online at **www.cengage.com/permissions.**
Further permissions questions can be e-mailed to
**permissionrequest@cengage.com**

Cover photograph: ©Lighthunter/Shutterstock.com.

While every effort has been made to ensure the reliability of the information presented in this publication, Gale, a part of Cengage Learning, does not guarantee the accuracy of the data contained herein. Gale accepts no payment for listing; and inclusion in the publication of any organization, agency, institution, publication, service, or individual does not imply endorsement of the editors or publisher. Errors brought to the attention of the publisher and verified to the satisfaction of the publisher will be corrected in future editions.

Gale
27500 Drake Rd.
Farmington Hills, MI 48331-3535

ISBN-13: 978-0-7876-5103-9 (set)
ISBN-13: 978-1-4103-2553-2

ISSN 1543-2556

This title is also available as an e-book.
ISBN-13: 978-1-4103-3270-7 (set)
Contact your Gale sales representative for ordering information.

Printed in the United States of America
1 2 3 4 5      21 20 19 18 17

CECIL COUNTY
PUBLIC LIBRARY

JUN 0 6 2017

301 Newark Ave
Elkton, MD 21921

# THE HEALTH CARE SYSTEM

JUN 06 2011

# TABLE OF CONTENTS

# PREFACE

*The Health Care System* is part of the *Information Plus Reference Series*. The purpose of each volume of the series is to present the latest facts on a topic of pressing concern in modern American life. These topics include the most controversial and studied social issues of the 21st century: abortion, capital punishment, care for the elderly, child abuse, energy, the environment, gambling, gun control, immigration, national security, social welfare, youth, and many more. Although this series is written especially for high school and undergraduate students, it is an excellent resource for anyone in need of factual information on current affairs.

By presenting the facts, it is the intention of Gale, Cengage Learning, to provide its readers with everything they need to reach an informed opinion on current issues. To that end, there is a particular emphasis in this series on the presentation of scientific studies, surveys, and statistics. These data are generally presented in the form of tables, charts, and other graphics placed within the text of each book. Every graphic is directly referred to and carefully explained in the text. The source of each graphic is presented within the graphic itself. The data used in these graphics are drawn from the most reputable and reliable sources, such as from the various branches of the U.S. government and from private organizations and associations. Every effort has been made to secure the most recent information available. Readers should bear in mind that many major studies take years to conduct and that additional years often pass before the data from these studies are made available to the public. Therefore, in many cases the most recent information available in 2017 is dated from 2014 or 2015. Older statistics are sometimes presented as well, if they are landmark studies or of particular interest and no more-recent information exists.

Although statistics are a major focus of the *Information Plus Reference Series*, they are by no means its only content. Each book also presents the widely held positions and important ideas that shape how the book's subject is discussed in the United States. These positions are explained in detail and, where possible, in the words of their proponents. Some of the other material to be found in these books includes historical background, descriptions of major events related to the subject, relevant laws and court cases, and examples of how these issues play out in American life. Some books also feature primary documents or have pro and con debate sections that provide the words and opinions of prominent Americans on both sides of a controversial topic. All material is presented in an evenhanded and unbiased manner; readers are never be encouraged to accept one view of an issue over another.

## HOW TO USE THIS BOOK

The U.S. health care system is multifaceted and consists of health care providers, patients, and treatment facilities, just to name a few components. This book examines the state of the nation's health care system, the education and training of health care providers, and the various types of health care institutions. Implementation of landmark health care reform legislation, efforts to control the cost of health care, prevalence of insurance, mental health care, and a comparison of health care systems throughout the world are also covered.

*The Health Care System* consists of nine chapters and three appendixes. Each chapter is devoted to a particular aspect of the health care system in the United States. For a summary of the information that is covered in each chapter, please see the synopses that are provided in the Table of Contents. Chapters generally begin with an overview of the basic facts and background information on the chapter's topic, then proceed to examine subtopics of particular interest. For example, Chapter 8: Change, Challenges, and Innovation in Health Care Delivery describes several of the most pressing challenges and opportunities faced by the U.S. health care system, including patient safety and information management. Next, the chapter details the qualities and characteristics of organizational culture that contribute to or detract from patient safety in hospitals. The chapter also looks at plans and programs to improve patient safety by preventing medical errors and adhering to practice guidelines. It also discusses the use of information management technologies to improve communication between health professionals, improve access to care, and educate health professionals and health care consumers. Readers can find their way through a chapter by looking for the section and subsection headings, which are clearly set off from the text. They can also refer to the book's extensive Index if they already know what they are looking for.

## Statistical Information

The tables and figures featured throughout *The Health Care System* will be of particular use to readers in learning about this issue. These tables and figures represent an extensive collection of the most recent and important statistics on the health care system, as well as related issues—for example, graphics cover the rate of supply and demand for registered nurses, the number of emergency department visits, the national health expenditure amounts, the percentage of people without health insurance, the estimated cost of repealing the Affordable Care Act, and public opinion on whether the health care reform law has helped or hurt their families. Gale, Cengage Learning, believes that making this information available to readers is the most important way to fulfill the goal of this book: to help readers understand the issues and controversies surrounding the health care system in the United States and reach their own conclusions.

Each table or figure has a unique identifier appearing above it, for ease of identification and reference. Titles for the tables and figures explain their purpose. At the end of each table or figure, the original source of the data is provided.

To help readers understand these often complicated statistics, all tables and figures are explained in the text. References in the text direct readers to the relevant statistics. Furthermore, the contents of all tables and figures are fully indexed. Please see the opening section of the Index at the back of this volume for a description of how to find tables and figures within it.

## Appendixes

Besides the main body text and images, *The Health Care System* has three appendixes. The first is the Important Names and Addresses directory. Here, readers will find contact information for a number of government and private organizations that can provide further information on aspects of the health care system. The second appendix is the Resources section, which can also assist readers in conducting their own research. In this section, the author and editors of *The Health Care System* describe some of the sources that were most useful during the compilation of this book. The final appendix is the Index. It has been greatly expanded from previous editions and should make it even easier to find specific topics in this book.

## COMMENTS AND SUGGESTIONS

The editors of the *Information Plus Reference Series* welcome your feedback on *The Health Care System*. Please direct all correspondence to:

Editors
*Information Plus Reference Series*
27500 Drake Rd.
Farmington Hills, MI 48331-3535

## CHAPTER 1
# THE U.S. HEALTH CARE SYSTEM

When asked to describe the U.S. health care system, most Americans would probably offer a description of just a single facet of a huge, complex interaction of people, institutions, and technology. Like snapshots, each account offers an image, frozen in time, of one of the many health care providers and the settings in which medical care is delivered. Examples of these include:

- Physician offices: for many Americans, health care may be described as the interaction between a primary care physician and a patient to address minor and urgent medical problems, such as colds, allergies, or back pain. A primary care physician (usually a general practitioner, family practitioner, internist, or pediatrician) is the frontline caregiver—the first practitioner to evaluate and treat the patient. Routine physical examinations, prevention management actions such as immunization and health screening to detect disease, and treatment of acute and chronic diseases commonly take place in physicians' offices.

- Medical clinics: these settings provide primary care services comparable to those provided in physicians' offices and may be organized to deliver specialized support such as prenatal care for expectant mothers, well-baby care for infants, or treatment for specific medical conditions such as hypertension (high blood pressure), diabetes, or asthma.

- Hospitals: these institutions contain laboratories, imaging centers (also known as radiology departments, where x-rays and other imaging studies are performed), and other equipment for diagnosis and treatment, as well as emergency departments, operating rooms, and highly specialized personnel.

Medical care is also provided through many other venues, including outpatient surgical centers, school health programs, pharmacies, urgent care and work-site clinics, and voluntary health agencies such as Planned Parenthood, the American Red Cross, and the American Lung Association.

## IS THE U.S. HEALTH CARE SYSTEM AILING?

Although medical care in the United States is often considered to be the best available, some observers feel the system that delivers it is fragmented and in serious disarray. This section offers some of the many opinions about the challenges of the present health care system and how to improve it. For example, Karen Davis et al. assert in *Mirror, Mirror on the Wall: How the Performance of the U.S. Health Care System Compares Internationally* (June 2014, http://www.commonwealthfund.org/~/media/files/publications/fund-report/2014/jun/1755_davis_mirror_mirror_2014.pdf) that the nation's health care system is the most expensive and ranks last among 11 countries (Australia, Canada, France, Germany, the Netherlands, New Zealand, Norway, Sweden, Switzerland, and the United Kingdom) in terms of access, equity, quality, efficiency, and key health indicators such as mortality amenable to health care (deaths from treatable conditions), infant mortality, and healthy life expectancy at age 60.

According to Gary Claxton et al. of the Kaiser Family Foundation (KFF), in "Measuring the Quality of Healthcare in the U.S." (September 9, 2015, http://www.healthsystemtracker.org/insight/measuring-the-quality-of-healthcare-in-the-u-s/), the U.S. health care system has improved in some measures of quality, such as mortality amenable to health care, the number of hospital-acquired infections, and the percentage of children receiving the recommended vaccines. Nevertheless, the health care system has also declined in some areas such as health-related quality of life (self-reported healthy days and days in which activities are interrupted by poor health) and the prevalence of obesity.

In *Viable Solutions: Six Steps to Transform Healthcare Now* (February 17, 2016, http://www.ndhi.org/files/6414/5565/8017/VIable_Solutions_Final_Report.pdf), a report to the Healthcare Leadership Council, a coalition of chief executive officers from all disciplines within the U.S. health care system, Cheryl Austein Casnoff et al. identify the following steps to improve the effectiveness of the health care system:

- Improve the operation of the U.S. Food and Drug Administration by relieving some of its administrative responsibilities and enabling it to improve timely patient access to new and innovative treatments.

- Ensure the ability of health care organizations to share data by requiring health information interoperability throughout the nation by the close of 2018.

- Enhance care of patients with chronic illnesses (e.g., heart disease, asthma, and diabetes) by using comprehensive care planning principles, which emphasize coordination of care.

- Implement medication therapy management to increase the percentage of patients who take their medication as prescribed.

- Expand Medicare (a federal health insurance program for people aged 65 years and older and people with disabilities) payment policies to encourage care coordination while preventing fraud and abuse.

- Standardize privacy laws and improve access to patient data for research.

In "Malcolm Gladwell on Fixing the US Healthcare Mess" (July 14, 2015, http://www.medscape.com/view article/847495), Eric J. Topol interviews Malcolm Gladwell, a journalist known for his penetrating industry investigations and analyses, who offers a number of suggestions to advance health care quality and reduce costs, including:

- Improving electronic medical records so that the health care providers who must use them do not perceive them as burdensome.

- Reserving insurance for catastrophic events (e.g., major, unanticipated expenses) and using a cash economy for simple, routine health services.

- Allowing health care providers to spend more time with patients.

In an interview with Robert Pearl, in "Malcolm Gladwell on American Health Care: An Interview" (Forbes .com, March 6, 2014), Gladwell proposes reducing payments to hospitals with high rates of patient complications that are attributable to medical errors. He advocates incentives to encourage hospitals and physicians to work together to better coordinate care and to improve its efficiency as well as measures to reduce the unnecessary costs that are associated with end-of-life care.

The previously described ideas are just a few of the wide variety of proposals to improve the existing health care system in the United States. The Patient Protection

and Affordable Care Act (also known as the Affordable Care Act [ACA]) that was signed into law by President Barack Obama (1961–) in 2010 promised to improve the health care system. Despite its problematic rollout—most notably the botched launch of HealthCare.gov, the technically flawed and often inoperable federal online marketplace—the ACA extended coverage to millions of uninsured Americans, instituted measures designed to control health care costs and improve system efficiency, and eliminated denial of health care coverage based on preexisting conditions.

## Reforming the U.S. Health Care System

The aim of the ACA was to expand coverage, contain health care costs, and improve the health care delivery system. More specifically, the ACA requires most U.S. citizens and legal residents to have health insurance, and it created health insurance exchanges and other mechanisms to enable people with low incomes and small businesses to purchase insurance coverage. Beginning in 2016 all employers with 50 or more full-time employees were required to offer coverage; failing to do so results in penalties as high as $3,000 per employee. The ACA expanded Medicaid (a state and federal health insurance program for low-income people) and the Children's Health Insurance Program to ensure that these public programs cover eligible people. It also strengthened Medicare prescription drug benefits. Furthermore, it eliminated lifetime and annual limits on insurance coverage.

Opposition to the ACA continued after it was passed. The ACA's opponents argued that some or all of the law was unconstitutional. Some challenged the individual mandate, arguing that the federal government could not legally require people to purchase health care. There were also challenges to the idea that the ACA could require states to expand their Medicaid programs. Robert Pear indicates in "Health Care Ruling, Vast Implications for Medicaid" (NYTimes.com, June 15, 2012) that more than half the states challenged the constitutionality of this aspect of the ACA.

The U.S. Supreme Court was called on to consider these issues. In June 2012, in *National Federation of Independent Business v. Sebelius, Secretary of Health and Human Services* (No. 11-393), the court voted 5–4 to uphold the core components of the ACA. Chief Justice John G. Roberts Jr. (1955–) wrote the majority opinion. In it, Roberts reasoned that requiring individuals who choose to forgo health insurance to pay a penalty is not unlike a tax, and thus was a constitutional exercise of Congress's powers. However, the court did limit the ACA's requirement that the states expand Medicaid coverage, rejecting the plan to deny federal payments to states that failed to do so.

While supporters of the ACA celebrated the Supreme Court decision, its detractors, many of whom were

**FIGURE 1.1**

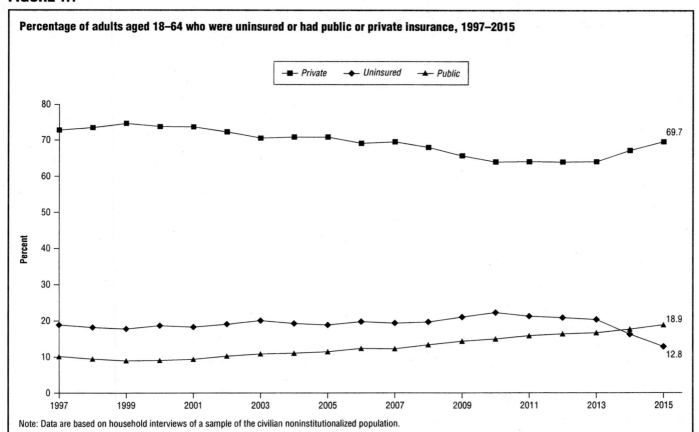

Percentage of adults aged 18–64 who were uninsured or had public or private insurance, 1997–2015

Note: Data are based on household interviews of a sample of the civilian noninstitutionalized population.

SOURCE: Robin A. Cohen, Michael E. Martinez, and Emily P. Zammitti, "Figure 1. Percentage of Adults Aged 18–64 Who Were Uninsured or Had Private or Public Coverage at the Time of Interview: United States, 1997–2015," in *Health Insurance Coverage: Early Release of Estimates from the National Health Interview Survey, 2015*, National Center for Health Statistics, May 2016, http://www.cdc.gov/nchs/data/nhis/earlyrelease/insur201605.pdf (accessed July 25, 2016)

Republican, vowed to continue their efforts to repeal it. For example, Robert E. Moffit of the Center for Health Policy Studies asserts in "Year Six of the Affordable Care Act: Obamacare's Mounting Problems" (April 2016, http://www.heritage.org/research/reports/2016/04/year-six-of-the-affordable-care-act-obamacares-mounting-problems) that in the sixth year since the ACA was enacted Americans were still dissatisfied with the legislation because it resulted in "increased costs for individuals, families, and businesses; excessive health care spending and middle-class taxation; and a seemingly endless series of managerial failures or unanticipated consequences."

By 2016 nearly 13 million Americans had signed up for coverage under the ACA, and a total of about 20 million Americans were covered by other provisions of the act such as Medicaid expansion and the ability of an estimated 5.7 million young adults up to the age of 26 years to remain on their parents' plan. According to the National Health Interview Survey (NHIS), an annual nationwide survey about Americans' health, the percentage of uninsured adults aged 18 to 64 years fell from 20% in 2010 to 12.8% in 2015. (See Figure 1.1.) The percentage of uninsured children aged zero to 17 years also fell, from 8% in 2010 to 4.5% in 2015. (See Figure 1.2.) Furthermore, the percentages of adults aged 18 to 64 years who were uninsured at the time of the NHIS interview, uninsured at least part of the year preceding the interview, and uninsured for more than a year steadily declined between 2013 and 2015. (See Figure 1.3.)

The KFF reports in "Current Status of Health Insurance Marketplace and Medicaid Expansion Decisions" (November 1, 2016, http://kff.org/health-reform/slide/current-status-of-health-insurance-marketplace-and-medicaid-expansion-decisions/) that as of July 2016, 16 states (California, Colorado, Connecticut, Delaware, Kentucky, Maryland, Massachusetts, Nevada, New Jersey, New Hampshire, New Mexico, New York, Oregon, Rhode Island, Vermont, and Washington) and the District of Columbia had adopted Medicaid expansion. In expansion states, the percentage of uninsured adults aged 18 to 64 years was lower and the percentages covered by public and private insurance were higher. (See Figure 1.4.)

Although opponents predicted that the ACA would have a negative impact on the economy, Cathy Schoen of

FIGURE 1.2

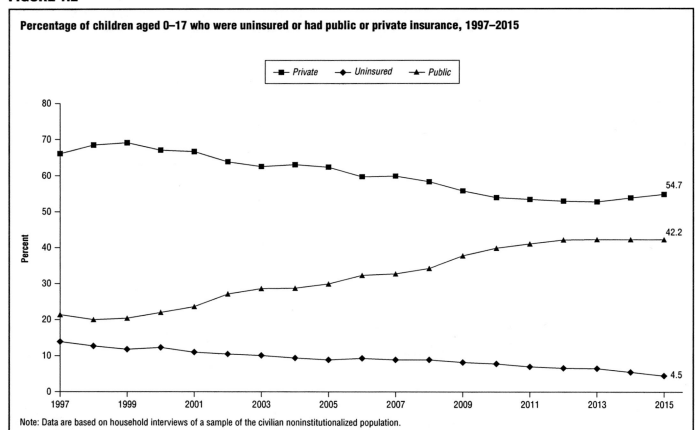

**Percentage of children aged 0–17 who were uninsured or had public or private insurance, 1997–2015**

Note: Data are based on household interviews of a sample of the civilian noninstitutionalized population.

SOURCE: Robin A. Cohen, Michael E. Martinez, and Emily P. Zammitti, "Figure 2. Percentage of Children Aged 0–17 Who Were Uninsured at the Time of Interview or Had Private or Public Coverage: United States, 1997–2015," in *Health Insurance Coverage: Early Release of Estimates from the National Health Interview Survey, 2015*, National Center for Health Statistics, May 2016, http://www.cdc.gov/nchs/data/nhis/earlyrelease/insur201605.pdf (accessed July 25, 2016)

the Commonwealth Fund finds in *The Affordable Care Act and the U.S. Economy: A Five-Year Perspective* (February 2016, http://www.commonwealthfund.org/~/media/files/publications/fund-report/2016/feb/1860_schoen_aca_and _us_economy_v2.pdf?la=en) that the ACA has had "no net negative economic impact and, in fact, has likely helped to stimulate growth by contributing to the slower rise in health care costs."

The early results of ACA reforms appear promising, but it is not yet known whether the restructuring of health care delivery that is currently under way will ultimately reduce costs and improve quality of health care. In "Do Health Care Delivery System Reforms Improve Value? The Jury Is Still Out" (*Medical Care*, vol. 54, no. 1, January 2016), Deborah Korenstein et al. reviewed 29 studies that evaluated the results of 28 reforms—programs or actions aimed at improving quality, cost, or utilization measures. The researchers find that health system reform, such as pay-for-performance initiatives (which offer financial rewards to providers who achieve, improve, or exceed their performance on specified quality and cost measures), do improve value.

Even so, Amy Goldstein notes in "Average Premiums for Popular ACA Plans Rising 25 Percent" (WashingtonPost.com, October 24, 2016) that in October 2016 the U.S. Department of Health and Human Services announced that 2017 insurance premiums were expected to rise by an average of 25%, which was three times higher than the percentage increase in premiums for 2016. Furthermore, several large health insurance companies announced that in 2017 they would participate in fewer state exchanges. According to Goldstein, this means there will likely be fewer health plan options available for consumers to choose from. Health policy experts opined that rising premiums and fewer options "injected a new round of uncertainty into the future" of the ACA.

## THE COMPONENTS OF THE HEALTH CARE SYSTEM

The health care system consists of all personal medical care services—prevention, diagnosis, treatment, and rehabilitation (services to restore function and independence)—plus the institutions and personnel that provide these

**FIGURE 1.3**

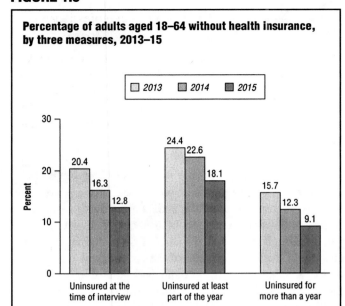

**Percentage of adults aged 18–64 without health insurance, by three measures, 2013–15**

Note: Data are based on household interviews of a sample of the civilian noninstitutionalized population.

SOURCE: Robin A. Cohen, Michael E. Martinez, and Emily P. Zammitti, "Figure 7. Percentage of Adults Aged 18–64 without Health Insurance, by Three Measures of Uninsurance: United States, 1997–2015," in *Health Insurance Coverage: Early Release of Estimates from the National Health Interview Survey, 2015*, National Center for Health Statistics, May 2016, http://www.cdc.gov/nchs/data/nhis/earlyrelease/insur201605.pdf (accessed July 25, 2016)

services and the government, public, and private organizations and agencies that finance service delivery.

The health care system may be viewed as a complex consisting of three interrelated components: health care consumers (people in need of health care services), health care providers (people who deliver health care—the professionals and practitioners), and the institutions and organizations of the health care system (the public and private agencies that organize, plan, regulate, finance, and coordinate services) that provide the systematic arrangements for delivering health care. The institutional component includes hospitals, clinics, and home-health agencies; the insurance companies and programs that pay for services (such as Blue Cross/Blue Shield); managed care plans (such as health maintenance and preferred provider organizations); and entitlement programs such as Medicare and Medicaid. Other institutions are the professional schools that train students for careers in medical, public health, dental, and allied health professions, such as nursing and laboratory technology. Also included are agencies and associations that research and monitor the quality of health care services; license and accreditation providers and institutions; local, state, and national professional societies; and the companies that produce medical technology, equipment, and pharmaceuticals.

Much of the interaction among the three components of the health care system occurs directly between individual

**FIGURE 1.4**

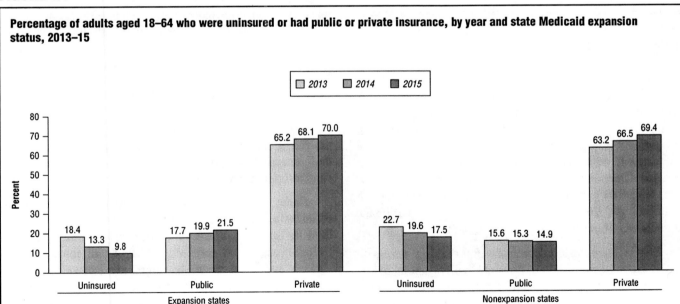

**Percentage of adults aged 18–64 who were uninsured or had public or private insurance, by year and state Medicaid expansion status, 2013–15**

Notes: For 2013 and 2014, there were 26 Medicaid expansion states; for 2015, there were 29 Medicaid expansion states. Data are based on household interviews of a sample of the civilian noninstitutionalized population.

SOURCE: Robin A. Cohen, Michael E. Martinez, and Emily P. Zammitti, "Figure 9. Percentage of Adults Aged 18–64 Who Were Uninsured or Had Private or Public Coverage at the Time of Interview, by Year and State Medicaid Expansion Status: United States, 2013–2015," in *Health Insurance Coverage: Early Release of Estimates from the National Health Interview Survey, 2015*, National Center for Health Statistics, May 2016, http://www.cdc.gov/nchs/data/nhis/earlyrelease/insur201605.pdf (accessed July 25, 2016)

health care consumers and providers. Other interactions are indirect, such as immunization programs or screenings to detect disease, which are performed by public health agencies for whole populations. All health care delivery relies on interactions among the three components. The ability to benefit from health care depends on an individual's or group's ability to gain entry to the health care system. The process of gaining entry to the health care system is referred to as access, and many factors can affect access to health care. This chapter provides an overview of how Americans access the health care system.

## ACCESS TO THE HEALTH CARE SYSTEM

In the 21st century, access to health care services is a key measure of the overall health and prosperity of a nation or a population, but access and availability were not always linked to good health status. In fact, many medical historians assert that until the beginning of the 20th century a visit with a physician was as likely to be harmful as it was helpful. Only since the early 20th century has medical care been considered to be a positive influence on health and longevity.

There are three aspects of accessibility: consumer access, comprehensive availability of services, and supply of services adequate to meet community demand. Quality health care services must be accessible to health care consumers when and where they are needed. The health care provider must have access to a full range of facilities, equipment, drugs, and services provided by other practitioners. The institutional component of health care delivery—the hospitals, clinics, and payers—must have timely access to information to enable them to plan an adequate supply of appropriate services for their communities.

### Consumer Access to Care

Access to health care services is influenced by a variety of factors. Characteristics of health care consumers strongly affect when, where, and how they access services. Differences in age, educational attainment, economic status, race, ethnicity, cultural heritage, and geographic location determine when consumers seek health care services, where they go to receive them, their expectations of treatment, and the extent to which they wish to participate in decisions about their own medical care.

People have different reasons for seeking access to health care services. Their personal beliefs about health and illness, motivations to obtain care, expectations of the care they will receive, and knowledge about how and where to receive care vary. For an individual to have access to quality care, there must be appropriately defined points of entry into the health care system. For many consumers, a primary care physician is their portal to the health care system. Besides evaluating and addressing the patient's immediate health care need, the primary care physician

also directs the consumer to other providers of care such as physician specialists or mental health professionals.

Some consumers access the health care system by seeking care from a clinic or hospital outpatient department, where teams of health professionals are available at one location. Others gain entry by way of a public health nurse, school nurse, social worker, or pharmacist, who refers them to an appropriate source, site, or health care practitioner.

### Comprehensive Availability of Health Care Services

Historically, the physician was the exclusive provider of all medical services. Until the 20th century the family doctor served as physician, surgeon, pharmacist, therapist, adviser, and dentist. He carried all the tools of his trade in a small bag and could easily offer state-of-the-art medical care in the patient's home, because hospitals had little more to offer in the way of equipment or facilities. In the 21st century it is neither practical nor desirable to ask one practitioner to serve in all these roles. It would be impossible for one professional to perform the full range of health care services, from primary prevention of disease and diagnosis to treatment and rehabilitation. Modern physicians and other health care practitioners must have access to a comprehensive array of trained personnel, facilities, and equipment so that they can, in turn, make them accessible to their patients.

Although many medical problems are effectively treated in a single office visit with a physician, even simple diagnosis and treatment relies on a variety of ancillary (supplementary) services and personnel. To make the diagnosis, the physician may order an imaging study, such as an x-ray that is performed by a radiology technician and interpreted by a radiologist (a physician specialized in imaging techniques). Laboratory tests may be performed by technicians and analyzed by pathologists (physicians specialized in microscopic analysis and diagnosis). More complicated medical problems involve teams of surgeons and high-tech surgical suites that are equipped with robotic assistants, and rehabilitation programs in which physical and occupational therapists assist patients to regain function and independence.

Some health care services are more effectively, efficiently, and economically provided to groups rather than to individuals. Immunization to prevent communicable diseases and screening to detect diseases in their earliest and most treatable stages are examples of preventive services best performed as cooperative efforts of voluntary health organizations, medical and other professional societies, hospitals, and public health departments.

### Access Requires Enough Health Care Services to Meet Community Needs

For all members of a community to have access to the full range of health care services, careful planning is required to ensure both the adequate supply and distribution of needed services. To evaluate community needs and effectively allocate health care resources, communities must gather demographic data and information about the social and economic characteristics of the population. They must also monitor the spread of disease and the frequency of specific medical conditions over time. All these population data must be considered in relation to available resources, including health care personnel; the distribution of facilities, equipment, and human resources (the available health care workforce); and advances in medicine and technology.

For example, a predicted shortage of nurses may prompt increased spending on nursing education; reviews of nurses' salary, benefits, and working conditions; and the cultivation of non-nursing personnel to perform specific responsibilities that were previously assigned to nurses. Similarly, when ongoing surveillance anticipates an especially virulent influenza (flu) season, public health officials, agencies, and practitioners intensify efforts to provide timely immunization to vulnerable populations such as older adults. Government agencies such as the Centers for Disease Control and Prevention (CDC), the National Institutes of Health, state and local health departments, professional societies, voluntary health agencies, and universities work together to research, analyze, and forecast health care needs. Their recommendations allow health care planners, policy makers, and legislators to allocate resources so that supply keeps pace with demand and to

ensure that new services and strategies are developed to address existing and emerging health care concerns.

## A Regular Source of Health Care Improves Access

According to the CDC, whether or not an individual has a regular source of health care (i.e., a regular provider or site) is a powerful predictor of access to health care services. Generally, people without regular sources have less access or access to fewer services, including key preventive medical services such as prenatal care, routine immunization, and health screening. Many factors have been found that contribute to keeping individuals from having regular sources of medical care, with income level being the best predictor of unmet medical needs or problems gaining access to health care services.

The National Center for Health Statistics (NCHS) analyzes the 2015 NHIS in *Early Release of Selected Estimates Based on Data from the 2015 National Health Interview Survey* (May 2016, http://www.cdc.gov/nchs/data/nhis/earlyrelease/earlyrelease201605_02.pdf). The NCHS finds that between 1997 and 2015 the percentage of people of all ages with a usual source of medical care did not substantially vary—ranging from a low of 85% in 2010, prior to enactment of the ACA, to a high of 88% in 2015. (See Figure 1.5.)

Still, the percentage of people who needed medical care but did not obtain it because of financial barriers to access increased fairly steadily between 1998 and 2010,

**FIGURE 1.5**

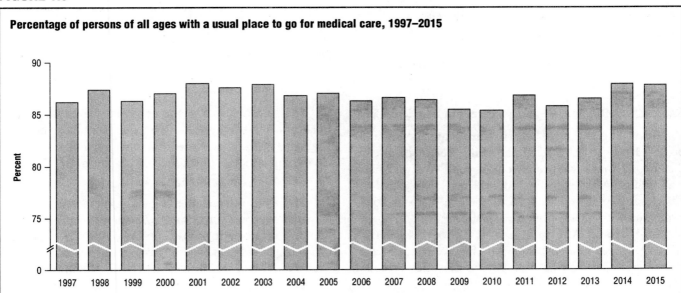

Percentage of persons of all ages with a usual place to go for medical care, 1997–2015

Notes: Data are based on household interviews of a sample of the civilian noninstitutionalized population. The usual place to go for medical care does not include a hospital emergency room. The analyses exclude persons with an unknown usual place to go for medical care (about 1.5% of respondents each year).

SOURCE: Brian W. Ward et al., "Figure 2.1. Percentage of Persons of All Ages with a Usual Place to Go for Medical Care: United States, 1997–2015," in *Early Release of Selected Estimates Based on Data from the 2015 National Health Interview Survey*, National Center for Health Statistics, May 2016, http://www.cdc.gov/nchs/data/nhis/earlyrelease/earlyrelease201605_02.pdf (accessed July 25, 2016)

**FIGURE 1.6**

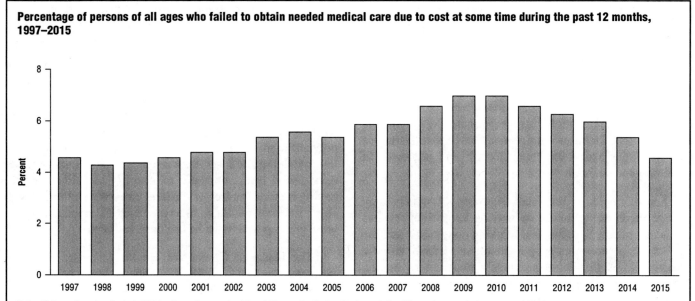

Percentage of persons of all ages who failed to obtain needed medical care due to cost at some time during the past 12 months, 1997–2015

Notes: Data are based on household interviews of a sample of the civilian noninstitutionalized population. The analyses exclude persons with unknown responses to the question on failure to obtain needed medical care due to cost (about 0.2% of respondents each year).

SOURCE: Brian W. Ward et al., "Figure 3.1. Percentage of Persons of All Ages Who Failed to Obtain Needed Medical Care Due to Cost at Some Time during the Past 12 Months: United States, 1997–2015," in *Early Release of Selected Estimates Based on Data from the 2015 National Health Interview Survey*, National Center for Health Statistics, May 2016, http://www.cdc.gov/nchs/data/nhis/earlyrelease/earlyrelease201605_03.pdf (accessed July 25, 2016)

when it peaked at 6.9%. (See Figure 1.6.) It subsequently decreased to 4.5% by 2015.

The NCHS finds that people aged 18 to 24 years were the least likely to have a regular source of care and that the likelihood of having a regular source of medical care increased among people aged 25 years and older. (See Figure 1.7.) Children under the age of 18 years were more likely than adults aged 18 to 64 years to have a usual place to go for medical care. Among adults (aged 18 to 64 years), women were more likely than men to have a usual place to seek medical care.

### Race, Ethnicity, and Regular Sources of Medical Care

According to the NCHS, Hispanic adults continue to be less likely to have a regular source for medical care than non-Hispanic white and non-Hispanic African American adults. After adjusting for age and sex, 82.6% of Hispanics had a usual source of medical care in 2015, compared with 88.8% of non-Hispanic whites and 86.7% of non-Hispanic African Americans. (See Figure 1.8.) Hispanics and non-Hispanic African Americans were more likely than non-Hispanic whites to suffer financial barriers to access. After adjusting for age and sex, 5.4% of Hispanics and 5.8% of non-Hispanic African Americans were unable to obtain needed medical care because of financial barriers, compared with 4.1% of non-Hispanic whites. (See Figure 1.9.) Health educators speculate that language barriers and the lack of information about the

availability of health care services may serve to widen this gap.

### Women Face Additional Obstacles

In *Women's Health Insurance Coverage* (October 2016, http://files.kff.org/attachment/fact-sheet-womens-health-insurance-coverage), the KFF notes that women fare worse than men in terms of access to health care services because they are more likely to be covered as a dependent on their spouse's plan and are at greater risk of losing their coverage should they divorce or if their spouse becomes unemployed or dies.

The NCHS also documents gender-based disparities in access. Women aged 18 to 64 years and those aged 65 years and older were more likely than men to have failed to obtain needed medical care because of financial barriers to access. (See Figure 1.10.)

The KFF observes that the ACA improved access to care and coverage for women by instituting insurance system reforms, lowering out-of-pocket costs, and mandating comprehensive benefits packages to meet the health service needs of women of all ages. In 2015, 8.8 million (9%) women purchased insurance on their own. More than 11 million women aged 19 to 64 years were uninsured in 2015. KFF notes that low-income women, racial and ethnic minorities, and single mothers were at greater risk of being uninsured and that more than two-thirds of uninsured women lived in households where someone was working.

FIGURE 1.7

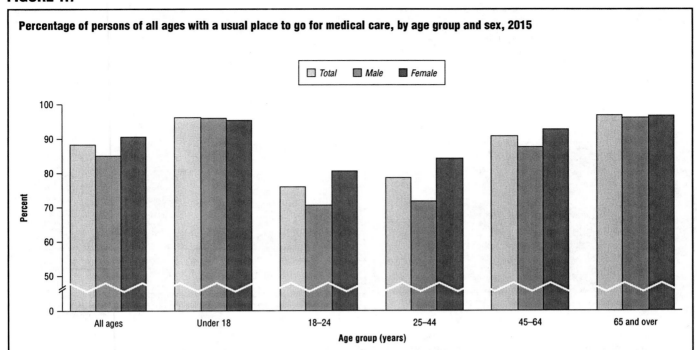

**Percentage of persons of all ages with a usual place to go for medical care, by age group and sex, 2015**

Notes: Data are based on household interviews of a sample of the civilian noninstitutionalized population. The usual place to go for medical care does not include a hospital emergency room. The analyses excluded the 0.8% of persons with an unknown usual place to go for medical care.

SOURCE: Brian W. Ward et al., "Figure 2.2. Percentage of Persons of All Ages with a Usual Place to Go for Medical Care, by Age Group and Sex: United States, 2015," in *Early Release of Selected Estimates Based on Data from the 2015 National Health Interview Survey*, National Center for Health Statistics, May 2016, http://www.cdc.gov/nchs/data/nhis/earlyrelease/earlyrelease201605_02.pdf (accessed July 25, 2016)

The rates of uninsured women varied geographically, from 5% in Rhode Island to 21% in Texas.

Although there has been a dramatic decline in the number of uninsured women since the ACA was implemented, the KFF reports that in 2016 one-third of uninsured women were not eligible for assistance from the ACA because they were undocumented (21%) or were not covered by Medicaid because their state did not choose to expand Medicaid (12%).

**Children Need Better Access to Health Care, Too**

The NCHS notes in *Health, United States, 2015: With Special Feature on Racial and Ethnic Health Disparities* (May 2016, http://www.cdc.gov/nchs/data/hus/hus15.pdf) that children are less likely to be uninsured than adults because they are more likely to qualify for public coverage, primarily Medicaid and the Children's Health Insurance Program. The percentage of children under the age of 18 years without health insurance coverage has steadily decreased, from 11.9% in 1999 to 4.5% during the first half of 2015. (See Table 1.1.)

According to the NCHS, the percentage of children that delayed or did not receive needed medical care in the year preceding the survey due to cost has also decreased, from 4.6% in 2000 to 2.8% in 2014.

The Federal Interagency Forum on Child and Family Statistics considers selected health measures, including children's access to care, in *America's Children in Brief: Key National Indicators of Well-Being, 2016* (July 2016, http://www.childstats.gov/pdf/ac2016/ac_16.pdf). The agency also analyzes NHIS data from 2000 to 2014.

The agency notes that the likelihood that children have insurance coverage and the type of insurance vary by race and ethnicity. In 2014 Hispanic children (10%) were more likely to be uninsured than were non-Hispanic white (4%) and non-Hispanic African American (4%) children. (See Figure 1.11.) Twice as many non-Hispanic white children (68%) had private insurance, compared with Hispanic (31%) and non-Hispanic African American (34%) children. For public insurance the percentages were roughly the opposite. Just 25% of non-Hispanic white children were covered by public insurance, compared with 57% of Hispanic children and 59% of non-Hispanic African American children.

According to the Federal Interagency Forum on Child and Family Statistics, between 2000 and 2014 the percentage of children covered by some form of health insurance increased seven percentage points, to 95%. Among all children, the percentages with no health insurance and with private health insurance decreased between 2000 and 2014. Conversely, the percentage with public coverage increased during the same period.

**FIGURE 1.8**

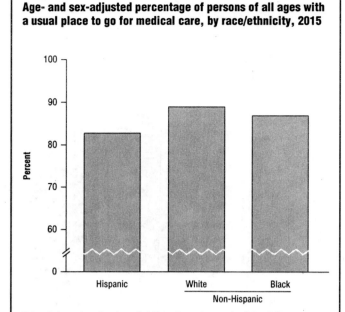

Age- and sex-adjusted percentage of persons of all ages with a usual place to go for medical care, by race/ethnicity, 2015

Notes: Data are based on household interviews of a sample of the civilian noninstitutionalized population. The usual place to go for medical care does not include a hospital emergency room. The analyses exclude the 0.8% of persons with an unknown usual place to go for medical care. Estimates are age-sex-adjusted using the projected 2000 U.S. population as the standard population and five age groups: under 18 years, 18–24, 25–44, 45–64, and 65 and over.

SOURCE: Brian W. Ward et al., "Figure 2.3. Age-Sex-Adjusted Percentage of Persons of All Ages with a Usual Place to Go for Medical Care, by Race/Ethnicity: United States, 2015," in *Early Release of Selected Estimates Based on Data from the 2015 National Health Interview Survey*, National Center for Health Statistics, May 2016, http://www.cdc.gov/nchs/data/nhis/earlyrelease/earlyrelease201605_02.pdf (accessed July 25, 2016)

**FIGURE 1.9**

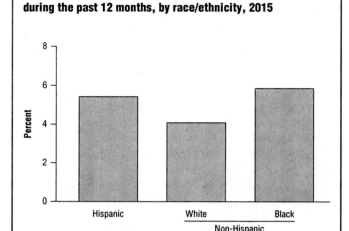

Age- and sex-adjusted percentage of persons of all ages who failed to obtain needed medical care due to cost at some time during the past 12 months, by race/ethnicity, 2015

Notes: Data are based on household interviews of a sample of the civilian noninstitutionalized population. The analyses exclude the 0.1% of persons with unknown responses to the question on failure to obtain needed medical care due to cost. Estimates are age sex-adjusted using the projected 2000 U.S. population as the standard population and three age groups: under 18 years, 18–64, and 65 and over.

SOURCE: Brian W. Ward et al., "Figure 3.3. Age-Sex-Adjusted Percentage of Persons of All Ages Who Failed to Obtain Needed Medical Care Due to Cost at Some Time during the Past 12 Months, by Race/Ethnicity: United States, 2015," in *Early Release of Selected Estimates Based on Data from the 2015 National Health Interview Survey*, National Center for Health Statistics, May 2016, http://www.cdc.gov/nchs/data/nhis/earlyrelease/earlyrelease201605_03.pdf (accessed July 25, 2016)

## ACA REDUCES DISPARITIES IN ACCESS TO CARE

Health care researchers believe many factors contribute to differences in access, including cultural perceptions and beliefs about health and illness, patient preferences, availability of services, and provider bias. They recommend special efforts to inform and educate minority health care consumers and to increase understanding and sensitivity among practitioners and other care providers. Besides acquiring factual information, minority consumers must overcome the belief that they are at a disadvantage because of their race or ethnicity. Along with action to dispel barriers to access, educating practitioners, policy makers, and consumers can help reduce the perception of disadvantage.

For decades, health care researchers have documented sharp differences in the ability of ethnic and racial groups to access medical services. The federal government has repeatedly called for an end to these disparities. Although some observers believe universal health insurance coverage is an important first step in eliminating disparities, there is widespread concern that

the challenge is more complicated and that additional analysis and action is needed.

In "Racial and Ethnic Disparities in Health Care Access and Utilization under the Affordable Care Act" (*Medical Care*, vol. 54, no. 2, February 2016), Jie Chen et al. analyze 2011–14 NHIS data to determine whether racial and ethnic disparities in health care access were reduced by the implementation of the ACA. The researchers find that since the ACA took full effect in 2014, it not only significantly improved insurance coverage for African Americans and Hispanics but also increased the likelihood that they visit primary care physicians and receive timely medical care.

According to Chen et al., African Americans showed greater improvement in both insurance coverage and access under the ACA when compared with whites because they were more likely to gain insurance coverage through the Health Insurance Marketplace and Medicaid expansion that has occurred under the ACA. The researchers explain that the relatively smaller declines in uninsured rates among Hispanics were attributable to the fact that many recent immigrants lived in states that were not participating in the Medicaid expansion, but

**FIGURE 1.10**

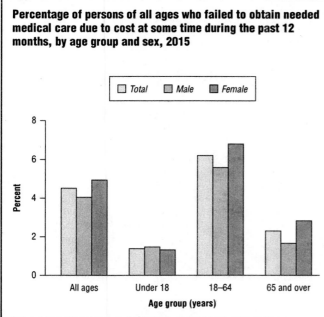

**Percentage of persons of all ages who failed to obtain needed medical care due to cost at some time during the past 12 months, by age group and sex, 2015**

Notes: Data are based on household interviews of a sample of the civilian noninstitutionalized population. The analyses exclude the 0.1% of persons with unknown responses to the question on failure to obtain needed medical care due to cost.

SOURCE: Brian W. Ward et al., "Figure 3.2. Percentage of Persons of All Ages Who Failed to Obtain Needed Medical Care Due to Cost at Some Time during the Past 12 Months, by Age Group and Sex: United States, 2015," in *Early Release of Selected Estimates Based on Data from the 2015 National Health Interview Survey*, National Center for Health Statistics, May 2016, http://www.cdc.gov/nchs/data/nhis/earlyrelease/earlyrelease201605_03.pdf (accessed July 25, 2016)

also cite ineffective outreach to the Hispanic community about ACA eligibility, subsidies, and enrollment.

Chen et al. point out that although Hispanics did not keep pace with African Americans in rates of insurance coverage, those who were eligible for health coverage were significantly less likely to delay or forgo health care, which is a key factor in improving health outcomes (how people fare as a result of treatment). The researchers conclude that their results "suggest that the ACA has the potential to reduce and eliminate racial and ethnic disparities if present trends continue."

**AHRQ Report Documents Disparities in Access**

In July 2003 the Agency for Healthcare Research and Quality (AHRQ) released its first *National Healthcare Disparities Report* (http://archive.ahrq.gov/qual/nhdr03/nhdr2003.pdf), a report requested by Congress that documented racial health disparities including access to care. Among other concerns, the agency found that African Americans and low-income Americans have higher mortality rates for cancer than the general population because they are less likely to receive screening tests for certain forms of the disease and other preventive services. Although the AHRQ asserted that differential access

may lead to disparities in quality, and observed that opportunities to provide preventive care are often missed, it conceded that knowledge about why disparities exist is limited.

The AHRQ's report generated fiery debate in the health care community and among legislators and painted a rather bleak view of disparities. The agency called for detailed data to support quality improvement initiatives and observed that "community-based participatory research has numerous examples of communities working to improve quality overall, while reducing healthcare disparities for vulnerable populations."

**Highlights from the *2015 National Healthcare Disparities Report***

In *2015 National Healthcare Disparities Report and 5th Anniversary Update on the National Quality Strategy* (April 2016, http://www.ahrq.gov/sites/default/files/wysiwyg/research/findings/nhqrdr/nhqdr15/2015nhqdr.pdf), the AHRQ tracks the measures of access to care that the first report, *National Healthcare Disparities Report*, identified in 2003. These measures include factors that facilitated access, such as having a primary care provider, and factors that were barriers to access, such as having no health insurance.

The AHRQ indicates that although some measures of access are improving, overall access to care is getting worse. Specifically, for at least one access measure, having a usual place to go for medical care, the gap related to race and ethnicity narrowed between 2010 and 2015. (See Figure 1.12.) Regardless, for most racial, ethnic, and income groups, the number of access measures that were worsening or unchanged were greater than the number that were improving. Figure 1.13 shows the number and proportion of access measures that improved, were unchanged, or worsened.

Racial and ethnic minorities continued to encounter disproportionate barriers to care. (Figure 1.13.) For about half of all access measures analyzed, African Americans had worse access to care than whites. Hispanics had worse access to care than whites across roughly two-thirds of the measures.

Socioeconomic status greatly affected access to care. The AHRQ finds that poor people (below $23,550 of the 2013 federal poverty level for a family of four) had worse access to care than high-income people across every measure. (See Figure 1.13.) Although there was an overall decrease between 2011 and the first half of 2015 in the percentage of people having trouble paying medical bills, poor and near-poor people were more likely to have trouble paying medical bills than people who were not poor. (See Figure 1.14.) Compared with whites, African Americans and Hispanics were more likely to have trouble paying medical bills, while Asian Americans were less likely to have

TABLE 1.1

**Children under age 18 without health insurance coverage, 1999–June 2015**

| | | | Race and Hispanic origin[a] | | |
|---|---|---|---|---|---|
| | | | | Not Hispanic or Latino | |
| Age and year | Total[b] | Hispanic or Latino | White only | Black only | Asian only |
| | | Percent without health insurance coverage[c] | | | |
| **Under 18 years** | | | | | |
| 1999 | 11.9 | 26.7 | 8.1 | 11.9 | 10.4 |
| 2000 | 12.6 | 25.9 | 8.7 | 12.2 | 12.5 |
| 2001 | 11.2 | 24.6 | 7.2 | 10.6 | 12.6 |
| 2002 | 10.9 | 21.9 | 7.5 | 10.0 | 13.4 |
| 2003 | 9.8 | 20.2 | 6.4 | 8.9 | 12.0 |
| 2004 | 9.2 | 19.5 | 6.4 | 6.9 | 10.5 |
| 2005 | 9.3 | 17.5 | 6.5 | 8.9 | 11.4 |
| 2006 | 9.5 | 19.4 | 6.2 | 7.8 | 8.3 |
| 2007 | 9.0 | 15.3 | 7.1 | 6.2 | 8.0 |
| 2008 | 9.0 | 16.8 | 6.7 | 7.5 | 6.5 |
| 2009 | 8.2 | 14.7 | 6.0 | 6.6 | 7.5 |
| 2010 | 7.8 | 13.0 | 5.8 | 6.4 | 8.7 |
| 2011 | 7.0 | 12.3 | 4.8 | 5.5 | 7.8 |
| 2012 | 6.6 | 10.9 | 5.2 | 4.4 | 7.8 |
| 2013 | 6.6 | 11.8 | 4.7 | 5.1 | 5.9 |
| 2014 | 5.4 | 9.7 | 4.1 | 3.5 | 4.3* |
| 2015, Jan–Jun[d] | 4.5 | 8.0 | 3.6 | 2.9 | * |

*Estimates are considered unreliable.
[a]Persons of Hispanic origin may be of any race. Race-specific estimates are tabulated according to the 1997 Revisions to the Standards for the Classification of Federal Data on Race and Ethnicity. The single-race categories plus multiple-race category shown in the table conform to the 1997 Standards. Starting with 2003 data, race responses of other race and unspecified multiple race were treated as missing, and then race was imputed if these were the only race responses. Almost all persons with a race response of other race were of Hispanic origin.
[b]Includes all persons not shown separately.
[c]Persons not covered by private insurance, Medicaid, Children's Health Insurance Program (CHIP), state-sponsored or other government-sponsored health plans (starting in 1997), Medicare, or military plans are considered to have no health insurance coverage. Persons with only Indian Health Service coverage are considered to have no health insurance coverage. Health insurance coverage is at the time of interview.
[d]Preliminary data based on the National Health Interview Survey's Early Release program. Estimates based on the preliminary 6-month file may differ from estimates based on the final annual file.

SOURCE: Adapted from "Data Table for Figure 26. No Health Insurance Coverage among Persons under Age 65, by Age and Race and Hispanic Origin: United States, 1999–June 2015 (Preliminary Data)," in *Health, United States, 2015: With Special Feature on Racial and Ethnic Health Disparities*, U.S. Department of Health and Human Services, Centers for Disease Control and Prevention, National Center for Health Statistics, May 2016, http://www.cdc.gov/nchs/data/hus/hus15.pdf (accessed July 25, 2016)

trouble paying their bills. This disparity did not change appreciably between 2011 and the first half of 2015.

## ACCESS TO MENTAL HEALTH CARE

Besides the range of barriers to access faced by all Americans trying to access the health care system, people seeking mental health care face unique challenges, not the least of which is that they are even less able than people in good health to successfully navigate the fragmented mental health service delivery system. Furthermore, because people with serious mental illness frequently suffer from unemployment and disability, they are likely to join the ranks of the impoverished, uninsured, and homeless, which only compounds access problems. Finally, the social stigmas (deeply held negative attitudes) that promote discrimination against people with mental illness are a powerful deterrent to seeking care.

Myths about mental illness persist, especially the mistaken beliefs that mental illness is a sign of moral weakness or that an affected individual can simply choose to "wish or will away" the symptoms of mental illness. People with mental illness cannot just "pull themselves together" and will themselves well. Without treatment, symptoms can worsen and persist for months or even years.

People with mental illness experience other types of social stigmas as well. They may face discrimination in the workplace, in school, and in finding housing. Thwarted in their efforts to maintain independence, people suffering from mental illness may become trapped in a cycle characterized by feelings of worthlessness and hopelessness and may be further isolated from the social and community supports and treatments most able to help them recover.

### Disparities in Access to Mental Health Care

The principal barriers to access of mental health care are the cost of mental health services, the lack of sufficient insurance for these services, the fragmented organization of these services, mistrust of providers, and the social stigmas about mental illness. These obstacles may act as deterrents for all Americans, but for racial and ethnic minorities they are compounded by language barriers, ethnic and cultural compatibility of practitioners, and geographic availability of services.

**FIGURE 1.11**

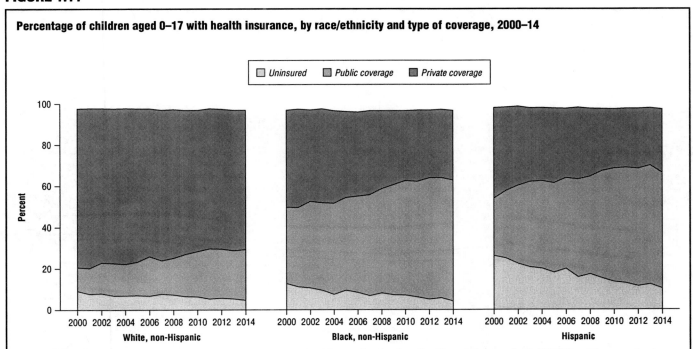

**Percentage of children aged 0–17 with health insurance, by race/ethnicity and type of coverage, 2000–14**

Notes: Persons of Hispanic origin may be of any race. Data on race and Hispanic origin are collected and combined for reporting according to 1997 Office of Management and Budget Standards for Data on Race and Ethnicity. A small percentage of children have coverage other than private or public health insurance.

SOURCE: "Figure 9. Percentage of Children Ages 0–17 by Race and Hispanic Origin and Health Insurance Coverage at the Time of Interview, 2000–2014," in *America's Children in Brief: Key National Indicators of Well-Being*, Federal Interagency Forum on Child and Family Statistics, July 2016, http://www .childstats.gov/pdf/ac2016/ac_16.pdf (accessed July 25, 2016)

## HEALTH CARE REFORM PROMISES TO IMPROVE ACCESS

The 2010 enactment of the ACA was hailed as landmark legislation—the most sweeping social legislation since the enactment of Social Security in 1935 and Medicare and Medicaid in 1965. The act intended to improve access to care by extending health care coverage to an estimated 27 million uninsured Americans by 2019 and by preventing health insurance companies from denying coverage to people with preexisting medical conditions or dropping them when they develop costly medical problems.

In the years after its passage, the ACA has remained controversial. Congressional Republicans, who had not supported the law's enactment, led numerous efforts to revise or repeal the ACA. Court challenges limited the ACA's effects in some ways, most notably by giving states the power to decide if they would expand Medicaid. Even the law's supporters were dismayed by highly visible problems with the ACA's rollout that caused difficulties for consumers.

Concerns about the mandate that medium-sized (50 to 99 full-time workers) and large (100 plus full-time workers) businesses offer health insurance to their employees led to these provisions being delayed by the Obama administration. Implementation of these rules was delayed until January 2016. Opponents of the ACA pointed to these repeated delays and the difficult rollout of the HealthCare.gov marketplace as indications that the law was unworkable. ACA opponents were heartened by the November 2016 election of Donald Trump (1946–), given that during his campaign the president-elect promised immediate repeal and replacement of the law.

### The ACA Delivers on Its Promise

Despite these problems and controversies, the ACA has improved access to care. In the fact sheet "The Affordable Care Act: Healthy Communities Six Years Later" (March 2, 2016, https://www.whitehouse.gov/the-press-office/2016/03/02/fact-sheet-affordable-care-act-healthy-communities-six-years-later), the White House states that 9 out of 10 Americans had health insurance in 2015. An estimated 137 million Americans with private insurance gained coverage for at least one free preventive health care service—such as mammograms, birth control, or immunizations—and 39 million Medicare beneficiaries received at least one preventive service with no out-of-pocket cost. Because 31 states and the District of Columbia opted to expand their Medicaid programs, 14 million more Americans were enrolled in Medicaid in 2015 than were in 2013. In addition, under the ACA, 105 million Americans no longer had to worry about losing their health benefits when they reach a lifetime limit.

FIGURE 1.12

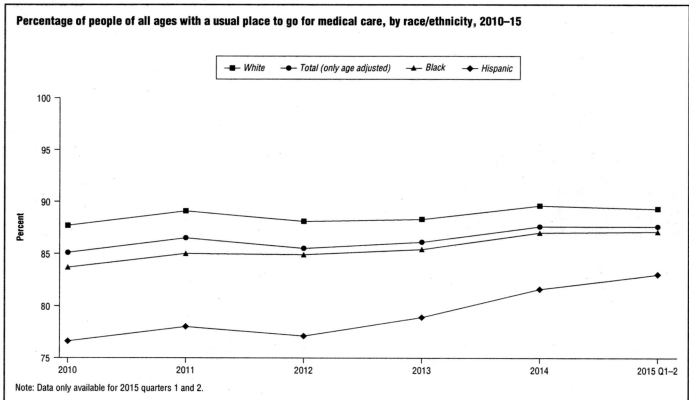

**Percentage of people of all ages with a usual place to go for medical care, by race/ethnicity, 2010–15**

Note: Data only available for 2015 quarters 1 and 2.

SOURCE: "Age-Sex Adjusted Percentage of People of All Ages with a Usual Place to Go for Medical Care, by Race/Ethnicity, 2010–2015 Q1–2," in *2015 National Healthcare Quality and Disparities Report and 5th Anniversary Update on the National Quality Strategy*, U.S. Department of Health and Human Services, Agency for Healthcare Research and Quality, April 2016, http://www.ahrq.gov/sites/default/files/wysiwyg/research/findings/nhqrdr/nhqdr15/2015nhqdr.pdf (accessed July 25, 2016)

## IS ACCESS TO HEALTH CARE A RIGHT OR A PRIVILEGE?

The United States is the only developed country in the world that does not have a government-funded universal or national program of health insurance. As a result, American families with greater incomes and assets are more likely than low-income families to have health insurance and have greater access to health care services. It is for this reason that many regard the ACA as groundbreaking. Supporters of this legislation assert that as previously uninsured people obtain insurance, access will be greatly improved.

However, the AHRQ and other health care researchers and policy makers observe that having health insurance does not necessarily ensure access to medical care. They contend that many other factors, including cost-containment measures put in place by private and public payers, have reduced access to care. They note that reduced access affects vulnerable populations—the poor, people with mental illness and other disabilities, and immigrants—more than others.

Various groups and organizations support the premise that health care is a fundamental human right, rather than a privilege. These organizations include Physicians for a National Health Program, the AARP, National Health Care for the Homeless, the Friends Committee on National Legislation (a Quaker public interest lobby), and the National Economic and Social Rights Initiative (NESRI). For example, the NESRI states in "Campaigning for the Human Right to Health Care" (2016, http://www.nesri.org/programs/health) that "after succeeding in passing the country's first commitment to implementing a universal health care law in Vermont, the Healthcare Is a Human Right movement is now opening political possibilities well beyond Vermont's borders.... We work with allies across the country to advance right-based health care policies and grassroots organizing. Together we are promoting a bold vision rooted in human rights, and a set of principles, tools and methods to build people power and advance equity and justice in health care and beyond."

In "Health Care Is a Right, Not a Privilege, Pope Says" (CatholicNews.com, May 9, 2016), Cindy Wooden quotes Pope Francis I (1936–), who affirmed in 2016 that "health is not a consumer good but a universal right, so access to health services cannot be a privilege." In a meeting with physicians, volunteers, and supporters of Doctors with Africa, a medical mission, the pope bemoaned the fact that

**FIGURE 1.13**

**Number and percentage of access measures for which members of selected groups experienced better, same, or worse access to care, 2015**

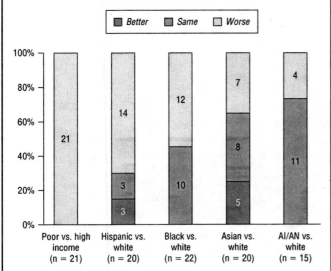

AI/AN = American Indian or Alaska Native.
n = number of measures.
Note: Numbers of measures differ across groups because of sample size limitations. The relative difference between a selected group and its reference group is used to assess disparities. For income, the reference group is "high income." For race and ethnicity, the reference group is white.
Better = Population had better access to care than reference group. Differences are statistically significant, are equal to or larger than 10%, and favor the selected group.
Same = Population and reference group had about the same access to care. Differences are not statistically significant or are smaller than 10%.
Worse = Population had worse access to care than reference group. Differences are statistically significant, are equal to or larger than 10%, and favor the reference group.

SOURCE: "Number and Percentage of Access Measures for Which Members of Selected Groups Experienced Better, Same, or Worse Access to Care Compared with Reference Group," in *2015 National Healthcare Quality and Disparities Report and 5th Anniversary Update on the National Quality Strategy*, U.S. Department of Health and Human Services, Agency for Healthcare Research and Quality, April 2016, http://www.ahrq.gov/sites/default/files/wysiwyg/research/findings/nhqrdr/nhqdr15/2015nhqdr.pdf (accessed July 25, 2016)

many people are denied basic health care and described health care as "not a right for all, but rather still a privilege for a few, for those who can afford it."

Others disagree with the notion that access to health care is a fundamental right. For example, Richard M. Salsman argues in "Memo to the Supreme Court: Health Care Is Not a Right" (Forbes.com, April 3, 2012) that "health care is not a right. It's a valuable service provided by intelligent, hard-working professionals with years of painstaking education and training, people who, like other Americans, deserve equal protection under the law, people who, like other Americans, have a right to their own life, liberty, property and the pursuit of their own happiness." Salsman believes that because people pay for health care, as they do for other goods and services, it is a privilege. Furthermore, he opposes the ACA, contending that mandating health coverage and requiring hospitals to treat patients who cannot pay violate both personal rights and the U.S. Constitution.

Concurring with Salsman, many groups and organizations assert that health care is not a fundamental right. These include Americans for Free Choice in Medicine, the Atlas Society, the United States Conference of Catholic Bishops, and the Heritage Foundation.

**FIGURE 1.14**

**People under age 65 who had problems paying medical bills in the past year, by poverty status and race/ethnicity, 2011–15**

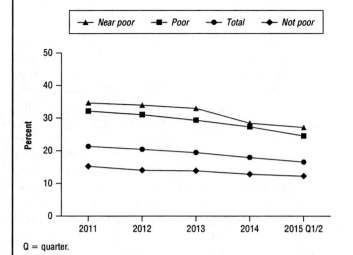

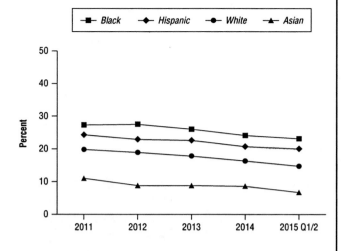

Q = quarter.

SOURCE: "Care Affordability: People under Age 65 Who Were in Families Having Problems Paying Medical Bills in the Past Year, by Poverty Status and Race/Ethnicity, 2011–2015 Q2," in *2015 National Healthcare Quality and Disparities Report and 5th Anniversary Update on the National Quality Strategy*, U.S. Department of Health and Human Services, Agency for Healthcare Research and Quality, April 2016, http://www.ahrq.gov/sites/default/files/wysiwyg/research/findings/nhqrdr/nhqdr15/2015nhqdr.pdf (accessed July 25, 2016)

# CHAPTER 2
# HEALTH CARE PRACTITIONERS

*The art of medicine consists of amusing the patient while nature cures the disease.*

—Voltaire

*One of the first duties of the physician is to educate the masses not to take medicine.*

—William Osler, *Sir William Osler: Aphorisms, from His Bedside Teachings and Writings* (1950)

## PHYSICIANS

Physicians routinely perform medical examinations, provide preventive medicine services, diagnose illness, treat patients suffering from injury or disease, and offer counsel about how to achieve and maintain good health. There are two types of physicians trained in traditional Western medicine: the Doctor of Medicine (MD) is schooled in allopathic medicine and the Doctor of Osteopathy (DO) learns osteopathy. Allopathy is the philosophy and system of curing disease by producing conditions that are incompatible with disease, such as prescribing antibiotics to combat bacterial infection. The philosophy of osteopathy is different; it is based on recognition of the body's capacity for self-healing, and it emphasizes structural and manipulative therapies such as postural education, manual treatment of the musculoskeletal system (osteopathic physicians are trained in hands-on diagnosis and treatment), and preventive medicine. Osteopathy is also considered a holistic practice because it considers the whole person, rather than simply the diseased organ or system.

In modern medical practice, the philosophical differences may not be obvious to most health care consumers because MDs and DOs use many comparable methods of treatment, including prescribing medication and performing surgery. In fact, the American Osteopathic Association (2016, https://www.osteopathic.org/inside-aoa/about/Pages/default.aspx), the national medical professional society that represents more than 123,000 DOs and DO

students, admits that many people who seek care from osteopathic physicians may be entirely unaware of their physician's training. Like MDs, DOs complete four years of medical school and postgraduate residency training; may specialize in areas such as surgery, psychiatry, or obstetrics; and must pass state licensing examinations to practice.

## Medical School, Postgraduate Training, and Qualifications

Modern medicine requires considerable skill and extensive training. The road to becoming a physician is long, difficult, and intensely competitive. Medical school applicants must earn excellent college grades, achieve high scores on entrance exams, and demonstrate emotional maturity and motivation to be admitted to medical school. Once admitted, they spend the first two years primarily in laboratories and classrooms learning basic medical sciences such as anatomy (detailed understanding of body structure), physiology (biological processes and vital functions), and biochemistry. They also learn how to take medical histories, perform complete physical examinations, and recognize symptoms of diseases. During their third and fourth years, medical students work under supervision at teaching hospitals and clinics. By completing clerkships—spending time in different specialties such as internal medicine, obstetrics and gynecology, pediatrics, psychiatry, and surgery—they acquire the necessary skills to diagnose and treat a wide variety of illnesses.

Following medical school, new physicians must complete a year of internship, also referred to as postgraduate year one, that emphasizes either general medical practice or one specific specialty and that provides clinical experience in various hospital services (e.g., inpatient care, outpatient clinics, emergency departments, and operating rooms). In the past, many physicians entered practice after this first year of postgraduate training. However, in the present era of specialization most physicians choose to continue in residency training, which lasts an additional three to six years, depending on the specialty. Those who choose a subspecialty such as cardiology, infectious diseases, oncology, or plastic surgery must spend additional years in residency and may then choose to complete fellowship training. Following residency, they are eligible to take an examination to earn board certification in their chosen specialty. Fellowship training involves a year or two of laboratory and clinical research work as well as opportunities to gain additional clinical and patient care expertise.

## Medical School Applicants

The Association of American Medical Colleges (AAMC; 2016, https://www.aamc.org/download/321442/data/factstablea1.pdf) indicates that the number of students entering medical school totaled 20,631 for the 2015–16 academic year. The students were selected from a pool of 781,602 applicants.

## The High Costs and Long Hours of Medical Training

Medical school is very expensive. According to the AAMC (2016, https://services.aamc.org/tsfreports/report_median.cfm?year_of_study=2016), based on 85 schools reporting, the average costs of attending public medical schools during the 2015–16 academic year were $33,895 for residents and $57,834 for nonresidents. For private medical schools, based on 57 schools reporting, costs averaged $53,951 for residents and $55,379 for nonresidents.

Many medical students borrow money to pay for their education. The AAMC indicates in "Medical Student Education: Debt, Costs, and Loan Repayment Fact Card" (October 2015, https://www.aamc.org/download/447254/data/debtfactcard.pdf) that for the class of 2015, 83% of public medical school graduates had education debt, as did 78% of private medical school graduates. (This education debt included debts incurred for education prior to medical school.) On average, indebted public medical school graduates had education debts of $180,000, and indebted private medical school graduates owed $200,000 in education debt.

Although a physician's earning power is considerable, and many students are able to repay their educational debt during their first years of practice, some observers believe the extent of medical students' indebtedness may unduly influence their career choices. They may train for higher-paying specialties and subspecialties rather than follow their natural interests, or opt not to practice in underserved geographic areas. The high cost of medical education is also believed to limit the number of minority applicants to medical school.

Historically, medical training has been difficult and involved long hours. This is particularly true for those in residency training. However, working long hours without

adequate rest has been found to increase the occurrence of preventable medical errors and thereby adversely affect patient safety. Since July 1, 2011, the Accreditation Council for Graduate Medical Education (ACGME) restricts the duty hours of the more than 100,000 medical residents in the United States. The ACGME Common Program Requirements (2011, http://www.acgme.org/acgmeweb/Portals/0/PDFs/Common_Program_Requirements_07012011%5B2%5D.pdf) stipulate that:

- Residents' "duty hours must be limited to 80 hours per week, averaged over a four-week period"

- "Residents must be scheduled for a minimum of one day free of duty every week"

- First-year residents (interns) must not work more than 16 hours and "should have 10 hours, and must have eight hours, free of duty between scheduled duty periods"

- Second-year residents and above "may be scheduled to a maximum of 24 hours of continuous duty in the hospital"

- "Programs must encourage residents to use alertness management strategies in the context of patient care responsibilities. Strategic napping, especially after 16 hours of continuous duty and between the hours of 10:00 p.m. and 8:00 a.m., is strongly suggested."

In "What Effects Have Resident Work-Hour Changes Had on Education, Quality of Life, and Safety? A Systematic Review" (*Clinical Orthopedics Related research*, vol. 473, no. 5, May 2015), Joshua D. Harris et al. report the results of a review of 11 studies to determine whether patient safety outcomes, residents' quality of life, and operative and technical skills improved after the 2011 residency work-hour changes. The researchers find evidence of improved resident quality of life, improved resident sleep, and less fatigue and burnout. However, they also observe that the work-hour changes are thought to have a negative impact on learning and training experiences resulting in less surgical operative and technical skill. Harris et al. report conflicting evidence about the impact of the limited hours on patient safety and outcomes and attitudes toward the work-hour changes.

## Conventional and Newer Medical Specialties

Rapid advances in medicine and changing needs have resulted in a variety of new medical and surgical specialties, subspecialties, and concentrations. For example, geriatrics, the medical subspecialty concerned with the prevention and treatment of diseases in older adults, has developed in response to growth in this population. The term *geriatrics* is derived from the Greek *geras* (old age) and *iatrikos* (physician). Geriatricians are physicians trained in primary care, such as internal medicine or family practice, who receive further training and gain certification as specialists in the medical care of older adults.

Another relatively new medical specialty has resulted in physician intensivists. Intensivists, as the name indicates, are trained to staff hospital intensive care units (ICUs; which are sometimes known as critical care units), where the most critically ill patients are cared for using a comprehensive array of state-of-the-art technology and equipment. This specialty arose in response to both the increasing complexity of care provided in ICUs and the demonstrated benefits of having highly trained physicians immediately available to care for critically ill patients. The Health Resources and Services Administration (HRSA) notes in *The Critical Care Workforce: A Study of the Supply and Demand for Critical Care Physicians* (July 2006, http://www.mc.vanderbilt.edu/documents/CAPNAH/files/criticalcare.pdf) that "demand for intensivists will continue to exceed available supply through the year 2020 if current supply and demand trends continue." Assuming optimal utilization, the HRSA predicts a shortfall of 1,500 intensivists in 2020. (See Figure 2.1.)

Although Jeremy M. Kahn and Gordon D. Rubenfeld note in "The Myth of the Workforce Crisis. Why the United States Does Not Need More Intensivist Physicians" (*American Journal of Respiratory and Critical Care Medicine*, vol. 191, no. 2, January 15, 2015) that intensivist staffing is associated with fewer deaths in the ICU, they argue against increasing the number intensivists. The researchers feel that training more intensivists is impractical, would prioritize intensive care over other necessary specialties, and would require excessive costs.

Instead of training additional intensivists, they propose the use of nonphysician providers (nurse practitioners and physician assistants), ICU telemedicine and enhanced information technologies, regionalization of care, and restrictions on the growth of new ICU beds.

Growing more than 8% per year, another newer specialty is hospitalists—physicians who are hospital based as opposed to office based and who provide a variety of services, such as caring for hospitalized patients who do not have personal physicians, explaining complex medical procedures to patients and families, and coordinating many aspects of inpatient care. The Society of Hospital Medicine (https://hospitalmedicine.org/Web/Partner_with_SHM/Hospitalists_About.aspx) estimates that there were more than 44,000 hospitalists in practice in 2016.

More traditional medical specialties include:

- Anesthesiologist—administers anesthesia (to induce partial or complete loss of sensation) and monitors patients during surgery

- Cardiologist—diagnoses and treats diseases of the heart and blood vessels

- Dermatologist—diagnoses and treats diseases of the skin, hair, and nails

- Family practitioner—delivers primary care to people of all ages and, when necessary, refers patients to other physician specialists

- Gastroenterologist—specializes in digestive system disorders

- Internist—provides diagnosis and nonsurgical treatment of a broad array of illnesses affecting adults

- Neurologist—specializes in the nervous system and diagnosis and treatment of brain, spinal cord, and nerve disorders

- Obstetrician-gynecologist—provides health care for women and their reproductive systems, as well as care for mothers and babies before, during, and immediately following delivery

- Oncologist—provides diagnosis and treatment of cancer

- Otolaryngologist—skilled in the medical and surgical treatment of ear, nose, and throat disorders and related structures of the face, head, and neck

- Pathologist—uses skills in microscopic chemical analysis and diagnostics to detect disease in body tissues and fluids

- Psychiatrist—specializes in the prevention, diagnosis, and treatment of mental health and emotional disorders

- Pulmonologist—specializes in diseases of the lungs and respiratory system

**FIGURE 2.1**

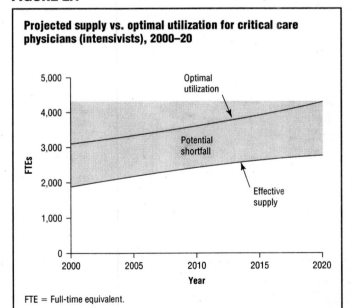

Projected supply vs. optimal utilization for critical care physicians (intensivists), 2000–20

FTE = Full-time equivalent.

SOURCE: Elizabeth M. Duke, "Exhibit 15. Projected Supply vs. Optimal Utilization for Intensivists, 2000–2020," in *Report to Congress—The Critical Care Workforce: A Study of the Supply and Demand for Critical Care Physicians*, U.S. Department of Health and Human Services, Health Resources and Services Administration, May 2006

- Urologist—provides diagnosis as well as medical and surgical treatment of the urinary tract in both men and women as well as male reproductive health services

## The Number of Physicians in Practice Is Increasing

There were 1,045,910 actively practicing physicians in the United States in 2013, of which 319,881 (37.4%) were primary care physicians. (See Table 2.1.) Primary care physicians are the front line of the health care system—the first health professionals most people see for medical problems or routine care. Family practitioners, internists, pediatricians, obstetrician/gynecologists, and general practitioners are considered to be primary care physicians. Primary care physicians tend to see the same patients regularly and develop relationships with patients over time as they offer preventive services, scheduled visits, follow-up, and urgent medical care. When necessary, they refer patients for consultation with, and care from, physician specialists.

In 2013, 600,863 physicians of all types maintained office-based practices. (See Table 2.2.) There were an additional 208,982 physicians working full time at hospitals, aided by 117,203 residents and interns. Another 44,853 active doctors were engaged in teaching, research, or other activities rather than patient care. Of the 854,698 active doctors in 2013, 636,707 (74.5%) were graduates of U.S. or Canadian medical schools, while the remaining 217,991 (25.5%) received their medical education elsewhere.

Some states have more physicians engaged in patient care relative to their populations than do other states, making it easier for patients living in those areas to find a doctor. In 2013 the District of Columbia (66.1 physicians per 10,000 civilian population) and Massachusetts (43 per 10,000) had the highest ratios. (See Table 2.3.) Idaho (18.6 per 10,000) and Mississippi (18.7 per 10,000) had the lowest ratios.

## Physician Working Conditions and Earnings

In *Occupational Outlook Handbook* (December 17, 2015, http://www.bls.gov/ooh), the U.S. Bureau of Labor Statistics (BLS) reports that most physicians and

**TABLE 2.1**

### Doctors in primary care, by specialty, selected years 1949–2013

[Data are based on reporting by physicians]

| Specialty | 1949[a] | 1960[a] | 1970 | 1980 | 1990 | 2000 | 2010 | 2012 | 2013 |
|---|---|---|---|---|---|---|---|---|---|
| | | | | | Number | | | | |
| **Total doctors of medicine[b]** | 201,277 | 260,484 | 334,028 | 467,679 | 615,421 | 813,770 | 985,375 | 1,026,788 | 1,045,910 |
| Active doctors of medicine[c] | 191,577 | 247,257 | 310,845 | 414,916 | 547,310 | 692,368 | 794,862 | 826,001 | 854,698 |
| General primary care specialists | 113,222 | 125,359 | 134,354 | 170,705 | 213,514 | 274,653 | 304,687 | 313,793 | 319,881 |
| General practice/family medicine | 95,980 | 88,023 | 57,948 | 60,049 | 70,480 | 86,312 | 94,746 | 96,552 | 98,298 |
| Internal medicine | 12,453 | 26,209 | 39,924 | 58,462 | 76,295 | 101,353 | 113,591 | 118,504 | 121,127 |
| Obstetrics/gynecology | — | — | 18,532 | 24,612 | 30,220 | 35,922 | 38,520 | 39,324 | 40,045 |
| Pediatrics | 4,789 | 11,127 | 17,950 | 27,582 | 36,519 | 51,066 | 57,830 | 59,413 | 60,411 |
| Primary care subspecialists | — | — | 3,161 | 16,642 | 30,911 | 52,294 | 76,122 | 83,532 | 90,147 |
| Family medicine | — | — | — | — | — | 483 | 1,445 | 1,764 | 1,991 |
| Internal medicine | — | — | 1,948 | 13,069 | 22,054 | 34,831 | 50,730 | 55,357 | 59,256 |
| Obstetrics/gynecology | — | — | 344 | 1,693 | 3,477 | 4,319 | 4,277 | 4,186 | 4,141 |
| Pediatrics | — | — | 869 | 1,880 | 5,380 | 12,661 | 19,670 | 22,225 | 24,759 |
| | | | | | Percent of active doctors of medicine | | | | |
| General primary care specialists | 59.1 | 50.7 | 43.2 | 41.1 | 39.0 | 39.7 | 38.3 | 38.0 | 37.4 |
| General practice/family medicine | 50.1 | 35.6 | 18.6 | 14.5 | 12.9 | 12.5 | 11.9 | 11.7 | 11.5 |
| Internal medicine | 6.5 | 10.6 | 12.8 | 14.1 | 13.9 | 14.6 | 14.3 | 14.3 | 14.2 |
| Obstetrics/gynecology | — | — | 6.0 | 5.9 | 5.5 | 5.2 | 4.8 | 4.8 | 4.7 |
| Pediatrics | 2.5 | 4.5 | 5.8 | 6.6 | 6.7 | 7.4 | 7.3 | 7.2 | 7.1 |
| Primary care subspecialists | — | — | 1.0 | 4.0 | 5.6 | 7.6 | 9.6 | 10.1 | 10.5 |
| Family medicine | — | — | — | — | — | 0.1 | 0.2 | 0.2 | 0.2 |
| Internal medicine | — | — | 0.6 | 3.1 | 4.0 | 5.0 | 6.4 | 6.7 | 6.9 |
| Obstetrics/gynecology | — | — | 0.1 | 0.4 | 0.6 | 0.6 | 0.5 | 0.5 | 0.5 |
| Pediatrics | — | — | 0.3 | 0.5 | 1.0 | 1.8 | 2.5 | 2.7 | 2.9 |

—Data not available.
0.0 Percentage greater than zero but less than 0.05.
[a]Estimated by the Bureau of Health Professions, Health Resources and Services Administration. Active doctors of medicine (MDs) include those with address unknown and primary specialty not classified.
[b]Data on federal and nonfederal doctors of medicine engaged in office- or hospital-based patient care and other professional activities.
[c]Starting with 1970 data, MDs who are inactive, have unknown address, or primary specialty not classified are excluded.
Notes: Data are as of December 31 except for 1990–1994 data, which are as of January 1, and 1949 data, which are as of midyear. Outlying areas include Puerto Rico, the U.S. Virgin Islands, and the U.S. Pacific Islands.

SOURCE: "Table 85. Doctors of Medicine in Primary Care, by Specialty: United States and Outlying U.S. Areas, Selected Years 1949–2013," in *Health, United States, 2015: With Special Feature on Racial and Ethnic Health Disparities*, U.S. Department of Health and Human Services, Centers for Disease Control and Prevention, National Center for Health Statistics, May 2016, http://www.cdc.gov/nchs/data/hus/hus15.pdf (accessed July 26, 2016). Data from the American Medical Association (AMA).

TABLE 2.2

**Medical doctors by activity and place of medical education, selected years 1975–2013**

[Data are based on reporting by physicians]

| Place of medical education and activity | 1975 | 1985 | 1995 | 2000 | 2005 | 2010 | 2012 | 2013 |
|---|---|---|---|---|---|---|---|---|
| | | | | Number of doctors of medicine | | | | |
| Total doctors of medicine | 393,742 | 552,716 | 720,325 | 813,770 | 902,053 | 985,375 | 1,026,788 | 1,045,910 |
| Active doctors of medicine[a] | 340,280 | 497,140 | 625,443 | 692,368 | 762,438 | 794,862 | 826,001 | 854,698 |
| **Place of medical education:** | | | | | | | | |
| U.S. medical graduates | — | 392,007 | 481,137 | 527,931 | 571,798 | 595,908 | 615,100 | 636,707 |
| International medical graduates[b] | — | 105,133 | 144,306 | 164,437 | 190,640 | 198,954 | 210,901 | 217,991 |
| **Activity:** | | | | | | | | |
| Patient care[c, d] | 287,837 | 431,527 | 564,074 | 631,431 | 718,473 | 752,572 | 784,633 | 809,845 |
| Office-based practice | 213,334 | 329,041 | 427,275 | 490,398 | 563,225 | 565,024 | 585,933 | 600,863 |
| General and family practice | 46,347 | 53,862 | 59,932 | 67,534 | 74,999 | 77,098 | 78,935 | 80,240 |
| Cardiovascular diseases | 5,046 | 9,054 | 13,739 | 16,300 | 17,519 | 17,454 | 17,512 | 17,657 |
| Dermatology | 3,442 | 5,325 | 6,959 | 7,969 | 8,795 | 9,272 | 9,669 | 9,910 |
| Gastroenterology | 1,696 | 4,135 | 7,300 | 8,515 | 9,742 | 10,466 | 10,985 | 11,322 |
| Internal medicine | 28,188 | 52,712 | 72,612 | 88,699 | 107,028 | 110,612 | 116,937 | 120,439 |
| Pediatrics | 12,687 | 22,392 | 33,890 | 42,215 | 51,854 | 53,054 | 56,692 | 58,719 |
| Pulmonary diseases | 1,166 | 3,035 | 4,964 | 6,095 | 7,321 | 7,846 | 8,365 | 8,870 |
| General surgery | 19,710 | 24,708 | 24,086 | 24,475 | 26,079 | 24,327 | 24,448 | 25,024 |
| Obstetrics and gynecology | 15,613 | 23,525 | 29,111 | 31,726 | 34,659 | 34,083 | 34,570 | 34,780 |
| Ophthalmology | 8,795 | 12,212 | 14,596 | 15,598 | 16,580 | 15,723 | 16,002 | 16,331 |
| Orthopedic surgery | 8,148 | 13,033 | 17,136 | 17,367 | 19,115 | 19,325 | 19,581 | 20,013 |
| Otolaryngology | 4,297 | 5,751 | 7,139 | 7,581 | 8,206 | 7,964 | 8,021 | 8,136 |
| Plastic surgery | 1,706 | 3,299 | 4,612 | 5,308 | 6,011 | 6,180 | 6,322 | 6,414 |
| Urological surgery | 5,025 | 7,081 | 7,991 | 8,460 | 8,955 | 8,606 | 8,558 | 8,563 |
| Anesthesiology | 8,970 | 15,285 | 23,770 | 27,624 | 31,887 | 31,819 | 32,604 | 33,218 |
| Diagnostic radiology | 1,978 | 7,735 | 12,751 | 14,622 | 17,618 | 17,503 | 17,916 | 18,203 |
| Emergency medicine | — | — | 11,700 | 14,541 | 20,173 | 20,654 | 22,223 | 23,414 |
| Neurology | 1,862 | 4,691 | 7,623 | 8,559 | 10,400 | 10,547 | 11,249 | 11,762 |
| Pathology, anatomical/clinical | 4,195 | 6,877 | 9,031 | 10,267 | 11,747 | 10,688 | 10,648 | 10,481 |
| Psychiatry | 12,173 | 18,521 | 23,334 | 24,955 | 27,638 | 25,690 | 26,171 | 26,696 |
| Radiology | 6,970 | 7,355 | 5,994 | 6,674 | 7,049 | 7,032 | 7,228 | 7,527 |
| Other specialty | 15,320 | 28,453 | 29,005 | 35,314 | 39,850 | 39,081 | 41,297 | 43,144 |
| Hospital-based practice | 74,503 | 102,486 | 136,799 | 141,033 | 155,248 | 187,548 | 198,700 | 208,982 |
| Residents and interns[e] | 53,527 | 72,159 | 93,650 | 95,125 | 95,391 | 108,142 | 116,460 | 117,203 |
| Full-time hospital staff | 20,976 | 30,327 | 43,149 | 45,908 | 59,857 | 79,406 | 82,240 | 91,779 |
| Other professional activity[f] | 24,252 | 44,046 | 40,290 | 41,556 | 43,965 | 42,290 | 41,368 | 44,853 |
| Inactive | 21,449 | 38,646 | 72,326 | 75,168 | 99,823 | 125,928 | 142,716 | 147,676 |
| Not classified | 26,145 | 13,950 | 20,579 | 45,136 | 39,304 | 64,153 | 57,649 | 43,536 |
| Unknown address | 5,868 | 2,980 | 1,977 | 1,098 | 488 | 432 | 422 | — |

—Data not available.

[a]Doctors of medicine who are inactive, have unknown address, or primary specialty not classified are excluded.
[b]International medical graduates received their medical education in schools outside of the United States and Canada.
[c]Specialty information is based on the physician's self-designated primary area of practice. Categories include generalists and specialists.
[d]Starting with 2003 data, federal and nonfederal doctors of medicine are included. Data prior to 2003 included nonfederal doctors of medicine only.
[e]Starting with 1990 data, clinical fellows are included in this category. In prior years, clinical fellows were included in the other professional activity category.
[f]Includes doctors of medicine in medical teaching, administration, research, and other nonpatient care activities. Prior to 1990, this category also included clinical fellows.
Notes: Data for doctors of medicine are as of December 31. Outlying areas include Puerto Rico, the U.S. Virgin Islands, and the U.S. Pacific Islands.

SOURCE: "Table 84. Doctors of Medicine, by Place of Medical Education and Activity: United States and Outlying U.S. Areas, Selected Years 1975–2013," in *Health, United States, 2015: With Special Feature on Racial and Ethnic Health Disparities*, U.S. Department of Health and Human Services, Centers for Disease Control and Prevention, National Center for Health Statistics, May 2016, http://www.cdc.gov/nchs/data/hus/hus15.pdf (accessed July 26, 2016). Data from the American Medical Association (AMA).

surgeons work full time, and that many "work long, irregular, and overnight hours." Physicians in salaried positions, such as those employed by health maintenance organizations, usually have more regular hours and enjoy more flexible work schedules than those in private practice. Instead of working as solo practitioners, growing numbers of physicians work in clinics or are partners in group practices or other integrated health care systems. Medical group practices allow physicians to have more flexible schedules, to realize purchasing economies of scale, to pool their money to finance expensive medical equipment, and to be better able to adapt to changes in health care delivery, financing, and reimbursement.

Physicians' earnings are among the highest of any profession. (See Figure 2.2.) The BLS notes that the median annual compensation (the middle value; half are lower and half are higher) for all physicians in 2015 was $187,200; however, many specialists earned more. In 2014 family practitioners had a median annual compensation of $221,419 and pediatricians had a median annual

**TABLE 2.3**

## Active physicians and physicians in patient care, by state, selected years 1975–2013

[Data are based on reporting by physicians]

| State | Active physicians[a, b] | | | | | | Physicians in patient care[a, b, c] | | | | | |
|---|---|---|---|---|---|---|---|---|---|---|---|---|
| | 1975 | 1985 | 2000[d] | 2010 | 2012 | 2013 | 1975 | 1985 | 2000[d] | 2010 | 2012 | 2013 |
| | Number per 10,000 civilian population | | | | | | | | | | | |
| **United States** | 15.3 | 20.7 | 25.8 | 27.2 | 28.3 | 29.4 | 13.5 | 18.0 | 22.7 | 24.0 | 26.9 | 27.6 |
| Alabama | 9.2 | 14.2 | 19.8 | 21.4 | 21.8 | 22.4 | 8.6 | 13.1 | 18.2 | 20.6 | 21.1 | 21.5 |
| Alaska | 8.4 | 13.0 | 18.5 | 24.3 | 24.2 | 25.0 | 7.8 | 12.1 | 16.3 | 23.3 | 23.2 | 23.7 |
| Arizona | 16.7 | 20.2 | 20.9 | 22.6 | 24.2 | 25.5 | 14.1 | 17.1 | 17.6 | 21.6 | 23.2 | 24.0 |
| Arkansas | 9.1 | 13.8 | 18.8 | 20.2 | 20.9 | 21.5 | 8.5 | 12.8 | 17.3 | 19.4 | 20.2 | 20.6 |
| California | 18.8 | 23.7 | 23.8 | 26.1 | 26.9 | 27.8 | 17.3 | 21.5 | 21.6 | 24.7 | 25.6 | 26.2 |
| Colorado | 17.3 | 20.7 | 24.0 | 26.9 | 27.6 | 29.1 | 15.0 | 17.7 | 20.9 | 25.5 | 26.3 | 27.4 |
| Connecticut | 19.8 | 27.6 | 33.7 | 36.0 | 37.6 | 38.4 | 17.7 | 24.3 | 30.3 | 33.6 | 35.2 | 35.8 |
| Delaware | 14.3 | 19.7 | 24.7 | 26.3 | 26.4 | 27.4 | 12.7 | 17.1 | 21.0 | 25.2 | 25.3 | 25.8 |
| District of Columbia | 39.6 | 55.3 | 62.5 | 76.9 | 73.8 | 74.7 | 34.6 | 45.6 | 54.5 | 68.8 | 65.9 | 66.1 |
| Florida | 15.2 | 20.2 | 24.1 | 26.0 | 26.5 | 27.2 | 13.4 | 17.8 | 21.2 | 25.0 | 25.5 | 25.7 |
| Georgia | 11.5 | 16.2 | 20.4 | 21.3 | 22.3 | 23.4 | 10.6 | 14.7 | 18.6 | 20.2 | 21.2 | 22.0 |
| Hawaii | 16.2 | 21.5 | 26.4 | 31.3 | 29.7 | 30.8 | 14.7 | 19.8 | 24.0 | 29.6 | 28.2 | 29.0 |
| Idaho | 9.5 | 12.1 | 15.8 | 18.4 | 18.4 | 19.2 | 8.9 | 11.4 | 14.4 | 17.9 | 18.0 | 18.6 |
| Illinois | 14.5 | 20.5 | 26.1 | 27.9 | 28.7 | 30.1 | 13.1 | 18.2 | 23.1 | 26.6 | 27.5 | 28.5 |
| Indiana | 10.6 | 14.7 | 20.0 | 22.2 | 22.6 | 23.3 | 9.6 | 13.2 | 18.0 | 21.3 | 21.7 | 22.2 |
| Iowa | 11.4 | 15.6 | 19.8 | 21.8 | 22.0 | 23.2 | 9.4 | 12.4 | 15.5 | 20.8 | 21.0 | 21.6 |
| Kansas | 12.8 | 17.3 | 21.8 | 24.0 | 24.5 | 25.4 | 11.2 | 15.1 | 18.8 | 23.1 | 23.6 | 24.1 |
| Kentucky | 10.9 | 15.1 | 20.6 | 23.1 | 23.3 | 24.6 | 10.1 | 13.9 | 19.1 | 22.2 | 22.5 | 23.6 |
| Louisiana | 11.4 | 17.3 | 23.8 | 25.4 | 26.8 | 27.2 | 10.5 | 16.1 | 22.4 | 24.5 | 25.9 | 26.3 |
| Maine | 12.8 | 18.7 | 26.8 | 31.8 | 32.0 | 33.7 | 10.7 | 15.6 | 21.7 | 30.2 | 30.5 | 31.7 |
| Maryland | 18.6 | 30.4 | 35.4 | 39.1 | 39.5 | 40.9 | 16.5 | 24.9 | 31.1 | 34.9 | 35.5 | 36.5 |
| Massachusetts | 20.8 | 30.2 | 38.6 | 43.4 | 44.6 | 47.0 | 18.3 | 25.4 | 34.4 | 40.0 | 41.3 | 43.0 |
| Michigan | 15.4 | 20.8 | 26.3 | 28.9 | 30.1 | 31.5 | 12.0 | 16.0 | 20.2 | 27.6 | 28.8 | 29.4 |
| Minnesota | 14.9 | 20.5 | 24.9 | 30.1 | 30.3 | 31.1 | 13.7 | 18.5 | 23.0 | 28.2 | 28.9 | 29.5 |
| Mississippi | 8.4 | 11.8 | 16.6 | 18.3 | 18.6 | 19.5 | 8.0 | 11.1 | 15.2 | 17.6 | 18.0 | 18.7 |
| Missouri | 15.0 | 20.5 | 24.7 | 26.3 | 27.4 | 28.9 | 11.6 | 16.3 | 20.2 | 25.1 | 26.2 | 26.9 |
| Montana | 10.6 | 14.0 | 20.4 | 22.5 | 22.4 | 23.1 | 10.1 | 13.2 | 18.8 | 21.8 | 21.7 | 22.3 |
| Nebraska | 12.1 | 15.7 | 21.7 | 24.5 | 24.8 | 26.0 | 10.9 | 14.4 | 20.1 | 23.4 | 23.8 | 24.8 |
| Nevada | 11.9 | 16.0 | 18.0 | 19.8 | 19.6 | 20.3 | 10.9 | 14.5 | 15.9 | 19.2 | 19.0 | 19.3 |
| New Hampshire | 14.3 | 18.1 | 23.8 | 29.5 | 30.6 | 32.0 | 13.1 | 16.7 | 21.7 | 28.2 | 29.3 | 30.4 |
| New Jersey | 16.2 | 23.4 | 31.1 | 31.8 | 32.5 | 33.5 | 14.0 | 19.8 | 26.2 | 30.1 | 30.9 | 31.5 |
| New Mexico | 12.2 | 17.0 | 20.9 | 23.8 | 24.1 | 25.2 | 10.1 | 14.7 | 18.5 | 22.5 | 22.9 | 23.6 |
| New York | 22.7 | 29.0 | 36.2 | 36.4 | 38.3 | 39.4 | 20.2 | 25.2 | 32.3 | 34.2 | 36.2 | 36.8 |
| North Carolina | 11.7 | 16.9 | 22.3 | 25.0 | 25.4 | 26.4 | 10.6 | 15.0 | 20.5 | 23.7 | 24.1 | 24.9 |
| North Dakota | 9.7 | 15.8 | 19.2 | 25.0 | 25.0 | 25.3 | 9.2 | 14.9 | 19.8 | 24.1 | 24.2 | 24.4 |
| Ohio | 14.1 | 19.9 | 25.4 | 28.5 | 29.5 | 31.4 | 12.2 | 16.8 | 21.3 | 27.3 | 28.3 | 29.5 |
| Oklahoma | 11.6 | 16.1 | 19.4 | 21.0 | 21.5 | 22.3 | 9.4 | 12.9 | 14.8 | 20.2 | 20.7 | 21.0 |
| Oregon | 15.6 | 19.7 | 22.9 | 28.3 | 29.1 | 30.7 | 13.8 | 17.6 | 20.5 | 26.9 | 27.8 | 29.0 |
| Pennsylvania | 16.6 | 23.6 | 31.6 | 32.6 | 33.1 | 35.1 | 13.9 | 19.2 | 25.4 | 30.7 | 31.2 | 32.5 |
| Rhode Island | 17.8 | 23.3 | 32.5 | 37.1 | 38.2 | 40.2 | 16.1 | 20.2 | 28.8 | 35.2 | 36.3 | 37.8 |
| South Carolina | 10.0 | 14.7 | 21.0 | 23.3 | 23.4 | 24.1 | 9.3 | 13.6 | 19.4 | 22.4 | 22.5 | 23.1 |
| South Dakota | 8.2 | 13.4 | 19.2 | 23.0 | 23.8 | 24.6 | 7.7 | 12.3 | 17.7 | 22.2 | 22.8 | 23.6 |
| Tennessee | 12.4 | 17.7 | 23.6 | 26.0 | 26.8 | 27.7 | 11.3 | 16.2 | 21.8 | 24.8 | 25.6 | 26.3 |
| Texas | 12.5 | 16.8 | 20.3 | 21.5 | 22.3 | 23.2 | 11.0 | 14.7 | 17.9 | 20.6 | 21.5 | 22.1 |
| Utah | 14.1 | 17.2 | 19.6 | 21.0 | 21.9 | 22.6 | 13.0 | 15.5 | 17.8 | 20.0 | 21.0 | 21.5 |
| Vermont | 18.2 | 23.8 | 32.0 | 35.7 | 36.2 | 38.2 | 15.5 | 20.3 | 28.8 | 33.4 | 34.0 | 35.6 |
| Virginia | 12.9 | 19.5 | 23.9 | 27.0 | 27.2 | 28.1 | 11.9 | 17.8 | 22.0 | 25.7 | 26.0 | 26.6 |
| Washington | 15.3 | 20.2 | 23.7 | 27.1 | 27.4 | 28.4 | 13.6 | 17.9 | 21.2 | 25.5 | 25.8 | 26.5 |
| West Virginia | 11.0 | 16.3 | 23.5 | 25.5 | 26.0 | 27.1 | 10.0 | 14.6 | 19.5 | 24.5 | 24.9 | 25.4 |
| Wisconsin | 12.5 | 17.7 | 23.1 | 26.8 | 27.3 | 27.9 | 11.4 | 15.9 | 20.9 | 25.6 | 26.2 | 26.6 |
| Wyoming | 9.5 | 12.9 | 17.3 | 19.7 | 19.2 | 19.5 | 8.9 | 12.0 | 15.7 | 19.1 | 18.8 | 18.9 |

[a]Includes active doctors of medicine (MDs) and active doctors of osteopathy (DOs).
[b]Starting with 2003 data, federal and nonfederal physicians are included. Data prior to 2003 included nonfederal physicians only.
[c]Prior to 2006, excludes DOs. Excludes physicians in medical teaching, administration, research, and other nonpatient care activities. Includes residents.
[d]Data for DOs are as of January 2001.
Notes: Data for MDs are as of December 31. Data for DOs are as of May 31, unless otherwise specified. Starting with *Health, United States, 2012*, data for DOs for 2009 and beyond are from the American Medical Association (AMA). Prior to 2009, data for DOs are from the American Osteopathic Association (AOA).

SOURCE: "Table 83. Active Physicians and Physicians in Patient Care, by State: United States, Selected Years 1975–2013," in *Health, United States, 2015: With Special Feature on Racial and Ethnic Health Disparities*, U.S. Department of Health and Human Services, Centers for Disease Control and Prevention, National Center for Health Statistics, May 2016, http://www.cdc.gov/nchs/data/hus/hus15.pdf (accessed July 26, 2016) Data from the American Medical Association (AMA).

compensation of $226,408. By contrast, the median annual compensation for general surgeons was $395,456 and for anesthesiologists it was $443,859. Salaries vary widely and are based on a physician's specialty, the number of years in practice, the hours worked, and the geographic location.

FIGURE 2.2

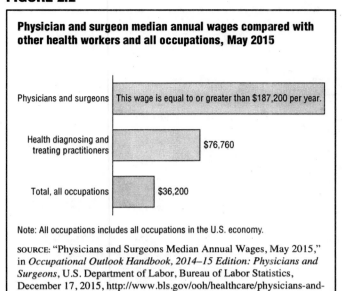

**Physician and surgeon median annual wages compared with other health workers and all occupations, May 2015**

Note: All occupations includes all occupations in the U.S. economy.

SOURCE: "Physicians and Surgeons Median Annual Wages, May 2015," in *Occupational Outlook Handbook, 2014–15 Edition: Physicians and Surgeons*, U.S. Department of Labor, Bureau of Labor Statistics, December 17, 2015, http://www.bls.gov/ooh/healthcare/physicians-and-surgeons.htm#tab-5 (accessed July 26, 2016)

**FIGURE 2.3**

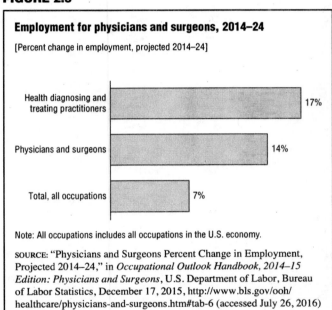

**Employment for physicians and surgeons, 2014–24**

[Percent change in employment, projected 2014–24]

Note: All occupations includes all occupations in the U.S. economy.

SOURCE: "Physicians and Surgeons Percent Change in Employment, Projected 2014–24," in *Occupational Outlook Handbook, 2014–15 Edition: Physicians and Surgeons*, U.S. Department of Labor, Bureau of Labor Statistics, December 17, 2015, http://www.bls.gov/ooh/healthcare/physicians-and-surgeons.htm#tab-6 (accessed July 26, 2016)

The BLS expects that physician employment will increase 14% between 2014 and 2024, outpacing many other occupations. (See Figure 2.3.) This increase is attributable to an aging population and continued demand for physician services.

### Effect of Health Care Reform on Physician Satisfaction

The results of a survey of 1,624 primary care physicians and their opinions about changing health care delivery were reported by Jamie Ryan et al. in *Primary Care Providers' Views of Recent Trends in Health Care Delivery and*

*Payment: Findings from the Commonwealth Fund/Kaiser Family Foundation 2015 National Survey of Primary Care Providers* (August 2015, http://www.commonwealthfund.org/publications/issue-briefs/2015/aug/primary-care-providers-views-delivery-payment). Physicians reported mixed feelings about new models of care and changes in payment such as financial incentives for quality or efficiency that have occurred in response to implementation of the Patient Protection and Affordable Care Act (also known as the Affordable Care Act [ACA]).

Physicians generally feel that health information technology, such as the use of electronic health records, has a favorable effect on quality of care, but they are unsure and divided about the increased use of medical homes (team-based care intended to provide comprehensive and continuous medical care to patients with the goal of obtaining maximized health outcomes) and accountable care organizations (groups of physicians, hospitals, health plans, and other providers that voluntarily join forces to deliver coordinated, quality care to defined patient populations). Physicians are also concerned and largely unhappy about the increased reliance on quality metrics used to assess their performance and the financial penalties for unnecessary hospital admissions or readmissions. Many physicians are frustrated with the speed and documentation requirements of Medicaid (a state and federal health insurance program for low-income people) and Medicare (a federal health insurance program for people aged 65 years and older and people with disabilities) payments.

### Physician Visits

In 2012 Americans made 928,630 physician-office visits. (See Table 2.4.) More than half (53.2%) of these visits were to primary care physicians. (See Table 2.5.) Younger Americans were particularly likely to see a primary care generalist when they visited a physician; 80.7% of visits by people aged 18 years and younger were to generalists, as were 57.4% of visits by those aged 18 to 44 years. Americans aged 45 years and older saw specialists for more than half of their physician visits in 2012.

### REGISTERED NURSES

Registered nurses (RNs) are licensed by the state to care for the sick and to promote health. RNs supervise hospital care, administer medication and treatment as prescribed by physicians, monitor the progress of patients, and provide health education. Nurses work in a variety of settings, including hospitals, nursing homes, physicians' offices, clinics, and schools.

### Education for Nurses

There are three types of education for RNs: associate's degree (two-year community college programs), baccalaureate degree (four-year programs), and postgraduate degree (master's and doctorate programs). The baccalaureate

TABLE 2.4

## Visits to physician offices by age, selected years 2000–12

[Data are based on reporting by a sample of office-based physicians, hospital outpatient departments, and hospital emergency departments]

| Age, sex, and race | All places[a] | | | | Physician offices | | | |
|---|---|---|---|---|---|---|---|---|
| | 2000 | 2010 | 2011 | 2012[b] | 2000 | 2010 | 2011 | 2012[b] |
| **Age** | | | | Number of visits, in thousands | | | | |
| **Total** | 1,014,848 | 1,239,387 | 1,249,047 | — | 823,542 | 1,008,802 | 987,029 | 928,630 |
| Under 18 years | 212,165 | 246,228 | 263,387 | — | 163,459 | 191,500 | 206,285 | 171,045 |
| 18–44 years | 315,774 | 342,797 | 333,427 | — | 243,011 | 261,941 | 239,224 | 234,645 |
| 45–64 years | 255,894 | 352,001 | 353,591 | — | 216,783 | 296,385 | 285,784 | 275,307 |
| 45–54 years | 142,233 | 171,039 | 173,334 | — | 119,474 | 140,819 | 136,429 | 129,816 |
| 55–64 years | 113,661 | 180,962 | 180,258 | — | 97,309 | 155,566 | 149,355 | 145,491 |
| 65 years and over | 231,014 | 298,362 | 298,642 | — | 200,289 | 258,976 | 255,736 | 247,634 |
| 65–74 years | 116,505 | 151,075 | 151,970 | — | 102,447 | 132,201 | 131,233 | 126,436 |
| 75 years and over | 114,510 | 147,287 | 146,672 | — | 97,842 | 126,775 | 124,503 | 121,197 |
| | | | | Number of visits per 100 persons | | | | |
| **Total, age-adjusted[c]** | 374 | 401 | 400 | — | 304 | 325 | 314 | 292 |
| **Total, crude** | 370 | 408 | 408 | — | 300 | 332 | 322 | 301 |
| Under 18 years | 293 | 331 | 357 | — | 226 | 257 | 280 | 232 |
| 18–44 years | 291 | 310 | 302 | — | 224 | 237 | 216 | 211 |
| 45–64 years | 422 | 441 | 431 | — | 358 | 371 | 349 | 335 |
| 45–54 years | 385 | 388 | 392 | — | 323 | 320 | 309 | 297 |
| 55–64 years | 481 | 505 | 477 | — | 412 | 434 | 395 | 380 |
| 65 years and over | 706 | 767 | 745 | — | 612 | 666 | 638 | 592 |
| 65–74 years | 656 | 713 | 683 | — | 577 | 624 | 590 | 532 |
| 75 years and over | 766 | 831 | 822 | — | 654 | 715 | 698 | 670 |
| **Sex and age** | | | | | | | | |
| Male, age-adjusted[c] | 325 | 350 | 354 | — | 261 | 283 | 280 | 254 |
| Male, crude | 314 | 350 | 356 | — | 251 | 283 | 281 | 258 |
| Under 18 years | 302 | 340 | 372 | — | 231 | 262 | 294 | 236 |
| 18–44 years | 203 | 205 | 208 | — | 148 | 151 | 145 | 140 |
| 45–54 years | 316 | 324 | 322 | — | 260 | 265 | 250 | 251 |
| 55–64 years | 428 | 460 | 430 | — | 367 | 396 | 351 | 343 |
| 65–74 years | 614 | 680 | 655 | — | 539 | 597 | 566 | 505 |
| 75 years and over | 771 | 871 | 869 | — | 670 | 760 | 758 | 685 |
| Female, age-adjusted[c] | 420 | 452 | 444 | — | 345 | 367 | 348 | 328 |
| Female, crude | 424 | 464 | 457 | — | 348 | 379 | 361 | 342 |
| Under 18 years | 285 | 322 | 341 | — | 221 | 252 | 265 | 229 |
| 18–44 years | 377 | 415 | 393 | — | 298 | 323 | 286 | 281 |
| 45–54 years | 451 | 450 | 459 | — | 384 | 372 | 364 | 340 |
| 55–64 years | 529 | 546 | 520 | — | 453 | 469 | 436 | 413 |
| 65–74 years | 692 | 741 | 707 | — | 609 | 647 | 611 | 556 |
| 75 years and over | 763 | 804 | 790 | — | 645 | 685 | 657 | 660 |
| **Race and age[d]** | | | | | | | | |
| White, age-adjusted[c] | 380 | 408 | 411 | — | 315 | 336 | 333 | 315 |
| White, crude | 381 | 421 | 424 | — | 316 | 349 | 345 | 330 |
| Under 18 years | 306 | 341 | 397 | — | 243 | 270 | 324 | 264 |
| 18–44 years | 301 | 319 | 312 | — | 239 | 249 | 233 | 231 |
| 45–54 years | 386 | 389 | 378 | — | 330 | 326 | 305 | 313 |
| 55–64 years | 480 | 505 | 474 | — | 416 | 440 | 400 | 400 |
| 65–74 years | 641 | 727 | 677 | — | 568 | 642 | 594 | 555 |
| 75 years and over | 764 | 838 | 815 | — | 658 | 723 | 698 | 693 |
| Black or African American, age-adjusted[c] | 353 | 439 | 430 | — | 239 | 316 | 277 | 229 |
| Black or African American, crude | 324 | 425 | 416 | — | 214 | 303 | 266 | 221 |
| Under 18 years | 264 | 351 | 275 | — | 167 | 241 | 153 | 168 |
| 18–44 years | 257 | 339 | 350 | — | 149 | 222 | 199 | 168 |
| 45–54 years | 383 | 466 | 550 | — | 269 | 339 | 378 | 252 |
| 55–64 years | 495 | 617 | 566 | — | 373 | 481 | 412 | 305 |
| 65–74 years | 656 | 715 | 733 | — | 512 | 565 | 539 | 421 |
| 75 years and over | 745 | 845 | 821 | — | 568 | 682 | 605 | 522 |

degree provides more knowledge of community health services, as well as the psychological and social aspects of caring for patients, than does the associate's degree. Those who complete the four-year baccalaureate degree and the other advanced degrees are generally better prepared to eventually attain administrative or management positions and may have greater opportunities for upward mobility in related disciplines such as research, teaching, and public health.

The BLS indicates in *Occupational Outlook Handbook* that in 2014 there were nearly 2.8 million RN jobs in the United States. It predicts that employment of RNs will grow 16% between 2014 and 2024, faster than it will for all occupations. (See Figure 2.4.)

**TABLE 2.4**

## Visits to physician offices by age, selected years 2000–12 [CONTINUED]

[Data are based on reporting by a sample of office-based physicians, hospital outpatient departments, and hospital emergency departments]

| Age, sex, and race | Hospital outpatient departments | | | | Hospital emergency departments | | | |
|---|---|---|---|---|---|---|---|---|
| | 2000 | 2010 | 2011 | 2012 | 2000 | 2010 | 2011 | 2012 |
| **Age** | Number of visits, in thousands | | | | | | | |
| Total | 83,289 | 100,742 | 125,721 | — | 108,017 | 129,843 | 136,296 | — |
| Under 18 years | 21,076 | 24,913 | 27,651 | — | 27,630 | 29,815 | 29,451 | — |
| 18–44 years | 26,947 | 28,159 | 37,557 | — | 45,816 | 52,697 | 56,646 | — |
| 45–64 years | 20,772 | 27,739 | 37,980 | — | 18,339 | 27,877 | 29,828 | — |
| 45–54 years | 11,558 | 13,639 | 19,310 | — | 11,201 | 16,581 | 17,595 | — |
| 55–64 years | 9,214 | 14,100 | 18,670 | — | 7,138 | 11,296 | 12,232 | — |
| 65 years and over | 14,494 | 19,932 | 22,534 | — | 16,232 | 19,454 | 20,372 | — |
| 65–74 years | 7,515 | 10,675 | 12,529 | — | 6,543 | 8,199 | 8,208 | — |
| 75 years and over | 6,979 | 9,257 | 10,005 | — | 9,690 | 11,255 | 12,163 | — |
| | Number of visits per 100 persons | | | | | | | |
| Total, age-adjusted[c] | 31 | 33 | 40 | — | 40 | 43 | 45 | — |
| Total, crude | 30 | 33 | 41 | — | 39 | 43 | 44 | — |
| Under 18 years | 29 | 33 | 37 | — | 38 | 40 | 40 | — |
| 18–44 years | 25 | 25 | 34 | — | 42 | 48 | 51 | — |
| 45–64 years | 34 | 35 | 46 | — | 30 | 35 | 36 | — |
| 45–54 years | 31 | 31 | 44 | — | 30 | 38 | 40 | — |
| 55–64 years | 39 | 39 | 49 | — | 30 | 32 | 32 | — |
| 65 years and over | 44 | 51 | 56 | — | 50 | 50 | 51 | — |
| 65–74 years | 42 | 50 | 56 | — | 37 | 39 | 37 | — |
| 75 years and over | 47 | 52 | 56 | — | 65 | 64 | 68 | — |
| **Sex and age** | | | | | | | | |
| Male, age-adjusted[c] | 26 | 27 | 32 | — | 38 | 40 | 42 | — |
| Male, crude | 25 | 27 | 33 | — | 38 | 39 | 41 | — |
| Under 18 years | 29 | 34 | 37 | — | 41 | 43 | 41 | — |
| 18–44 years | 17 | 16 | 20 | — | 38 | 38 | 43 | — |
| 45–54 years | 26 | 24 | 34 | — | 30 | 35 | 38 | — |
| 55–64 years | 32 | 32 | 45 | — | 30 | 32 | 34 | — |
| 65–74 years | 38 | 47 | 52 | — | 36 | 37 | 37 | — |
| 75 years and over | 42 | 50 | 49 | — | 59 | 60 | 62 | — |
| Female, age-adjusted[c] | 35 | 38 | 48 | — | 41 | 47 | 48 | — |
| Female, crude | 35 | 39 | 49 | — | 41 | 46 | 48 | — |
| Under 18 years | 29 | 33 | 38 | — | 35 | 37 | 39 | — |
| 18–44 years | 33 | 35 | 47 | — | 46 | 57 | 59 | — |
| 45–54 years | 36 | 37 | 53 | — | 31 | 40 | 41 | — |
| 55–64 years | 45 | 46 | 54 | — | 31 | 31 | 31 | — |
| 65–74 years | 46 | 54 | 60 | — | 37 | 40 | 37 | — |
| 75 years and over | 49 | 53 | 61 | — | 69 | 66 | 72 | — |
| **Race and age[d]** | | | | | | | | |
| White, age-adjusted[c] | 28 | 31 | 37 | — | 37 | 41 | 42 | — |
| White, crude | 28 | 32 | 38 | — | 37 | 40 | 41 | — |
| Under 18 years | 27 | 33 | 37 | — | 36 | 39 | 37 | — |
| 18–44 years | 23 | 25 | 31 | — | 39 | 45 | 47 | — |
| 45–54 years | 28 | 28 | 37 | — | 28 | 34 | 35 | — |
| 55–64 years | 36 | 36 | 44 | — | 28 | 29 | 30 | — |
| 65–74 years | 38 | 48 | 49 | — | 35 | 37 | 34 | — |
| 75 years and over | 44 | 52 | 52 | — | 63 | 62 | 65 | — |
| Black or African American, age-adjusted[c] | 51 | 51 | 69 | — | 62 | 73 | 85 | — |
| Black or African American, crude | 48 | 50 | 68 | — | 62 | 72 | 83 | — |
| Under 18 years | 40 | 48 | 50* | — | 57 | 62 | 72 | — |
| 18–44 years | 40 | 37 | 55 | — | 68 | 81 | 96 | — |
| 45–54 years | 61 | 54 | 89 | — | 53 | 73 | 83 | — |
| 55–64 years | 70 | 73 | 94 | — | 52 | 62 | 60 | — |
| 65–74 years | 85 | 85* | 121* | — | 59 | 66 | 73 | — |
| 75 years and over | 85 | 74* | 98* | — | 92 | 89 | 118 | — |

**NEED FOR NURSES EXCEEDS SUPPLY.** Although the number of RNs holding baccalaureate degrees increased sharply during the 1990s, there is still a shortage of nurses that is predicted to persist through 2020. Figure 2.5 shows that the gap between supply and demand for RNs is projected to widen between 2000 and 2020. In "How the Educational Funding Provisions of the Patient Protection and Affordable Care Act Will Affect the Nursing Shortage in the United States" (*Northwestern Journal of Law and Social Policy*, vol. 11, no. 1, Spring 2016), Kathleen Fischer forecasts a national RN deficit of 36% of demand in 2020. She attributes the shortage to "(1) a deficit of nursing faculty, classrooms, and clinical space in graduate and undergraduate nursing programs, (2) the retirement of nurses in the 'Baby Boom' generation, (3) low job

[Data are based on reporting by a sample of office-based physicians, hospital outpatient departments, and hospital emergency departments]

—Data not available.
*Estimates are considered unreliable.
<sup>a</sup>All places includes visits to physician offices and hospital outpatient and emergency departments.
<sup>b</sup>In 2012, data for all places and physician offices exclude visits to community health centers; in 2006–2011, data for all places and physician offices include visits to community health centers (2%–3% of visits to physician offices in 2006–2011 were to community health centers). Prior to 2006, visits to community health centers were not included in the survey.
<sup>c</sup>Estimates are age-adjusted to the year 2000 standard population using six age groups: under 18 years, 18–44 years, 45–54 years, 55–64 years, 65–74 years, and 75 years and over.
<sup>d</sup>Estimates by racial group should be used with caution because information on race was collected from medical records and race is imputed for records missing that information. Information on the race imputation process used in each data year is available in the public-use file documentation. Starting with 1999 data, the instruction for the race item on the Patient Record Form was changed so that more than one race could be recorded. In previous years only one race could be recorded. Estimates for race in this table are for visits where only one race was recorded. Because of the small number of responses with more than one racial group recorded, estimates for visits with multiple races recorded are unreliable and are not presented.
Notes: Rates for 1995–2000 were computed using 1990-based postcensal estimates of the civilian noninstitutionalized population as of July 1, adjusted for net underenumeration using the 1990 National Population Adjustment Matrix from the U.S. Census Bureau. For 2001–2010 data, rates were computed using 2000-based postcensal estimates of the civilian noninstitutionalized population as of July 1. For 2011 data and beyond, rates were computed using 2010-based postcensal estimates of the civilian noninstitutionalized population as of July 1. Rates using the civilian noninstitutionalized population will be overestimated to the extent that visits by institutionalized persons are counted in the numerator (for example, hospital emergency department visits by nursing home residents) but institutionalized persons are omitted from the denominator (the civilian noninstitutionalized population). Starting with *Health, United States, 2005*, data for physician offices for 2001 and beyond use a revised weighting scheme.

SOURCE: Adapted from "Table 76. Visits to Physician Offices, Hospital Outpatient Departments, and Hospital Emergency Departments, by Age, Sex, and Race: United States, Selected Years 2000–2012," in *Health, United States, 2015: With Special Feature on Racial and Ethnic Health Disparities*, U.S. Department of Health and Human Services, Centers for Disease Control and Prevention, National Center for Health Statistics, May 2016, http://www.cdc.gov/nchs/data/hus/hus15.pdf (accessed July 26, 2016)

satisfaction that causes nurses to leave the profession prematurely, (4) the increased demand for health care services related to the rapid aging of the United States' population, (5) the Affordable Care Act's expansion of access to health care to many currently uninsured Americans, and (6) economic pressures faced by nursing employers."

Industry observers believe other factors have contributed to the shortage, including expanding opportunities for women to pursue other careers, a sicker population of hospitalized patients requiring more labor-intensive care, and the public perception that nursing is a thankless, unglamorous job that requires grueling physical labor, long hours, and low pay. Observers also note that the public, particularly high school students who are considering careers in health care, are unaware of the many new opportunities in nursing, such as advanced practice nursing, which offers additional independence and increased earning potential, and the technology-driven field of applied informatics (computer management of information).

The article "The 100 Best Jobs" (http://money.usnews.com/careers/best-jobs/rankings/the-100-best-jobs) explains that in 2016 registered nurse ranked number 22 in terms of all career options with the brightest prospects, and number 16 among health care jobs, based on the high projected demand—an estimated 439,300 new jobs by 2024—for these workers.

## ADVANCED PRACTICE NURSES AND PHYSICIAN ASSISTANTS

Much of the preventive medical care and treatment usually delivered by physicians may also be provided by midlevel practitioners—health professionals with less formal education and training than physicians. Advanced practice nurses make up a group that includes certified nurse midwives, nurse practitioners (NPs; RNs with advanced academic and clinical experience), and clinical nurse specialists (RNs with advanced nursing degrees who specialize in areas such as mental health, gerontology, cardiac or cancer care, or community or neonatal health). Physician assistants (PAs) are midlevel practitioners who work under the auspices, supervision, or direction of physicians. They conduct physical examinations, order and interpret laboratory and radiological studies, and prescribe medication. They even perform procedures (e.g., biopsy, suturing, casting, and administering anesthesia) that were once performed exclusively by physicians.

The origins of each profession are key to understanding the differences between them. Nursing has the longer history, and nurses are recognized members of the health care team. For this reason, NPs were easily integrated into many practice settings.

PA is the newer of the two disciplines. PAs have been practicing in the United States since the early 1970s. The career originated as civilian employment for returning Vietnam War (1954–1975) veterans who had worked as medics. The veterans needed immediate employment and few had the educational prerequisites, time, or resources to pursue the training necessary to become physicians. At the same time, the United States was projecting a dire shortage of primary care physicians, especially in rural and inner-city practices. The use of NPs and PAs was seen as an ideal rapid response to the demand for additional medical services. They could be deployed quickly to serve remote communities or underserved populations for a fraction of the costs associated with physicians.

**TABLE 2.5**

**Visits to physician offices, by selected characteristics, selected years 1980–2012**

[Data are based on reporting by a sample of office-based physicians]

| | Type of primary care generalist physician[a] | | | | | | | | | | | |
| | All primary care generalists | | | | General and family practice | | | | Internal medicine | | | |
| Age, sex, and race | 1980 | 2000 | 2010 | 2012[b] | 1980 | 2000 | 2010 | 2012[b] | 1980 | 2000 | 2010 | 2012[b] |
|---|---|---|---|---|---|---|---|---|---|---|---|---|
| **Age** | | | | | Percent distribution | | | | | | | |
| Total | **66.2** | **58.9** | **55.2** | **53.2** | **33.5** | **24.1** | **21.1** | **20.3** | **12.1** | **15.3** | **13.9** | **12.7** |
| Under 18 years | 77.8 | 79.7 | 80.9 | 80.7 | 26.1 | 19.9 | 15.3 | 12.4 | 2.0 | * | * | 1.3* |
| 18–44 years | 65.3 | 62.1 | 62.7 | 57.4 | 34.3 | 28.2 | 27.8 | 24.2 | 8.6 | 12.7 | 11.6 | 10.2 |
| 45–64 years | 60.2 | 51.2 | 46.7 | 44.6 | 36.3 | 26.4 | 23.1 | 23.0 | 19.5 | 20.1 | 18.5 | 16.3 |
| 45–54 years | 60.2 | 52.3 | 48.7 | 47.0 | 37.4 | 27.8 | 26.2 | 24.4 | 17.1 | 18.7 | 15.7 | 15.2 |
| 55–64 years | 60.2 | 49.9 | 44.8 | 42.5 | 35.4 | 24.7 | 20.4 | 21.7 | 21.8 | 21.7 | 21.0 | 17.2 |
| 65 years and over | 61.6 | 46.5 | 38.3 | 39.7 | 37.5 | 20.2 | 16.4 | 19.0 | 22.7 | 24.5 | 20.5 | 19.0 |
| 65–74 years | 61.2 | 46.6 | 37.3 | 39.8 | 37.4 | 19.7 | 17.5 | 20.0 | 22.1 | 24.5 | 18.2 | 17.6 |
| 75 years and over | 62.3 | 46.4 | 39.2 | 39.6 | 37.6 | 20.8 | 15.4 | 18.0 | 23.5 | 24.5 | 22.8 | 20.4 |
| **Sex and age** | | | | | | | | | | | | |
| **Male:** | | | | | | | | | | | | |
| Under 18 years | 77.3 | 77.7 | 80.1 | 78.6 | 25.6 | 18.3 | 15.7 | 12.3 | 2.0 | * | * | 1.0* |
| 18–44 years | 50.8 | 51.5 | 51.7 | 46.1 | 38.0 | 34.2 | 33.7 | 29.9 | 11.5 | 14.4 | 16.4 | 14.3 |
| 45–64 years | 55.6 | 49.4 | 43.7 | 43.5 | 34.4 | 28.7 | 24.4 | 25.2 | 20.5 | 19.8 | 19.1 | 18.2 |
| 65 years and over | 58.2 | 43.1 | 36.6 | 37.5 | 35.6 | 19.3 | 16.2 | 18.9 | 22.3 | 23.8 | 20.3 | 18.5 |
| **Female:** | | | | | | | | | | | | |
| Under 18 years | 78.5 | 82.0 | 81.7 | 82.9 | 26.6 | 21.7 | 14.9 | 12.6 | 2.0 | * | * | 1.7* |
| 18–44 years | 72.1 | 67.2 | 67.9 | 62.8 | 32.5 | 25.3 | 25.0 | 21.5 | 7.3 | 11.9 | 9.4 | 8.2 |
| 45–64 years | 63.4 | 52.5 | 48.9 | 45.4 | 37.7 | 24.9 | 22.2 | 21.3 | 18.9 | 20.2 | 18.1 | 14.8 |
| 65 years and over | 63.9 | 48.9 | 39.6 | 41.3 | 38.7 | 20.9 | 16.7 | 19.1 | 22.9 | 25.0 | 20.5 | 19.3 |
| **Race and age[c]** | | | | | | | | | | | | |
| **White:** | | | | | | | | | | | | |
| Under 18 years | 77.6 | 78.5 | 79.6 | 80.5 | 26.4 | 21.2 | 15.6 | 13.0 | 2.0 | * | * | 1.4* |
| 18–44 years | 64.8 | 61.4 | 61.2 | 56.4 | 34.5 | 29.2 | 27.9 | 24.8 | 8.6 | 11.0 | 11.1 | 9.6 |
| 45–64 years | 59.6 | 49.3 | 45.2 | 43.7 | 36.0 | 27.3 | 22.8 | 23.4 | 19.2 | 17.1 | 17.5 | 14.9 |
| 65 years and over | 61.4 | 45.1 | 37.6 | 39.4 | 36.6 | 20.3 | 16.6 | 19.4 | 23.3 | 23.0 | 19.7 | 18.2 |
| **Black or African American:** | | | | | | | | | | | | |
| Under 18 years | 79.9 | 87.3 | 88.0 | 81.0 | 23.7 | * | 16.5* | 10.2 | 2.2* | * | * | * |
| 18–44 years | 68.5 | 65.0 | 72.6 | 61.1 | 31.7 | 22.0 | 29.4 | 23.1 | 9.0 | 20.9 | 14.0* | 12.2 |
| 45–64 years | 66.1 | 61.7 | 57.0 | 48.7 | 38.6 | 23.3 | 26.7 | 24.7 | 22.6 | 35.9 | 24.5 | 18.7 |
| 65 years and over | 64.6 | 52.8 | 45.2 | 41.5 | 49.0 | 18.5* | 18.6* | 18.2 | 14.2 | 33.4 | 25.4* | 21.8 |

| | Type of primary care generalist physician[a] | | | | | | | | | | | |
| | Obstetrics and gynecology | | | | Pediatrics | | | | Specialty care physicians | | | |
| Age, sex, and race | 1980 | 2000 | 2010 | 2012[b] | 1980 | 2000 | 2010 | 2012[b] | 1980 | 2000 | 2010 | 2012[b] |
|---|---|---|---|---|---|---|---|---|---|---|---|---|
| **Age** | | | | | Percent distribution | | | | | | | |
| Total | **9.6** | **7.8** | **7.8** | **7.6** | **10.9** | **11.7** | **12.4** | **12.5** | **33.8** | **41.1** | **44.8** | **46.8** |
| Under 18 years | 1.3 | 1.1* | 1.3* | 0.8 | 48.5 | 57.3 | 63.4 | 66.1 | 22.2 | 20.3 | 19.1 | 19.3 |
| 18–44 years | 21.7 | 20.4 | 22.3 | 21.6 | 0.7 | 0.9* | 1.0 | 1.3 | 34.7 | 37.9 | 37.3 | 42.6 |
| 45–64 years | 4.2 | 4.5 | 4.9 | 5.3 | * | * | * | * | 39.8 | 48.8 | 53.3 | 55.4 |
| 45–54 years | 5.6 | 5.6 | 6.7 | 7.2 | * | * | * | * | 39.8 | 47.7 | 51.3 | 53.0 |
| 55–64 years | 2.9 | 3.3 | 3.3 | 3.5 | * | * | * | * | 39.8 | 50.1 | 55.2 | 57.5 |
| 65 years and over | 1.4 | 1.5 | 1.3 | 1.7 | * | * | * | * | 38.4 | 53.5 | 61.7 | 60.3 |
| 65–74 years | 1.7 | 2.0 | 1.7 | 2.1 | * | * | * | * | 38.8 | 53.4 | 62.7 | 60.2 |
| 75 years and over | 1.0 | 1.0* | 1.0* | 1.2 | * | * | * | * | 37.7 | 53.6 | 60.8 | 60.4 |
| **Sex and age** | | | | | | | | | | | | |
| **Male:** | | | | | | | | | | | | |
| Under 18 years | — | — | — | — | 49.4 | 58.0 | 63.7 | 65.2 | 22.7 | 22.3 | 19.9 | 21.4 |
| 18–44 years | — | — | — | — | 1.0 | 1.7* | 1.4* | 1.8 | 49.2 | 48.5 | 48.3 | 53.9 |
| 45–64 years | — | — | — | — | * | * | * | * | 44.4 | 50.6 | 56.3 | 56.5 |
| 65 years and over | — | — | — | — | * | * | * | * | 41.8 | 56.9 | 63.4 | 62.5 |
| **Female:** | | | | | | | | | | | | |
| Under 18 years | 2.5 | 2.1 | 2.8* | 1.6 | 47.4 | 56.5 | 63.1 | 67.0 | 21.5 | 18.0 | 18.3 | 17.1 |
| 18–44 years | 31.7 | 29.6 | 32.5 | 32.0 | 0.6 | * | 0.9* | 1.1 | 27.9 | 32.8 | 32.1 | 37.2 |
| 45–64 years | 6.7 | 7.3 | 8.5 | 9.0 | * | * | * | * | 36.6 | 47.5 | 51.1 | 54.6 |
| 65 years and over | 2.1 | 2.6 | 2.4 | 2.9 | * | * | * | * | 36.1 | 51.1 | 60.4 | 58.7 |

The numbers of NPs and PAs have increased dramatically since the beginning of the 1990s. According to the American Association of Nurse Practitioners, in "NP Fact Sheet" (October 25, 2016, https://www.aanp.org/all-about-nps/np-fact-sheet), there are more than 222,000 NPs licensed in the United States and about 20,000

**TABLE 2.5**

**Visits to physician offices, by selected characteristics, selected years 1980–2012** [CONTINUED]

[Data are based on reporting by a sample of office-based physicians]

| Age, sex, and race | Type of primary care generalist physician[a] | | | | | | | | Specialty care physicians | | | |
|---|---|---|---|---|---|---|---|---|---|---|---|---|
| | Obstetrics and gynecology | | | | Pediatrics | | | | | | | |
| | 1980 | 2000 | 2010 | 2012[b] | 1980 | 2000 | 2010 | 2012[b] | 1980 | 2000 | 2010 | 2012[b] |
| **Race and age[c]** | | | | | | Percent distribution | | | | | | |
| **White:** | | | | | | | | | | | | |
| Under 18 years | 1.1 | 1.2* | 1.3* | 0.8 | 48.2 | 54.7 | 61.7 | 65.3 | 22.4 | 21.5 | 20.4 | 19.5 |
| 18–44 years | 21.0 | 20.4 | 21.1 | 20.6 | 0.7 | 0.8* | 1.1* | 1.4 | 35.2 | 38.6 | 38.8 | 43.6 |
| 45–64 years | 4.1 | 4.7 | 4.7 | 5.2 | * | * | * | * | 40.4 | 50.7 | 54.8 | 56.3 |
| 65 years and over | 1.4 | 1.5 | 1.3* | 1.7 | * | * | * | * | 38.6 | 54.9 | 62.4 | 60.6 |
| **Black or African American:** | | | | | | | | | | | | |
| Under 18 years | 2.8 | * | * | * | 51.2 | 75.0 | 70.2 | 67.9 | 20.1 | 12.7* | 12.0* | 19.0 |
| 18–44 years | 27.1 | 20.7 | 28.4 | 24.9 | * | * | * | * | 31.5 | 35.0 | 27.4 | 38.9 |
| 45–64 years | 4.8 | 2.4* | 5.6* | 5.3 | * | * | * | * | 33.9 | 38.3 | 43.0 | 51.3 |
| 65 years and over | * | * | 1.2* | * | * | * | * | 0.0 | 35.4 | 47.2 | 54.8 | 58.5 |

*Estimates are considered unreliable. Data preceded by an asterisk have a relative standard error (RSE) of 20%–30%. Data not shown have a RSE greater than 30%.
—Category not applicable.
[a]Type of physician is based on physician's self-designated primary area of practice. Primary care generalist physicians are defined as practitioners in the fields of general and family practice, general internal medicine, general obstetrics and gynecology, and general pediatrics and exclude primary care specialists. Primary care generalists in general and family practice exclude primary care specialties, such as sports medicine and geriatrics. Primary care internal medicine physicians exclude internal medicine specialists, such as allergists, cardiologists, and endocrinologists. Primary care obstetrics and gynecology physicians exclude obstetrics and gynecology specialties, such as gynecological oncology, maternal and fetal medicine, obstetrics and gynecology critical care medicine, and reproductive endocrinology. Primary care pediatricians exclude pediatric specialists, such as adolescent medicine specialists, neonatologists, pediatric allergists, and pediatric cardiologists.
[b]In 2012, data exclude visits to community health centers; in 2006–2011, data include visits to community health centers (2%–3% of visits to physician offices in 2006–2011 were to community health centers). Prior to 2006, visits to community health centers were not included in the survey.
[c]Estimates by racial group should be used with caution because information on race was collected from medical records. In 2012, race data were missing and imputed for 34% of visits. Starting with 1999 data, the instruction for the race item on the Patient Record Form was changed so that more than one race could be recorded. In previous years only one racial category could be checked. Estimates for racial groups presented in this table are for visits where only one race was recorded. Because of the small number of responses with more than one racial group checked, estimates for visits with multiple races checked are unreliable and are not presented.
Notes: This table presents data on visits to physician offices and excludes visits to other sites, such as hospital outpatient and emergency departments. In 1980, the survey excluded Alaska and Hawaii. Data for all other years include all 50 states and the District of Columbia. Visits with specialty of physician unknown are excluded. Starting with *Health, United States, 2005*, data for 2001 and later years for physician offices use a revised weighting scheme.

SOURCE: "Table 77. Visits to Primary Care Generalist and Specialty Care Physicians, by Selected Characteristics and Type of Physician: United States, Selected Years 1980–2012," in *Health, United States, 2015: With Special Feature on Racial and Ethnic Health Disparities*, U.S. Department of Health and Human Services, Centers for Disease Control and Prevention, National Center for Health Statistics, May 2016, http://www.cdc.gov/nchs/data/hus/hus15.pdf (accessed July 26, 2016)

completed their training between 2014 and 2015. The BLS notes in *Occupational Outlook Handbook* that in 2014 there were 38,200 nurse anesthetists, 5,300 nurse midwives, and 94,400 PAs.

**Training, Certification, and Practice**

Advanced practice nurses usually have considerable clinical nursing experience before completing certificate or master's degree NP programs. Key components of NP programs are instruction in nursing theory and practice and a period of direct supervision by a physician or NP. The American Association of Nurse Practitioners explains in "State Practice Environment" (2016, https://www.aanp.org/legislation-regulation/state-legislation/state-practice-environment) that NPs are a scope of practice that varies from state to state. For example, some states require state certification as well as national certification and some states permit independent practice for NPs (not requiring any physician involvement).

The Commission on Accreditation of Allied Health Education Programs accredits PA training programs. In "Become a PA" (2016, https://www.aapa.org/become-a-pa/), the American Academy of Physician Assistants notes that most students have an undergraduate degree and health care experience before they enter a PA training program, which lasts about 26 months. Graduates sit for a national certifying examination and, once certified, must earn 100 hours of continuing medical education every two years and pass a recertification exam every six years. PAs must also obtain a state license.

PA practice is always delegated by the physician and conducted with physician supervision. The extent and nature of physician supervision varies from state to state. For example, Connecticut permits a physician to supervise up to six PAs, whereas California limits a supervising physician to two. Although PAs work interdependently with physicians, supervision is not necessarily direct and on-site; some PAs working in remote communities are supervised primarily by telephone.

According to the article "The 100 Best Jobs," PA was ranked number 5 and NP was ranked number six in terms of the best jobs in 2016. In *Occupational Outlook Handbook*, the BLS notes that in 2015 the median salary

FIGURE 2.4

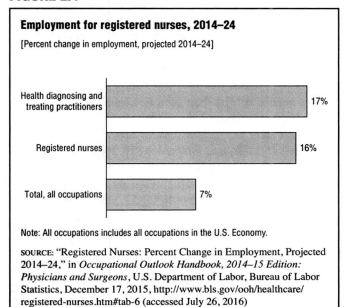

**Employment for registered nurses, 2014–24**

[Percent change in employment, projected 2014–24]

Note: All occupations includes all occupations in the U.S. Economy.

SOURCE: "Registered Nurses: Percent Change in Employment, Projected 2014–24," in *Occupational Outlook Handbook, 2014–15 Edition: Physicians and Surgeons*, U.S. Department of Labor, Bureau of Labor Statistics, December 17, 2015, http://www.bls.gov/ooh/healthcare/registered-nurses.htm#tab-6 (accessed July 26, 2016)

**FIGURE 2.5**

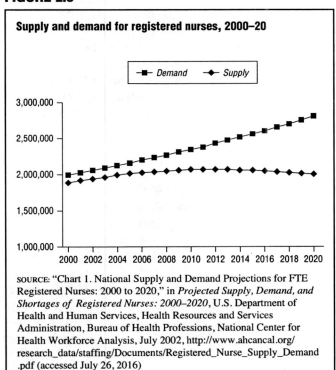

**Supply and demand for registered nurses, 2000–20**

SOURCE: "Chart 1. National Supply and Demand Projections for FTE Registered Nurses: 2000 to 2020," in *Projected Supply, Demand, and Shortages of Registered Nurses: 2000–2020*, U.S. Department of Health and Human Services, Health Resources and Services Administration, Bureau of Health Professions, National Center for Health Workforce Analysis, July 2002, http://www.ahcancal.org/research_data/staffing/Documents/Registered_Nurse_Supply_Demand.pdf (accessed July 26, 2016)

of NPs was $98,190 and the median salary for PAs was $98,180.

### Expanding Role of Midlevel Practitioners

The role of NPs has been gradually expanding over time, but the ACA may accelerate the broadening of responsibilities of NPs, because it extends health insurance coverage to millions of previously uninsured Americans. This creates additional demand for services—especially time-consuming preventive care—that cannot be met by physicians alone.

Amanda Van Vleet and Julia Paradise of the Kaiser Family Foundation explain in "Tapping Nurse Practitioners to Meet Rising Demand for Primary Care" (January 2015, http://files.kff.org/attachment/issue-brief-tapping-nurse-practitioners-to-meet-rising-demand-for-primary-care) that expanded roles for NPs and PAs could help ease the projected physician shortage. However, the researchers note that fewer than half the states permit NPs full-practice authority (the ability to evaluate, diagnose, initiate, and manage the treatment of patients, including prescribing medication) and the restrictive regulations in many states limit NPs from reaching more patients.

ACA funds have been used to expand the role of nurses by encouraging training and increasing compensation. These include:

- $50 million to clinics managed by nurses that provide care to low-income patients

- $50 million annually for three years for hospitals to train nurses with advanced degrees to care for Medicare patients

- 10% bonuses from Medicare through 2016 to primary care providers, including NPs, who work in physician-shortage areas

- Grants to nursing schools to increase full-time enrollment in NP and nurse midwife programs

According to the American Association of Nurse Practitioners, in "State Practice Environment," as of 2016, 21 states and the District of Columbia allowed NPs to work independently (without a supervising physician). In 2016 the U.S. Department of Veterans Affairs said it was considering giving NPs full-practice authority. In "VA Would Join 21 States Already Lifting Nurse Practitioner Hurdles" (Forbes.com, May 26, 2016), Bruce Jepsen reports that Veterans Administration (VA) facilities employ 4,800 NPs and that expanding their scope of practice without physician supervision would increase "veterans' access to VA healthcare by expanding the pool of qualified healthcare professionals who are authorized to provide primary healthcare and other related healthcare services."

### DENTISTS

Dentists diagnose and treat problems of the teeth, gums, and mouth, take x-rays, apply protective plastic sealants to teeth, fill cavities, straighten teeth, and treat gum disease. The BLS reports in *Occupational Outlook Handbook* that dentists held about 151,500 jobs in 2014.

Fluoridation of community water supplies and improved dental hygiene have dramatically improved the dental health of Americans. Dental caries (cavities) among all age groups have declined significantly. As a result, many dental services are shifting focus from young people to adults. In the 21st century many adults are choosing to have orthodontic services, such as straightening their teeth. In addition, the growing older adult population generally requires more complex dental procedures, such as endodontic (root canal) services, bridges, and dentures.

Many dentists own solo dental practices, where only one dentist operates in each office. Others are partners in a practice with other general dentists or dental specialists. Most dentists manage a small staff, which may include dental hygienists and assistants. The BLS reports that most dentists work full time and many work evenings and weekends to accommodate their patients.

### Dental Specialists

In "Specialty Definitions" (2016, http://www.ada.org/495.aspx), the American Dental Association identifies recognized specialties. Orthodontists, who straighten teeth, make up the largest group of specialists. The next largest group, oral and maxillofacial surgeons, operates on the mouth and jaw. Other specialties are pediatric dentistry (dentistry for children), periodontics (treating the gums), prosthodontics (making dentures and artificial teeth), endodontics (root canals), public health dentistry (community dental health), and oral and maxillofacial pathology (diseases of the mouth).

### Training to Become a Dentist

Entry into dental schools requires two to four years of college-level pre-dental education—most dental students have earned excellent grades and have at least a bachelor's degree when they enter dental school. Dentists should have good visual memory, excellent judgment about space and shape, a high degree of manual dexterity, and scientific ability. Development and maintenance of a successful private practice requires business acumen, the ability to manage and organize people and materials, and strong interpersonal skills.

Dental schools require applicants to take the Dental Admission Test (DAT). During the admission process schools consider scores earned on the DAT, applicants' grade-point averages, and information gleaned from recommendations and interviews. Dental school usually lasts four academic years. Students begin by studying the basic sciences, including anatomy, microbiology, biochemistry, and physiology. During the last two years students receive practical experience by treating patients, usually in dental clinics that are supervised by licensed dentists.

### Visiting a Dentist

In 2014, 66.6% of Americans aged two years and older had visited a dentist at least once in the past year. (See Table 2.6.) Children aged two to 17 years (83%) were more likely to have visited a dentist than any other age group. Women (68.9%) were somewhat more likely to have seen a dentist than men (64.1%). The proportion of non-Hispanic whites (67.7%) who had visited a dentist was higher than the proportions of non-Hispanic African Americans (60.7%) and Hispanics (59.7%) who had done so. People who were poor or near poor were much less likely to have visited a dentist in the past year than those who were not poor. For example, 52.5% of people who were below the poverty level had visited a dentist in the past year, compared with 80.4% of people who with incomes above 400% of the poverty level.

### Shortages of Dentists in Some Areas

Although the United States boasts the highest concentration of dentists of any country in the world, large swaths of the country have few dentists. Not unexpectedly, poor, rural regions are disproportionately affected. The National Center for Health Statistics reports in *Health, United States, 2015: With Special Feature on Racial and Ethnic Health Disparities* (May 2016, http://www.cdc.gov/nchs/data/hus/hus15.pdf) that Arkansas had just 40.9 dentists per 100,000 people in the civilian population in 2013, compared with the District of Columbia, which boasted 89.2 dentists per 100,000 population. (See Table 2.7.) For the entire country, there were 60.5 dentists per 100,000 people in the civilian population.

## ALLIED HEALTH CARE PROVIDERS

Many health care services are provided by an interdisciplinary team of health professionals. The complete health care team may include not just physicians and nurses, but a variety of allied health professionals. Table 2.8 describes some of these allied health professions. Specific health care teams are assembled to meet the varying needs of patients. For example, a team involved in stroke rehabilitation might include a physician, a nurse, a speech pathologist, a social worker, and physical and occupational therapists.

Table 2.9 shows the growth in numbers of health care practitioners, allied health professionals, and health care support occupations such as assistants, aides, and massage therapists as well as their mean (average) hourly wages in 2000, 2010, 2013, and 2014. For example, hourly wages for dieticians and nutritionists were essentially unchanged between 2010 and 2014, whereas hourly wages for medical records and health information technicians and medical and clinical laboratory technicians increased during the same period.

TABLE 2.6

## Dental visits in the past year by selected characteristics, 1997–2014

[Data are based on household interviews of a sample of the civilian noninstitutionalized population]

| Characteristic | 2 years and over | | | 2–17 years | | | 18–64 years | | | 65 years and over[a] | | |
|---|---|---|---|---|---|---|---|---|---|---|---|---|
| | 1997 | 2010 | 2014 | 1997 | 2010 | 2014 | 1997 | 2010 | 2014 | 1997 | 2010 | 2014 |
| | Percent of persons with a dental visit in the past year[b] | | | | | | | | | | | |
| **Total[c]** | **65.1** | **64.7** | **66.6** | **72.7** | **78.9** | **83.0** | **64.1** | **61.1** | **62.0** | **54.8** | **57.7** | **62.4** |
| **Sex** | | | | | | | | | | | | |
| Male | 62.9 | 61.7 | 64.1 | 72.3 | 78.3 | 82.3 | 60.4 | 56.8 | 58.1 | 55.4 | 56.2 | 62.2 |
| Female | 67.1 | 67.5 | 68.9 | 73.0 | 79.6 | 83.8 | 67.7 | 65.4 | 65.8 | 54.4 | 58.9 | 62.5 |
| **Race[d]** | | | | | | | | | | | | |
| White only | 66.4 | 65.6 | 67.7 | 74.0 | 79.2 | 83.4 | 65.7 | 62.4 | 63.3 | 56.8 | 59.3 | 64.9 |
| Black or African American only | 58.9 | 58.8 | 60.7 | 68.8 | 79.0 | 83.0 | 57.0 | 53.1 | 54.8 | 35.4 | 40.6 | 42.7 |
| American Indian or Alaska Native only | 55.1 | 57.4 | 59.4 | 66.8 | 73.2 | 88.6 | 49.9 | 49.8 | 46.8 | * | 72.2 | 51.8 |
| Asian only | 62.5 | 66.5 | 66.5 | 69.9 | 74.8 | 78.9 | 60.3 | 64.6 | 64.8 | 53.9 | 61.9 | 55.0 |
| Native Hawaiian or other Pacific Islander only | — | * | * | — | * | * | — | * | * | — | * | * |
| 2 or more races | — | 65.2 | 66.4 | — | 77.9 | 79.2 | — | 54.7 | 56.8 | — | 48.1 | 53.8 |
| Black or African American; White | — | 72.5 | 72.3 | — | 78.4 | 77.6 | — | 62.1 | 62.3 | — | * | 78.4 |
| American Indian or Alaska Native; White | — | 54.7 | 54.9 | — | 70.0 | 81.2 | — | 49.0 | 45.5 | — | 54.5* | 45.1 |
| **Hispanic origin and race[d]** | | | | | | | | | | | | |
| Hispanic or Latino | 54.0 | 56.5 | 59.7 | 61.0 | 74.8 | 81.4 | 50.8 | 48.5 | 50.2 | 47.8 | 42.1 | 51.3 |
| Not Hispanic or Latino | 66.4 | 66.2 | 68.0 | 74.7 | 80.1 | 83.5 | 65.7 | 63.4 | 64.5 | 55.2 | 59.0 | 63.3 |
| White only | 68.0 | 67.6 | 69.7 | 76.4 | 80.9 | 84.4 | 67.5 | 65.4 | 66.5 | 57.2 | 60.9 | 66.2 |
| Black or African American only | 58.8 | 58.7 | 60.6 | 68.8 | 79.2 | 83.0 | 56.9 | 53.1 | 55.1 | 35.3 | 40.5 | 42.6 |
| **Percent of poverty level[e]** | | | | | | | | | | | | |
| Below 100% | 50.5 | 50.6 | 52.5 | 62.0 | 73.2 | 78.2 | 46.9 | 41.0 | 41.9 | 31.5 | 32.8 | 35.1 |
| 100%–199% | 50.8 | 51.6 | 54.4 | 62.5 | 73.4 | 78.2 | 48.3 | 44.1 | 47.1 | 40.8 | 43.8 | 44.1 |
| 200%–399% | 66.2 | 63.5 | 65.8 | 76.1 | 79.0 | 83.6 | 63.4 | 59.6 | 60.9 | 60.7 | 57.9 | 62.1 |
| 400% or more | 78.9 | 79.3 | 80.4 | 85.7 | 88.0 | 90.5 | 77.7 | 77.5 | 77.8 | 74.7 | 77.2 | 81.5 |
| **Hispanic origin and race and percent of poverty level[d, e]** | | | | | | | | | | | | |
| Hispanic or Latino: | | | | | | | | | | | | |
| Below 100% | 45.7 | 50.8 | 54.2 | 55.9 | 74.3 | 80.3 | 39.2 | 34.7 | 37.6 | 33.6 | 32.4 | 39.3 |
| 100%–199% | 47.2 | 50.8 | 55.1 | 53.8 | 71.1 | 78.3 | 43.5 | 40.2 | 43.7 | 47.9 | 39.5 | 46.8 |
| 200%–399% | 61.2 | 59.1 | 62.7 | 70.5 | 76.5 | 83.9 | 57.5 | 54.1 | 55.5 | 57.0 | 46.0 | 55.2 |
| 400% or more | 73.0 | 73.3 | 74.0 | 82.4 | 84.2 | 89.4 | 70.8 | 71.6 | 69.6 | 64.9 | 54.3 | 74.3 |
| **Not Hispanic or Latino:** | | | | | | | | | | | | |
| White only: | | | | | | | | | | | | |
| Below 100% | 51.7 | 49.3 | 51.0 | 64.4 | 69.1 | 73.8 | 50.6 | 44.4 | 45.4 | 32.0 | 36.4 | 36.0 |
| 100%–199% | 52.4 | 52.7 | 53.1 | 66.1 | 75.3 | 78.2 | 50.4 | 47.2 | 47.4 | 42.2 | 45.4 | 45.7 |
| 200%–399% | 67.5 | 64.7 | 67.1 | 77.1 | 79.6 | 83.7 | 65.0 | 61.4 | 62.7 | 61.9 | 59.8 | 64.5 |
| 400% or more | 79.7 | 79.8 | 81.8 | 86.8 | 88.6 | 91.6 | 78.5 | 77.9 | 79.3 | 75.5 | 78.8 | 83.2 |
| Black or African American only: | | | | | | | | | | | | |
| Below 100% | 52.8 | 52.0 | 52.5 | 66.1 | 78.0 | 82.0 | 46.2 | 39.7 | 39.2 | 27.7 | 20.9 | 27.4 |
| 100%–199% | 48.7 | 50.0 | 57.2 | 61.2 | 75.9 | 81.5 | 46.3 | 41.5 | 51.7 | 26.9 | 33.6 | 32.9 |
| 200%–399% | 63.3 | 61.2 | 61.5 | 75.0 | 81.2 | 84.0 | 60.7 | 57.2 | 57.3 | 41.5 | 45.3 | 43.6 |
| 400% or more | 74.6 | 77.2 | 75.6 | 81.8 | 87.2 | 88.8 | 73.4 | 75.9 | 74.8 | 66.1 | 69.8 | 66.8 |

*Estimates are considered unreliable. Data not available.
—Category not applicable.
[a]Based on the 1997–2014 National Health Interview Surveys, about 21%–30% of persons aged 65 and over were edentulous (having lost all their natural teeth). In 1997–2014, about 69%–73% of older dentate persons, compared with 17%–24% of older edentate persons, had a dental visit in the past year.
[b]Respondents were asked, "About how long has it been since you last saw or talked to a dentist?"
[c]Includes all other races not shown separately and unknown disability status.
[d]The race groups, white, black, American Indian or Alaska Native, Asian, Native Hawaiian or other Pacific Islander, and 2 or more races, include persons of Hispanic and non-Hispanic origin. Persons of Hispanic origin may be of any race. Starting with 1999 data, race-specific estimates are tabulated according to the 1997 Revisions to the Standards for the Classification of Federal Data on Race and Ethnicity and are not strictly comparable with estimates for earlier years. The five single-race categories plus multiple-race categories shown in the table conform to the 1997 Standards. Starting with 1999 data, race-specific estimates are for persons who reported only one racial group; the category 2 or more races includes persons who reported more than one racial group. Prior to 1999, data were tabulated according to the 1977 Standards with four racial groups, and the Asian only category included Native Hawaiian or Other Pacific Islander. Estimates for single-race categories prior to 1999 included persons who reported one race or, if they reported more than one race, identified one race as best representing their race. Starting with 2003 data, race responses of other race and unspecified multiple race were treated as missing, and then race was imputed if these were the only race responses. Almost all persons with a race response of other race were of Hispanic origin.
[e]Percent of poverty level is based on family income and family size and composition using U.S. Census Bureau poverty thresholds. Missing family income data were imputed for 1997 and beyond.

SOURCE: Adapted from "Table 78. Dental Visits in the Past Year, by Selected Characteristics: United States, Selected Years 1997–2014," in *Health, United States, 2015: With Special Feature on Racial and Ethnic Health Disparities*, U.S. Department of Health and Human Services, Centers for Disease Control and Prevention, National Center for Health Statistics, May 2016, http://www.cdc.gov/nchs/data/hus/hus15.pdf (accessed July 26, 2016)

TABLE 2.7

## Active dentists by state, selected years 2001–13

[Data are based on reporting by dentists]

| State | Number of dentists | | | | | Number of dentists per 100,000 civilian population | | | | |
|---|---|---|---|---|---|---|---|---|---|---|
| | 2001 | 2006 | 2011 | 2012 | 2013 | 2001 | 2006 | 2011 | 2012 | 2013 |
| United States | 163,345 | 172,603 | 186,025 | 188,820 | 191,347 | 57.32 | 57.85 | 59.68 | 60.11 | 60.46 |
| Alabama | 1,880 | 1,921 | 2,056 | 2,107 | 2,128 | 42.08 | 41.50 | 42.82 | 43.74 | 44.02 |
| Alaska | 457 | 489 | 555 | 571 | 577 | 72.11 | 72.41 | 76.81 | 78.10 | 78.26 |
| Arizona | 2,374 | 3,061 | 3,465 | 3,515 | 3,617 | 45.02 | 50.77 | 53.53 | 53.61 | 54.51 |
| Arkansas | 1,047 | 1,114 | 1,161 | 1,187 | 1,210 | 38.90 | 39.48 | 39.51 | 40.25 | 40.90 |
| California | 22,709 | 26,388 | 28,680 | 29,119 | 29,425 | 65.86 | 73.26 | 76.07 | 76.50 | 76.57 |
| Colorado | 2,844 | 3,098 | 3,486 | 3,563 | 3,623 | 64.26 | 65.63 | 68.09 | 68.63 | 68.72 |
| Connecticut | 2,590 | 2,587 | 2,721 | 2,695 | 2,742 | 75.45 | 73.55 | 75.78 | 74.98 | 76.18 |
| Delaware | 352 | 383 | 409 | 422 | 420 | 44.24 | 44.57 | 45.05 | 46.03 | 45.39 |
| District of Columbia | 603 | 533 | 564 | 568 | 579 | 104.96 | 93.40 | 90.91 | 89.44 | 89.20 |
| Florida | 8,158 | 8,754 | 9,583 | 9,774 | 9,947 | 49.87 | 48.19 | 50.15 | 50.50 | 50.75 |
| Georgia | 3,614 | 4,115 | 4,574 | 4,629 | 4,701 | 43.14 | 44.94 | 46.61 | 46.67 | 47.03 |
| Hawaii | 1,022 | 1,009 | 1,047 | 1,048 | 1,060 | 83.36 | 77.04 | 75.97 | 75.25 | 75.23 |
| Idaho | 690 | 864 | 927 | 913 | 932 | 52.27 | 58.83 | 58.53 | 57.22 | 57.79 |
| Illinois | 8,154 | 7,994 | 8,416 | 8,476 | 8,599 | 65.29 | 63.22 | 65.45 | 65.84 | 66.71 |
| Indiana | 2,870 | 2,842 | 3,074 | 3,066 | 3,116 | 46.84 | 44.88 | 47.17 | 46.90 | 47.42 |
| Iowa | 1,516 | 1,526 | 1,601 | 1,601 | 1,604 | 51.71 | 51.16 | 52.24 | 52.05 | 51.87 |
| Kansas | 1,314 | 1,347 | 1,437 | 1,442 | 1,461 | 48.63 | 48.75 | 50.07 | 49.97 | 50.45 |
| Kentucky | 2,256 | 2,287 | 2,452 | 2,427 | 2,488 | 55.46 | 54.20 | 56.11 | 55.37 | 56.55 |
| Louisiana | 2,058 | 2,017 | 2,189 | 2,240 | 2,221 | 45.96 | 46.88 | 47.84 | 48.65 | 47.98 |
| Maine | 598 | 642 | 650 | 660 | 693 | 46.51 | 48.50 | 48.95 | 49.68 | 52.16 |
| Maryland | 3,955 | 3,989 | 4,160 | 4,248 | 4,268 | 73.59 | 70.89 | 71.19 | 72.10 | 71.87 |
| Massachusetts | 4,898 | 4,797 | 5,181 | 5,234 | 5,232 | 76.56 | 74.84 | 78.35 | 78.64 | 77.99 |
| Michigan | 5,783 | 5,928 | 5,972 | 6,036 | 6,075 | 57.88 | 59.07 | 60.47 | 61.06 | 61.37 |
| Minnesota | 2,880 | 3,105 | 3,210 | 3,254 | 3,284 | 57.80 | 60.13 | 60.02 | 60.48 | 60.57 |
| Mississippi | 1,117 | 1,140 | 1,220 | 1,253 | 1,275 | 39.15 | 39.24 | 40.96 | 41.96 | 42.61 |
| Missouri | 2,634 | 2,666 | 2,846 | 2,897 | 2,900 | 46.69 | 45.63 | 47.35 | 48.08 | 47.97 |
| Montana | 511 | 525 | 613 | 616 | 598 | 56.34 | 55.11 | 61.44 | 61.28 | 58.92 |
| Nebraska | 1,103 | 1,117 | 1,166 | 1,201 | 1,203 | 64.13 | 63.01 | 63.29 | 64.73 | 64.37 |
| Nevada | 846 | 1,177 | 1,396 | 1,432 | 1,448 | 40.32 | 46.66 | 51.35 | 51.97 | 51.87 |
| New Hampshire | 735 | 815 | 833 | 840 | 847 | 58.54 | 62.29 | 63.20 | 63.57 | 64.04 |
| New Jersey | 6,054 | 6,922 | 7,181 | 7,264 | 7,238 | 71.28 | 79.92 | 81.21 | 81.84 | 81.22 |
| New Mexico | 814 | 861 | 1,023 | 1,055 | 1,062 | 44.44 | 43.88 | 49.22 | 50.61 | 50.89 |
| New York | 14,309 | 14,062 | 14,211 | 14,262 | 14,468 | 74.98 | 73.61 | 72.80 | 72.74 | 73.46 |
| North Carolina | 3,474 | 4,016 | 4,588 | 4,674 | 4,719 | 42.31 | 45.04 | 47.54 | 47.95 | 47.91 |
| North Dakota | 305 | 311 | 370 | 383 | 394 | 47.73 | 47.89 | 54.00 | 54.58 | 54.43 |
| Ohio | 5,929 | 5,797 | 5,932 | 6,012 | 6,003 | 52.07 | 50.49 | 51.38 | 52.05 | 51.88 |
| Oklahoma | 1,664 | 1,749 | 1,912 | 1,924 | 1,943 | 47.99 | 48.66 | 50.49 | 50.41 | 50.43 |
| Oregon | 2,197 | 2,431 | 2,643 | 2,643 | 2,708 | 63.35 | 66.22 | 68.34 | 67.79 | 68.94 |
| Pennsylvania | 7,595 | 7,454 | 7,529 | 7,676 | 7,698 | 61.75 | 59.58 | 59.08 | 60.11 | 60.23 |
| Rhode Island | 588 | 576 | 581 | 582 | 566 | 55.62 | 54.18 | 55.23 | 55.29 | 53.73 |
| South Carolina | 1,839 | 1,958 | 2,228 | 2,267 | 2,288 | 45.24 | 44.93 | 47.68 | 48.00 | 47.95 |
| South Dakota | 348 | 382 | 443 | 440 | 457 | 45.91 | 48.78 | 53.75 | 52.73 | 54.05 |
| Tennessee | 2,912 | 2,947 | 3,131 | 3,195 | 3,246 | 50.64 | 48.40 | 48.93 | 49.50 | 49.96 |
| Texas | 9,642 | 10,365 | 12,451 | 12,861 | 13,391 | 45.23 | 44.37 | 48.53 | 49.29 | 50.52 |
| Utah | 1,409 | 1,559 | 1,852 | 1,878 | 1,892 | 61.70 | 61.73 | 65.78 | 65.77 | 65.18 |
| Vermont | 354 | 343 | 357 | 361 | 365 | 57.82 | 55.07 | 56.99 | 57.66 | 58.23 |
| Virginia | 4,189 | 4,367 | 4,854 | 5,068 | 5,194 | 58.19 | 56.91 | 59.85 | 61.85 | 62.80 |
| Washington | 3,957 | 4,312 | 4,856 | 4,917 | 4,951 | 66.11 | 67.68 | 71.18 | 71.30 | 70.99 |
| West Virginia | 863 | 835 | 873 | 874 | 890 | 47.91 | 45.68 | 47.06 | 47.08 | 48.01 |
| Wisconsin | 3,069 | 2,860 | 3,072 | 3,137 | 3,215 | 56.76 | 51.28 | 53.81 | 54.80 | 55.98 |
| Wyoming | 266 | 266 | 294 | 306 | 309 | 53.77 | 50.89 | 51.79 | 53.04 | 52.98 |

Notes: Data include professionally active dentists only. Professionally active dentists include those whose primary occupation is one of the following: private practice (full- or part-time), dental school/faculty staff member, armed forces, other federal services (i.e., Veterans' Affairs, Public Health Service), state or local government employee, hospital staff dentist, graduate student/intern/resident, or other health/dental organization staff member. U.S. totals include dentists with unknown state of practice not shown separately and may include missing data.

SOURCE: "Table 86. Active Dentists, by State: United States, Selected Years 2001–2013," in *Health, United States, 2015: With Special Feature on Racial and Ethnic Health Disparities*, U.S. Department of Health and Human Services, Centers for Disease Control and Prevention, National Center for Health Statistics, May 2016, http://www.cdc.gov/nchs/data/hus/hus15.pdf (accessed July 26, 2016)

## Physical and Occupational Therapists

Physical therapists (PTs) are licensed practitioners who work with patients to preserve and restore function, improve capabilities and mobility, and regain independence following an illness or injury. They also aim to prevent or limit disability and slow the progress of debilitating diseases. Treatment involves exercise to improve range of motion, balance, coordination, flexibility, strength, and endurance. PTs may also use electrical stimulation to promote healing, hot and cold packs to relieve pain and inflammation (swelling), and therapeutic massage.

**TABLE 2.8**

**Allied health care providers**

**Dental hygienists** provide services for maintaining oral health. Their primary duty is to clean teeth.

**Emergency medical technicians (EMTs)** provide immediate care to critically ill or injured people in emergency situations.

**Home health aides** provide nursing, household, and personal care services to patients who are homebound or disabled.

**Licensed practical nurse (LPNs)** are trained and licensed to provide basic nursing care under the supervision of registered nurses and doctors.

**Medical records personnel** analyze patient records and keep them up-to-date, complete, accurate, and confidential.

**Medical technologists** perform laboratory tests to help diagnose diseases and to aid in identifying their causes and extent.

**Nurses' aides, orderlies, and attendants** help nurses in hospitals, nursing homes, and other facilities.

**Occupational therapists** help disabled persons adapt to their disabilities. This may include helping a patient relearn basic living skills or modifying the environment.

**Optometrists** measure vision for corrective lenses and prescribe glasses.

**Pharmacists** are trained and licensed to make up and dispense drugs in accordance with a physician's prescription.

**Physician assistants (PAs)** work under a doctor's supervision. Their duties include performing routine physical exams, prescribing certain drugs, and providing medical counseling.

**Physical therapists** work with disabled patients to help restore function, strength and mobility. PTs use exercise, heat, cold, water, and electricity to relieve pain and restore function.

**Podiatrists** diagnose and treat diseases, injuries, and abnormalities of the feet. They may use drugs and surgery to treat foot problems.

**Psychologists** are trained in human behavior and provide counseling and testing services related to mental health.

**Radiation technicians** take and develop x-ray photographs for medical purposes.

**Registered dietitians (RDs)** are licensed to use dietary principles to maintain health and treat disease.

**Respiratory therapists** treat breathing problems under a doctor's supervision and help in respiratory rehabilitation.

**Social workers** help patients to handle social problems such as finances, housing, and social and family problems that arise out of illness or disability.

**Speech pathologists** diagnose and treat disorders of speech and communication.

SOURCE: "Allied Health Care Providers," U.S. Department of Commerce, Washington, DC

According to the BLS, in *Occupational Outlook Handbook*, PTs worked at 210,900 jobs in 2014. Employment of PTs was forecast to increase 34% between 2014 and 2024. (See Figure 2.6.) PTs work in hospitals and physicians' offices, outpatient rehabilitation clinics, nursing homes, and home health agencies. Although most work in rehabilitation, PTs may specialize in areas such as sports medicine, pediatrics, or neurology. The BLS notes that the median annual wage for a PT was $84,020 in 2015.

According to the BLS, PTs are required to earn a master's or doctorate degree from an accredited physical therapy program. To practice physical therapy, PTs must obtain state licensure. Although the requirements vary by state, licensure generally requires graduation from an accredited physical therapy education program and passing a national examination. Many states also require continuing education as a condition of maintaining licensure.

Occupational therapists (OTs) help people relearn how to perform the "activities of daily living," meaning the tasks they perform during the course of their work and home life. Examples of activities of daily living that OTs help patients regain are dressing, bathing, and meal preparation. For people with long-term or permanent disabilities, OTs may assist them to find new ways to accomplish their responsibilities on the job, sometimes by using adaptive equipment or by asking employers to accommodate workers with special needs such as people in wheelchairs. OTs use computer simulations to help patients restore fine motor skills and practice reasoning, decision making, and problem solving.

A master's degree or higher in occupational therapy is the minimum educational requirement. The American Occupational Therapy Association states in "Occupational Therapy's Role in Health Care Reform" (2016, http://www.aota.org/About-Occupational-Therapy/Professionals/HCR.aspx) that in addition to providing some of the essential benefits of the ACA such as rehabilitation, OTs focus on prevention and helping people remain in the community as opposed to entering long-term-care facilities. All these services help improve health outcomes and decrease costs.

The BLS notes that in 2014 OTs filled 114,600 jobs. It also indicates that their median annual wage was $80,150 in 2015.

The demand for OTs is expected to exceed the available supply through 2024, growing 27% between 2014 and 2024. (See Figure 2.7.) Besides hospital and rehabilitation center jobs, it is anticipated that PTs and OTs will increasingly be involved in school program efforts to meet the needs of disabled and special education students.

**Pharmacists**

Pharmacists are involved in many more aspects of patient care than simply compounding and dispensing medication from behind a drugstore counter. According to the American Pharmacists Association, pharmacists provide pharmaceutical care that both improves patient adherence to prescribed drug treatment and reduces the frequency of drug therapy mishaps, which can have serious and even life-threatening consequences.

Studies citing the value of pharmacists in patient care describe pharmacists improving the rates of immunization against disease (pharmacists can provide immunization in all 50 states, the District of Columbia, and Puerto Rico), assisting patients to better control chronic diseases such as asthma and diabetes, reducing the frequency and severity of drug interactions and adverse reactions, and helping patients effectively manage pain and symptoms of disease, especially at the end of life. Pharmacists also offer public health education programs about prescription medication safety, prevention of poisoning, appropriate use of nonprescription (over-the-counter [OTC]) drugs, and medical self-care.

Pharmacists must obtain a doctoral degree, called a PharmD, from an accredited school of pharmacy. Training

TABLE 2.9

## Health care workers and wages, selected years 2000–14

[Data are based on a semiannual mail survey of nonfarm establishments]

| Occupation title | Employment[a] | | | | Mean hourly wage[b] | | | |
|---|---|---|---|---|---|---|---|---|
| | 2000 | 2010 | 2013 | 2014 | 2000 | 2010 | 2013 | 2014 |
| **Healthcare practitioners and technical occupations** | | | | | | | | |
| Audiologists | 11,530 | 12,860 | 11,550 | 12,250 | $22.92 | $33.58 | $35.75 | $36.92 |
| Cardiovascular technologists and technicians | 40,080 | 48,720 | 51,010 | 51,080 | 16.81 | 24.38 | 25.95 | 26.54 |
| Dental hygienists | 148,460 | 177,520 | 192,330 | 196,520 | 24.99 | 33.02 | 34.39 | 34.60 |
| Diagnostic medical sonographers | 31,760 | 53,010 | 58,250 | 59,760 | 22.03 | 31.20 | 32.29 | 32.88 |
| Dietetic technicians | 28,010 | 23,890 | 26,420 | 28,690 | 10.98 | 13.86 | 13.74 | 13.75 |
| Dietitians and nutritionists | 43,030 | 53,510 | 59,530 | 59,490 | 18.76 | 26.13 | 27.07 | 27.62 |
| Emergency medical technicians and paramedics | 165,530 | 221,760 | 237,660 | 235,760 | 11.89 | 16.01 | 16.77 | 16.88 |
| Licensed practical and licensed vocational nurses | 679,470 | 730,290 | 705,200 | 695,610 | 14.65 | 19.88 | 20.63 | 20.87 |
| Magnetic resonance imaging technologists | — | — | 32,000 | 33,130 | — | — | 31.71 | 32.36 |
| Medical and clinical laboratory technicians | 146,060 | 156,480 | 157,080 | 160,460 | 13.93 | 18.36 | 19.35 | 19.59 |
| Medical and clinical laboratory technologists | 144,530 | 164,430 | 162,630 | 161,710 | 19.84 | 27.34 | 28.59 | 29.12 |
| Medical records and health information technicians | 143,870 | 176,090 | 180,760 | 184,740 | 11.74 | 16.83 | 18.13 | 18.68 |
| Nuclear medicine technologists | 18,030 | 21,600 | 20,020 | 20,320 | 21.56 | 33.20 | 34.60 | 35.21 |
| Nurse anesthetists | — | — | 35,430 | 36,590 | — | — | 75.81 | 76.40 |
| Nurse midwives | — | — | 5,460 | 5,110 | — | — | 44.34 | 46.97 |
| Nurse practitioners | — | — | 113,370 | 122,050 | — | — | 45.71 | 47.11 |
| Occupational therapists | 75,150 | 100,300 | 108,410 | 110,520 | 24.10 | 35.28 | 37.45 | 38.46 |
| Opticians, dispensing | 66,580 | 62,200 | 68,390 | 73,110 | 12.67 | 16.73 | 17.17 | 17.43 |
| Pharmacists | 212,660 | 268,030 | 287,420 | 290,780 | 33.39 | 52.59 | 56.01 | 56.96 |
| Pharmacy technicians | 190,940 | 333,500 | 362,690 | 368,760 | 10.38 | 14.10 | 14.83 | 14.95 |
| Physical therapists | 120,410 | 180,280 | 195,670 | 200,670 | 27.62 | 37.50 | 39.51 | 40.35 |
| Physician assistants | 55,490 | 81,420 | 88,110 | 91,670 | 29.17 | 41.89 | 45.36 | 46.77 |
| Psychiatric technicians | 53,350 | 72,650 | 66,760 | 64,540 | 12.53 | 15.15 | 16.09 | 16.91 |
| Radiation therapists | 13,100 | 16,590 | 16,950 | 16,380 | 25.59 | 37.64 | 39.30 | 40.25 |
| Radiologic technologists[c] | 172,080 | 216,730 | 194,000 | 193,400 | 17.93 | 26.80 | 27.29 | 27.65 |
| Recreational therapists | 26,940 | 20,830 | 18,640 | 17,950 | 14.23 | 19.92 | 21.88 | 22.14 |
| Registered nurses[d] | 2,189,670 | 2,655,020 | 2,661,890 | 2,687,310 | 22.31 | 32.56 | 33.13 | 33.55 |
| Respiratory therapists | 82,670 | 109,270 | 118,640 | 119,410 | 18.37 | 26.54 | 27.83 | 28.12 |
| Respiratory therapy technicians | 28,230 | 13,570 | 12,070 | 10,610 | 16.46 | 22.28 | 23.01 | 23.46 |
| Speech-language pathologists | 82,850 | 112,530 | 125,050 | 126,500 | 23.31 | 33.60 | 35.56 | 36.01 |
| **Healthcare support occupations** | | | | | | | | |
| Dental assistants | 250,870 | 294,030 | 309,540 | 314,330 | 12.86 | 16.41 | 17.13 | 17.43 |
| Home health aides | 561,120 | 982,840 | 806,710 | 799,080 | 8.71 | 10.46 | 10.60 | 10.77 |
| Massage therapists | 24,620 | 60,040 | 79,040 | 87,670 | 15.51 | 19.12 | 19.42 | 20.09 |
| Medical assistants | 330,830 | 523,260 | 571,690 | 584,970 | 11.46 | 14.31 | 14.80 | 15.01 |
| Medical equipment preparers | 32,760 | 47,310 | 51,300 | 50,550 | 10.68 | 14.59 | 16.02 | 16.28 |
| Medical transcriptionists | 97,330 | 78,780 | 68,350 | 61,210 | 12.37 | 16.12 | 16.95 | 17.11 |
| Nursing assistants[e] | 1,273,460 | 1,451,090 | 1,427,830 | 1,427,740 | 9.18 | 12.09 | 12.51 | 12.62 |
| Occupational therapy aides | 8,890 | 7,180 | 8,710 | 8,570 | 11.21 | 14.95 | 13.90 | 13.96 |
| Occupational therapy assistants | 15,910 | 27,720 | 30,450 | 32,230 | 16.76 | 24.66 | 26.56 | 27.53 |
| Pharmacy aides | 59,890 | 49,580 | 42,250 | 41,240 | 9.10 | 10.98 | 11.78 | 12.28 |
| Physical therapist aides | 34,620 | 45,900 | 48,630 | 48,730 | 10.06 | 12.02 | 12.50 | 12.82 |
| Physical therapist assistants | 44,120 | 65,960 | 72,640 | 76,910 | 16.52 | 23.95 | 25.63 | 26.12 |
| Psychiatric aides | 57,680 | 64,730 | 75,340 | 72,860 | 10.79 | 12.84 | 12.98 | 13.67 |

—Data not available.

[a]Employment is the number of filled positions. This table includes both full-time and part-time wage and salary positions. Estimates do not include the self-employed, owners and partners in unincorporated firms, household workers, or unpaid family workers. Estimates were rounded to the nearest 10.

[b]The mean hourly wage rate for an occupation is the total wages that all workers in the occupation earn in an hour, divided by the total number of employees in the occupation.

[c]2012–2014 data are not comparable with earlier data. Starting with 2012 data, the radiologic technologists and technicians occupation category was split into two occupations as part of the 2010 Standard Occupational Classification (SOC) revision: Radiologic technologists (29–2034) and Magnetic resonance imaging technologists (29–2035).

[d]2012–2014 data are not comparable to earlier data. Starting with 2012 data, the registered nurses occupation category was split into four occupations as part of the 2010 SOC revision: Registered nurses (29–1141), plus three advanced practice nursing occupations: Nurse anesthetists (29–1151), Nurse midwives (29–1161), and Nurse practitioners (29–1171).

[e]2012–2014 data are not comparable to earlier data. Starting with 2012 data, the nursing aides, orderlies, and attendants occupation category was split into two occupations as part of the 2010 SOC revision: Nursing assistants (31–1014) and Orderlies (31–1015).

Notes: This table excludes occupations such as dentists, physicians, and chiropractors, which have a large percentage of workers who are self-employed. Challenges in using Occupational Employment Statistics (OES) data as a time series include changes in the occupational, industrial, and geographical classification systems; changes in the way data are collected; changes in the survey reference period; and changes in mean wage estimation methodology, as well as permanent features of the methodology.

SOURCE: "Table 87. Healthcare Employment and Wages, by Selected Occupations: United States, Selected Years 2000–2014," in *Health, United States, 2015: With Special Feature on Racial and Ethnic Health Disparities*, U.S. Department of Health and Human Services, Centers for Disease Control and Prevention, National Center for Health Statistics, May 2016, http://www.cdc.gov/nchs/data/hus/hus15.pdf (accessed July 26, 2016)

for the PharmD generally takes four years to complete, and some PharmD graduates obtain additional training. All states require prospective pharmacists to pass two exams to obtain a license to practice pharmacy. Some states also require additional exams and all require a stipulated number of hours of experience in a practice setting as a prerequisite for licensure.

**FIGURE 2.6**

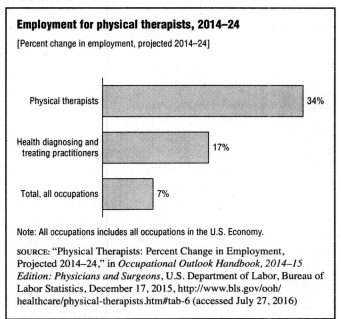

**Employment for physical therapists, 2014–24**

[Percent change in employment, projected 2014–24]

Note: All occupations includes all occupations in the U.S. Economy.

SOURCE: "Physical Therapists: Percent Change in Employment, Projected 2014–24," in *Occupational Outlook Handbook, 2014–15 Edition: Physicians and Surgeons*, U.S. Department of Labor, Bureau of Labor Statistics, December 17, 2015, http://www.bls.gov/ooh/healthcare/physical-therapists.htm#tab-6 (accessed July 27, 2016)

**FIGURE 2.7**

**Employment for occupational therapists, 2014–24**

[Percent change in employment, projected 2014–24]

Note: All occupations includes all occupations in the U.S. economy.

SOURCE: "Occupational Therapists: Percent Change in Employment, Projected 2014–24," in *Occupational Outlook Handbook, 2014–15 Edition: Physicians and Surgeons*, U.S. Department of Labor, Bureau of Labor Statistics, December 17, 2015, http://www.bls.gov/ooh/healthcare/occupational-therapists.htm#tab-6 (accessed July 27, 2016)

According to the BLS, in *Occupational Outlook Handbook*, pharmacists worked at 297,100 jobs in 2014. The median annual wage of pharmacists in 2015 was $121,500.

## MENTAL HEALTH PROFESSIONALS

The mental health sector includes a range of professionals—psychiatrists, psychologists, psychiatric nurses, clinical social workers, and counselors—whose training, orientation, philosophy, and practice styles differ, even within a single discipline. For example, different clinical psychologists may endorse and offer dramatically different forms of therapy—ranging from long-term psychoanalytic psychotherapy to short-term cognitive-behavioral therapy.

### Psychiatrists

Psychiatrists are physicians who have completed residency training in the prevention, diagnosis, and treatment of mental illness, mental retardation, and substance abuse disorders. Because they are trained physicians, psychiatrists are especially well equipped to care for people who have coexisting medical diseases and mental health problems. They can prescribe medication including psychoactive drugs. Psychiatrists may also obtain additional training that prepares them to treat certain populations, such as children and adolescents or older adults (this subspecialty is called geriatric psychiatry or geropsychiatry), or they may specialize in a specific treatment modality.

### Psychologists

Psychologists are professionals trained in the study and treatment of people's cognitive, emotional, and social issues. They are distinct from psychiatrists in that they are not trained as physicians. Psychologists can engage in a wide variety of specialties and subspecialties, only some of which involve providing health care.

Research psychologists investigate the physical, cognitive, emotional, or social aspects of human behavior. They work at academic and private research centers and for business, nonprofit, and governmental organizations.

Clinical psychologists help mentally and emotionally disturbed clients better manage their symptoms and behaviors. Some work in rehabilitation, treating patients with spinal cord injuries, chronic pain or illness, stroke, arthritis, and neurologic conditions. Others help people cope during times of personal crisis, such as divorce or the death of a loved one. Psychologists are also called on to help communities recover from the trauma of natural or human-made disasters by working with, for example, people who have lost their homes to earthquakes, fires, or floods, or with students who have witnessed school violence.

Subspecialties open to clinical psychologists include health psychology, neuropsychology, and geropsychology. Health psychologists promote healthy lifestyles and behaviors and provide counseling such as smoking cessation, weight reduction, and stress management to assist people to reduce their health risks. Neuropsychologists often work in stroke rehabilitation and head injury programs, and geropsychologists work with older adults in institutional and community settings.

School psychologists identify, diagnose, and address students' learning and behavior problems. They work with teachers and school personnel to improve classroom management strategies and to design educational programs for students with disabilities or gifted and talented students. They also work with parents to help improve parenting skills.

Industrial-organizational psychologists aim to improve productivity and quality of life in the workplace. They screen prospective employees and conduct training and development, counseling, and organizational development and analysis. Industrial-organizational psychologists examine aspects of work life. They work in organizational consultation, market research, systems design, or other applied psychology fields. For example, industrial-organizational psychologists may be involved in efforts to understand and influence consumer-purchasing behaviors.

Social psychologists consider interpersonal relationships and interactions with the social environment and social experience. Many social psychologists specialize in particular aspects of social psychology, such as group behavior, leadership, aggression, attitudinal change, or social perception.

EDUCATION, TRAINING, LICENSURE, AND EARNINGS. Most psychologists hold a doctorate degree in psychology, which requires between five and seven years of graduate study. Clinical psychologists usually earn a Doctor of Philosophy or a Doctor of Psychology degree and complete an internship that lasts at least one year. An educational specialist degree qualifies an individual to work as a school psychologist; however, most school psychologists complete a master's degree followed by a one-year internship. People with a master's degree in psychology might also work as industrial-organizational psychologists, or as psychological assistants under the supervision of doctoral-level psychologists, and conduct research or psychological evaluations. Vocational and guidance counselors usually need two years of graduate education in counseling and one year of counseling experience. A master's degree in psychology requires at least two years of full-time graduate study. People with undergraduate degrees in psychology assist psychologists and other professionals in community mental health centers, vocational rehabilitation offices, and correctional programs.

Psychologists in clinical practice must be certified or licensed in all states and the District of Columbia. The BLS indicates in *Occupational Outlook Handbook* that the median annual wage for psychologists was $72,580 in 2015.

## Psychiatric Nurses

Psychiatric nurses must have a degree in nursing, be licensed as RNs, and have additional experience in psychiatry. Advanced practice psychiatric nurses (RNs prepared at the master's level) may prescribe psychotropic medications and conduct individual, group, and family psychotherapy as well as perform crisis intervention and case management functions. Along with primary care physicians, they are often the first points of contact for people seeking mental health help.

The American Psychiatric Nurses Association is the professional society that represents psychiatric nurses. In "Psychiatric-Mental Health Nurses" (2015, http://www .apna.org/i4a/pages/index.cfm?pageid=3292), the association explains that the pay scale for psychiatric nurses and psychiatric nurse practitioners "depends on many factors, such as level of education, years of experience, size of the agency or hospital, and geographic location." According to PayScale (October 28, 2016, http://www.payscale.com/ research/US/Job=Psychiatric_Nurse_(RN)/Hourly_Rate), a service that collects salary data, psychiatric nurses' salaries range from $45,790 to $80,143.

## Social Workers

Social workers help people cope with challenges in their lives. They work in a variety of settings and specialties, only some of which are specifically related to health care.

Health care social workers help people deal with illnesses and disabilities. For instance, they help people transition from care in a hospital back to living in their home and community, a process that may include making adjustments to lifestyle and housing. Mental health and substance abuse social workers specialize in helping people deal with mental illnesses and addictions, such as by directing them to 12-step programs.

Some social workers are specifically licensed to diagnose and treat mental, behavioral, and emotional disorders. They are known as clinical social workers or licensed clinical social workers. They offer psychotherapy or counseling and a range of diagnostic services in public agencies, clinics, and private practice.

In *Occupational Outlook Handbook*, the BLS notes that social workers held 649,300 positions in the United States in 2014. The median annual wage for social workers was $45,900 in 2015.

EDUCATION, CERTIFICATION, AND LICENSURE. A bachelor's degree in social work is usually the minimum requirement for employment as a social worker, and an advanced degree has become the standard for many positions. A master's degree in social work is necessary for positions in health and mental health settings and is typically required for certification for clinical work. Licensed clinical social workers hold a master's degree in social work along with additional clinical training. Supervisory, administrative, and staff training positions usually require an advanced degree, and university teaching positions and research appointments normally require a doctorate in social work.

All the states and the District of Columbia have licensing, certification, or registration requirements that delineate the scope of social work practice and the use of professional titles; however, standards for licensing vary by state. The National Association of Social Workers (2016, https://www.socialworkers.org/nasw/default.asp) represents 132,000 professional social workers and "works to enhance the professional growth and development of its members, to create and maintain professional standards, and to advance sound social policies."

## Counselors

Counselors assist people with personal, family, educational, mental health, and job-related challenges and problems. Their roles and responsibilities depend on the clients they serve and on the settings in which they work; only some types of counselors are involved in providing health care. The BLS indicates in *Occupational Outlook Handbook* that a master's degree is required to become a licensed counselor. The American Counseling Association (2016, http://www.counseling.org) is the world's largest association for professional counselors and represents 56,000 professional counselors in various practice settings. The association advocates for certification, licensure, and registry of counselors.

Rehabilitation counselors help people gain independence and employment despite personal, social, and vocational challenges that stem from birth defects, illness, disease, accidents, or the stress of daily life. They help design and coordinate activities for people in rehabilitation treatment facilities and perform client evaluations. Rehabilitation counselors plan and implement programs that may include personal and vocational counseling, training, and job placement. The BLS notes that a master's degree is required to become a rehabilitation counselor. There were 101,630 jobs in this field in 2014, with a mean annual wage of $38,040.

Mental health counselors work in prevention programs to promote optimum mental health and provide a range of counseling services. They work closely with other mental health professionals, including psychiatrists, psychologists, clinical social workers, psychiatric nurses, and school counselors. Marriage and family therapists help people with problems with their personal relationships. According to the BLS, there were 168,200 jobs for these types of counselors and therapists in 2014, with a mean annual salary of $43,190. A master's degree and a license to practice are typically required for these positions.

Substance abuse and behavioral disorder counselors help people overcome addictions to alcohol, drugs, gambling, and eating disorders. They counsel individuals, families, and groups in clinics, hospital-based outpatient treatment programs, community mental health centers, and inpatient chemical dependency treatment programs.

The BLS states that "educational requirements can vary from a high school diploma and certification to a master's degree," depending on the location, but that workers with more education are typically permitted to provide more services with less supervision. There were 94,900 jobs in this field in 2014, paying a mean annual salary of $39,980.

Pastoral counselors offer a type of psychotherapy that combines spiritual resources with psychological understanding for healing and growth. According to the American Association of Pastoral Counselors (AAPC; 2016, http://www.aapc.org/home/mission-statement.aspx), this therapeutic modality is more than simply the comfort, support, and encouragement a religious community can offer; instead, it aims to provide "healing, hope, and wholeness to individuals, families, and communities by expanding and equipping spiritually grounded and psychologically informed care, counseling, and psychotherapy." Typically, an AAPC-certified counselor has obtained a bachelor's degree from a college or university, a three-year professional degree from a seminary, and a specialized master's or doctorate degree in the mental health field.

The AAPC asserts that demand for spiritually based counseling is on the rise, in part because interest in spirituality is on the rise in the United States. For many Americans, free or low-cost counseling from pastoral counselors is the most accessible, available, affordable, and acceptable form of mental health care.

## PRACTITIONERS OF COMPLEMENTARY AND ALTERNATIVE MEDICINE

The field of complementary and alternative medicine (CAM) is attracting a growing number of professionals. In "Complementary, Alternative, or Integrative Health: What's in a Name?" (June 28, 2016, https://nccih.nih.gov/health/integrative-health), the federal government's National Center for Complementary and Integrative Health (NCCIH) explains that the term *complementary medicine* refers to "a non-mainstream practice is used together with conventional medicine," while *alternative medicine* is "a non-mainstream practice is used in place of conventional medicine." The term *integrative medicine* involves "bringing conventional and complementary approaches together in a coordinated way."

CAM techniques and products are considered nonmainstream by the NCCIH because they are not a part of conventional medical training and because they have generally not undergone the sort of scientific testing associated with mainstream medicine.

Examples of CAM include acupuncture, dietary supplements, meditation, spinal manipulation, and traditional Chinese medicine. Although these and other CAM approaches are not considered conventional medicine in the United

FIGURE 2.8

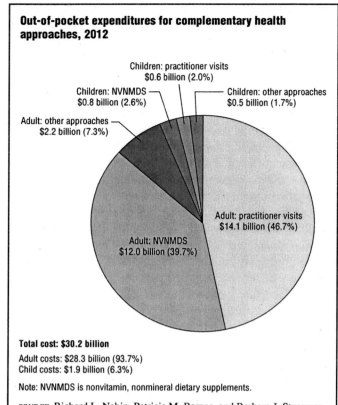

**Out-of-pocket expenditures for complementary health approaches, 2012**

Children: practitioner visits
$0.6 billion (2.0%)

Children: NVNMDS
$0.8 billion (2.6%)

Children: other approaches
$0.5 billion (1.7%)

Adult: other approaches
$2.2 billion (7.3%)

Adult: practitioner visits
$14.1 billion (46.7%)

Adult: NVNMDS
$12.0 billion (39.7%)

**Total cost: $30.2 billion**

Adult costs: $28.3 billion (93.7%)
Child costs: $1.9 billion (6.3%)

Note: NVNMDS is nonvitamin, nonmineral dietary supplements.

SOURCE: Richard L. Nahin, Patricia M. Barnes, and Barbara J. Stussman, "Figure 1. Out-of-Pocket Expenditures for Complementary Health Approaches among Children Aged 4–17 Years and Adults Aged 18 and over: United States, 2012," in "Expenditures on Complementary Health Approaches: United States, 2012," *National Health Statistics Reports*, no. 95, June 22, 2016, http://www.cdc.gov/nchs/data/nhsr/nhsr095.pdf (accessed July 27, 2016)

States, that does not mean they are uncommon. There is considerable enthusiasm for, and use of, CAM approaches and practices. For example, in *Expenditures on Complementary Health Approaches: United States, 2012* (June 22, 2016, http://www.cdc.gov/nchs/data/nhsr/nhsr095.pdf), Richard L. Nahin, Patricia M. Barnes, and Barbara J. Stussman report that in 2012, 59 million people aged four years and older had at least one expenditure for some form of complementary health care, resulting in total out-of-pocket expenditures of $30.2 billion. (See Figure 2.8.) More was spent on visits to CAM practitioners than for purchases of dietary supplements or self-care approaches.

### Homeopathic Medicine

Homeopathic medicine (also called homeopathy) is based on the belief that "like cures like" and uses very diluted amounts of natural substances to encourage the body's own self-healing mechanisms. Homeopathy was developed by the German physician Samuel Hahnemann (1755–1843) during the 1790s. Hahnemann found that he could produce symptoms of particular diseases by injecting small doses of various herbal substances. This discovery inspired him to administer to sick people extremely diluted formulations of substances that would produce the same symptoms they suffered from in an effort to stimulate natural recovery and regeneration.

According to Lex Rutten et al., in "Plausibility and Evidence: The Case of Homeopathy" (*Medicine, Health Care and Philosophy*, vol. 16, no. 3, August 2013), studies evaluating homeopathy report varied results from "comparable to conventional medicine" to "no evidence of effects beyond placebo." (Patients sometimes report improvement even when their treatment is a placebo—something that has no physical effects—because people expect to feel better when they are being treated and this expectation colors the perception of their condition.) Rutten et al. observe that there are many unanswered questions and unresolved issues about the efficacy (the ability of an intervention to produce the intended diagnostic or therapeutic effect in optimal circumstances) of homeopathy, but they "remain convinced that these will eventually be resolved by application of authentic scientific method."

Aeysha Sultan, Bushra Nisar, and Noreen Sajjad observe in "Allopathy versus Homeopathy: A Never Ending Tacit War" (*Medicinal Chemistry*, vol. 6, no. 4, May 2016) that despite widespread allopathic physicians' disapproval, homeopathy is sought by increasing numbers of people, and that homeopathic hospitals and clinics are flourishing. The NCCIH explains in "Homeopathy" (April 4, 2016, https://nccih.nih.gov/health/homeopathy) that although homeopathic remedies are regulated by the U.S. Food and Drug Administration (FDA), they are not evaluated for safety or effectiveness. Laws governing the practice of homeopathy vary by state. Licensed physicians may practice homeopathy in most states, and some states permit nonlicensed professionals to practice it as well. In some states homeopathy is within the scope of practice of chiropractic, naturopathy, and physical therapy.

### Naturopathic Medicine

As its name suggests, naturopathic medicine (also called naturopathy) uses naturally occurring substances to prevent, diagnose, and treat disease. Although it is now considered to be an alternative medicine system, it is one of the oldest medicine systems and has its origins in Native American culture and even draws from Greek, Chinese, and East Indian ideas about health and illness.

The guiding principles of modern naturopathic medicine are "first, do no harm" and "nature has the power to heal." Naturopathy seeks to treat the whole person, because disease is seen as arising from many causes rather than from a single cause. Naturopathic physicians are taught that "prevention is as important as cure" and to view creating and maintaining health as equally important as curing disease. They are instructed to identify and treat the causes of diseases rather than to act only to relieve symptoms.

Naturopathic treatment methods include nutritional counseling; use of dietary supplements, herbs, and vitamins; hydrotherapy (water-based therapies, usually involving whirlpool or other baths); exercise; manipulation; massage; heat therapy; and electrical stimulation. Because naturopathy draws on Chinese and Indian medical techniques, naturopathic physicians often use Chinese herbs, acupuncture, and East Indian medicines to treat disease.

In "Integrating Naturopathy: Can We Move Forward?" (*Permanente Journal*, vol. 17, no. 4, Fall 2013), Charles R. Elder describes naturopathy as "a whole system medical practice guiding the selection and prescription of relatively complex, individualized treatment regimens." Elder claims that naturopathy is potentially effective for many conditions including osteoarthritis, menopausal symptoms, irritable bowels, headache, chronic fatigue, and eczema.

The NCCIH notes in "Naturopathy" (February 24, 2016, https://nccih.nih.gov/health/naturopathy) that some states license naturopathic physicians. In states with licensing requirements, naturopathic physicians must graduate from a four-year naturopathic medical college and pass an examination to be licensed. Other health professionals such as physicians, chiropractors, and nurses may also offer naturopathic treatment.

## Traditional Chinese Medicine

Traditional Chinese medicine (TCM) uses nutrition, acupuncture, massage, herbal medicine, and Qigong (exercises to improve the flow of vital energy through the body) to help people achieve balance and unity of their mind, body, and spirit. Practiced for more than 3,000 years by about a quarter of the world's population, TCM has been adopted by naturopathic physicians, chiropractors, and other CAM practitioners in the United States.

TCM views balancing qi (pronounced chee), the vital life force that flows over the surface of the body and through internal organs, as central to health, wellness, disease prevention, and treatment. This vital force or energy is thought to flow through the human body in meridians (channels). TCM practitioners believe that pain and disease develop when there is any sort of disturbance in the natural flow. TCM also seeks to balance the feminine and masculine qualities of yin and yang by using other techniques such as moxibustion, which is the stimulation of acupuncture points with heat, and cupping, in which the practitioner increases circulation by putting a heated jar on the skin of a body part. Herbal medicine is the most commonly prescribed treatment.

According to the NCCIH, in "Traditional Chinese Medicine: In Depth" (April 21, 2016, https://nccih.nih .gov/health/whatiscam/chinesemed.htm), some of the herbal medicine used in TCM may be marketed as dietary supplements. Although the FDA oversees the sale of supplements, the regulations are not as strict as those for prescription and OTC drugs. The FDA requires manufacturers of prescription and OTC drugs to provide evidence that their claims are true, whereas supplement manufacturers do not have to provide such proof. The safety of Chinese herbs varies. There have been reports of contamination with drugs, toxins, and heavy metals, and some formulations do not contain the ingredients listed on their labels.

## Acupuncture

Acupuncture is a Chinese practice that dates back more than 5,000 years. Chinese medicine describes acupuncture—the insertion of extremely thin, sterile needles to any of 360 specific points on the body—as a way to balance qi. When an acupuncturist determines that there is an imbalance in the flow of energy, needles are inserted at specific points along the meridians. Each point controls a different part of the body. Once the needles are in place, they are rotated gently or are briefly charged with a small electric current.

Traditional Western medicine explains the acknowledged effectiveness of acupuncture as the result of triggering the release of neurotransmitters and neuropeptides that influence brain chemistry and of pain-relieving substances called endorphins that occur naturally in the body. Besides providing lasting pain relief, acupuncture has demonstrated success in helping people with substance abuse problems, relieving nausea, heightening immunity by increasing total white blood cells and T-cell production, and assisting patients to recover from stroke and other neurological impairments. Imaging techniques confirm that acupuncture acts to alter brain chemistry and function.

The NCCIH explains in "Traditional Chinese Medicine: In Depth" that the FDA considers acupuncture needles to be medical devices and requires the needles to be "sterile, nontoxic, and labeled for single use by qualified practitioners only." Although complications arising from acupuncture are rare, there have been reports of the use of nonsterile needles or improper provision of acupuncture treatment.

## Chiropractic Physicians

Chiropractic physicians treat patients whose health problems are associated mainly with the body's structural and neurological systems, especially the spine. These practitioners believe that interference with these systems can impair normal functions and lower resistance to disease. Chiropractic medicine asserts that misalignment or compression of, for example, the spinal nerves can alter many important body functions. Chiropractic care is used most often to treat neuromusculoskeletal complaints, including but not limited to back pain, neck pain, pain in the joints of the arms or legs, and headaches. Chiropractors do not use or prescribe pharmaceutical drugs or perform surgery. Instead, they rely on adjustment and manipulation of the musculoskeletal system, particularly the spinal column.

Many chiropractors use nutritional therapy and prescribe dietary supplements; some employ a technique known as applied kinesiology to diagnose and treat disease. Applied kinesiology is based on the belief that every organ problem is associated with weakness of a specific muscle. Chiropractors who use this technique claim they can accurately identify organ system dysfunction without any laboratory or other diagnostic tests.

Besides manipulation, chiropractors use a variety of other therapies to support healing and relax muscles before they make manual adjustments. These treatments include:

- Heat and cold therapy to relieve pain, speed healing, and reduce swelling

- Hydrotherapy to relax muscles and stimulate blood circulation

- Immobilization such as casts, wraps, traction, and splints to protect injured areas

- Electrotherapy to deliver deep tissue massage and boost circulation

- Ultrasound to relieve muscle spasms and reduce swelling

All states and the District of Columbia license chiropractors that meet the educational and examination requirements established by the state. According to the BLS, in *Occupational Outlook Handbook*, chiropractors worked at 45,200 jobs in 2014, and most were self-employed and in solo practice. In 2015 the median annual wage for chiropractors was $64,440. Visits to chiropractors are most often for treatment of lower back pain, neck pain, and headaches.

## INCREASE IN HEALTH CARE EMPLOYMENT

The number of people working in health care services has increased steadily since the middle of the 20th century. Table 2.10 shows the 15 fastest-growing occupations and their projected growth between 2014 and 2024. Of these, nine are health care occupations. The largest employment increases forecasted are for occupational and physical therapist assistants, followed by physical therapist aides, home health aides, nurse practitioners, physical therapists, ambulance drivers and attendants, occupational therapy aides, and physician assistants.

### Why Is Health Care Booming?

Three major factors appear to have influenced the escalation in health care employment: advances in technology, the increasing amounts of money spent on health care, and the aging of the U.S. population. In other sectors of the economy, technology often replaces humans in the labor force. However, health care technology has increased the demand for highly trained specialists to operate the sophisticated equipment. Because of technological advances, patients are likely to undergo more tests and diagnostic procedures, take more drugs, see more specialists, and be subjected to more aggressive treatments than ever before.

**TABLE 2.10**

**Fastest growing occupations, 2014–24**

[Numbers in thousands]

| Occupation | Employment | | Change, 2014–24 | | Median annual wage, 2014 | Typical education needed for entry |
|---|---|---|---|---|---|---|
| | 2014 | 2024 | Number | Percent | | |
| Total, all occupations | 150,539.9 | 160,328.8 | 9,788.9 | 6.5 | $35,540 | — |
| Wind turbine service technicians | 4.4 | 9.2 | 4.8 | 108.0 | 48,800 | Some college, no degree |
| Occupational therapy assistants | 33.0 | 47.1 | 14.1 | 42.7 | 56,950 | Associate's degree |
| Physical therapist assistants | 78.7 | 110.7 | 31.9 | 40.6 | 54,410 | Associate's degree |
| Physical therapist aides | 50.0 | 69.5 | 19.5 | 39.0 | 24,650 | High school diploma or equivalent |
| Home health aides | 913.5 | 1,261.9 | 348.4 | 38.1 | 21,380 | No formal educational credential |
| Commercial divers | 4.4 | 6.0 | 1.6 | 36.9 | 45,890 | Postsecondary nondegree award |
| Nurse practitioners | 126.9 | 171.7 | 44.7 | 35.2 | 95,350 | Master's degree |
| Physical therapists | 210.9 | 282.7 | 71.8 | 34.0 | 82,390 | Doctoral or professional degree |
| Statisticians | 30.0 | 40.1 | 10.1 | 33.8 | 79,990 | Master's degree |
| Ambulance drivers and attendants, except emergency medical technicians | 19.6 | 26.1 | 6.5 | 33.0 | 24,080 | High school diploma or equivalent |
| Occupational therapy aides | 8.8 | 11.6 | 2.7 | 30.6 | 26,550 | High school diploma or equivalent |
| Physician assistants | 94.4 | 123.2 | 28.7 | 30.4 | 95,820 | Master's degree |
| Operations research analysts | 91.3 | 118.9 | 27.6 | 30.2 | 76,660 | Bachelor's degree |
| Personal financial advisors | 249.4 | 323.2 | 73.9 | 29.6 | 81,060 | Bachelor's degree |
| Cartographers and photogrammetrists | 12.3 | 15.9 | 3.6 | 29.3 | 60,930 | Bachelor's degree |

SOURCE: "Table 5. Fastest Growing Occupations, 2014–24," in *Economic News Release*, U.S. Bureau of Labor Statistics, December 8, 2015, http://www.bls.gov/news.release/ecopro.t05.htm (accessed July 27, 2016)

The second factor involves the amount of money the nation spends on keeping its citizens in good health. The Centers for Medicare and Medicaid Services forecasts in *National Health Expenditure Projections 2015–2025* (July 14, 2016, https://www.cms.gov/Research-Statistics-Data-and-Systems/Statistics-Trends-and-Reports/NationalHealth ExpendData/NationalHealthAccountsProjected.html) that national health expenditures will rise from an average of $10,775 per person in 2017 to $16,032 per person in 2025. For each year that the amount of money spent on health care continues to grow, employment in the field grows as well. Some health care industry observers believe that government and private financing for the health care industry, unlike most other fields, is virtually unlimited.

The third factor contributing to the rise in the number of health care workers is the aging of the nation's population. There are greater numbers of older adults in the United States than ever before, and they are living longer. The U.S. Census Bureau states in the press release "The Next Four Decades: The Older Population in the United States: 2010 to 2050" (May 2010, https://www.census .gov/prod/2010pubs/p25-1138.pdf) that the U.S. population aged 65 years and older will more than double by 2050, rising from 40.2 million in 2010 to 88.5 million in 2050.

The increase in the number of older people is expected to boost the demand for home health care services, assisted living, and nursing home care. Many nursing homes now offer special care for stroke patients, people with Alzheimer's disease (a progressive cognitive impairment), and people who need a respirator to breathe. To care for such patients, nursing homes need more PTs, nursing aides, and respiratory therapists.

Another factor that is increasing the demand for health care workers is the full implementation of the ACA. Millions of previously uninsured Americans have obtained coverage and entered the health care system and require additional health care resources (i.e., workers and facilities). The ACA is also improving the way in which physicians and other health care workers deliver care. For example, previously uninsured Americans who may have used hospital emergency departments to obtain needed medical care are able, after obtaining insurance coverage, to access preventive services in physicians' offices and clinics. People with insurance are more likely to seek care when the symptoms of sickness first appear, when diseases and disorders are more amenable to treatment, rather than waiting until their illnesses require emergency treatment.

The ACA expanded training programs for health professionals and established the National Health Care Workforce Commission to meet the growing demand for health care professionals. In *Projecting the Supply and Demand for Primary Care Practitioners through 2020* (November 2013, http://bhw.hrsa.gov/sites/default/files/ bhw/nchwa/projectingprimarycare.pdf), the National Center for Health Workforce Analysis attributes 81% of the increased demand for primary care services between 2010 and 2020 to population growth and the aging population. The balance of the projected increase in demand is associated with expanded coverage under the ACA. There will be a corresponding demand for services from clinical laboratory professionals, imaging technicians, pharmacists and other pharmacy personnel, and health educators.

Bianca K. Frogner et al. note in "The Demand for Health Care Workers Post-ACA" (*International Journal of Health Economics and Management*, vol. 15, no. 1, March 2015) that increasing demand for health services will exacerbate strain on the already overloaded health care system. The researchers project that by 2022 the health care industry will need between 3 million and 4 million additional workers. The need for a full 40% of these additional health care workers is attributable to the increased demand for services from people newly insured under the ACA.

## THE FUTURE OF THE ACA

The Republican president-elect Donald Trump (1946–) promised to repeal and replace the ACA during his campaign. However, many industry observers believe that only specific provisions of the law, such as subsidies to help low- and moderate-income Americans pay for health insurance, will be targeted. In "The Future of U.S. Health Reform under the Trump Administration" (ScientificAmerican.com, November 14, 2016), John E. McDonough, a professor at the Harvard T. H. Chan School of Public Health, explains that full repeal of the ACA will be challenging for the 115th Congress, which will open in January 2017, because it will require 60 U.S. Senate votes; the Republicans will have just 52 seats, and Democrats will likely oppose repeal.

# CHAPTER 3
# HEALTH CARE INSTITUTIONS

*A hospital is no place to be sick.*

—Samuel Goldwyn

## HOSPITALS

The first hospitals in the United States were established more than 200 years ago. No records of hospitals in the early colonies exist, but almshouses, which sheltered the poor, also cared for those who were ill. The first almshouse opened in 1662 in the Massachusetts Bay Colony. In 1756 the Pennsylvania Hospital in Philadelphia became the first U.S. institution devoted entirely to care of the sick.

Until the late 1800s, U.S. hospitals had a bad reputation. The upper classes viewed hospitals as places for the poor who could not afford home care, and the poor saw hospitalization as a humiliating consequence of personal economic failure. People from all walks of life thought hospitals were places to go to die. These attitudes changed as the quality of care available in hospitals improved.

## TYPES OF HOSPITALS

The American Hospital Association (AHA) notes in "Fast Facts on US Hospitals" (January 2016, http://www.aha.org/research/rc/stat-studies/fast-facts.shtml) that there were 5,627 registered hospitals in the United States in 2014. These included both short-stay and long-term facilities. Short-stay facilities include community, teaching, and public hospitals. Sometimes short-stay hospitals are referred to as acute care facilities because the services provided within them focus on pressing problems or medical conditions, such as a heart attack, rather than on long-term chronic conditions, such as the need for rehabilitation following a head injury. Long-term hospitals are usually rehabilitation and psychiatric hospitals or facilities for the management of illnesses that require longer periods

of treatment, such as tuberculosis or other pulmonary (respiratory) diseases.

Hospitals are also distinguished by their ownership, scope of services, and whether they are teaching hospitals with academic affiliations. Hospitals may be operated as proprietary (for-profit) businesses—owned either by corporations or individuals, such as physicians and staff—or they may be voluntary—owned by nonprofit corporations or religious organizations or operated by federal, state, or city governments. Voluntary, nonprofit hospitals are usually governed by a board of trustees, who are selected from among community business and civic leaders and who serve without pay to oversee hospital operations.

Most community hospitals offer emergency services as well as a range of inpatient and outpatient medical and surgical services. There are more than 1,000 tertiary hospitals in the United States, which provide highly specialized services such as neonatal intensive care units (for care of sick newborns), trauma services, or cardiovascular surgery programs. A majority of tertiary hospitals serve as teaching hospitals.

Teaching hospitals are those community and tertiary hospitals affiliated with medical schools, nursing schools, or allied health professions training programs. Teaching hospitals are the primary sites for training new physicians, where interns and residents work under the supervision of experienced physicians. Nonteaching hospitals may also maintain affiliations with medical schools and some serve as sites for nursing and allied health professions students as well as for physicians-in-training.

Table 3.1 shows that the total number of U.S. hospitals declined from 7,156 in 1975 to 5,686 in 2013. Occupancy rates also declined during this period. Although the number of community nonprofit and state and local hospitals declined during this period, the number of for-profit hospitals grew, from 775 in 1975 to 1,060 in 2013.

TABLE 3.1

**Hospitals, beds, and occupancy rates, by type of ownership and size of hospital, selected years 1975–2013**

[Data are based on reporting by a census of hospitals]

| Type of ownership and size of hospital | 1975 | 1980 | 1990 | 2000 | 2005 | 2010 | 2012 | 2013 |
|---|---|---|---|---|---|---|---|---|
| **Hospitals** | | | | Number | | | | |
| All hospitals | 7,156 | 6,965 | 6,649 | 5,810 | 5,756 | 5,754 | 5,723 | 5,686 |
| Federal | 382 | 359 | 337 | 245 | 226 | 213 | 211 | 213 |
| Nonfederal[a] | 6,774 | 6,606 | 6,312 | 5,565 | 5,530 | 5,541 | 5,512 | 5,473 |
| Community[b] | 5,875 | 5,830 | 5,384 | 4,915 | 4,936 | 4,985 | 4,999 | 4,974 |
| Nonprofit | 3,339 | 3,322 | 3,191 | 3,003 | 2,958 | 2,904 | 2,894 | 2,904 |
| For profit | 775 | 730 | 749 | 749 | 868 | 1,013 | 1,068 | 1,060 |
| State-local government | 1,761 | 1,778 | 1,444 | 1,163 | 1,110 | 1,068 | 1,037 | 1,010 |
| 6–24 beds | 299 | 259 | 226 | 288 | 370 | 424 | 462 | 469 |
| 25–49 beds | 1,155 | 1,029 | 935 | 910 | 1,032 | 1,167 | 1,192 | 1,186 |
| 50–99 beds | 1,481 | 1,462 | 1,263 | 1,055 | 1,001 | 970 | 954 | 959 |
| 100–199 beds | 1,363 | 1,370 | 1,306 | 1,236 | 1,129 | 1,029 | 1,012 | 995 |
| 200–299 beds | 678 | 715 | 739 | 656 | 619 | 585 | 570 | 571 |
| 300–399 beds | 378 | 412 | 408 | 341 | 368 | 352 | 348 | 334 |
| 400–499 beds | 230 | 266 | 222 | 182 | 173 | 185 | 189 | 183 |
| 500 beds or more | 291 | 317 | 285 | 247 | 244 | 273 | 272 | 277 |
| **Beds** | | | | | | | | |
| All hospitals | 1,465,828 | 1,364,516 | 1,213,327 | 983,628 | 946,997 | 941,995 | 920,829 | 914,513 |
| Federal | 131,946 | 117,328 | 98,255 | 53,067 | 45,837 | 44,940 | 38,557 | 38,747 |
| Nonfederal[a] | 1,333,882 | 1,247,188 | 1,115,072 | 930,561 | 901,160 | 897,055 | 882,272 | 875,766 |
| Community[b] | 941,844 | 988,387 | 927,360 | 823,560 | 802,311 | 804,943 | 800,566 | 795,603 |
| Nonprofit | 658,195 | 692,459 | 656,755 | 582,988 | 561,106 | 555,768 | 545,287 | 543,929 |
| For profit | 73,495 | 87,033 | 101,377 | 109,883 | 113,510 | 124,652 | 135,008 | 134,643 |
| State-local government | 210,154 | 208,895 | 169,228 | 130,689 | 127,695 | 124,523 | 120,271 | 117,031 |
| 6–24 beds | 5,615 | 4,932 | 4,427 | 5,156 | 6,316 | 7,261 | 7,791 | 7,763 |
| 25–49 beds | 41,783 | 37,478 | 35,420 | 33,333 | 33,726 | 37,446 | 38,338 | 38,039 |
| 50–99 beds | 106,776 | 105,278 | 90,394 | 75,865 | 71,737 | 69,470 | 67,879 | 67,892 |
| 100–199 beds | 192,438 | 192,892 | 183,867 | 175,778 | 161,593 | 148,090 | 145,556 | 143,760 |
| 200–299 beds | 164,405 | 172,390 | 179,670 | 159,807 | 151,290 | 142,616 | 139,212 | 140,113 |
| 300–399 beds | 127,728 | 139,434 | 138,938 | 117,220 | 126,899 | 121,749 | 120,554 | 115,511 |
| 400–499 beds | 101,278 | 117,724 | 98,833 | 80,763 | 76,894 | 82,071 | 84,007 | 81,148 |
| 500 beds or more | 201,821 | 218,259 | 195,811 | 175,638 | 173,856 | 196,240 | 197,229 | 201,377 |
| **Occupancy rate[c]** | | | | Percent | | | | |
| All hospitals | 76.7 | 77.7 | 69.5 | 66.1 | 69.3 | 66.6 | 65.2 | 64.7 |
| Federal | 80.7 | 80.1 | 72.9 | 68.2 | 66.0 | 65.3 | 63.5 | 64.5 |
| Nonfederal[a] | 76.3 | 77.4 | 69.2 | 65.9 | 69.5 | 66.6 | 65.3 | 64.7 |
| Community[b] | 75.0 | 75.2 | 66.8 | 63.9 | 67.3 | 64.5 | 63.4 | 62.9 |
| Nonprofit | 77.5 | 78.2 | 69.3 | 65.5 | 69.1 | 66.2 | 64.9 | 64.5 |
| For profit | 65.9 | 65.2 | 52.8 | 55.9 | 59.6 | 57.1 | 56.8 | 56.2 |
| State-local government | 70.4 | 71.1 | 65.3 | 63.2 | 66.7 | 64.4 | 63.8 | 62.9 |
| 6–24 beds | 48.0 | 46.8 | 32.3 | 31.7 | 33.5 | 32.3 | 30.8 | 30.5 |
| 25–49 beds | 56.7 | 52.8 | 41.3 | 41.3 | 47.1 | 44.8 | 43.1 | 42.7 |
| 50–99 beds | 64.7 | 64.2 | 53.8 | 54.8 | 59.0 | 55.1 | 55.2 | 55.1 |
| 100–199 beds | 71.2 | 71.4 | 61.5 | 60.0 | 63.2 | 60.4 | 58.1 | 57.6 |
| 200–299 beds | 77.1 | 77.4 | 67.1 | 65.0 | 67.7 | 64.0 | 63.2 | 61.6 |
| 300–399 beds | 79.7 | 79.7 | 70.0 | 65.7 | 70.1 | 67.4 | 65.1 | 64.9 |
| 400–499 beds | 81.1 | 81.2 | 73.5 | 69.1 | 71.2 | 68.5 | 67.5 | 67.6 |
| 500 beds or more | 80.9 | 82.1 | 77.3 | 72.2 | 75.9 | 73.0 | 72.6 | 72.1 |

[a]The category of nonfederal hospitals comprises psychiatric hospitals, tuberculosis and other respiratory diseases hospitals, and long-term and short-term general and other special hospitals.

[b]Community hospitals are nonfederal short-term general and special hospitals whose facilities and services are available to the public. The types of facilities included in the community hospitals category have changed over time.

[c]Estimated percentage of staffed beds that are occupied. Occupancy rate is calculated as the average daily census (from the American Hospital Association) divided by the number of hospital beds.

SOURCE: "Table 89. Hospitals, Beds, and Occupancy Rates, by Type of Ownership and Size of Hospital: United States, Selected Years 1975–2013," in *Health, United States, 2015: With Special Feature on Racial and Ethnic Health Disparities*, U.S. Department of Health and Human Services, Centers for Disease Control and Prevention, National Center for Health Statistics, May 2016, http://www.cdc.gov/nchs/data/hus/hus15.pdf (accessed July 28, 2016).

## Community Hospitals

The most common type of hospital in the United States is the community, or general, hospital. Community hospitals, where most people receive care, are typically small, with 50 to 500 beds. The AHA reports in "Fast Facts on US Hospitals" that in 2014 there were 4,926 community hospitals, with 786,874 staffed beds, in the United States. These hospitals normally provide quality care for routine medical and surgical problems. Since the 1980s many smaller hospitals have closed down because they are no longer profitable. The larger ones, usually located in cities and adjacent suburbs, are often equipped with a full complement of medical and surgical personnel and state-of-the-art equipment.

Some community hospitals are nonprofit corporations that are supported by local funding. These include hospitals supported by religious, cooperative, or osteopathic organizations. During the 1990s increasing numbers of nonprofit community hospitals converted their ownership status, becoming proprietary hospitals that are owned and operated on a for-profit basis by corporations. These hospitals joined investor-owned corporations because they needed additional financial resources to maintain their existence in an increasingly competitive industry. Investor-owned corporations acquire nonprofit hospitals to build market share, expand their provider networks, and penetrate new health care markets. According to the AHA, there were 2,870 nonprofit community hospitals and 1,053 investor-owned, for-profit community hospitals in 2014.

## Teaching Hospitals

Teaching hospitals, which provide clinical training for medical students and other health care professionals, are affiliated with a medical school and have several hundred beds. Many of the physicians on staff at the hospital also hold teaching positions at the university that is affiliated with the hospital. These physicians may serve as classroom instructors as well as teaching physicians-in-training at the bedsides of the patients. Patients in teaching hospitals understand that they may be examined by medical students and residents as well as by their primary attending physician.

One advantage of obtaining care at a university-affiliated teaching hospital is the opportunity to receive treatment from highly qualified physicians with access to the most advanced technology and equipment. A disadvantage is the inconvenience and invasion of privacy that may result from multiple examinations performed by residents and students. When compared with smaller community hospitals, some teaching hospitals have reputations for being impersonal; however, patients with complex, unusual, or difficult diagnoses usually benefit from the presence of acknowledged medical experts and more comprehensive resources that are available at these facilities.

## Public Hospitals

Public hospitals are owned and operated by federal, state, or city governments. Many have a continuing tradition of caring for the poor. They are usually located in the inner cities and are often in precarious financial situations because many of their patients are unable to pay for services. These hospitals depend heavily on Medicaid payments that are supplied by federal and state agencies or on grants from local governments. Medicaid is a program run by both the federal and state governments for the provision of health care insurance to people younger than age 65 who

cannot afford to pay for private health insurance. The federal government matches the states' contribution to provide a certain minimal level of available coverage, and the states may offer additional services at their own expense. In "Fast Facts on US Hospitals," the AHA indicates that there were 1,003 state and local government community hospitals and 213 federal government hospitals in 2014.

**TREATING SOCIETY'S MOST VULNERABLE MEMBERS.** Increasingly, public hospitals must bear the burden of the weaknesses in the nation's health care system. Many of the major problems in U.S. society are readily apparent in the emergency departments and corridors of public hospitals: poverty, drug and alcohol abuse, crime victimization, domestic violence, untreated or inadequately treated chronic conditions such as high blood pressure and diabetes, and infectious diseases such as acquired immunodeficiency syndrome (AIDS) and tuberculosis.

**LOSING MONEY.** Historically, the typical public hospital provided millions of dollars in health care and often failed to recoup these costs from reimbursement by private insurance, Medicaid, and Medicare (a federal health insurance program for people aged 65 years and older and people with disabilities). In response to these fiscal pressures, some hospitals closed and others decreased the range of services provided. Others responded by streamlining services and pursuing paying patients.

According to Rich Daly, in "Outlook Improves for Not-for-Profit Hospitals" (HFMA.org, September 14, 2015), under the Patient Protection and Affordable Care Act (also known as the Affordable Care Act [ACA]) the financial outlook for public hospitals in states that expanded Medicaid enrollment has improved because hospitals are experiencing an increase in patient volume and a more favorable patient mix—meaning, more patients with health coverage.

**PROVIDING NEEDED SERVICES.** America's Essential Hospitals (2016, https://essentialhospitals.org/about-americas-essential-hospitals/) is an association of hospitals and health systems dedicated to serving vulnerable patients. In 2016 the organization represented nearly 275 hospitals and health care systems that provided care to patients and served as community resources.

Many of the members of America's Essential Hospitals are disproportionate share hospitals (DSHs), meaning that an especially large percentage of their patients (about 50% were uninsured in 2014 and the balance were covered by Medicaid) cannot pay their medical bills. In *2014 Essential Data: Our Hospitals, Our Patients* (June 2016, https://essentialhospitals.org/wp-content/uploads/2016/06/2014-Essential-Data-Our-Hospitals-Our-Patients.pdf), America's Essential Hospitals reports that although its members represented a scant 2% of all acute care hospitals in the United States, they provided $7.8 billion in uncompensated care in 2014, which was 18.3% of all uncompensated care nationally, up from 16.8% in 2013. They also operated 45% of all level I trauma centers (the most comprehensive trauma services available), 79% of burn care beds, and 35% of psychiatric care beds in the nation's 10 largest cities.

Carl Graziano, the director of communications for America's Essential Hospitals, reports in "Essential Hospitals Make Pitch for ACA Enrollment" (January 29, 2016, https://essentialhospitals.org/essential-hospitals-pitch-in-again-for-aca-enrollment-campaign/) that public hospitals have made a concerted effort to help uninsured people obtain health insurance coverage under the ACA. Graziano explains, "To sustain their mission, our hospitals must sustain themselves, and more covered patients means less uncompensated care. With an aggregate operating margin of negative 3.2 percent, our hospitals need to reduce uncompensated care."

The ACA requires all insurance plans offered on the insurance marketplace it created to include some "essential community providers." These are health care providers that care for people who are low income or medically underserved and include critical access hospitals, federally qualified health centers, and Ryan White HIV/AIDS providers (which provide care for people with human immunodeficiency virus [HIV] and who do not have sufficient coverage or resources).

Under the ACA, safety net providers have opportunities to coordinate care and serve as medical homes (sources of patient-centered, comprehensive, and coordinated care). The law also offers states the option to receive federal matching funds to implement or expand health home programs for Medicaid beneficiaries with chronic conditions, which are akin to medical homes. Furthermore, the law funds implementation and assessment of novel delivery system and payment models, especially those that incentivize providers to coordinate and integrate care for vulnerable populations. For example, the Medicare Shared Savings Program creates incentives for providers to work together in accountable care organizations to improve health care quality and efficiency.

Safety net hospitals continue to care for the nation's most vulnerable populations; even when previously uninsured patients gain coverage, they do not choose other hospitals. In "Massachusetts Health Reform's Effect on Hospitals' Racial Mix of Patients and on Patients' Use of Safety-Net Hospitals" (*Medical Care*, vol. 54, no. 9, September 2016), Karen E. Lasser et al. analyze Massachusetts data after that state's reforms expanded health coverage to previously uninsured people, many of whom were racial and ethnic minorities. According to the researchers, their study refutes the notion that when patients can seek care anywhere, they will forgo safety net hospitals, and that safety net hospitals will no longer need additional funding for uncompensated care or for the special programs they provide.

## HOSPITAL EMERGENCY DEPARTMENTS: MORE THAN THEY CAN HANDLE

For many Americans, the hospital emergency department (ED) has replaced the physician's office as the place to seek health care services. With no insurance and little money, many people go to the only place that will take them without question. Insurance companies and health care planners estimate that more than half of all ED visits are for nonemergency treatment.

In 2014, 16.7% of all children under the age of 18 years visited an ED at least once. (See Table 3.2.) The poorest children were the most likely to have visited an ED. Almost a quarter (24.7%) of children whose families lived below the poverty level visited an ED in 2014, as did 18.5% of children whose families were between 100% and 199% of the poverty level. By comparison, only 11.4% of children whose families were at or above 400% of the poverty level visited an ED that year. In 2014, 22.9% of children on Medicaid (at the time the government surveyed them) had visited EDs at least once, as opposed to 12.4% of children who were privately insured and 14.7% of uninsured children.

In the 18 years and older age group, 18.6% of the population visited an ED at least once in 2014. (See Table 3.3.) As with children, poorer adults were the most likely to have visited an ED, with 28.6% of people living below 100% of the poverty level and 23.4% of those living between 100% and 199% of the poverty level making at least one visit that year. By contrast, only 13.5% of those with incomes at or above 400% of the poverty level had visited an ED. Among adults aged 18 to 64 years, 34.9% of people who were insured under Medicaid had visited an ED at least once in 2014, as opposed to 14.5% of those who were privately insured and 16.5% of those who were uninsured.

### Lack of Access to Other Providers Prompts Many ED Visits

Because people without health insurance or a usual source of care often resort to using hospital EDs, industry observers sometimes assume that the crowding and long waits in EDs are at least in part caused by uninsured patients seeking care for routine problems such as colds, allergies, or back pain. It was hoped that under the ACA, states that extended and expanded Medicaid to cover people previously uninsured would increase access to primary care and reduce ED use. Renee M. Gindi, Lindsey I. Black, and Robin A. Cohen of the Centers for Disease Control and Prevention analyze in *Reasons for Emergency Room Use among U.S. Adults Aged 18–64: National Health Interview Survey, 2013 and 2014* (February 18, 2016, http://www.cdc.gov/nchs/data/nhsr/nhsr090.pdf) 2013 and 2014 National Health Interview Survey data to assess why and how often people sought care in an ED. Data from 2014

**TABLE 3.2**

**Emergency department visits within the past 12 months among children under age 18, by selected characteristics, selected years 1997–2014**

[Data are based on household interviews of a sample of the civilian noninstitutionalized population]

| Characteristic | Under 18 years | | | Under 6 years | | | 6–17 years | | |
|---|---|---|---|---|---|---|---|---|---|
| | 1997 | 2010 | 2014 | 1997 | 2010 | 2014 | 1997 | 2010 | 2014 |
| | Percent of children with one or more emergency department visits | | | | | | | | |
| **All children**[a] | **19.9** | **22.1** | **16.7** | **24.3** | **27.8** | **22.6** | **17.7** | **19.1** | **13.8** |
| **Sex** | | | | | | | | | |
| Male | 21.5 | 23.3 | 16.9 | 25.2 | 29.3 | 22.1 | 19.6 | 20.1 | 14.4 |
| Female | 18.3 | 20.9 | 16.4 | 23.3 | 26.3 | 23.2 | 15.7 | 18.2 | 13.2 |
| **Race**[b] | | | | | | | | | |
| White only | 19.4 | 21.2 | 15.9 | 22.6 | 26.6 | 21.5 | 17.8 | 18.4 | 13.2 |
| Black or African American only | 24.0 | 27.6 | 21.3 | 33.1 | 34.0 | 30.0 | 19.4 | 24.2 | 17.1 |
| American Indian or Alaska Native only | 24.1* | 20.9 | 28.7 | 24.3* | 35.4* | 31.3* | 24.0* | * | 27.5* |
| Asian only | 12.6 | 15.0 | 10.4 | 20.8 | 18.4 | 13.2 | 8.6 | 13.3 | 8.8 |
| Native Hawaiian or other Pacific Islander only | — | * | * | — | * | * | — | * | * |
| 2 or more races | — | 27.2 | 19.4 | — | 34.9 | 25.3 | — | 21.6 | 15.6 |
| **Hispanic origin and race**[b] | | | | | | | | | |
| Hispanic or Latino | 21.1 | 23.6 | 17.1 | 25.7 | 30.2 | 21.8 | 18.1 | 19.4 | 14.6 |
| Not Hispanic or Latino | 19.7 | 21.7 | 16.6 | 24.0 | 27.0 | 22.9 | 17.6 | 19.0 | 13.6 |
| White only | 19.2 | 20.4 | 15.8 | 22.2 | 25.1 | 21.8 | 17.7 | 18.2 | 13.0 |
| Black or African American only | 23.6 | 27.2 | 20.7 | 32.7 | 34.4 | 30.1 | 19.2 | 23.3 | 16.4 |
| **Percent of poverty level**[c] | | | | | | | | | |
| Below 100% | 25.1 | 30.6 | 24.7 | 29.5 | 35.4 | 31.2 | 22.2 | 27.6 | 21.1 |
| 100%–199% | 22.0 | 25.7 | 18.5 | 28.0 | 31.6 | 23.4 | 19.0 | 22.3 | 16.0 |
| 200%–399% | 18.0 | 18.4 | 13.8 | 21.4 | 22.7 | 20.1 | 16.4 | 16.4 | 10.7 |
| 400% or more | 16.3 | 15.9 | 11.4 | 19.1 | 21.7 | 16.0 | 15.1 | 13.3 | 9.3 |
| **Hispanic origin and race and percent of poverty level**[b, c] | | | | | | | | | |
| Hispanic or Latino: Percent of poverty level: | | | | | | | | | |
| Below 100% | 21.9 | 27.0 | 21.0 | 25.0 | 32.0 | 26.3 | 19.6 | 23.4 | 17.8 |
| 100%–199% | 20.8 | 23.3 | 16.6 | 28.8 | 31.6 | 21.7 | 15.6 | 18.0 | 14.1 |
| 200%–399% | 21.4 | 19.5 | 14.4 | 24.6 | 25.2 | 16.5 | 19.6 | 16.1 | 13.4 |
| 400% or more | 17.7 | 21.4 | 11.3 | 20.2* | 28.6 | 16.2* | 16.4 | 18.0 | 8.8* |
| **Not Hispanic or Latino:** | | | | | | | | | |
| White only: Percent of poverty level: | | | | | | | | | |
| Below 100% | 25.5 | 33.7 | 28.8 | 27.2 | 37.4 | 32.2 | 24.4 | 31.6 | 27.2 |
| 100%–199% | 22.3 | 26.3 | 19.0 | 25.8 | 29.2 | 23.2 | 20.7 | 24.7 | 16.9 |
| 200%–399% | 17.8 | 17.6 | 13.8 | 20.9 | 21.2 | 20.9 | 16.3 | 15.9 | 10.1 |
| 400% or more | 16.5 | 15.5 | 11.4 | 19.0 | 21.0 | 17.5 | 15.4 | 13.2 | 9.0 |
| Black or African American only: Percent of poverty level: | | | | | | | | | |
| Below 100% | 29.3 | 32.4 | 24.8 | 39.5 | 41.6 | 37.0 | 23.0 | 26.6 | 18.2 |
| 100%–199% | 22.5 | 27.5 | 20.6 | 31.7 | 34.5 | 28.6 | 18.5 | 23.7 | 16.7 |
| 200%–399% | 18.5 | 22.3 | 14.6 | 23.9 | 24.6 | 19.5* | 16.3 | 21.4 | 13.2 |
| 400% or more | 16.1 | 18.9 | 17.1 | 18.8* | 24.1* | 19.5* | 15.2 | 16.1 | 16.0* |
| **Health insurance status at the time of interview**[d] | | | | | | | | | |
| Insured | 19.8 | 22.3 | 16.9 | 24.4 | 28.1 | 22.7 | 17.5 | 19.2 | 14.0 |
| Private | 17.5 | 17.1 | 12.4 | 20.9 | 21.8 | 17.6 | 15.9 | 14.9 | 10.1 |
| Medicaid | 28.2 | 30.0 | 22.9 | 33.0 | 35.5 | 28.5 | 24.1 | 26.4 | 19.6 |
| Uninsured | 20.2 | 19.4 | 14.7 | 23.0 | 24.0 | 22.9 | 18.9 | 17.6 | 12.0 |
| **Health insurance status prior to interview**[d] | | | | | | | | | |
| Insured continuously all 12 months | 19.6 | 22.2 | 16.8 | 24.1 | 28.1 | 22.8 | 17.3 | 19.1 | 13.9 |
| Uninsured for any period up to 12 months | 24.0 | 23.7 | 18.0 | 27.1 | 28.0 | 20.7 | 21.9 | 21.3 | 16.6 |
| Uninsured more than 12 months | 18.4 | 17.6 | 11.3 | 19.3 | 21.3* | * | 18.1 | 16.7 | 9.0* |

(the year that ACA coverage provisions went into effect) reveal that the percentage of adults visiting an ED did not significantly differ from the previous year, despite the fact that about 8 million people gained coverage between 2013 and 2014. (See Figure 3.1.)

Gindi, Black, and Cohen indicate that in 2014, 77% of ED visits were prompted by the seriousness of a medical problem, 12% because their physician's office was not open, and 7% because of a lack of access to other providers. Figure 3.1 shows that there were no significant

**TABLE 3.2**

**Emergency department visits within the past 12 months among children under age 18, by selected characteristics, selected years 1997–2014** [CONTINUED]

[Data are based on household interviews of a sample of the civilian noninstitutionalized population]

*Estimates are considered unreliable.
—Data not available.
ªIncludes all other races not shown separately and unknown health insurance status.
ᵇThe race groups, white, black, American Indian or Alaska Native, Asian, Native Hawaiian or other Pacific Islander, and 2 or more races, include persons of Hispanic and non-Hispanic origin. Persons of Hispanic origin may be of any race. Starting with 1999 data, race-specific estimates are tabulated according to the 1997 Revisions to the Standards for the Classification of Federal Data on Race and Ethnicity and are not strictly comparable with estimates for earlier years. The five single-race categories plus multiple-race categories shown in the table conform to the 1997 Standards. Starting with 1999 data, race-specific estimates are for persons who reported only one racial group; the category 2 or more races includes persons who reported more than one racial group. Prior to 1999, data were tabulated according to the 1977 Standards with four racial groups, and the Asian only category included Native Hawaiian or other Pacific Islander. Estimates for single-race categories prior to 1999 included persons who reported one race or, if they reported more than one race, identified one race as best representing their race. Starting with 2003 data, race responses of other race and unspecified multiple race were treated as missing, and then race was imputed if these were the only race responses. Almost all persons with a race response of other race were of Hispanic origin.
ᶜPercent of poverty level is based on family income and family size and composition using U.S. Census Bureau poverty thresholds. Missing family income data were imputed for 1997 and beyond.
ᵈHealth insurance categories are mutually exclusive. Persons who reported both Medicaid and private coverage are classified as having private coverage. Starting with 1997 data, state-sponsored health plan coverage is included as Medicaid coverage. Starting with 1999 data, coverage by the Children's Health Insurance Program (CHIP) is included with Medicaid coverage. In addition to private and Medicaid, the insured category also includes military, other government, and Medicare coverage. Persons not covered by private insurance, Medicaid, CHIP, state-sponsored or other government-sponsored health plans (starting in 1997), Medicare, or military plans are considered to have no health insurance coverage. Persons with only Indian Health Service coverage are considered to have no health insurance coverage.

SOURCE: Adapted from "Table 73. Emergency Department Visits within the Past 12 Months among Children under Age 18, by Selected Characteristics: United States, Selected Years 1997–2014," in *Health, United States, 2015: With Special Feature on Racial and Ethnic Health Disparities*, U.S. Department of Health and Human Services, Centers for Disease Control and Prevention, National Center for Health Statistics, May 2016, http://www.cdc.gov/nchs/data/hus/hus15.pdf (accessed July 29, 2016)

---

differences in the percentages of ED visits by health insurance status. By contrast, the percentage of people seeking ED care because they lacked access to other providers was markedly higher among people who were uninsured than among those with Medicaid coverage or private insurance. (See Figure 3.2.)

The short-term increase in ED visits observed during the first year of ACA implementation is attributed in part to the increased number of Americans with coverage for ED visits and the fact that many of these previously uninsured Americans historically relied on EDs as sites where they could obtain urgent and nonemergency care. Furthermore, although the ACA contains incentives to train additional health care workers, demand for care from the newly insured has outpaced the supply of physicians and other health care practitioners. In "Six Problems with the ACA That Aren't Going Away" (HealthAffairs.org, June 25, 2015), John Goodman notes that many of the newly insured are covered by Medicaid and that Medicaid enrollees have 40% more ED use than people who are uninsured. Goodman laments, "So traffic to our safety-net institutions will be going up, not down, at the very time the ACA will be reducing federal subsidies to these facilities for uncompensated care."

**Hospitals EDs Cater to Older Adults**

The oldest Americans are the most likely age group to visit an ED. Table 3.3 shows that in 2014, 24.4% of those aged 75 years and older did so at least once, and 8.6% did so two or more times. This fact has led some hospitals to create special areas in the EDs for them, or even dedicating EDs to meet their needs. For example, Anna Gorman reports in "Geriatric ERs Reduce Stress, Risks for Older Patients" (CNN.com, July 27, 2016) that Mount Sinai Hospital in New York City is among a growing number of hospitals with an ED dedicated to serving older adults. Gorman explains that senior EDs are designed to be quieter and more tranquil than conventional EDs and are equipped with thicker mattresses, raised toilet seats, hand rails in hallways, and reduced-noise curtains. Because they are better able to screen older patients, senior EDs have the potential to lower costs by preventing unnecessary hospital admissions.

**HOSPITALIZATION**

In *Health, United States, 2015:With Special Feature on Racial and Ethnic Health Disparities* (May 2016, http://www.cdc.gov/nchs/data/hus/hus15.pdf), the National Center for Health Statistics (NCHS) reports that there were 34.5 million admissions to nonfederal short-stay hospitals in 2013. The average length of stay was 6 days, down from 6.6 days in 2000.

**Organ Transplants**

Organ transplants are a viable means of saving lives. According to the United Network for Organ Sharing's (UNOS) Organ Procurement and Transplantation Network (OPTN; http://optn.transplant.hrsa.gov), 27,605 transplants were performed as of November 11, 2016. The UNOS compiles data on organ transplants, distributes organ donor cards, and maintains a registry of patients waiting for organ transplants. It reports that as of November 11, 2016, 119,871 Americans were waiting

**TABLE 3.3**

**Emergency department visits within the past 12 months among adults, by selected characteristics, selected years 1997–2014**

[Data are based on household interviews of a sample of the civilian noninstitutionalized population]

| Characteristic | One or more emergency department visits | | | | Two or more emergency department visits | | | |
|---|---|---|---|---|---|---|---|---|
| | 1997 | 2000 | 2010 | 2014 | 1997 | 2000 | 2010 | 2014 |
| | Percent of adults with emergency department visits | | | | | | | |
| 18 years and over, age-adjusted[a, b] | 19.6 | 20.2 | 21.4 | 18.6 | 6.7 | 6.9 | 7.8 | 6.7 |
| 18 years and over, crude[a] | 19.6 | 20.1 | 21.3 | 18.6 | 6.7 | 6.8 | 7.7 | 6.7 |
| **Age** | | | | | | | | |
| 18–44 years | 20.7 | 20.5 | 22.0 | 18.4 | 6.8 | 7.0 | 8.4 | 6.7 |
| 18–24 years | 26.3 | 25.7 | 25.4 | 20.9 | 9.1 | 8.8 | 9.6 | 8.2 |
| 25–44 years | 19.0 | 18.8 | 20.7 | 17.5 | 6.2 | 6.4 | 8.0 | 6.1 |
| 45–64 years | 16.2 | 17.6 | 19.2 | 17.5 | 5.6 | 5.6 | 6.7 | 6.4 |
| 45–54 years | 15.7 | 17.9 | 18.6 | 16.2 | 5.5 | 5.8 | 6.6 | 5.8 |
| 55–64 years | 16.9 | 17.0 | 19.8 | 18.9 | 5.7 | 5.3 | 6.8 | 7.0 |
| 65 years and over | 22.0 | 23.7 | 23.7 | 21.2 | 8.1 | 8.6 | 7.7 | 7.1 |
| 65–74 years | 20.3 | 21.6 | 20.7 | 18.9 | 7.1 | 7.4 | 6.4 | 6.1 |
| 75 years and over | 24.3 | 26.2 | 27.4 | 24.4 | 9.3 | 10.0 | 9.4 | 8.6 |
| **Sex[b]** | | | | | | | | |
| Male | 19.1 | 18.7 | 18.5 | 16.9 | 5.9 | 5.7 | 6.0 | 5.3 |
| Female | 20.2 | 21.6 | 24.3 | 20.3 | 7.5 | 7.9 | 9.6 | 8.1 |
| **Race[b, c]** | | | | | | | | |
| White only | 19.0 | 19.4 | 20.7 | 17.7 | 6.2 | 6.4 | 7.2 | 6.1 |
| Black or African American only | 25.9 | 26.5 | 28.6 | 26.3 | 11.1 | 10.8 | 12.6 | 11.1 |
| American Indian or Alaska Native only | 24.8 | 30.3 | 22.6 | 31.1 | 13.1 | 12.6* | 11.8* | 18.6 |
| Asian only | 11.6 | 13.6 | 13.3 | 11.0 | 2.9* | 3.8* | 3.3 | 2.8 |
| Native Hawaiian or other Pacific Islander only | — | * | * | * | — | * | * | * |
| 2 or more races | — | 32.5 | 29.7 | 23.8 | — | 11.3 | 11.1 | 8.1 |
| American Indian or Alaska Native; white | — | 33.9 | 31.1 | 25.5 | — | 9.4* | 15.2* | 9.1* |
| **Hispanic origin and race[b, c]** | | | | | | | | |
| Hispanic or Latino | 19.2 | 18.3 | 19.8 | 17.0 | 7.4 | 7.0 | 6.9 | 6.0 |
| Mexican | 17.8 | 17.4 | 18.1 | 17.4 | 6.4 | 7.1 | 6.1 | 6.1 |
| Not Hispanic or Latino | 19.7 | 20.6 | 21.9 | 19.0 | 6.7 | 6.9 | 8.1 | 6.9 |
| White only | 19.1 | 19.8 | 21.1 | 18.1 | 6.2 | 6.4 | 7.4 | 6.3 |
| Black or African American only | 25.9 | 26.5 | 29.0 | 26.6 | 11.0 | 10.8 | 12.7 | 11.2 |
| **Percent of poverty level[b, d]** | | | | | | | | |
| Below 100% | 28.1 | 29.0 | 30.6 | 28.6 | 12.8 | 13.3 | 14.9 | 12.9 |
| 100%–199% | 23.8 | 23.9 | 25.6 | 23.4 | 9.3 | 9.6 | 10.5 | 9.5 |
| 200%–399% | 18.3 | 19.8 | 20.4 | 17.2 | 5.9 | 6.3 | 6.8 | 6.2 |
| 400% or more | 15.9 | 16.8 | 17.0 | 13.5 | 3.9 | 4.5 | 4.7 | 3.4 |
| **Hispanic origin and race and percent of poverty level[b, d, e]** | | | | | | | | |
| Hispanic or Latino: | | | | | | | | |
| Below 100% | 22.1 | 22.4 | 23.6 | 22.6 | 9.8 | 9.7 | 11.5 | 10.2 |
| 100%–199% | 19.2 | 18.1 | 19.9 | 17.0 | 8.1 | 6.7 | 6.3 | 5.7 |
| 200%–399% | 18.5 | 17.3 | 18.1 | 14.7 | 6.0 | 7.4 | 5.2 | 4.9 |
| 400% or more | 14.6 | 16.4 | 18.8 | 13.6 | 3.8* | 4.3* | 5.5* | 3.4* |
| Not Hispanic or Latino: | | | | | | | | |
| White only: | | | | | | | | |
| Below 100% | 29.5 | 30.1 | 33.3 | 30.7 | 13.0 | 13.9 | 15.5 | 13.4 |
| 100%–199% | 24.3 | 25.5 | 26.8 | 25.4 | 9.1 | 10.4 | 11.2 | 10.8 |
| 200%–399% | 18.1 | 20.1 | 20.3 | 17.1 | 5.8 | 6.3 | 6.5 | 6.1 |
| 400% or more | 15.8 | 16.3 | 16.9 | 13.5 | 3.8 | 4.1 | 4.9 | 3.3 |
| Black or African American only: | | | | | | | | |
| Below 100% | 34.6 | 35.4 | 36.9 | 35.3 | 17.5 | 17.4 | 20.2 | 17.7 |
| 100%–199% | 29.2 | 28.5 | 33.5 | 30.4 | 12.8 | 12.2 | 15.9 | 12.9 |
| 200%–399% | 20.8 | 23.2 | 25.7 | 22.0 | 8.1 | 8.0 | 10.2 | 8.8 |
| 400% or more | 18.2 | 22.6 | 18.8 | 18.2 | 5.9 | 8.8 | 4.0* | 5.6 |
| **Health insurance status at the time of interview[e, f]** | | | | | | | | |
| 18–64 years: | | | | | | | | |
| Insured | 18.8 | 19.5 | 20.8 | 18.2 | 6.1 | 6.4 | 7.5 | 6.7 |
| Private | 16.9 | 17.6 | 17.4 | 14.5 | 4.7 | 5.1 | 5.2 | 4.2 |
| Medicaid | 37.6 | 42.2 | 40.2 | 34.9 | 19.7 | 21.0 | 21.1 | 18.4 |
| Uninsured | 20.0 | 19.3 | 21.3 | 16.5 | 7.5 | 6.9 | 8.9 | 5.9 |

for a transplant. Because demand for organs continues to outpace supply, many patients die while waiting for an organ transplant.

In February 2004 the UNOS/OPTN revised and strengthened its policies to guard against potential medical errors in transplant candidate and donor matching.

**TABLE 3.3**

**Emergency department visits within the past 12 months among adults, by selected characteristics, selected years 1997–2014** [CONTINUED]

[Data are based on household interviews of a sample of the civilian noninstitutionalized population]

| Characteristic | One or more emergency department visits | | | | Two or more emergency department visits | | | |
| --- | --- | --- | --- | --- | --- | --- | --- | --- |
| | 1997 | 2000 | 2010 | 2014 | 1997 | 2000 | 2010 | 2014 |
| | Percent of adults with emergency department visits | | | | | | | |
| **Health insurance status prior to interview[e, f]** | | | | | | | | |
| 18–64 years: | | | | | | | | |
| Insured continuously all 12 months | 18.3 | 19.0 | 20.2 | 17.6 | 5.8 | 6.1 | 7.1 | 6.4 |
| Uninsured for any period up to 12 months | 25.5 | 28.2 | 26.0 | 22.9 | 9.4 | 10.3 | 12.5 | 9.3 |
| Uninsured more than 12 months | 18.9 | 17.3 | 20.6 | 15.4 | 7.1 | 6.4 | 8.1 | 5.4 |
| **Percent of poverty level and health insurance status prior to interview[d, e, f]** | | | | | | | | |
| 18–64 years: | | | | | | | | |
| Below 100%: | | | | | | | | |
| Insured continuously all 12 months | 30.2 | 31.6 | 35.2 | 32.7 | 14.7 | 15.4 | 18.3 | 16.0 |
| Uninsured for any period up to 12 months | 34.1 | 43.7 | 34.2 | 29.6 | 16.1 | 18.1 | 16.5 | 14.5 |
| Uninsured more than 12 months | 20.8 | 20.5 | 23.4 | 20.2 | 8.1 | 9.1 | 11.7 | 6.9 |
| 100%–199%: | | | | | | | | |
| Insured continuously all 12 months | 24.5 | 25.5 | 26.1 | 25.0 | 8.9 | 10.2 | 10.8 | 11.0 |
| Uninsured for any period up to 12 months | 28.7 | 27.7 | 29.7 | 29.0 | 12.3 | 11.7 | 15.6 | 11.6 |
| Uninsured more than 12 months | 19.0 | 17.4 | 21.2 | 14.2 | 8.3 | 6.4 | 7.8 | 5.8 |
| 200%–399%: | | | | | | | | |
| Insured continuously all 12 months | 17.5 | 19.5 | 19.6 | 16.3 | 5.3 | 6.3 | 6.0 | 6.0 |
| Uninsured for any period up to 12 months | 21.6 | 24.6 | 25.4 | 19.9 | 6.6 | 7.3 | 12.2 | 7.2 |
| Uninsured more than 12 months | 16.8 | 15.6 | 17.6 | 12.6 | 5.9 | 4.5 | 5.7 | 4.2* |
| 400% or more: | | | | | | | | |
| Insured continuously all 12 months | 14.9 | 15.5 | 15.9 | 12.5 | 3.7 | 3.7 | 4.5 | 2.8 |
| Uninsured for any period up to 12 months | 18.0 | 20.1 | 12.5 | 9.2 | 3.1* | 6.4 | * | * |
| Uninsured more than 12 months | 19.1 | 15.8 | 19.4 | 10.7* | * | 5.2* | * | * |
| **Disability measure[b, g]** | | | | | | | | |
| Any basic actions difficulty or complex activity limitation | 30.8 | 32.0 | 34.9 | 32.2 | 13.5 | 14.6 | 16.8 | 14.8 |
| Any basic actions difficulty | 30.5 | 32.4 | 35.0 | 32.6 | 13.5 | 14.9 | 17.2 | 15.0 |
| Any complex activity limitation | 39.7 | 41.5 | 43.8 | 41.5 | 19.9 | 21.2 | 24.5 | 21.7 |
| No disability | 14.5 | 15.3 | 16.1 | 13.2 | 3.7 | 3.9 | 4.4 | 3.6 |
| **Geographic region[b]** | | | | | | | | |
| Northeast | 19.5 | 20.0 | 22.6 | 18.3 | 6.9 | 6.2 | 8.4 | 6.4 |
| Midwest | 19.3 | 20.1 | 22.3 | 20.6 | 6.2 | 6.9 | 8.2 | 7.7 |
| South | 20.9 | 21.2 | 22.1 | 19.1 | 7.3 | 7.6 | 8.0 | 6.9 |
| West | 17.7 | 18.6 | 18.9 | 16.0 | 6.0 | 6.3 | 6.7 | 5.4 |
| **Location of residence[b, h]** | | | | | | | | |
| Within MSA | 19.1 | 19.6 | 20.8 | 18.1 | 6.4 | 6.6 | 7.5 | 6.4 |
| Outside MSA | 21.5 | 22.5 | 25.5 | 22.0 | 7.8 | 7.8 | 9.8 | 8.9 |

The policy revisions were developed in response to a systematic review of a medical error in February 2003, when a teenager named Jésica Sántillan (1985–2003) died after receiving a heart-lung transplant from a blood-type incompatible donor at Duke University Medical Center. News of this tragic error immediately prompted transplant centers throughout the United States to perform internal audits of their protocols and procedures to ensure appropriate donor-recipient matching.

The key policy revisions included stipulations that:

- The blood type of each transplant candidate and donor must be independently verified by two staff members at the institution involved at the time blood type is entered into the national database.

- Each transplant program and organ procurement organization must establish a protocol to ensure blood-type data for transplant candidates and donors are accurately entered into the national database and communicated to transplant teams. The UNOS will verify the existence and effective use of these protocols during routine audits of organ procurement organizations and transplant programs.

- Organs must only be offered to candidates specifically identified on the computer-generated list of medically suitable transplant candidates for a given organ offer. If the organ offer is not accepted for any candidate on a given match run, an organ procurement organization may give transplant programs the opportunity to update transplant candidate data and rerun a match to see if any additional candidates are identified.

The UNOS resolved to continuously review national policies and procedures for organ placement and to recommend policy and procedure enhancements to maximize the efficiency of organ placement and the safety of transplant candidates and recipients. As of 2016, there

**TABLE 3.3**

**Emergency department visits within the past 12 months among adults, by selected characteristics, selected years 1997–2014** [CONTINUED]

[Data are based on household interviews of a sample of the civilian noninstitutionalized population]

*Estimates are considered unreliable.
—Data not available.
aIncludes all other races not shown separately, unknown health insurance status, and unknown disability status.
bEstimates are for persons aged 18 and over and are age-adjusted to the year 2000 standard population using five age groups: 18–44 years, 45–54 years, 55–64 years, 65–74 years, and 75 years and over.
cThe race groups, white, black, American Indian or Alaska Native, Asian, Native Hawaiian or other Pacific Islander, and 2 or more races, include persons of Hispanic and non-Hispanic origin. Persons of Hispanic origin may be of any race. Starting with 1999 data, race-specific estimates are tabulated according to the 1997 *Revisions to the Standards for the Classification of Federal Data on Race and Ethnicity* and are not strictly comparable with estimates for earlier years. The five single-race categories plus multiple-race categories shown in the table conform to the 1997 Standards. Starting with 1999 data, race-specific estimates are for persons who reported only one racial group; the category 2 or more races includes persons who reported more than one racial group. Prior to 1999, data were tabulated according to the 1977 Standards with four racial groups, and the Asian only category included Native Hawaiian or Other Pacific Islander. Estimates for single-race categories prior to 1999 included persons who reported one race or, if they reported more than one race, identified one race as best representing their race. Starting with 2003 data, race responses of other race and unspecified multiple race were treated as missing, and then race was imputed if these were the only race responses. Almost all persons with a race response of other race were of Hispanic origin.
dPercent of poverty level is based on family income and family size and composition using U.S. Census Bureau poverty thresholds. Missing family income data were imputed for 1997 and beyond.
eEstimates for persons aged 18–64 are age-adjusted to the year 2000 standard population using three age groups: 18–44 years, 45–54 years, and 55–64 years.
fHealth insurance categories are mutually exclusive. Persons who reported both Medicaid and private coverage are classified as having private coverage. Starting with 1997 data, state-sponsored health plan coverage is included as Medicaid coverage. Starting with 1999 data, coverage by the Children's Health Insurance Program (CHIP) is included with Medicaid coverage. In addition to private and Medicaid, the insured category also includes military plans, other government-sponsored health plans, and Medicare, not shown separately. Persons not covered by private insurance, Medicaid, CHIP, state-sponsored or other government-sponsored health plans (starting in 1997), Medicare, or military plans are considered to have no health insurance coverage. Persons with only Indian Health Service coverage are considered to have no health insurance coverage.
gAny basic actions difficulty or complex activity limitation is defined as having one or more of the following limitations or difficulties: movement difficulty, emotional difficulty, sensory (seeing or hearing) difficulty, cognitive difficulty, self-care (activities of daily living or instrumental activities of daily living) limitation, social limitation, or work limitation. Starting with 2007 data, the hearing question, a component of the basic actions difficulty measure, was revised. Consequently, data prior to 2007 are not comparable with data for 2007 and beyond.
hMSA is metropolitan statistical area. Starting with 2006 data, MSA status is determined using 2000 census data and the 2000 standards for defining MSAs.

SOURCE: Adapted from "Table 74. Emergency Department Visits within the Past 12 Months among Adults Aged 18 Years and over, by Selected Characteristics: United States, Selected Years 1997–2014," in *Health, United States, 2015: With Special Feature on Racial and Ethnic Health Disparities*, U.S. Department of Health and Human Services, Centers for Disease Control and Prevention, National Center for Health Statistics, May 2016, http://www.cdc.gov/nchs/data/hus/hus15.pdf (accessed July 29, 2016)

were no further reported occurrences of unintentional blood-type incompatible transplants.

The risks associated with organ transplant were, however, publicized again in 2005 and 2006, when two transplant recipients from the same organ donor contracted West Nile virus, a potentially serious illness that is transmitted by mosquitoes. Both developed encephalitis (a brain infection), fell into comas, and died. These cases catalyzed transplant physicians and public health officials to intensify organ safety protocols and procedures.

Following a review of more than 200 reports of unexpected disease transmission through organ transplantation, Debbie L. Seem et al. published "Public Health Service Guideline for Reducing Transmission of Human Immunodeficiency Virus (HIV), Hepatitis B Virus (HBV), and Hepatitis C Virus (HCV) through Solid Organ Transplantation" (September 21, 2011, http://www.regulations.gov/#!docketDetail;dct=FR%252BPR%252BN%252BO%252BSR;rpp=10;po=0;D=CDC-2011-0011) to reduce the risk and occurrence of unintended disease in organ recipients. The guidelines recommend enhancing donor screening practices and improving organ testing procedures to enable patients and physicians to make more informed risk-benefit decisions about organs that are available for transplant.

The UNOS continually updates its policies. In *Policies* (November 10, 2016, https://optn.transplant.hrsa.gov/media/1200/optn_policies.pdf), the organization details rules that govern the operation of transplant hospitals, organ procurement organizations, and histocompatibility labs (labs that determine whether tissues from different individuals are compatible, so that a graft from one person will not trigger an immune response in another) in the United States.

## SURGICAL CENTERS AND URGENT CARE CENTERS

Ambulatory surgery centers (also called surgicenters) are equipped to perform routine surgical procedures that do not require an overnight hospital stay. A surgical center requires less sophisticated and expensive equipment than a hospital operating room. Minor surgery, such as biopsies, abortions, hernia repair, and many cosmetic surgery procedures, are performed at outpatient surgical centers. Most procedures are done under local anesthesia, and patients go home the same day.

Most ambulatory surgery centers are freestanding, but some are located on hospital campuses or are next to physicians' offices or clinics. Facilities are licensed by their state and must be equipped with at least one operating room, an area for preparing patients for procedures, a patient recovery area, and x-ray and clinical laboratory services. Also, surgical centers must have a registered nurse on the premises when patients are in the facility.

Urgent care centers (also called urgicenters) are usually operated by private, for-profit organizations and provide up

FIGURE 3.1

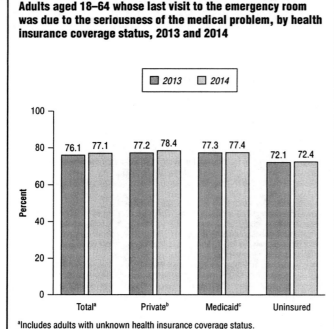

**Adults aged 18–64 whose last visit to the emergency room was due to the seriousness of the medical problem, by health insurance coverage status, 2013 and 2014**

aIncludes adults with unknown health insurance coverage status.
bSignificantly different from uninsured in both 2013 and 2014.
cSignificantly different from uninsured in 2013.
Note: Seriousness of the medical problem was based on a positive response to at least one of the following reasons: health provider advised to go, problem was too serious for the doctor's office or clinic, only a hospital could help, or arrived by ambulance or other emergency vehicle.

SOURCE: Renee M. Gindi, Lindsey I. Black, and Robin A. Cohen, "Figure 2. Adults Aged 18–64 with a Visit to the Emergency Room Whose Last Visit Was Due to the Seriousness of the Medical Problem, by Year and Health Insurance Coverage Status: United States, 2013 and 2014," in "Reasons for Emergency Room Use among U.S. Adults Aged 18–64: National Health Interview Survey, 2013 and 2014," *National Health Statistics Report*, no. 90, February 18, 2016, http://www.cdc.gov/nchs/data/nhsr/nhsr090.pdf (accessed July 29, 2016)

FIGURE 3.2

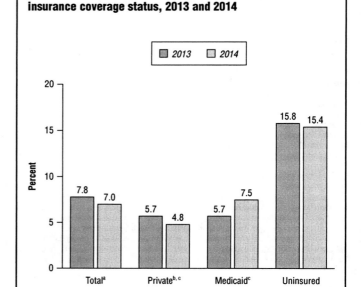

**Adults aged 18–64 whose last visit to the emergency room was due to lack of access to other providers, by health insurance coverage status, 2013 and 2014**

aIncludes adults with unknown health insurance coverage status.
bSignificantly different from Medicaid in 2014.
cSignificantly different from uninsured in 2013 and 2014.
Note: Lack of access to other providers was based on a positive response to at least one of the following: didn't have another place to go, emergency room is the closest provider, or get most of care at the emergency room. This category excludes those who selected reasons related to seriousness of the medical problem or doctor's office or clinic was not open.

SOURCE: Renee M. Gindi, Lindsey I. Black and Robin A. Cohen, "Figure 4. Adults Aged 18–64 with a Visit to the Emergency Room Whose Last Visit Was Due Lack of Access to Other Providers, by Year, Health Insurance Coverage Status, and Demographic Characteristics: United States, 2013 and 2014," in "Reasons for Emergency Room Use among U.S. Adults Aged 18–64: National Health Interview Survey, 2013 and 2014," *National Health Statistics Report*, no. 90, February 18, 2016, http://www.cdc.gov/nchs/data/nhsr/nhsr090.pdf (accessed July 29, 2016)

to 24-hour care on a walk-in basis. These centers fill several special needs in a community. They provide convenient, timely, and easily accessible care when the nearest hospital may be miles away. The centers are often open during the hours when most physicians' offices are closed, and they are economical to operate because they do not provide hospital beds. They usually treat problems such as cuts that require sutures, sprains and bruises from accidents, and various infections. Many provide inexpensive immunizations, and some offer routine health care for people who do not have a regular source of medical care. Urgent care may be more expensive than a visit to the family physician, but an urgent care center visit is usually less expensive than treatment from a traditional hospital ED.

### Clinics in Stores and Malls

Retail-based clinics in grocery stores, drug stores, or big-box stores offer more than simply convenient locations. Many welcome walk-in patients and offer urgent care as well as extended hours, flat fees for physician

visits, low-cost immunizations, and comfortable surroundings. They also emphasize unscheduled care much more than do most primary care practices. Furthermore, some clinics telephone all patients within 48 hours of being seen for care, a measure that serves to improve both quality of care and patient satisfaction.

The Robert Wood Johnson Foundation observes in "Growing Retail Clinic Industry Employs, Empowers Nurse Practitioners" (February 20, 2015, http://www.rwjf.org/en/library/articles-and-news/2015/02/growing-retail-clinic-industry-employs--empowers-nurse-practitio.html) that the number of retail-based clinics was expected to reach 3,000 by 2016 and notes that many clinics planned to increase access to care. As a result, the number of retail-based clinics is anticipated to increase. Although studies suggest that the care the clinics provide is comparable and costs less than care in other settings such as hospital EDs, the foundation notes that the American Academy of Pediatrics (AAP) asserts that the clinics do not provide infants, children, and adolescents with the "continuous, coordinated care" they need.

Specifically, in the policy statement "AAP Principles Concerning Retail-Based Clinics" (*Pediatrics*, vol. 133, no. 3, March 2014), the AAP cites concerns, including fragmentation of care; lack of access to complete, central health records; use of diagnostic tests without proper follow-up; and potential public health problems when patients with infectious diseases such as measles, mumps, or strep throat are seen in a retail environment rather than isolated to prevent the spread of infection. The AAP also notes that visits with pediatricians in conventional offices offer opportunities to identify and discuss problems, catch up on immunizations, and strengthen relationships with children and their families.

## LONG-TERM-CARE FACILITIES

Families are the primary caretakers for older, dependent, and disabled individuals in U.S. society. However, the number of people aged 65 years and older living in long-term-care facilities such as nursing homes is rising because the population in this age group is increasing rapidly. Although many older people now live longer, healthier lives, the increase in overall length of life has expanded the need for long-term-care facilities.

Growth of the home health care industry during the early 1990s only slightly slowed the increase in the numbers of Americans entering nursing homes. Assisted-living and continuing-care retirement communities offer other alternatives to nursing home care. When it is possible, many older adults prefer to remain in the community and receive health care in their home.

### Types of Nursing Homes

Nursing homes fall into three broad categories: residential care facilities, intermediate care facilities, and skilled nursing facilities. Each provides a different range and intensity of services:

- A residential care facility normally provides meals and housekeeping for its residents, plus some basic medical monitoring, such as administering medications. This type of home is for people who are fairly independent and do not need constant medical attention but need help with tasks such as laundry and cleaning. Many residential care facilities also provide social activities and recreational programs for their residents.

- An intermediate care facility offers room and board and nursing care as necessary for people who can no longer live independently. As in the residential care facility, exercise and social programs are provided, and some intermediate care facilities also offer physical therapy and rehabilitation programs.

- A skilled nursing facility provides around-the-clock nursing care, plus on-call physician coverage. A skilled nursing facility is for patients who need intensive nursing care and services such as occupational therapy, physical therapy, respiratory therapy, and rehabilitation.

### Nursing Home Beds, Residents, and Occupancy Rates

The NCHS reports that in 2014 there were 15,643 certified nursing homes in the United States, which housed nearly 1.7 million beds and had an average occupancy rate of 80.8%. (See Table 3.4.)

In *Long-Term Care Providers and Services Users in the United States: Data from the National Study of Long-Term Care Providers, 2013–2014* (February 2016, http://www.cdc.gov/nchs/data/series/sr_03/sr03_038.pdf), Lauren Harris-Kojetin et al. of the NCHS provide information about supply, organizational characteristics, staffing, and services that are offered by regulated providers of long-term-care services and the patients they serve. For example, the researchers find that the percentage of patients requiring assistance with the activities of daily living (walking, bathing, dressing, toileting, and eating) was higher among nursing home residents and people receiving home health care services than among residents living in residential care communities and people at adult day services centers. (See Figure 3.3.)

Kojetin et al. note that in 2013 and 2014, 41.6% residents of nursing homes were the "oldest old" (people aged 85 years and older). (See Figure 3.4.) Nursing home residents aged 75 to 85 years accounted for 27.2% of all nursing home residents. About two-thirds (62.9%) of long-term-care patients' nursing home care in 2013 and 2014 was paid for by Medicaid. (See Figure 3.5.)

In 2008 the Centers for Medicare and Medicaid Services (CMS) began the Five-Star Quality Rating System for the nation's certified nursing homes. The CMS offers the online "Nursing Home Compare" (http://www.medicare.gov/NHCompare/Include/DataSection/Questions/ProximitySearch.asp), which contains detailed information, updated every month, about every Medicare- and Medicaid-certified nursing home in the country.

### Diversification of Nursing Homes

To remain competitive with home health care and the increasing array of alternative living arrangements for the elderly, many nursing homes offer alternative services and programs. These services include adult day care and visiting nurse services for people who still live at home. Other programs include respite plans that allow caregivers who need to travel for business or vacation to leave an elderly relative in a nursing home temporarily.

One of the most popular nontraditional services is subacute care, which is comprehensive inpatient treatment

TABLE 3.4

**Nursing home beds, residents, and occupancy rates, selected years 1995–2014**

[Data are based on a census of certified nursing facilities]

| State | Nursing homes | | | | Beds | | | |
|---|---|---|---|---|---|---|---|---|
| | 1995 | 2000 | 2013 | 2014 | 1995 | 2000 | 2013 | 2014 |
| | | | | | Number | | | |
| **United States** | **16,389** | **16,886** | **15,663** | **15,643** | **1,751,302** | **1,795,388** | **1,697,484** | **1,693,943** |
| Alabama | 221 | 225 | 228 | 226 | 23,353 | 25,248 | 26,685 | 26,388 |
| Alaska | 15 | 15 | 17 | 18 | 814 | 821 | 779 | 693 |
| Arizona | 152 | 150 | 146 | 147 | 16,162 | 17,458 | 16,607 | 16,605 |
| Arkansas | 256 | 255 | 230 | 229 | 29,952 | 25,715 | 24,546 | 24,558 |
| California | 1,382 | 1,369 | 1,226 | 1,217 | 140,203 | 131,762 | 121,381 | 119,866 |
| Colorado | 219 | 225 | 211 | 214 | 19,912 | 20,240 | 20,371 | 20,431 |
| Connecticut | 267 | 259 | 231 | 229 | 32,827 | 32,433 | 27,841 | 27,673 |
| Delaware | 42 | 43 | 46 | 46 | 4,739 | 4,906 | 4,986 | 4,876 |
| District of Columbia | 19 | 20 | 19 | 19 | 3,206 | 3,078 | 2,766 | 2,766 |
| Florida | 627 | 732 | 687 | 689 | 72,656 | 83,365 | 83,178 | 83,545 |
| Georgia | 352 | 363 | 358 | 357 | 38,097 | 39,817 | 39,883 | 39,975 |
| Hawaii | 34 | 45 | 47 | 46 | 2,513 | 4,006 | 4,215 | 4,213 |
| Idaho | 76 | 84 | 77 | 78 | 5,747 | 6,181 | 5,930 | 5,951 |
| Illinois | 827 | 869 | 769 | 761 | 103,230 | 110,766 | 98,883 | 98,348 |
| Indiana | 556 | 564 | 515 | 528 | 59,538 | 56,762 | 58,764 | 59,555 |
| Iowa | 419 | 467 | 444 | 443 | 39,959 | 37,034 | 32,183 | 31,950 |
| Kansas | 429 | 392 | 345 | 345 | 30,016 | 27,067 | 25,653 | 25,730 |
| Kentucky | 288 | 307 | 283 | 287 | 23,221 | 25,341 | 26,170 | 26,300 |
| Louisiana | 337 | 337 | 280 | 280 | 37,769 | 39,430 | 35,189 | 35,066 |
| Maine | 132 | 126 | 107 | 105 | 9,243 | 8,248 | 7,020 | 6,953 |
| Maryland | 218 | 255 | 230 | 228 | 28,394 | 31,495 | 28,487 | 28,115 |
| Massachusetts | 550 | 526 | 421 | 416 | 54,532 | 56,030 | 48,660 | 48,320 |
| Michigan | 432 | 439 | 432 | 433 | 49,473 | 50,696 | 46,970 | 46,521 |
| Minnesota | 432 | 433 | 380 | 377 | 43,865 | 42,149 | 30,405 | 30,319 |
| Mississippi | 183 | 190 | 205 | 205 | 16,059 | 17,068 | 18,550 | 18,434 |
| Missouri | 546 | 551 | 513 | 512 | 52,679 | 54,829 | 55,106 | 55,273 |
| Montana | 100 | 104 | 83 | 83 | 7,210 | 7,667 | 6,713 | 6,732 |
| Nebraska | 231 | 236 | 217 | 219 | 18,169 | 17,877 | 15,855 | 16,005 |
| Nevada | 42 | 51 | 51 | 52 | 3,998 | 5,547 | 5,979 | 6,040 |
| New Hampshire | 74 | 83 | 76 | 76 | 7,412 | 7,837 | 7,510 | 7,501 |
| New Jersey | 300 | 361 | 365 | 361 | 43,967 | 52,195 | 52,417 | 52,051 |
| New Mexico | 83 | 80 | 71 | 71 | 6,969 | 7,289 | 6,716 | 6,869 |
| New York | 624 | 665 | 631 | 628 | 107,750 | 120,514 | 116,448 | 117,131 |
| North Carolina | 391 | 410 | 421 | 422 | 38,322 | 41,376 | 44,598 | 45,088 |
| North Dakota | 87 | 88 | 81 | 81 | 7,125 | 6,954 | 6,138 | 6,131 |
| Ohio | 943 | 1,009 | 955 | 954 | 106,884 | 105,038 | 91,563 | 90,653 |
| Oklahoma | 405 | 392 | 311 | 309 | 33,918 | 33,903 | 29,396 | 28,962 |
| Oregon | 161 | 150 | 138 | 137 | 13,885 | 13,500 | 12,276 | 12,210 |
| Pennsylvania | 726 | 770 | 703 | 699 | 92,625 | 95,063 | 88,284 | 88,236 |
| Rhode Island | 94 | 99 | 84 | 84 | 9,612 | 10,271 | 8,715 | 8,720 |
| South Carolina | 166 | 178 | 189 | 188 | 16,682 | 18,102 | 19,689 | 19,631 |
| South Dakota | 114 | 114 | 111 | 111 | 8,296 | 7,844 | 6,909 | 6,945 |
| Tennessee | 322 | 349 | 320 | 321 | 37,074 | 38,593 | 37,140 | 37,268 |
| Texas | 1,266 | 1,215 | 1,205 | 1,212 | 123,056 | 125,052 | 135,350 | 136,000 |
| Utah | 91 | 93 | 98 | 99 | 7,101 | 7,651 | 8,500 | 8,577 |
| Vermont | 23 | 44 | 38 | 37 | 1,862 | 3,743 | 3,199 | 3,174 |
| Virginia | 271 | 278 | 286 | 288 | 30,070 | 30,595 | 32,638 | 32,497 |
| Washington | 285 | 277 | 225 | 221 | 28,464 | 25,905 | 21,641 | 21,286 |
| West Virginia | 129 | 139 | 126 | 127 | 10,903 | 11,413 | 10,888 | 10,888 |
| Wisconsin | 413 | 420 | 392 | 389 | 48,754 | 46,395 | 34,730 | 33,959 |
| Wyoming | 37 | 40 | 39 | 39 | 3,035 | 3,119 | 2,984 | 2,965 |

for people recovering from acute illnesses such as pneumonia, injuries such as a broken hip, and chronic diseases such as arthritis that do not require intensive, hospital-level treatment. This level of care also enables nursing homes to expand their markets by offering services to younger patients.

## Innovation Improves Quality of Nursing Home Care

Industry observers and the media frequently raise concerns about the care provided in nursing homes and publicize instances of elder abuse and other quality of care issues. Several organizations have actively sought to develop models of health service delivery that improve the clinical care and quality of life for nursing home residents. In *Evaluation of the Wellspring Model for Improving Nursing Home Quality* (August 2002, http://www.cmwf.org/usr_doc/stone_wellspringevaluation.pdf), a benchmark report that examines one such model in eastern Wisconsin, Robyn I. Stone et al. evaluate the Wellspring model of nursing home quality improvement.

**TABLE 3.4**

**Nursing home beds, residents, and occupancy rates, selected years 1995–2014** [CONTINUED]

[Data are based on a census of certified nursing facilities]

| State | Residents | | | | Occupancy rate* | | | |
|---|---|---|---|---|---|---|---|---|
| | 1995 | 2000 | 2013 | 2014 | 1995 | 2000 | 2013 | 2014 |
| | | | | Number | | | | |
| United States | 1,479,550 | 1,480,076 | 1,371,926 | 1,368,667 | 84.5 | 82.4 | 80.8 | 80.8 |
| Alabama | 21,691 | 23,089 | 22,764 | 22,731 | 92.9 | 91.4 | 85.3 | **86.1** |
| Alaska | 634 | 595 | 498 | 612 | 77.9 | 72.5 | 63.9 | 88.3 |
| Arizona | 12,382 | 13,253 | 11,344 | 11,428 | 76.6 | 75.9 | 68.3 | 68.8 |
| Arkansas | 20,823 | 19,317 | 17,774 | 17,688 | 69.5 | 75.1 | 72.4 | 72.0 |
| California | 109,805 | 106,460 | 102,324 | 102,245 | 78.3 | 80.8 | 84.3 | 85.3 |
| Colorado | 17,055 | 17,045 | 15,957 | 16,309 | 85.7 | 84.2 | 78.3 | 79.8 |
| Connecticut | 29,948 | 29,657 | 24,610 | 24,250 | 91.2 | 91.4 | 88.4 | 87.6 |
| Delaware | 3,819 | 3,900 | 4,217 | 4,314 | 80.6 | 79.5 | 84.6 | 88.5 |
| District of Columbia | 2,576 | 2,858 | 2,569 | 2,539 | 80.3 | 92.9 | 92.9 | 91.8 |
| Florida | 61,845 | 69,050 | 72,679 | 73,487 | 85.1 | 82.8 | 87.4 | 88.0 |
| Georgia | 35,933 | 36,559 | 33,889 | 33,930 | 94.3 | 91.8 | 85.0 | 84.9 |
| Hawaii | 2,413 | 3,558 | 3,714 | 3,663 | 96.0 | 88.8 | 88.1 | 86.9 |
| Idaho | 4,697 | 4,640 | 3,909 | 3,841 | 81.7 | 75.1 | 65.9 | 64.5 |
| Illinois | 83,696 | 83,604 | 72,856 | 72,563 | 81.1 | 75.5 | 73.7 | 73.8 |
| Indiana | 44,328 | 42,328 | 38,649 | 38,893 | 74.5 | 74.6 | 65.8 | 65.3 |
| Iowa | 27,506 | 29,204 | 24,980 | 24,859 | 68.8 | 78.9 | 77.6 | 77.8 |
| Kansas | 25,140 | 22,230 | 18,400 | 18,337 | 83.8 | 82.1 | 71.7 | 71.3 |
| Kentucky | 20,696 | 22,730 | 22,818 | 23,008 | 89.1 | 89.7 | 87.2 | 87.5 |
| Louisiana | 32,493 | 30,735 | 25,600 | 25,854 | 86.0 | 77.9 | 72.8 | 73.7 |
| Maine | 8,587 | 7,298 | 6,342 | 6,239 | 92.9 | 88.5 | 90.3 | 89.7 |
| Maryland | 24,716 | 25,629 | 24,360 | 24,430 | 87.0 | 81.4 | 85.5 | 86.9 |
| Massachusetts | 49,765 | 49,805 | 41,595 | 41,255 | 91.3 | 88.9 | 85.5 | 85.4 |
| Michigan | 43,271 | 42,615 | 39,288 | 39,374 | 87.5 | 84.1 | 83.6 | 84.6 |
| Minnesota | 41,163 | 38,813 | 27,201 | 26,695 | 93.8 | 92.1 | 89.5 | 88.0 |
| Mississippi | 15,247 | 15,815 | 16,165 | 16,129 | 94.9 | 92.7 | 87.1 | 87.5 |
| Missouri | 39,891 | 38,586 | 37,828 | 38,326 | 75.7 | 70.4 | 68.7 | 69.3 |
| Montana | 6,415 | 5,973 | 4,689 | 4,619 | 89.0 | 77.9 | 69.9 | 68.6 |
| Nebraska | 16,166 | 14,989 | 12,070 | 12,043 | 89.0 | 83.8 | 76.1 | 75.2 |
| Nevada | 3,645 | 3,657 | 4,749 | 4,821 | 91.2 | 65.9 | 79.4 | 79.8 |
| New Hampshire | 6,877 | 7,158 | 6,813 | 6,767 | 92.8 | 91.3 | 90.7 | 90.2 |
| New Jersey | 40,397 | 45,837 | 45,450 | 45,185 | 91.9 | 87.8 | 86.7 | 86.8 |
| New Mexico | 6,051 | 6,503 | 5,531 | 5,439 | 86.8 | 89.2 | 82.4 | 79.2 |
| New York | 103,409 | 112,957 | 105,965 | 105,390 | 96.0 | 93.7 | 91.0 | 90.0 |
| North Carolina | 35,511 | 36,658 | 36,908 | 37,058 | 92.7 | 88.6 | 82.8 | 82.2 |
| North Dakota | 6,868 | 6,343 | 5,702 | 5,664 | 96.4 | 91.2 | 92.9 | 92.4 |
| Ohio | 79,026 | 81,946 | 77,129 | 76,325 | 73.9 | 78.0 | 84.2 | 84.2 |
| Oklahoma | 26,377 | 23,833 | 19,376 | 19,108 | 77.8 | 70.3 | 65.9 | 66.0 |
| Oregon | 11,673 | 9,990 | 7,373 | 7,343 | 84.1 | 74.0 | 60.1 | 60.1 |
| Pennsylvania | 84,843 | 83,880 | 79,554 | 79,598 | 91.6 | 88.2 | 90.1 | 90.2 |
| Rhode Island | 8,823 | 9,041 | 7,986 | 8,011 | 91.8 | 88.0 | 91.6 | 91.9 |
| South Carolina | 14,568 | 15,739 | 16,744 | 16,773 | 87.3 | 86.9 | 85.0 | 85.4 |
| South Dakota | 7,926 | 7,059 | 6,335 | 6,381 | 95.5 | 90.0 | 91.7 | 91.9 |
| Tennessee | 33,929 | 34,714 | 29,990 | 28,897 | 91.5 | 89.9 | 80.7 | 77.5 |
| Texas | 89,354 | 85,275 | 93,712 | 93,170 | 72.6 | 68.2 | 69.2 | 68.5 |
| Utah | 5,832 | 5,703 | 5,383 | 5,515 | 82.1 | 74.5 | 63.3 | 64.3 |
| Vermont | 1,792 | 3,349 | 2,726 | 2,686 | 96.2 | 89.5 | 85.2 | 84.6 |
| Virginia | 28,119 | 27,091 | 28,249 | 28,486 | 93.5 | 88.5 | 86.6 | 87.7 |
| Washington | 24,954 | 21,158 | 17,199 | 17,005 | 87.7 | 81.7 | 79.5 | 79.9 |
| West Virginia | 10,216 | 10,334 | 9,524 | 9,535 | 93.7 | 90.5 | 87.5 | 87.6 |
| Wisconsin | 43,998 | 38,911 | 28,062 | 27,485 | 90.2 | 83.9 | 80.8 | 80.9 |
| Wyoming | 2,661 | 2,605 | 2,377 | 2,364 | 87.7 | 83.5 | 79.7 | 79.7 |

*Percentage of beds occupied (number of nursing home residents per 100 nursing home beds).

Notes: Annual numbers of nursing homes, beds, and residents are based on the Centers for Medicare & Medicaid Services' reporting cycle. Starting with 2013 data, a new editing rule was used for number of beds. For the U.S., the number of beds decreased by less than 1%. For most states, this caused little or no change in the data. The change in the number of beds also caused a change in some occupancy rates. Because of the methodology change, trends should be interpreted with caution.

SOURCE: "Table 92. Nursing Homes, Beds, Residents, and Occupancy Rates, by State: United States, Selected Years 1995–2014," in *Health, United States, 2015: With Special Feature on Racial and Ethnic Health Disparities*, U.S. Department of Health and Human Services, Centers for Disease Control and Prevention, National Center for Health Statistics, May 2016, http://www.cdc.gov/nchs/data/hus/hus15.pdf (accessed July 29, 2016)

Wellspring is a group of nonprofit nursing homes that are governed by a group called the Wellspring Alliance. Founded in 1994, the alliance aims to improve the clinical care delivered to its nursing home residents and the work environment for its employees. Based on the Wellspring philosophy that education and collaboration are paramount to success, the program began by equipping nursing home personnel with the skills needed to perform their jobs and by organizing employees in teams working toward shared goals. The Wellspring model of service delivery uses a

**FIGURE 3.3**

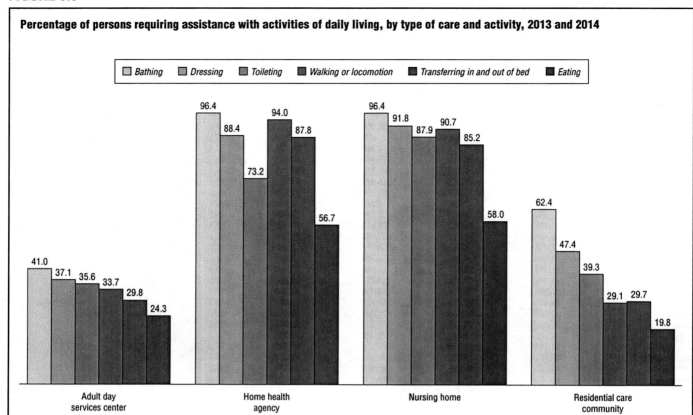

**Percentage of persons requiring assistance with activities of daily living, by type of care and activity, 2013 and 2014**

Legend: Bathing · Dressing · Toileting · Walking or locomotion · Transferring in and out of bed · Eating

Notes: Denominators used to calculate percentages for adult day services centers, nursing homes, and residential care communities were the number of current participants enrolled in adult day services centers, the number of current residents in nursing homes, and the number of current residents in residential care communities in 2014, respectively. The denominator used to calculate percentages for home health agencies was the number of patients whose episode of care ended at any time in 2013. Participants, patients, or residents were considered needing any assistance with a given activity if they needed help or supervision from another person or used special equipment to perform the activity. Data on need for assistance with activities of daily living were not available for hospice patients. Percentages are based on the unrounded numbers.

SOURCE: Lauren Harris-Kojetin et al., "Figure 27. Percentage of Long-Term Care Services Users Needing Any Assistance with Activities of Daily Living, by Sector and Activity: United States, 2013 and 2014," in "Long-Term Care Providers and Services Users in the United States: Data from the National Study of Long-Term Care Providers, 2013–2014," *Vital and Health Statistics*, series 3, no. 38, February 2016, http://www.cdc.gov/nchs/data/series/sr_03/sr03_038.pdf (accessed July 30, 2016)

multidisciplinary clinical team approach (nurse practitioners, social service professionals, food service personnel, nursing assistants, and facility and housekeeping personnel) to solve problems and develop approaches to better meet residents' needs. Each of these teams represents an important innovation because it allows health professionals and other workers to interact as peers and share resources, information, and decision making in a cooperative, supportive environment.

Stone et al. observe that there was more cooperation, responsibility, and accountability within the teams and the institutions than what was noted at other comparable facilities. Besides finding a strong organizational culture that seemed committed to quality patient care, the researchers document measurable improvements in specific areas, including:

- Wellspring facilities had lower rates of staff turnover than comparable Wisconsin facilities during the same period, probably because Wellspring workers felt

valued by management and experienced greater job satisfaction than other nursing home personnel

- The Wellspring model did not require additional resources to institute, and Wellspring facilities operated at lower costs than comparable facilities

- Wellspring facilities' performance, as measured by a federal survey, improved

- Wellspring personnel appeared more attentive to residents' needs and problems and sought to anticipate and promptly resolve problems

- An organizational commitment to training and shared decision making, along with improved quality of interactions and relationships among staff and between staff and residents, significantly contributed to enhanced quality of life for residents

Mary Jane Koren of the Commonwealth Fund enumerates in "Person-Centered Care for Nursing Home Residents: The Culture-Change Movement" (*Health*

**FIGURE 3.4**

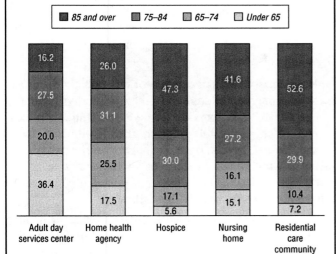

Persons using long-term care services, by age and type of care, 2013 and 2014

Legend: ■ 85 and over  ▨ 75–84  ▨ 65–74  □ Under 65

| Age group | Adult day services center | Home health agency | Hospice | Nursing home | Residential care community |
|---|---|---|---|---|---|
| 85 and over | 16.2 | 26.0 | 47.3 | 41.6 | 52.6 |
| 75–84 | 27.5 | 31.1 | | 27.2 | 29.9 |
| 65–74 | 20.0 | 25.5 | 30.0 | 16.1 | 10.4 |
| Under 65 | 36.4 | 17.5 | 17.1 | 15.1 | 7.2 |
| | | | 5.6 | | |

Notes: Denominators used to calculate percentages for adult day services centers, nursing homes, and residential care communities were the number of current participants enrolled in adult day services centers, the number of current residents in nursing homes, and the number of current residents in residential care communities in 2014, respectively. Denominators used to calculate percentages for home health agencies and hospices were the number of patients who received care from Medicare-certified home health agencies at any time in 2013 and the number of patients who received care from Medicare-certified hospices at any time in 2013, respectively. Percentages may not add to 100 because of rounding. Percentages are based on the unrounded numbers.

SOURCE: Lauren Harris-Kojetin et al., "Figure 22. Percentage of Long-Term Care Services Users, by Sector and Age Group: United States, 2013 and 2014," in "Long-Term Care Providers and Services Users in the United States: Data from the National Study of Long-Term Care Providers, 2013–2014," *Vital and Health Statistics*, series 3, no. 38, February 2016, http://www.cdc.gov/nchs/data/series/sr_03/sr03_038.pdf (accessed July 30, 2016)

**FIGURE 3.5**

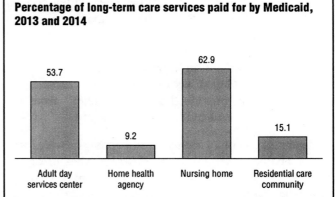

Percentage of long-term care services paid for by Medicaid, 2013 and 2014

| | Adult day services center | Home health agency | Nursing home | Residential care community |
|---|---|---|---|---|
| | 53.7 | 9.2 | 62.9 | 15.1 |

Notes: Denominators used to calculate percentages for adult day services centers, nursing homes, and residential care communities were the number of current participants enrolled in adult day services centers, the number of current residents in nursing homes, and the number of current residents in residential care communities in 2014, respectively. The denominator used to calculate percentages for home health agencies was the number of patients whose episode of care ended at any time in 2013. Data on Medicaid as payer source were not available for hospice patients.

SOURCE: Lauren Harris-Kojetin et al., "Figure 25. Percentage of Long-Term Care Services Users, with Medicaid as Payer Source, by Sector: United States, 2013 and 2014," in "Long-Term Care Providers and Services Users in the United States: Data from the National Study of Long-Term Care Providers, 2013–2014," *Vital and Health Statistics*, series 3, no. 38, February 2016, http://www.cdc.gov/nchs/data/series/sr_03/sr03_038.pdf (accessed July 30, 2016)

*Affairs*, vol. 29, no. 2, February 2010) the principles of the culture-change movement championed by organizations such as Wellspring. These include:

- Resident direction—supporting residents to make their own choices and decisions about personal issues such as food choices, clothing, and activities

- Homelike environment—using strategies such as replacing larger institutional units with smaller groups of residents and eliminating public address systems

- Relationship cultivation—improving continuity of care by having the same staff provide care to a resident

- Staff empowerment—by providing necessary training and granting them authority, staff are better able to respond to residents' needs

- Collaborative decision making—direct caregivers, working in teams, should have the authority to make decisions about residents' care

- Quality improvement—culture change should be understood as continuous performance improvement

Koren observes that about one-third of nursing homes have adopted some culture-change practices and an additional one-third are planning to make some changes. She encourages policy changes to support the wider adoption of comprehensive culture change.

The Green House Project (2016, http://www.the green houseproject.org/about/discover) explains that it "provides a home for 10–12 people, with private room/baths, that harmonizes with the neighboring community." Also, it "creates a real home environment with an open kitchen, great room, and easy access to the outdoors." According to the Green House Project (2016, http://www.thegreenhouseproject.org/), its model is "the new standard in long-term and post-acute care, with national brand power, higher measurable quality outcomes, consumer demand, and caregiver satisfaction." In "A New Model for Nursing Home Care" (Kiplinger.com, April 2016), Susan B. Garland reports that in 2016 there were 187 Green Houses operating in 28 states, with 150 more in development. Research confirms that Green House residents are happier and healthier than those in conventional nursing homes and less likely to be hospitalized or to experience declining ability to perform the activities of daily living.

# MENTAL HEALTH FACILITIES

In earlier centuries mental illness was often considered to be a sign of possession by the devil or, at best, a moral weakness. A change in these attitudes began during the late 18th century, when mental illness was perceived to be a treatable condition. It was then that the concept of asylums was developed, not only to lock the mentally ill away but also to provide them with "relief" from the conditions they found troubling.

In the 21st century mental health care is provided in a variety of treatment settings by different types of organizations. The following mental health organizations offer diagnostic and therapeutic mental health services:

- Psychiatric hospitals (public or private) provide 24-hour inpatient care to people with mental illnesses in a hospital setting. They may also offer 24-hour residential care and less than 24-hour care, but these are not requirements. Psychiatric hospitals are operated under state, county, private for-profit, and private nonprofit auspices.

- General hospitals with separate psychiatric services, units, or designated beds are under governmental or nongovernmental auspices and maintain assigned staff for 24-hour inpatient care, 24-hour residential care, and less than 24-hour care (outpatient care or partial hospitalization) to provide mental health diagnosis, evaluation, and treatment.

- Veterans Administration (VA) hospitals are operated by the U.S. Department of Veterans Affairs and include VA general hospital psychiatric services and VA psychiatric outpatient clinics that exclusively serve people entitled to VA benefits.

- Outpatient mental health clinics that provide only ambulatory mental health services. Generally, a psychiatrist has overall medical responsibility for clients and establishes the philosophy and orientation of the mental health program.

- Community mental health centers were funded under the Federal Community Mental Health Centers Act of 1963 and subsequent amendments to the act. During the early 1980s, when the federal government reverted to funding mental health services through block grants to the states rather than by funding them directly, the federal government stopped tracking these mental health organizations individually, and statistical reports include them in the category "all other mental health organizations." This category also includes freestanding psychiatric outpatient clinics, freestanding partial care organizations, and multiservice mental health organizations such as residential treatment centers. These so-called community mental health centers have sliding scale fees and accept Medicaid, Medicare, private health insurance, and private fee-for-service (paid for each visit, procedure, or treatment that is delivered) payment. Mental health care is also available from nonprofit mental health or counseling services offered by health and social service agencies, such as Catholic Social Services, family and children's service agencies, Jewish Family Services, and Lutheran Social Services, that are staffed by qualified mental health professionals to provide counseling services.

- Residential treatment centers for emotionally disturbed children serve children and youth primarily under the age of 18 years, provide 24-hour residential services, and offer a clinical program that is directed by a psychiatrist, psychologist, social worker, or psychiatric nurse who holds a master's or doctorate degree.

## Where Are People with Mental Illness?

People with chronic mental illness reside in mental hospitals, in intermediate care facilities, or in community settings, such as with families, in boarding homes and shelters, in single-room-occupancy hotels (usually inexpensive hotels or boardinghouses), in prison, or even on the streets as part of the homeless population. The institutionalized mentally ill are those people with psychiatric diagnoses who have lived in mental hospitals for more than one year or those with diagnosed mental illness who are living in nursing homes.

Declining mental health expenditures have resulted in fewer available services for specific populations of the mentally ill, particularly those who could benefit from inpatient or residential care. Even for people without conditions requiring institutional care there are barriers to access. The U.S. surgeon general describes in the landmark report *Mental Health: A Report of the Surgeon General, 1999* (1999, http://profiles.nlm.nih.gov/ps/retrieve/Resource Metadata/NNBBHS) the U.S. mental health service system as largely uncoordinated and fragmented, in part because it involves so many different sectors—health and social welfare agencies, public and private hospitals, housing, criminal justice, and education—and because it is funded through many different sources. Finally, inequalities in insurance coverage for mental health, coupled with the stigma associated with mental illness and treatment, have also limited access to services.

The NCHS reveals in *Health, United States, 2011: With Special Feature on Socioeconomic Status and Health* (May 2012, http://www.cdc.gov/nchs/data/hus/hus11.pdf), the most recent year for which these data were available as of November 2016, that the number of mental health organizations for 24-hour inpatient treatment steadily declined from 3,942 in 1990 to 3,130 in 2008. Except for Department of Veterans Affairs medical centers and residential treatment centers for children, all other service sites and types of organizations diminished in capacity. The number of beds per 100,000 civilian population fell from 128.5 in 1990 to just 78.6 in 2008. There was a similar decline in the number of intermediate care facilities specializing in psychiatric care—the number of beds declined from 689 in 1995 to 508 in 2010. This decline was not necessarily a result of better treatment for the mentally ill but a consequence of reduced funding for inpatient facilities. Many patients who were once housed in mental institutions (including some who had been lifelong residents in these facilities) were forced to fend for themselves on the streets or in prison.

Besides mental health units or beds in acute care medical/surgical hospitals and physicians' offices, mental health care and treatment is offered in the offices of other mental health clinicians such as psychologists, clinical social workers, and marriage and family therapists, as well as in other settings. Private psychiatric hospitals provide outpatient mental health evaluation and therapy in day programs as well as inpatient care. Like acute care hospitals, these facilities are accredited by the Joint Commission and may offer outpatient services by way of referral to a local network of qualified mental health providers.

### National Goals for Mental Health Service Delivery

The federal government's Healthy People initiative sets 10-year national objectives for improving the health of Americans. In "Mental Health and Mental Disorders" (2016, https://www.healthypeople.gov/2020/topics-objectives/topic/mental-health-and-mental-disorders/objectives), the initiative describes the 12 mental health objectives that the government hopes to achieve by 2020:

1. Reduce the suicide rate

2. Reduce suicide attempts by adolescents

3. Reduce the proportion of adolescents who engage in disordered eating behaviors in an attempt to control their weight

4. Reduce the proportion of persons who experience major depressive episodes [a serious depression with symptoms such as despondency, feelings of worthlessness, and even suicidal thoughts]

5. Increase the proportion of primary care facilities that provide mental health treatment onsite or by paid referral

6. Increase the proportion of children with mental health problems who receive treatment

7. Increase the proportion of juvenile residential facilities that screen admissions for mental health problems

8. Increase the proportion of persons with serious mental illness who are employed

9. Increase the proportion of adults with mental health disorders who receive treatment

10. Increase the proportion of persons with co-occurring substance abuse and mental disorders who receive treatment for both disorders

11. Increase depression screening by primary care providers

12. Increase the proportion of homeless adults with mental health problems who receive mental health services

## HOME HEALTH CARE

The concept of home health care began as postacute care after hospitalization, an alternative to longer, costlier lengths of stay in regular hospitals. Home health care services have grown tremendously since the 1980s, when prospective payment (payments made before, rather than after, care is received) for Medicare patients sharply reduced hospital lengths of stay. During the mid-1980s Medicare began reimbursing hospitals using a rate scale based on diagnosis-related groups—hospitals received a fixed amount for providing services to Medicare patients based on their diagnoses. This form of payment gave hospitals powerful financial incentives to use fewer resources because they could keep the difference between the prospective payment and the amount they actually spent to provide care. Hospitals experienced losses when patients had longer lengths of stay and used more services than were covered by the standardized diagnosis-related group prospective payment.

According to the article "Home Health Care" (*Family Economics and Nutrition Review*, Spring 1996), home health care grew faster during the early 1990s than any other segment of health services. Its growth may be attributable to the fact that in many cases caring for patients at home is preferable to, and more cost effective than, care provided in a hospital, nursing home, or some other residential facility. Oftentimes, older adults are more comfortable and much happier living in their own home or with family members. People with disabilities may also be able to function better at home with limited assistance than in a residential setting with full-time monitoring.

Home health care agencies provide a wide variety of services, from helping with activities of daily living to skilled nursing care, such as the nursing care needed by AIDS or cancer patients. According to the NCHS, in *Health, United States 2013: With Special Feature on Prescription Drugs* (May 2014, http://www.cdc.gov/nchs/data/hus/hus13.pdf), the number of Medicare-certified home health agencies has varied in response to reimbursement, growing from 2,924 in 1980 to 8,437 in 1996, then declining to 7,857 in 2000. In 2014 the number of Medicare-certified home health agencies

FIGURE 3.6

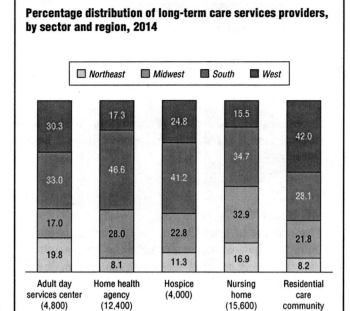

**Percentage distribution of long-term care services providers, by sector and region, 2014**

Northeast   Midwest   South   West

| | Adult day services center (4,800) | Home health agency (12,400) | Hospice (4,000) | Nursing home (15,600) | Residential care community (30,200) |
|---|---|---|---|---|---|
| West | 30.3 | 17.3 | 24.8 | 15.5 | 42.0 |
| South | 33.0 | 46.6 | 41.2 | 34.7 | 28.1 |
| Midwest | 17.0 | 28.0 | 22.8 | 32.9 | 21.8 |
| Northeast | 19.8 | 8.1 | 11.3 | 16.9 | 8.2 |

Note: Percentages are based on the unrounded numbers.

SOURCE: Lauren Harris-Kojetin et al., "Figure 1. Percentage Distribution of Long-Term Care Services Providers, by Sector and Region: United States, 2014," in "Long-Term Care Providers and Services Users in the United States: Data from the National Study of Long-Term Care Providers, 2013–2014," *Vital and Health Statistics*, series 3, no. 38, February 2016, http://www.cdc.gov/nchs/data/series/sr_03/sr03_038.pdf (accessed July 30, 2016)

rose to 12,400, the highest level since the mid-1970s. (See Figure 3.6.)

In 1972 Medicare extended home health care coverage to people under 65 years of age only if they were disabled or suffered from end-stage renal disease. Before 2000 Medicare coverage for home health care was limited to patients immediately following discharge from the hospital. By 2000 Medicare covered beneficiaries' home health care services with no requirement for previous hospitalization. There were also no limits to the number of professional visits or to the length of coverage. As long as the patient's condition warranted it, the following services were provided:

- Part-time or intermittent skilled nursing and home health aide services
- Speech-language pathology services
- Physical and occupational therapy
- Medical social services
- Medical supplies
- Durable medical equipment (with a 20% co-payment)

Over time, the population receiving home health care services has changed. Since 2000 much of home health

care is associated with rehabilitation from critical illnesses, and fewer users are long-term patients with chronic conditions. This changing pattern of utilization reflects a shift from longer-term care for chronic conditions to short-term, postacute care. Compared with postacute care users, the long-term patients are older, more functionally disabled, more likely to be incontinent, and more expensive to serve.

**Medicare Limits Home Health Care Services**

The Balanced Budget Act of 1997 cut approximately $16.2 billion from the federal government's home health care expenditures over a period of five years. The act sought to return home health care to its original concept of short-term care plus skilled nursing and therapy services. As a result of this shift away from personal care and "custodial care" services and toward short-term, skilled nursing services, some Medicare beneficiaries who received home health care lost coverage for certain personal care services, such as assistance with activities of daily living.

The Balanced Budget Act sharply curtailed the growth in home health care spending, which affected health care providers. Nonetheless, the aging population and the financial imperative to prevent or minimize institutionalization (hospitalization or placement in a long-term-care facility) combined to generate increasing expenditures for home health care services. Medicare expenditures for home health care rose from $4 billion in 2000 to $6.6 billion in 2014, which represented 2.5% of Medicare expenditures. (See Table 3.5.) In contrast, payments to skilled nursing facilities accounted for 10.7% ($28.8 billion) of expenditures in 2014, and inpatient hospital expenditures were 50.4% ($135.6 billion) of the total.

Sharply reduced Medicare spending for home health care under the ACA reduced planned funding for home care 14% between 2014 and 2018, and was expected to slow the growth of home health care jobs and services. Connie Dolin opines in "The ACA's Cuts to Medicare Threaten Home Health Care Jobs, Patients" (News Observer.com, February 5, 2014) that the cuts "will directly affect nearly 5,000 small-business providers that today serve nearly 1.5 million seniors and are responsible for nearly 500,000 jobs from coast to coast." In "Home Healthcare Industry Braces for Another Medicare Cut" (ModernHealthcare.com, June 28, 2016), Lisa Schencker notes that in 2016 about 11,400 home health agencies were caring for Medicare beneficiaries, a decrease from 11,781 in 2014. According to Schencker, a November 2015 survey of home care providers found that more than half were taking steps such as reducing caregiver hours and scheduling cases to avoid paying overtime and reduce costs.

TABLE 3.5

## Medicare enrollees and expenditures by type of service, selected years 1970–2014

[Data are compiled from various sources by the Centers for Medicare & Medicaid Services]

| Medicare program and type of service | 1970 | 1980 | 1990 | 1995 | 2000 | 2005 | 2010 | 2011 | 2012 | 2013 | 2014[a] |
|---|---|---|---|---|---|---|---|---|---|---|---|
| **Enrollees** | | | | | | Number, in millions | | | | | |
| **Total Medicare**[b] | **20.4** | **28.4** | **34.3** | **37.6** | **39.7** | **42.6** | **47.7** | **48.9** | **50.9** | **52.5** | **53.8** |
| Hospital insurance | 20.1 | 28.0 | 33.7 | 37.2 | 39.3 | 42.2 | 47.4 | 48.5 | 50.5 | 52.1 | 53.5 |
| Supplementary medical insurance (SMI)[c] | 19.5 | 27.3 | 32.6 | 35.6 | 37.3 | — | — | — | — | — | — |
| Part B | 19.5 | 27.3 | 32.6 | 35.6 | 37.3 | 39.8 | 43.9 | 44.9 | 46.5 | 47.9 | 49.3 |
| Part D[d] | — | — | — | — | — | 1.8 | 34.8 | 35.7 | 37.4 | 39.1 | 40.5 |
| **Expenditures** | | | | | | Amount, in billions | | | | | |
| **Total Medicare** | **$7.5** | **$36.8** | **$111.0** | **$184.2** | **$221.8** | **$336.4** | **$522.9** | **$549.1** | **$574.2** | **$582.9** | **$613.3** |
| **Total hospital insurance (HI)** | **5.3** | **25.6** | **67.0** | **117.6** | **131.1** | **182.9** | **247.9** | **256.7** | **266.8** | **266.2** | **269.3** |
| HI payments to managed care organizations[e] | — | 0.0 | 2.7 | 6.7 | 21.4 | 24.9 | 60.7 | 64.6 | 70.2 | 73.1 | 74.0 |
| HI payments for fee-for-service utilization | 5.1 | 25.0 | 63.4 | 109.5 | 105.1 | 156.6 | 183.3 | 187.0 | 189.2 | 184.7 | 186.4 |
| Inpatient hospital | 4.8 | 24.1 | 56.9 | 82.3 | 87.1 | 123.3 | 135.9 | 133.9 | 138.9 | 134.1 | 135.6 |
| Skilled nursing facility | 0.2 | 0.4 | 2.5 | 9.1 | 11.1 | 19.3 | 27.1 | 31.9 | 28.4 | 28.4 | 28.8 |
| Home health agency | 0.1 | 0.5 | 3.7 | 16.2 | 4.0 | 6.0 | 7.2 | 7.1 | 6.8 | 6.9 | 6.6 |
| Hospice | — | — | 0.3 | 1.9 | 2.9 | 8.0 | 13.1 | 14.0 | 15.0 | 15.3 | 15.5 |
| Other programs[f] | — | — | — | — | — | — | — | 0.9 | 2.8 | 3.5 | 3.7 |
| Home health agency transfer[g] | — | — | — | — | 1.7 | — | — | — | — | — | — |
| Medicare Advantage premiums[h] | — | — | — | — | — | — | 0.2 | 0.2 | 0.2 | 0.3 | 0.3 |
| Accounting error (CY 2005–2008)[i] | — | — | — | — | — | −1.9 | — | — | — | — | — |
| Administrative expenses[j] | 0.2 | 0.5 | 0.9 | 1.4 | 2.9 | 3.3 | 3.8 | 4.0 | 4.3 | 4.7 | 4.9 |
| **Total supplementary medical insurance (SMI)[c]** | **2.2** | **11.2** | **44.0** | **66.6** | **90.7** | **153.5** | **274.9** | **292.5** | **307.4** | **316.7** | **344.0** |
| **Total Part B** | **2.2** | **11.2** | **44.0** | **66.6** | **90.7** | **152.4** | **212.9** | **225.3** | **240.5** | **247.1** | **265.9** |
| Part B payments to managed care organizations[e] | 0.0 | 0.2 | 2.8 | 6.6 | 18.4 | 22.0 | 55.2 | 59.1 | 66.0 | 72.7 | 85.7 |
| Part B payments for fee-for-service utilization[k] | 1.9 | 10.4 | 39.6 | 58.4 | 72.2 | 125.0 | 154.3 | 162.3 | 170.3 | 170.8 | 175.8 |
| Physician/supplier[l] | 1.8 | 8.2 | 29.6 | — | — | — | — | — | — | — | — |
| Outpatient hospital[m] | 0.1 | 1.9 | 8.5 | — | — | — | — | — | — | — | — |
| Independent laboratory[n] | 0.0 | 0.1 | 1.5 | — | — | — | — | — | — | — | — |
| Physician fee schedule | — | — | — | 31.7 | 37.0 | 57.7 | 64.0 | 67.5 | 69.5 | 68.6 | 69.2 |
| Durable medical equipment | — | — | — | 3.7 | 4.7 | 8.0 | 8.3 | 8.2 | 8.2 | 7.2 | 6.3 |
| Laboratory[o] | — | — | — | 4.3 | 4.4 | 6.9 | 8.4 | 8.4 | 9.2 | 9.1 | 8.2 |
| Other[p] | — | — | — | 9.9 | 13.6 | 26.7 | 34.1 | 36.0 | 38.3 | 38.3 | 39.6 |
| Hospital[q] | — | — | — | 8.7 | 8.1 | 18.7 | 27.6 | 30.2 | 33.6 | 36.1 | 41.4 |
| Home health agency | 0.0 | 0.2 | 0.1 | 0.2 | 4.5 | 7.1 | 12.0 | 12.1 | 11.4 | 11.6 | 11.2 |
| Home health agency transfer[g] | — | — | — | — | −1.7 | — | — | — | — | — | — |
| Medicare Advantage premiums[h] | — | — | — | — | — | — | 0.2 | 0.2 | 0.2 | 0.3 | 0.3 |
| Accounting error (CY 2005–2008)[i] | — | — | — | — | — | 1.9 | — | — | — | — | — |
| Administrative expenses[j] | 0.2 | 0.6 | 1.5 | 1.6 | 1.8 | 2.8 | 3.2 | 3.7 | 4.0 | 3.4 | 4.1 |
| Part D start-up costs[r] | — | — | — | — | — | 0.7 | — | — | — | — | — |
| **Total Part D[d]** | **—** | **—** | **—** | **—** | **—** | **1.1** | **62.1** | **67.1** | **66.9** | **69.7** | **78.1** |
| | | | | | | Percent distribution of expenditures | | | | | |
| **Total hospital insurance (HI)** | **100.0** | **100.0** | **100.0** | **100.0** | **100.0** | **100.0** | **100.0** | **100.0** | **100.0** | **100.0** | **100.0** |
| HI payments to managed care organizations[e] | — | 0.0 | 4.0 | 5.7 | 16.3 | 13.6 | 24.5 | 25.2 | 26.3 | 27.5 | 27.5 |
| HI payments for fee-for-service utilization | 97.0 | 97.9 | 94.6 | 93.1 | 80.2 | 85.6 | 73.9 | 72.8 | 70.9 | 69.4 | 69.2 |
| Inpatient hospital | 91.4 | 94.3 | 85.0 | 70.0 | 66.4 | 67.4 | 54.8 | 52.2 | 52.1 | 50.4 | 50.3 |
| Skilled nursing facility | 4.7 | 1.5 | 3.7 | 7.8 | 8.5 | 10.6 | 10.9 | 12.4 | 10.7 | 10.7 | 10.7 |
| Home health agency | 1.0 | 2.1 | 5.5 | 13.8 | 3.1 | 3.3 | 2.9 | 2.8 | 2.6 | 2.6 | 2.5 |
| Hospice | — | — | 0.5 | 1.6 | 2.2 | 4.4 | 5.3 | 5.5 | 5.6 | 5.7 | 5.7 |
| Other programs[f] | — | — | — | — | — | — | — | 0.3 | 1.1 | 1.3 | 1.4 |
| Home health agency transfer[g] | — | — | — | — | 1.3 | — | — | — | — | — | — |
| Medicare Advantage premiums[h] | — | — | — | — | — | — | 0.1 | 0.1 | 0.1 | 0.1 | 0.1 |
| Accounting error (CY 2005–2008)[i] | — | — | — | — | — | −1.0 | — | — | — | — | — |
| Administrative expenses[j] | 3.0 | 2.1 | 1.4 | 1.2 | 2.2 | 1.8 | 1.5 | 1.6 | 1.6 | 1.8 | 1.8 |

## HOSPICE CARE

In medieval times hospices were refuges for the sick, the needy, and travelers. The modern hospice movement developed in response to the need to provide humane care to terminally ill patients, while at the same time offering support to their families. The British physician Cicely Saunders (1918–2005) pioneered the hospice concept in Britain during the late 1960s and helped introduce it in the United States during the 1970s. The care provided by hospice workers is called palliative care, and it aims to relieve patients' pain and the accompanying symptoms of terminal illness without seeking to cure the illness.

Hospice is a philosophy, an approach to care for the dying, and it is not necessarily a physical facility. Hospice may refer to a place—a freestanding facility or a designated floor in a hospital or nursing home—or to a

CY = calendar year.
—Category not applicable or data not available.
0.0 Quantity more than zero but less than 0.05.
[a]Preliminary estimates.
[b]Average number enrolled in the hospital insurance (HI) and/or supplementary medical insurance (SMI) programs for the period.
[c]Starting with 2004 data, the SMI trust fund consists of two separate accounts: Part B (which pays for a portion of the costs of physicians' services, outpatient hospital services, and other related medical and health services for voluntarily enrolled individuals) and Part D (Medicare Prescription Drug Account, which pays private plans to provide prescription drug coverage).
[d]The Medicare Modernization Act, enacted December 8, 2003, established within SMI two Part D accounts related to prescription drug benefits: the Medicare Prescription Drug Account and the Transitional Assistance Account. The Medicare Prescription Drug Account is used in conjunction with the broad, voluntary prescription drug benefits that began in 2006. The Transitional Assistance Account was used to provide transitional assistance benefits, beginning in 2004 and extending through 2005, for certain low-income beneficiaries prior to the start of the new prescription drug benefit. The amounts shown for Total Part D expenditures—and thus for total SMI expenditures and total Medicare expenditures—for 2006 and later years include estimated amounts for premiums paid directly from Part D beneficiaries to Part D prescription drug plans.
[e]Medicare-approved managed care organizations.
[f]Includes Community-Based Care Transitions Program ($0.1 billion in each of 2011–2014) and Electronic Health Records Incentive Program ($0.7 billion in 2011, $2.7 billion in 2012, $3.4 billion in 2013, and $3.6 billion in 2014).
[g]For 1998 to 2003, data reflects annual home health HI to SMI transfer amounts.
[h]When a beneficiary chooses a Medicare Advantage plan whose monthly premium exceeds the benchmark amount, the additional premiums (that is, amounts beyond those paid by Medicare to the plan) are the responsibility of the beneficiary. Beneficiaries subject to such premiums may choose to either reimburse the plans directly or have the additional premiums deducted from their Social Security checks. The amounts shown here are only those additional premiums deducted from Social Security checks. These amounts are transferred to the HI trust and SMI trust funds and then transferred from the trust funds to the plans.
[i]Represents misallocation of benefit payments between the HI trust fund and the Part B account of the SMI trust fund from May 2005 to September 2007, and the transfer made in June 2008 to correct the misallocation.
[j]Includes expenditures for research, experiments and demonstration projects, peer review activity (performed by Peer Review Organizations from 1983 to 2001 and by Quality Review Organizations from 2002 to present), and to combat and prevent fraud and abuse.
[k]Type-of-service reporting categories for fee-for-service reimbursement differ before and after 1991.
[l]Includes payment for physicians, practitioners, durable medical equipment, and all suppliers other than independent laboratory through 1990. Starting with 1991 data, physician services subject to the physician fee schedule are shown. Payments for laboratory services paid under the laboratory fee schedule and performed in a physician office are included under Laboratory beginning in 1991. Payments for durable medical equipment are shown separately beginning in 1991. The remaining services from the Physician/supplier category are included in Other.
[m]Includes payments for hospital outpatient department services, skilled nursing facility outpatient services, Part B services received as an inpatient in a hospital or skilled nursing facility setting, and other types of outpatient facilities. Starting with 1991 data, payments for hospital outpatient department services, except for laboratory services, are listed under Hospital. Hospital outpatient laboratory services are included in the Laboratory line.
[n]Starting with 1991 data, those independent laboratory services that were paid under the laboratory fee schedule (most of the independent laboratory category) are included in the Laboratory line; the remaining services are included in the Physician fee schedule and Other lines.
[o]Payments for laboratory services paid under the laboratory fee schedule performed in a physician office, independent laboratory, or in a hospital outpatient department.
[p]Includes payments for physician-administered drugs; freestanding ambulatory surgical center facility services; ambulance services; supplies; freestanding end-stage renal disease (ESRD) dialysis facility services; rural health clinics; outpatient rehabilitation facilities; psychiatric hospitals; and federally qualified health centers.
[q]Includes the hospital facility costs for Medicare Part B services that are predominantly in the outpatient department, with the exception of hospital outpatient laboratory services, which are included on the Laboratory line. Physician reimbursement is included on the Physician fee schedule line.
[r]Part D start-up costs were funded through the SMI Part B account in 2004–2008.
Notes: Estimates are subject to change as more recent data become available. Totals may not equal the sum of the components because of rounding. Estimates are for Medicare-covered services furnished to Medicare enrollees residing in the United States, Puerto Rico, Virgin Islands, Guam, other outlying areas, foreign countries, and unknown residence.

SOURCE: Adapted from "Table 107. Medicare Enrollees and Expenditures and Percent Distribution, by Medicare Program and Type of Service: United States and Other Areas, Selected Years 1970–2014," in *Health, United States, 2015: With Special Feature on Racial and Ethnic Health Disparities*, U.S. Department of Health and Human Services, Centers for Disease Control and Prevention, National Center for Health Statistics, May 2016, http://www.cdc.gov/nchs/data/hus/hus15.pdf (accessed July 29, 2016)

program such as hospice home care, where a team of health professionals helps the dying patient and family at home. Hospice teams may involve physicians, nurses, social workers, pastoral counselors, and trained volunteers. The goal of hospice care is to provide support and care for people at the end of life, enabling them to remain as comfortable as possible.

Hospice workers consider the patient and family as the "unit of care" and focus their efforts on attending to emotional, psychological, and spiritual needs as well as to physical comfort and well-being. The programs provide respite care, which offers relief at any time for families that may be overwhelmed and exhausted by the demands of caregiving and may be neglecting their own needs for rest and relaxation. Finally, hospice programs work to prepare relatives and friends for the loss of their loved ones. Hospice offers bereavement support groups and counseling to help deal with grief and may even help with funeral arrangements.

The hospice concept is different from most other health care services because it focuses on care rather than on cure. Hospice workers try to minimize the two greatest fears associated with dying: fear of isolation and fear of pain. Potent, effective medications are offered to patients in pain, with the goal of controlling pain without impairing alertness so that patients may be as comfortable as possible.

Hospice care also emphasizes living life to its fullest. Patients are encouraged to stay active for as long as possible, to do things they enjoy, and to learn something new each day. Quality of life, rather than length of life, is the focus. In addition, whenever it is possible, family and friends are urged to be the primary caregivers in the home. Care at home helps both patients and family members enrich their lives and face death together.

Ira Byock, the former president of the American Academy of Hospice and Palliative Medicine, explains the concept of hospice care in *Dying Well: The Prospect for Growth at the End of Life* (1997): "Hospice care differs noticeably from the modern medical approach to dying. Typically, as a hospice patient nears death, the medical details become almost automatic and attention focuses on the personal nature of this final transition—what the patient and family are going through emotionally and spiritually. In the more established system, even as people die, medical procedures remain the first priority. With hospice, they move to the background as the personal comes to the fore."

According to the National Hospice and Palliative Care Organization (NHPCO), in *NHPCO's Facts and Figures: Hospice Care in America 2015 Edition* (2015, http://www.nhpco.org/sites/default/files/public/Statistics_Research/2015_Facts_Figures.pdf), the use of hospice care is increasing in the United States. The NHPCO estimates that between 1.6 million and 1.7 million patients received hospice care in 2014. That same year Medicare expenditures for hospice care totaled $15.5 billion and accounted for 5.8% of Medicare expenditures. (See Table 3.5.)

## MANAGED CARE ORGANIZATIONS

Managed health care is the sector of the health insurance industry in which health care providers are not independent businesses run by, for example, private medical practitioners, but are instead administrative firms that manage the allocation of health care benefits. In contrast to conventional indemnity insurers that do not govern the provision of medical care services and simply pay for them, managed care firms have a significant voice in how services are administered to enable them to exert better control over health care costs. (Indemnity insurance is traditional fee-for-service coverage in which providers are paid according to the service performed.)

The beneficiaries of employer-funded health plans (people who receive health benefits from their employers), as well as Medicare and Medicaid recipients, often find themselves in this type of health care program. The term *managed care organization* covers several types of health care delivery systems, such as health maintenance organizations (HMOs), preferred provider organizations (PPOs), and utilization review groups that oversee diagnoses, recommend treatments, and manage costs for their beneficiaries.

### Health Maintenance Organizations

HMOs began to grow during the 1970s as alternatives to traditional health insurance, which was becoming increasingly expensive. The HMO Act of 1973 was a federal law requiring employers with more than 24 employees to offer an alternative to conventional indemnity insurance in the form of a federally qualified HMO. The intent of the act was to stimulate HMO development,

and the federal government has continued to promote them since then, maintaining that groups of physicians following certain rules of practice can slow rising medical costs and improve health care quality.

HMOs are health insurance programs organized to provide complete coverage for subscribers' (also known as enrollees or members) health needs for negotiated, prepaid prices. The subscribers (and/or their employers) pay a fixed amount each month; in turn, the HMO provides, at no extra charge, preventive care, such as routine checkups, screening, and immunizations, and care for any illness or accident. The monthly fee also covers inpatient hospitalization and referral services. HMO members benefit from reduced out-of-pocket costs (they do not pay deductibles), they do not have to file claims or fill out insurance forms, and they generally pay only nominal co-payments for each office visit. Members are usually locked into the plan for a specified period—typically one year. If the necessary service is available within the HMO, patients must normally use an HMO doctor. There are several types of HMOs:

- Staff model—the "purest" form of managed care. All primary care physicians are employees of the HMO and practice in a centralized location such as an outpatient clinic that may also house a laboratory, pharmacy, and facilities for other diagnostic testing. The staff model offers the HMO the greatest opportunity to manage both cost and quality of health care services.

- Group model—in which the HMO contracts with a group of primary care and multispecialty health providers. The group is paid a fixed amount per patient to provide specific services. The administration of the medical group determines how the HMO payments will be distributed among the physicians and other health care providers. Group model HMOs are usually located in hospitals or in clinic settings and have on-site pharmacies. Participating physicians usually do not have any fee-for-service patients.

- Network model—in which the HMO contracts with two or more groups of health providers that agree to provide health care at negotiated prices to all members enrolled in the HMO.

- Independent practice association (IPA) model—in which the HMO contracts with individual physicians or medical groups that then provide medical care to HMO members at their own offices. The individual physicians agree to follow the practices and procedures of the HMO when caring for the HMO members; however, they generally also maintain their own private practices and see fee-for-service patients as well as HMO members. IPA physicians are paid by capitation (literally, per head) for the HMO patients and by conventional methods for their fee-for-service patients. Physician members of the IPA guarantee that the care for each HMO member for which they are responsible will be delivered within a fixed budget. They guarantee this by allowing the HMO to withhold an amount of their payments (usually about 20% per year). If at year's end the physician's cost for providing care falls within the preset amount, then the physician receives all the monies withheld. If the physician's costs of care exceed the agreed-on amount, the HMO may retain any portion of the monies it has withheld. This arrangement places physicians and other providers such as hospitals, laboratories, and imaging centers at risk for keeping down treatment costs, and this at-risk formula is the key to HMO cost-containment efforts.

Some HMOs offer an open-ended or point-of-service (POS) option that allows members to choose their own physicians and hospitals, either within or outside the HMO. However, a member who chooses an outside provider will generally have to pay a larger portion of the expenses. Physicians not contracting with the HMO but who see HMO patients are paid according to the services performed. POS members are given an incentive to seek care from contracted network physicians and other health care providers through comprehensive coverage offerings.

The Kaiser Family Foundation (KFF) is a nonprofit organization that studies health care issues. In "Health Insurance & Managed Care" (http://kff.org/state-category/health-insurance-managed-care/hmos/), the KFF reports that as of January 2016, 92.4 million HMO members were served by 470 HMOs operating in the United States. Approximately 29% of the U.S population was enrolled in HMOs.

HMO enrollment varies by geographic region. According to the KFF, in "State HMO Penetration Rate" (http://kff.org/other/state-indicator/hmo-penetration-rate/?currentTimeframe=0&sortModel=%7B%22colId%22:%22Location%22,%22sort%22:%22asc%22%7D), 67.3% of the population of Puerto Rico was enrolled in an HMO in January 2016, as was 58.2% of the population in Hawaii and 59.2% in California. In contrast, 0.2% of the population of Alaska, 0.8% of Wyoming's population, and 4.4% of people in Montana were covered by HMOs.

## HMOs Have Fans and Critics

HMOs have been the subject of considerable debate among physicians, payers, policy makers, and health care consumers. Many physicians feel HMOs interfere in the physician-patient relationship and effectively prevent them from practicing medicine the way they have traditionally practiced. These physicians claim they know their patients' conditions and are, therefore, in the best position to recommend treatment. The physicians resent

being advised and overruled by insurance administrators. (Physicians can recommend the treatment they believe is best, but if the insurance company will not cover the costs, patients may be unwilling to undergo the recommended treatment.)

The HMO industry counters that its evidence-based determinations (judgments about the appropriateness of care that reflect scientific research) are based on the experiences of many thousands of physicians and, therefore, it knows which treatments are most likely to be successful. The industry maintains that, in the past, physician-chosen treatments were not scrutinized or even assessed for effectiveness, and as a result most physicians did not really know whether the treatment they prescribed was optimal for the specific medical condition.

Furthermore, the HMO industry cites the slower increase in health care expenses as another indicator of its management success. Industry spokespeople note that any major change in how the HMO industry is run would lead to increasing costs. They claim that HMOs and other managed care programs are bringing a more rational approach to the health care industry while maintaining health care quality and controlling costs.

Still, many physicians resent that, with a few exceptions, HMOs are not financially liable for their decisions. When a physician chooses to forgo a certain procedure and negative consequences result, the physician may be held legally accountable. When an HMO informs a physician that it will not cover a recommended procedure and the HMO's decision is found to be wrong, it cannot be held directly liable. Many physicians assert that because HMOs make such choices, they are practicing medicine and should, therefore, be held accountable. The HMOs counter that these are administrative decisions and deny that they are practicing medicine.

The legal climate seemed to be changing for HMOs during the mid-1990s. Both the Third Circuit Federal Court of Appeals in *Dukes v. U.S. Healthcare* (57 F.3d 350 [1995]) and the 10th Circuit Federal Court of Appeals in *PacifiCare of Oklahoma, Inc. v. Burrage* (59 F.3rd 151 [1995]) agreed that HMOs were liable for malpractice and negligence claims against the HMO and HMO physicians. In *Frappier Estate v. Wishnov* (678 So.2d 884 [1996]), the Florida District Court of Appeals, Fourth District, agreed with the earlier findings. It appeared that these court decisions would be backed by a new federal law when both houses of Congress passed legislation (the Patients' Bill of Rights) that would give patients more recourse to contest the decisions of HMOs. However, disagreements about the specific rights to be provided under the law ultimately led to its defeat.

In June 2004 the U.S. Supreme Court struck down a law in California and in several other states that allowed patients to sue their health plans for denying them health care services. Although patients can still sue in federal court for reimbursement of denied benefits, they no longer may sue for damages in federal or state courts.

## Preferred Provider Organizations

In response to HMOs and other efforts by insurance groups to cut costs, physicians began forming or joining PPOs during the 1990s. PPOs are managed care organizations that offer integrated delivery systems (networks of providers) available through a wide array of health plans and are readily accountable to purchasers for access, cost, quality, and services of their networks. They use provider selection standards, utilization management, and quality assessment programs to complement negotiated fee reductions (discounted rates from participating physicians, hospitals, and other health care providers) as effective strategies for long-term cost control. Under a PPO benefit plan, covered people retain the freedom of choice of providers but are offered financial incentives such as lower out-of-pocket costs to use the preferred provider network. PPO members may use other physicians and hospitals, but they usually have to pay a higher proportion of the costs. PPOs are marketed directly to employers and to third-party administrators who then market PPOs to their employer clients.

Exclusive provider organizations (EPOs) are a more restrictive variation of PPOs in which members must seek care from providers on the EPO panel. If a member visits an outside provider who is not on the EPO panel, then the EPO will offer either limited or no coverage for the office or hospital visit.

According to the KFF, in "2015 Employer Health Benefits Survey" (September 22, 2015, http://kff.org/report-section/ehbs-2015-summary-of-findings/), 52% of U.S. workers with insurance through their jobs were enrolled in PPO plans in 2015. By contrast, only 14% of workers were enrolled in HMO plans and 10% in POS plans.

## Accountable Care Organizations

Accountable care organizations (ACOs) are groups of health care providers that offer coordinated care and chronic disease management in an effort to improve the quality of care Medicare patients receive. Under the ACA, the CMS has established the Medicare Shared Savings Program for ACOs. ACOs that choose to join the program commit to containing or reducing costs while also achieving health care quality goals set by the CMS. (There were 34 quality measures in place as of January 2016.) ACOs that meet these standards share in the savings they achieve, receiving payments equal to as much as 60% of the money they saved the Medicare program. However, if an ACO fails to generate savings, and instead charges more for its services than the standards call for, it is required to pay back some of these funds to the Medicare program.

The CMS indicates in "Fast Facts: All Medicare Shared Savings Program (Shared Savings Program) ACOs" (April 2016, https://www.cms.gov/Medicare/Medicare-Fee-for-Service-Payment/sharedsavingsprogram/Downloads/All-Starts-MSSP-ACO.pdf) that in 2016 there were 433 ACOs serving 7.7 million Medicare beneficiaries in 49 states and the District of Columbia. In "Accountable Care Organizations in 2016: Private and Public-Sector Growth and Dispersion" (HealthAffairs.com, April 21, 2016), David Muhlestein and Mark McClellan report that in January 2016 there were a total of 838 active ACOs, an increase of 12.6% over 2015, covering an estimated 28.3 million people—about 8.9% of the total U.S. population and 22% of Medicare beneficiaries.

In August 2015 the CMS issued 2014 quality and financial performance results showing that ACOs continue to improve the quality of care for Medicare beneficiaries, while producing cost savings. In "Medicare ACOs Continue to Improve Quality of Care, Generate Shared Savings" (https://www.cms.gov/Newsroom/MediaRelease Database/Press-releases/2015-Press-releases-items/2015-08-25.html), the CMS reports that 20 Pioneer and 333 Shared Savings Program ACOs had collectively saved Medicare more than $411 million and that "Pioneer ACOs showed improvements in 28 of 33 quality measures and experienced average improvements of 3.6% across all quality measures. Shared Savings Program ACOs that reported quality measures in 2013 and 2014 improved on 27 of 33 quality measures."

## CHAPTER 4
# RESEARCHING, MEASURING, AND MONITORING
# THE QUALITY OF HEALTH CARE

Many agencies, institutions, and organizations are dedicated to researching, quantifying (measuring), monitoring, and improving health in the United States. Some are federally funded public entities such as the many institutes and agencies governed by the U.S. Department of Health and Human Services (HHS). Others are professional societies and organizations that develop standards of care, represent the views and interests of health care providers, and ensure the quality of health care facilities, such as the American Medical Association and the Joint Commission. Still other voluntary health organizations, such as the American Heart Association, the American Cancer Society, and the March of Dimes, promote research and education about prevention and treatment of specific diseases.

## AFFORDABLE CARE ACT INITIATIVES
## AND MEASURES TO IMPROVE QUALITY

The Patient Protection and Affordable Care Act (also known as the Affordable Care Act [ACA]) of 2010 authorized a wide range of quality initiatives, including measures that "pay-for-performance"—offering financial incentives for health care providers to achieve optimal outcomes for patients. These incentives may include bonuses for meeting or exceeding agreed on quality standards and penalties for failing to meet specified objectives. Examples of ACA quality measures include:

- Development of quality data collection and reporting tools such as a quality rating system and a quality improvement strategy, as well as an enrollee satisfaction survey system to assess health plans offered by health insurance marketplaces and exchanges

- Requiring health plans to report their quality improvement activities—benefits or coverage and provider reimbursement that improve health outcomes, prevent hospital readmissions, improve patient safety, and reduce medical errors

- Use of core measures to assess the quality of health care received by Medicaid enrollees

- Instituting quality reporting requirements for inpatient rehabilitation facilities

- Research on health delivery system improvement and best practices to improve the quality, safety, and efficiency of health care delivery

Effectively implementing these measures requires cooperation and collaboration between federal government agencies and state and local agencies, as well as health care providers and voluntary health organizations.

## U.S. DEPARTMENT OF HEALTH
## AND HUMAN SERVICES

The HHS is the nation's lead agency for ensuring the health of Americans by planning, operating, and funding delivery of essential human services, especially for society's most vulnerable populations. According to the HHS, in "About HHS" (2016, http://www.hhs.gov/about), it includes 11 divisions, 10 regional offices, and the Office of the Secretary. It is the largest grant-making agency in the federal government, funding several thousand grants each year as well as the HHS Medicare program, the nation's largest health insurer, which processes more than 1 billion claims every year. In *HHS FY2017 Budget in Brief* (2016, http://www.hhs.gov/sites/default/files/fy2017-budget-in-brief.pdf), the HHS indicates that for fiscal year (FY) 2017 it had a budget of $1.1 trillion, which was an increase of $117.2 billion over FY 2015. (See Figure 4.1.)

### HHS Milestones

The HHS notes in "Historical Highlights" (2016, http://www.hhs.gov/about/hhshist.html) that it began with the 1798 opening of the first Marine Hospital in Boston, Massachusetts, to care for sick and injured merchant seamen. Under President Abraham Lincoln (1809–1865) the

FIGURE 4.1

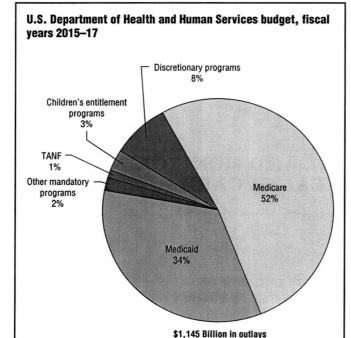

**U.S. Department of Health and Human Services budget, fiscal years 2015–17**

Discretionary programs
8%

Children's entitlement programs
3%

TANF
1%

Other mandatory programs
2%

Medicare
52%

Medicaid
34%

**$1,145 Billion in outlays**

TANF = Temporary Assistance for Needy Families.

Notes: Details in this document may not add to the totals due to rounding. Budget data in this book are presented "comparably" to the fiscal year 2017 budget, since the location of programs may have changed in prior years or be proposed for change in fiscal year 2017. This approach allows increases and decreases in this book to reflect true funding changes. The fiscal year 2016 and fiscal year 2017 mandatory figures reflect current law and mandatory proposals reflected in the budget.

SOURCE: "FY 2017 President's Budget for HHS," in *HHS FY2017 Budget in Brief*, U.S. Department of Health and Human Services, 2016, http://www.hhs.gov/sites/default/files/fy2017-budget-in-brief.pdf (accessed August 1, 2016)

agency that would become the U.S. Food and Drug Administration was established in 1862. The National Institutes of Health (NIH) dates back to 1887 and eventually became part of the Public Health Service. The 1935 enactment of the Social Security Act spurred the development of the Federal Security Agency in 1939 to direct programs in health, human services, insurance, and education. In 1946 the Communicable Disease Center, which would become the Centers for Disease Control and Prevention (CDC), was established, and 19 years later, in 1965, Medicare (a federal health insurance program for people aged 65 years and older and people with disabilities) and Medicaid (a state and federal health insurance program for low-income people) were enacted to improve access to health care for older, disabled, and low-income Americans. That same year the Head Start program was developed to provide education, health, and social services to preschool-aged children.

In 1970 the National Health Service Corps was established to help meet the health care needs of underserved areas and populations. The following year the National Cancer Act became law, which established cancer research

as a national research priority. In 1984 the human immunodeficiency virus (HIV), the virus that causes acquired immunodeficiency syndrome (AIDS), was identified by the Public Health Service and French research scientists. The National Organ Transplant Act became law in 1984, and in 1990 the Human Genome Project was initiated.

In 1994 NIH-funded research isolated the genes responsible for inherited breast cancer, colon cancer, and the most frequently occurring type of kidney cancer. In 1998 efforts were launched to eliminate racial and ethnic disparities (differences) in health, and in 2000 the human genome sequencing was published. In 2001 the Health Care Financing Administration was replaced by the Centers for Medicare and Medicaid Services, and the HHS responded to the first reported cases of bioterrorism (anthrax attacks) and developed new strategies to detect and prevent threats of bioterrorism. In 2003 the Medicare Prescription Drug Improvement and Modernization Act expanded Medicare and included prescription drug benefits. In 2010 the ACA was enacted.

In the press release "HHS Forges Unprecedented Partnership to Combat Antimicrobial Resistance" (July 28, 2016, http://www.hhs.gov/about/news/2016/07/28/hhs-forges-unprecedented-partnership-combat-antimicrobial-resistance.html), the HHS describes its new partnership with the Wellcome Trust of London, the AMR Centre of Alderley Park (Cheshire, United Kingdom), and Boston University School of Law to address antibiotic resistance (the ability of a microorganism to withstand the effects of a drug that would normally kill it or limit its growth), which is a global threat to public health. The new public-private partnership, called the Combating Antibiotic Resistant Bacteria Biopharmaceutical Accelerator, will discover and develop new antimicrobial (antibiotic) products.

## HHS Agencies and Institutes Provide Comprehensive Health and Social Services

Besides the CDC and the NIH, the HHS explains in *HHS FY2017 Budget in Brief* that the following agencies and programs research, plan, direct, oversee, administer, and provide health care services:

- Administration for Community Living (ACL) consists of the Administration on Aging, the Office on Disability, and the Administration on Developmental Disabilities and provides services aimed at helping older Americans and people with disabilities retain their independence. The ACL develops policies that support and direct programs that provide transportation, in-home services, and other community living services. For FY 2017 the ACL planned for a budget of $2.1 billion.

- Administration for Children and Families (ACF) provides services for families and children in need, administers Head Start, and works with state foster care and adoption programs. The ACF was allotted a budget of $63 billion for FY 2017.

- Agency for Healthcare Research and Quality (AHRQ) researches access to health care, quality of care, and efforts to control health care costs. It also looks at the safety of health care services and the ways to prevent medical errors. Figure 4.2 shows how the AHRQ researches health system problems by performing a continuous process of needs assessment, gaining knowledge, interpreting and communicating information, and evaluating the effects of this process on the health problem. Figure 4.3 shows the process that transforms new information about health care issues into actions to improve access, costs, outcomes (how patients fare as a result of the care they receive), and quality. For FY 2017 the AHRQ planned for a budget of $470 million.

- Agency for Toxic Substances and Disease Registry seeks to prevent exposure to hazardous waste. The agency's FY 2017 budget of $75 million represented no change from FY 2016.

- Centers for Medicare and Medicaid Services (CMS) administers programs that provide health insurance for about 100 million Americans (older adults, those in financial need, and uninsured children); manages the Health Insurance Marketplace (also known as exchanges, the ACA created the marketplace, which enables consumers to compare health plans based on price, benefits, and other features); and regulates all laboratory testing, except testing performed for research purposes, in the United States. For FY 2017 the CMS planned for a budget of $1 trillion. Figure 4.4 shows the allocation of the CMS budget for FY 2017—59.5% was devoted to Medicare, 37.9% to Medicaid, 1.5% to the Children's Health Insurance Plan, 1.3% to private health insurance programs, 0.2% to the Innovation Center, and 0.1% to state grants and demonstrations.

- Medicare Access and Children's Health Insurance Program Reauthorization Act (which is implemented by the AHRQ) identified an initial core set of 24 health care quality measures for voluntary use by Medicaid, and the Children's Health Insurance Program strengthened measures to prevent and reduce fraud.

- U.S. Food and Drug Administration (FDA) acts to ensure the safety and efficacy (the ability of an intervention to produce the intended diagnostic or therapeutic effect in optimal circumstances) of dietary supplements, pharmaceutical drugs, and medical devices and monitors food safety and purity. The FDA planned for a budget of $5.1 billion in FY 2017. Its budget included an increase of $358 million

more than the FY 2016 budget to ensure the safety and security of the food supply and to provide other safety and prevention measures.

- Health Resources and Services Administration provides services for medically underserved populations such as migrant workers, the homeless, and public housing residents. This agency oversees the nation's organ transplant program, directs efforts to improve maternal and child health, and delivers services through the Ryan White CARE Act to people with AIDS. In FY 2017 it had a budget of $10.7 billion.

- Indian Health Service (IHS) serves nearly 2 million Native Americans and Alaskan Natives through a network of hospitals, clinics, and health stations. In FY 2017 the IHS had a budget of $6.6 billion.

- General Departmental Management provides the HHS's leadership and oversees the 11 staff divisions and offices of the HHS. It also advises the president about health, welfare, human service, and income security issues. In FY 2017 it had a budget of $555 million.

- Substance Abuse and Mental Health Services Administration (SAMHSA) seeks to improve access to, and availability of, substance abuse prevention and treatment programs as well as other mental health services. SAMHSA was budgeted $4.3 billion in FY 2017.

**FIGURE 4.2**

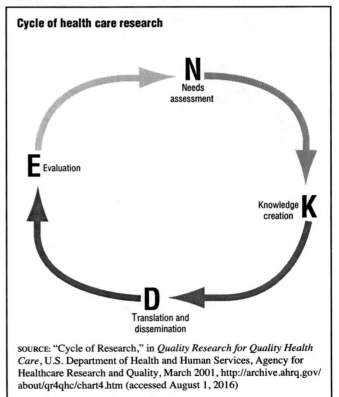

**Cycle of health care research**

SOURCE: "Cycle of Research," in *Quality Research for Quality Health Care*, U.S. Department of Health and Human Services, Agency for Healthcare Research and Quality, March 2001, http://archive.ahrq.gov/about/qr4qhc/chart4.htm (accessed August 1, 2016)

## FIGURE 4.3

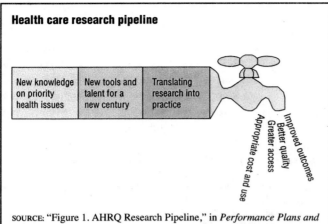

**Health care research pipeline**

SOURCE: "Figure 1. AHRQ Research Pipeline," in *Performance Plans and Performance Report*, U.S. Department of Health and Human Services, Agency for Healthcare Research and Quality, March 2001, http://archive .ahrq.gov/about/gpra2001/gprafig1.htm (accessed August 1, 2016)

## FIGURE 4.4

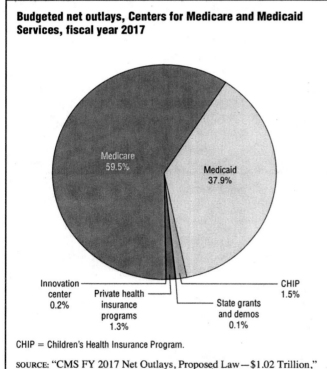

**Budgeted net outlays, Centers for Medicare and Medicaid Services, fiscal year 2017**

CHIP = Children's Health Insurance Program.

SOURCE: "CMS FY 2017 Net Outlays, Proposed Law—$1.02 Trillion," in *HHS FY2017 Budget in Brief*, U.S. Department of Health and Human Services, 2016, http://www.hhs.gov/sites/default/files/fy2017-budget-in-brief.pdf (accessed August 1, 2016)

The HHS agencies work with state, local, and tribal governments as well as with public and private organizations to coordinate and deliver a wide range of services including:

- Conducting preventive health services such as surveillance to detect outbreaks of disease and immunization programs through efforts directed by the CDC and the NIH

- Ensuring food, drug, and cosmetic safety through efforts of the FDA

- Improving maternal and child health and preschool education in programs such as Head Start, which serves nearly 1 million children per year, according to the National Head Start Association (2016, http://www.nhsa.org/facts)

- Preventing child abuse, domestic violence, and substance abuse, as well as funding substance abuse treatment through programs directed by the ACF

- Administering Medicare and Medicaid via the CMS

- Providing financial assistance and support services for low-income and older Americans, such as home-delivered meals (Meals on Wheels) coordinated by the Administration on Aging

**SUBSTANTIAL BUDGET HELPS THE HHS TO ACHIEVE ITS OBJECTIVES.** Table 4.1 displays how the FY 2017 HHS budget was allocated and provides comparisons between the outlays for FYs 2015, 2016, and 2017. The FY 2017 budget is a net increase of $117.2 billion over the FY 2015 budget and aims to provide funds to help improve access to and quality of health care, prevent disease, and support scientific research. In "HHS FY 2017 Budget in Brief" (February 8, 2016, http://www .hhs.gov/about/budget/fy2017/budget-in-brief/), the HHS explains that it allocates funds to "[find] better ways to deliver care, pay providers, and distribute information. The Budget includes targeted proposals that focus on improving care for all Americans and spending federal dollars more wisely."

**U.S. PUBLIC HEALTH SERVICE COMMISSIONED CORPS.** The U.S. Public Health Service Commissioned Corps (November 22, 2011, http://www.usphs.gov/aboutus/history.aspx) was originally the uniformed service component of the early Marine Hospital Service, which adopted a military model for a group of career health professionals who traveled from one marine hospital to another as their services were needed. By examining newly arrived immigrants and directing state quarantine (the period and place where people suspected of having contagious diseases are detained and isolated) functions, it also assisted the Marine Hospital Service to prevent infectious diseases from entering the country. A law enacted in 1889 established this group as the Commissioned Corps, and in 1912 the Marine Hospital Service was renamed the Public Health Service (PHS) to reflect its broader scope of activities.

Throughout the 20th century the corps grew to include a wide range of health professionals. Besides physicians, the corps employed nurses, dentists, research scientists, planners, pharmacists, sanitarians, engineers, and other public health professionals. These PHS-commissioned

TABLE 4.1

**U.S. Department of Health and Human Services budget, by operating division, fiscal years 2015–17**

[Dollars in millions]

| | 2015 | 2016 | 2017 |
|---|---|---|---|
| **Food and Drug Administration** | | | |
| Budget authority | 2,525 | 2,730 | 2,821 |
| Outlays | 2,393 | 2,463 | 2,624 |
| **Health Resources and Services Administration** | | | |
| Budget authority | 10,547 | 10,770 | 10,866 |
| Outlays | 9,122 | 10,296 | 11,537 |
| **Indian Health Service** | | | |
| Budget authority | 4,799 | 4,965 | 5,368 |
| Outlays | 4,550 | 5,074 | 5,260 |
| **Centers for Disease Control and Prevention** | | | |
| Budget authority | 9,096 | 7,658 | 7,455 |
| Outlays | 7,019 | 7,242 | 7,877 |
| **National Institutes of Health** | | | |
| Budget authority | 29,863 | 31,547 | 32,305 |
| Outlays | 29,294 | 30,221 | 32,302 |
| **Substance Abuse and Mental Health Services Administration** | | | |
| Budget authority | 3,486 | 3,646 | 4,107 |
| Outlays | 3,141 | 3,810 | 3,701 |
| **Agency for Healthcare Research and Quality** | | | |
| Budget authority | 364 | 334 | 280 |
| Program level | 443 | 428 | 470 |
| Outlays | 175 | 195 | 394 |
| **Centers for Medicare & Medicaid Services\*** | | | |
| Budget authority | 928,716 | 998,028 | 1,019,936 |
| Outlays | 917,644 | 992,531 | 1,017,627 |
| **Administration for Children and Families** | | | |
| Budget authority | 51,725 | 53,141 | 63,005 |
| Outlays | 50,231 | 52,385 | 58,266 |
| **Administration for Community Living** | | | |
| Budget authority | 1,835 | 1,939 | 1,969 |
| Outlays | 1,680 | 2,208 | 1,929 |
| **Office of the National Coordinator** | | | |
| Budget authority | 60 | 60 | — |
| Outlays | 105 | 154 | 2 |
| **Medicare hearings and appeals** | | | |
| Budget authority | 88 | 107 | 120 |
| Outlays | 88 | 143 | 120 |
| **Office for Civil Rights** | | | |
| Budget authority | 39 | 39 | 43 |
| Outlays | 39 | 39 | 44 |
| **Departmental management** | | | |
| Budget authority | 471 | 479 | 504 |
| Outlays | 844 | 1,154 | 1,216 |
| **Public Health and Social Services Emergency Fund** | | | |
| Budget authority | 1,951 | 1,533 | 1,431 |
| Outlays | 1,711 | 2,266 | 1,849 |
| **Office of Inspector General** | | | |
| Budget authority | 73 | 77 | 86 |
| Outlays | 90 | 93 | 116 |
| **Program Support Center (retirement pay, medical benefits, misc. trust funds)** | | | |
| Budget authority | 740 | 717 | 751 |
| Outlays | 601 | 1,085 | 732 |
| **Offsetting Collections** | | | |
| Budget authority | −1,121 | −767 | −765 |
| Outlays | −1,121 | −767 | −765 |

officers played important roles in disease prevention and detection, acted to ensure food and drug safety, conducted research, provided medical care to underserved groups such as Native Americans and Alaskan Natives, and assisted in disaster relief programs. As one of the seven uniformed services in the United States (the other six are

**TABLE 4.1**

[Dollars in millions]

| | 2015 | 2016 | 2017 |
|---|---|---|---|
| **Other Collections** | | | |
| Budget authority | −47 | −30 | −30 |
| Outlays | −47 | −30 | −30 |
| **Total, Health and Human Services** | | | |
| Budget authority | 1,045,210 | 1,116,973 | 1,150,252 |
| Outlays | 1,027,559 | 1,110,562 | 1,144,801 |
| Full-time equivalents | 75,567 | 77,583 | 79,406 |

*Budget Authority includes Non-CMS Budget Authority for Hospital Insurance and Supplementary Medical Insurance for the Social Security Administration and MEDPAC.

SOURCE: "HHS Budget by Operating Division," in *HHS FY2017 Budget in Brief*, U.S. Department of Health and Human Services, 2016, http://www.hhs.gov/sites/default/files/fy2017-budget-in-brief.pdf (accessed August 1, 2016)

the U.S. Navy, the U.S. Army, the U.S. Marine Corps, the U.S. Air Force, the U.S. Coast Guard, and the National Oceanic and Atmospheric Administration Commissioned Corps), the PHS Commissioned Corps continues to perform all these functions and identifies environmental threats to health and safety, promotes healthy lifestyles for Americans, and is involved with international agencies to help address global health problems.

The Office of the Surgeon General notes in "U.S. Public Health Service Commissioned Corps" (http://www.surgeongeneral.gov/about/corps/index.html) that as of 2016 the PHS Commissioned Corps numbered more than 6,700 health professionals. These people report to the U.S. surgeon general, who holds the rank of vice admiral in the PHS. Corps officers work in PHS agencies and in other agencies including the U.S. Bureau of Prisons, the U.S. Coast Guard, the U.S. Environmental Protection Agency, and the Commission on Mental Health of the District of Columbia. The surgeon general is a physician who is appointed by the U.S. president to serve in a medical leadership position for a four-year term of office. The surgeon general reports to the assistant secretary of health, and the Office of the Surgeon General (2016, http://www.surgeongeneral.gov/about/index.html) is part of the Office of Public Health and Science. Eighteen surgeons general, plus nine acting surgeons general, have served since the 1870s. In December 2014 Vice Admiral Vivek Murthy (1977–; http://www.surgeongeneral.gov/about/biographies/biosg.html) was confirmed as the surgeon general.

## CENTERS FOR DISEASE CONTROL AND PREVENTION

The CDC is the primary HHS agency responsible for ensuring the health and safety of the nation's citizens in the United States and abroad. The CDC's responsibilities include researching and monitoring health, detecting and investigating health problems, researching and instituting prevention programs, developing health policies, ensuring environmental health and safety, and offering education and training.

In "Fast Facts about CDC" (February 19, 2016, http://www.cdc.gov/about/facts/cdcfastfacts/cdcfacts.html), the CDC indicates that it employs approximately 14,000 people in nearly 170 disciplines and in more than 50 countries. Besides research scientists, physicians, nurses, and other health practitioners, the CDC employs epidemiologists, who study disease in populations as opposed to individuals. Epidemiologists measure disease occurrences, such as incidence and prevalence of disease, and work with clinical researchers to answer questions about causation (how particular diseases arise and the factors that contribute to their development), whether new treatments are effective, and how to prevent specific diseases.

The CDC lists in "CDC Organization" (September 6, 2016, http://www.cdc.gov/about/organization/cio.htm) the national centers and various institutes and offices that it is home to. Among the best known are the National Center for Health Statistics, which collects vital statistics, and the National Institute for Occupational Safety and Health, which seeks to prevent workplace injuries and accidents through research and prevention. Thomas R. Frieden (1960–) was named the director of the CDC in June 2009. Figure 4.5 shows the organization and leadership of the CDC in 2016.

### CDC Actions to Protect the Health of the Nation

The CDC is part of the first response to natural disasters, outbreaks of disease, other public health emergencies, and urgent public health problems. For example, the agency produces *Public Health Grand Rounds* (http://www.cdc.gov/cdcgrandrounds/), a monthly webcast intended to stimulate discussion of significant public health issues. Each session describes a specific health challenge and considers leading-edge scientific evidence and the possible impact of different interventions. In 2016 the series focused

**FIGURE 4.5**

Centers for Disease Control and Prevention organization and leadership, 2016

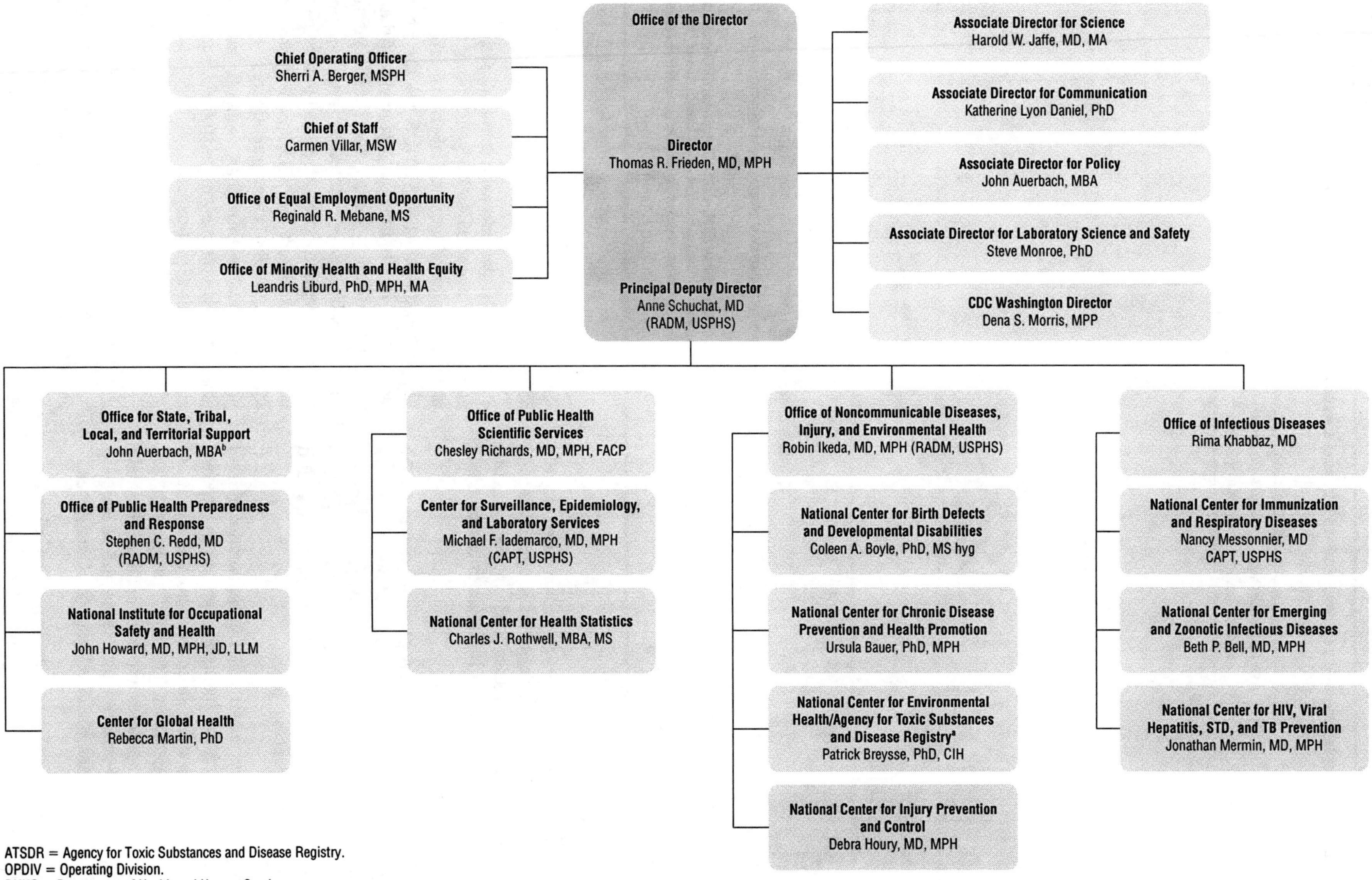

**Office of the Director**

**Director**
Thomas R. Frieden, MD, MPH

**Principal Deputy Director**
Anne Schuchat, MD
(RADM, USPHS)

**Associate Director for Science**
Harold W. Jaffe, MD, MA

**Associate Director for Communication**
Katherine Lyon Daniel, PhD

**Associate Director for Policy**
John Auerbach, MBA

**Associate Director for Laboratory Science and Safety**
Steve Monroe, PhD

**CDC Washington Director**
Dena S. Morris, MPP

**Chief Operating Officer**
Sherri A. Berger, MSPH

**Chief of Staff**
Carmen Villar, MSW

**Office of Equal Employment Opportunity**
Reginald R. Mebane, MS

**Office of Minority Health and Health Equity**
Leandris Liburd, PhD, MPH, MA

**Office of Public Health Scientific Services**
Chesley Richards, MD, MPH, FACP

**Center for Surveillance, Epidemiology, and Laboratory Services**
Michael F. Iademarco, MD, MPH (CAPT, USPHS)

**National Center for Health Statistics**
Charles J. Rothwell, MBA, MS

**Office of Noncommunicable Diseases, Injury, and Environmental Health**
Robin Ikeda, MD, MPH (RADM, USPHS)

**National Center for Birth Defects and Developmental Disabilities**
Coleen A. Boyle, PhD, MS hyg

**National Center for Chronic Disease Prevention and Health Promotion**
Ursula Bauer, PhD, MPH

**National Center for Environmental Health/Agency for Toxic Substances and Disease Registry[a]**
Patrick Breysse, PhD, CIH

**National Center for Injury Prevention and Control**
Debra Houry, MD, MPH

**Office of Infectious Diseases**
Rima Khabbaz, MD

**National Center for Immunization and Respiratory Diseases**
Nancy Messonnier, MD CAPT, USPHS

**National Center for Emerging and Zoonotic Infectious Diseases**
Beth P. Bell, MD, MPH

**National Center for HIV, Viral Hepatitis, STD, and TB Prevention**
Jonathan Mermin, MD, MPH

**Office for State, Tribal, Local, and Territorial Support**
John Auerbach, MBA[b]

**Office of Public Health Preparedness and Response**
Stephen C. Redd, MD (RADM, USPHS)

**National Institute for Occupational Safety and Health**
John Howard, MD, MPH, JD, LLM

**Center for Global Health**
Rebecca Martin, PhD

ATSDR = Agency for Toxic Substances and Disease Registry.
OPDIV = Operating Division.
DHHS = Department of Health and Human Services.
[a]ATSDR is an OPDIV within DHHS but is managed by a common director's office.
[b]Acting.

SOURCE: "Organizational Chart," in *CDC Organization*, Centers for Disease Control and Prevention, April 4, 2016, http://www.cdc.gov/about/pdf/organization/cdc-photo-org-chart.pdf (accessed August 1, 2016)

FIGURE 4.6

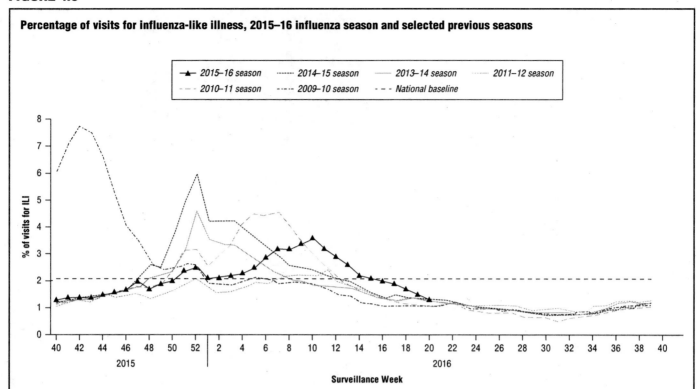

**Percentage of visits for influenza-like illness, 2015–16 influenza season and selected previous seasons**

Notes: Illness defined as a temperature of ≥100.0°F (≥37.8°C), oral or equivalent, and cough or sore throat, in the absence of a known cause other than influenza. Data reported as of June 3, 2016.

SOURCE: Stacy L. Davlin et al. "Figure 3. Percentage of Visits for Influenza-Like Illness (ILI) Reported to CDC—U.S. Outpatient Influenza-Like Illness Surveillance Network, United States, 2015–16 Influenza Season and Selected Previous Seasons," in "Influenza Activity—United States, 2015–16 Season and Composition of the 2016–17 Influenza Vaccine," *MMWR*, vol. 65, no. 22, June 10, 2016, http://www.cdc.gov/mmwr/volumes/65/wr/mm6522a3.htm#suggestedcitation (accessed August 1, 2016)

on a variety of topics, including health disparities in early childhood, prevention and treatment of strokes, detecting and tracking foodborne illness, and the Zika virus (a mosquito-borne infection that is known to cause certain birth defects).

The CDC also monitors and plans responses to the emerging threat of seasonal influenza and other influenza viruses. Figure 4.6 compares the percentage of visits for influenza in selected seasons, including the 2009–10 pandemic flu, and reveals that the 2015–16 season was mild compared with other recent years.

Among the many recent CDC initiatives to address threats to public health are intensified efforts to improve antibiotic use and prevent infection and the spread of antibiotic-resistant infections. The CDC works with federal, state, and local agencies and organizations to obtain data about antibiotic-resistant infections and to develop diagnostic tests to track the development of resistance.

The CDC also focuses on reducing prescription drug abuse and overdose. Efforts aim to reduce misuse and the number of deaths from painkiller overdoses while simultaneously ensuring that patients with pain receive safe, effective pain relief.

The CDC partners with national, state, local, public, and private agencies and organizations to deliver services. Examples of these collaborative efforts include the global battle against HIV/AIDS via the Leadership and Investment in Fighting an Epidemic initiative and the CDC Coordinating Center for Health Information and Service, which was created to improve public health through increased efficiencies and to foster stronger collaboration between the CDC and international health foundations, health care practitioners, community and philanthropic organizations, schools and universities, nonprofit and voluntary organizations, and state and local public health departments.

## NATIONAL INSTITUTES OF HEALTH

The NIH (January 22, 2016, http://www.nih.gov/about/history.htm) began as a one-room laboratory in 1887 and eventually became the world's premier medical research center. The NIH conducts research in its own facilities and supports research in universities, medical schools, and hospitals throughout and outside the United States. The NIH trains research scientists and other investigators and serves to communicate medical and health information to professional and consumer audiences.

The NIH (August 20, 2013, http://www.nih.gov/about/organization.htm) consists of 27 centers and institutes and is housed in more than 75 buildings on a 300-acre (121-ha) campus in Bethesda, Maryland. Among the better-known centers and institutes are the National Cancer Institute, the National Human Genome Research Institute, and the National Institute of Mental Health.

In "Facts at a Glance" (May 23, 2016, http://clinical center.nih.gov/about/welcome/fact.html), the NIH explains that patients arrive at the NIH Warren Grant Magnuson Clinical Center in Bethesda to participate in clinical research trials. About 5,400 patients per year are treated as inpatients, and an additional 100,500 receive outpatient treatment. The National Library of Medicine—which maintains MEDLINE (June 23, 2016, https://www.nlm .nih.gov/pubs/factsheets/medline.html), a comprehensive medical bibliographic database with more than 23 million references to articles published in around 5,600 biomedical journals in about 40 languages—is in the NIH Lister Hill Center.

In 2010 the National Library of Medicine released ReUnite, an iPhone application to improve post-disaster family reunification. Within one week of its release, ReUnite was downloaded by more than 1,000 people. By 2016 the NIH offered 15 apps (https://www.nlm.nih .gov/mobile/), ranging from Health Hotlines, a directory of nearly 9,000 biomedical organizations and resources with toll-free telephone numbers, to the Wireless System for Emergency Responders, which assists emergency responders in hazardous materials incidents.

The NIH budget for FY 2017 was $33.1 billion. Table 4.2 shows NIH funding allocation by institute. In "About the National Institutes of Health" (2016, https:// www.science.education.nih.gov/supplements/nih2/oral-health/about/NIDCR-print.pdf), the NIH states that it works to achieve its ambitious research objectives "to acquire new knowledge to help prevent, detect, diagnose, and treat disease and disability, from the rarest genetic disorder to the common cold" by investing in promising biomedical research. The NIH (April 4, 2016, https://www.nih.gov/about-nih/what-we-do/budget) makes grants and contracts to support research and training in every state in the country, at more than 2,500 institutions. The NIH allocated more than half (54.9%) of its FY 2017 budget to research project grants, 10.9% to intramural research (work conducted at NIH facilities), 9.6% to research and development contracts, and 7.8% to research centers. (See Figure 4.7.)

## Establishing Research Priorities

By law, all 27 institutes and centers of the NIH must be funded, and each institute and center must allocate its funding to specific areas and aspects of research within its domain. About half of each institute's or center's budget is dedicated to supporting the best research proposals presented, in terms of their potential to contribute to advances that will combat the diseases the institute or center is charged with researching. Some of the other criteria that are used to determine research priorities include:

- Public health need—the NIH responds to health problems and diseases based on their incidence (the rate of development of a disease in a group during a given period) and severity and on the costs associated with them. Examples of other measures used to weigh and assess need are the mortality rate (the number of deaths caused by disease), the morbidity rate (the degree of disability caused by disease), the economic and social consequences of the disease, and whether rapid action is required to control the spread of the disease.

- Rigorous peer review—proposals are scrutinized by accomplished researchers to determine the potential return on investment of resources.

- Flexibility and expansiveness—the NIH experience demonstrates that important findings for commonly occurring diseases may come from research on rarer ones. The NIH attempts to fund the broadest possible array of research opportunities to stimulate creative solutions to pressing problems.

- Commitment to human resources and technology—the NIH invests in people and equipment in the pursuit of scientific advancement.

Because not even the most gifted scientists can accurately predict the next critical discovery or stride in biomedical research, the NIH must analyze each research opportunity in terms of competition for the same resources, public interest, scientific merit, and the potential to build on current knowledge.

## NIH Achievements

The HHS notes in *HHS FY2017 Budget in Brief* that in FY 2017 the NIH had 18,000 employees. The NIH recruits and attracts the most capable research scientists in the world. In fact, the NIH indicates in "The NIH Almanac: Nobel Laureates" (https://www.nih.gov/about-nih/what-we-do/nih-almanac/nobel-laureates) that as of October 2016, 149 scientists who conducted NIH research or were supported by NIH grants had received Nobel Prizes. Several Nobel Prize winners made their prize-winning discoveries in NIH laboratories.

TABLE 4.2

**National Institutes of Health total funding, fiscal years 2015–17**

[Dollars in millions]

| | 2015[a] | 2016 | 2017 | 2017 +/− 2016 |
|---|---|---|---|---|
| **Institutes/centers** | | | | |
| National Cancer Institute | 4,953 | 5,214 | 5,894 | +680 |
| National Heart, Lung and Blood Institute | 2,996 | 3,114 | 3,114 | — |
| National Institute of Dental and Craniofacial Research | 398 | 413 | 413 | — |
| National Inst. of Diabetes & Digestive & Kidney Diseases | 1,899 | 1,966 | 1,966 | — |
| National Institute of Neurological Disorders and Stroke | 1,605 | 1,695 | 1,695 | — |
| National Institute of Allergy and Infectious Diseases | 4,418 | 4,716 | 4,716 | — |
| National Institute of General Medical Sciences | 2,372 | 2,512 | 2,512 | — |
| Eunice K. Shriver Natl. Inst. of Child Health & Human Development | 1,287 | 1,338 | 1,338 | — |
| National Eye Institute | 677 | 708 | 708 | — |
| National Institute of Environmental Health Sciences: Labor/HHS Appropriation | 667 | 694 | 694 | — |
| National Institute of Environmental Health Sciences: Interior Appropriation | 77 | 77 | 77 | — |
| National Institute on Aging | 1,198 | 1,598 | 1,598 | — |
| Natl. Inst. of Arthritis & Musculoskeletal & Skin Diseases | 522 | 542 | 542 | — |
| Natl. Inst. on Deafness and Communication Disorders | 405 | 423 | 423 | — |
| National Institute of Mental Health | 1,434 | 1,519 | 1,519 | — |
| National Institute on Drug Abuse | 1,016 | 1,051 | 1,051 | — |
| National Institute on Alcohol Abuse and Alcoholism | 447 | 467 | 467 | — |
| National Institute of Nursing Research | 141 | 146 | 146 | — |
| National Human Genome Research Institute | 499 | 513 | 513 | — |
| Natl. Institute of Biomedical Imaging and Bioengineering | 327 | 344 | 344 | — |
| Natl. Institute on Minority Health and Health Disparities | 271 | 281 | 281 | — |
| Natl. Center for Complementary and Integrative Health | 124 | 130 | 130 | — |
| National Center for Advancing Translational Sciences | 633 | 685 | 685 | — |
| Fogarty International Center | 68 | 70 | 70 | — |
| National Library of Medicine | 337 | 396 | 396 | — |
| Office of the Director | 1,414 | 1,571 | 1,716 | +145 |
| Buildings and facilities | 129 | 129 | 129 | — |
| **Total, program level** | **30,311** | **32,311** | **33,136** | **+825** |
| **Less funds from other sources** | | | | |
| PHS evaluation funds | −715 | −780 | −847 | −67 |
| Type 1 Diabetes Research (NIDDK)[b] | −150 | −150 | −150 | — |
| Additional mandatory funds | — | — | −1,825 | −1,825 |
| **Total, discretionary budget authority** | **29,446** | **31,381** | **30,314** | **−1,067** |
| **Appropriations** | | | | |
| Labor/HHS appropriation | 29,370 | 31,304 | 30,237 | −1,067 |
| Interior Appropriation | 77 | 77 | 77 | — |
| Full-time equivalents | 17,823 | 18,000 | 18,000 | — |

NIDDK = National Inst. of Diabetes & Digestive & Kidney Diseases.

[a]In addition, the fiscal year 2015 appropriation (P.L. 113-235) provided $239 million of emergency resources for ebola response and preparedness research activities.

[b]These mandatory funds were appropriated in P.L. 114-10, the Medicare Access and CHIP Reauthorization Act of 2015, and P.L. 113-93, the Protecting Access to Medicare Act of 2014.

SOURCE: "National Institutes of Health," in *HHS FY2017 Budget in Brief*, U.S. Department of Health and Human Services, 2016, http://www.hhs.gov/sites/default/files/fy2017-budget-in-brief.pdf (accessed August 1, 2016)

Equally important, NIH research has contributed to great improvements in the health of the nation. The following are some of the NIH's (October 27, 2016, http://www.nih.gov/about/almanac/historical/chronology_of_events.htm) recent achievements (from 2011 to 2015):

- A large NIH-funded clinical trial found that early treatment of HIV-positive patients significantly lowers their risk of transmitting HIV.

- NIH research found that a "primer" vaccine followed by an avian flu vaccine dramatically increased flu-fighting antibodies compared with the flu vaccine alone.

- Using computers and genomic data (information about the full set of chromosomes and all the inheritable traits), researchers identified new applications for existing FDA-approved drugs.

- NIH established the National Center for Advancing Translational Sciences, which aims to develop new methods and technologies to reduce, remove, or bypass bottlenecks in delivering new drugs, diagnostics, and medical devices to patients.

- The Human Connectome Project, which is mapping connections between the brain's neurons, showed that nerve fibers in the brain are not a jumble of overlapping wires. Instead, they form a structured three-dimensional grid—nerve pathways run parallel to one another and cross at right angles.

- NIH-funded research enabled paralyzed patients to reach and grasp objects using a robotic arm controlled by their thoughts.

**FIGURE 4.7**

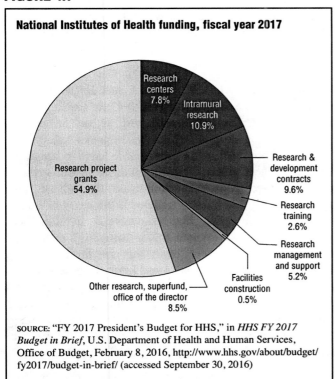

National Institutes of Health funding, fiscal year 2017

Research centers 7.8%

Intramural research 10.9%

Research project grants 54.9%

Research & development contracts 9.6%

Research training 2.6%

Research management and support 5.2%

Other research, superfund, office of the director 8.5%

Facilities construction 0.5%

SOURCE: "FY 2017 President's Budget for HHS," in *HHS FY 2017 Budget in Brief*, U.S. Department of Health and Human Services, Office of Budget, February 8, 2016, http://www.hhs.gov/about/budget/fy2017/budget-in-brief/ (accessed September 30, 2016)

- NIH-supported research found that programs that help prevent or delay the onset of type 2 diabetes are cost-effective because these programs reduce overall medical care costs and improve quality of life.

- NIH launched a partnership with 10 biopharmaceutical companies and several nonprofits to transform the model for identifying promising targets for new diagnostics and drug development.

- NIH researchers and investigators at the Walter Reed Army Institute developed an experimental Ebola (an infectious disease spread by contact with infected body fluid that is generally fatal) vaccine that was tested in Africa. Other researchers developed treatment for people infected with Ebola, which was tested in Sierra Leone.

NIH press releases report more recent achievements. For example, in "HIV Therapy for Breastfeeding Mothers Can Virtually Eliminate Transmission to Babies" (July 18, 2016, https://www.nih.gov/news-events/news-releases/hiv-therapy-breastfeeding-mothers-can-virtually-eliminate-transmission-babies), the NIH reports the results of a study that demonstrates that a three-drug antiretroviral regimen during breastfeeding prevents mother-to-child transmission of HIV to infants. Other NIH research, described in the press release "Testing of Investigational Inactivated Zika Vaccine in Humans Begins" (November 7, 2016, https://www.nih.gov/news-events/news-releases/testing-investigational-inactivated-zika-vaccine-humans-begins), announces the launch of clinical trials of an investigational Zika vaccine to determine whether it is safe and effective.

## ACCREDITATION

Accreditation of health care providers (facilities and organizations) offers consumers, payers, and other stakeholders the assurance that accredited facilities and organizations have been certified as meeting or exceeding predetermined standards. Accreditation refers to both the process during which the quality of care delivered is measured and the resulting official endorsement that quality standards have been met. Besides promoting accreditation to health care consumers and other purchasers of care such as employer groups, accreditation assists health care facilities and organizations to recruit and retain qualified staff, increase organizational efficiencies to reduce costs, identify ways to improve service delivery, and reduce liability insurance premiums.

### The Joint Commission

The Joint Commission (2016, http://www.jointcommission.org/about_us/fact_sheets.aspx) surveys and accredits more than 21,000 health care organizations and programs throughout the United States. The Joint Commission is a nonprofit organization and is headquartered in Oakbrook Terrace, Illinois, with a satellite office in Washington, D.C. The Joint Commission notes in "Facts about the Joint Commission" (July 8, 2016, http://www.jointcommission.org/about_us/who_we_are.aspx) that it has more than 1,000 surveyors (physicians, nurses, pharmacists, hospital and health care organization administrators, laboratory medical technologists, and other health professionals) who are qualified and trained to evaluate specific aspects of health care quality.

Working closely with medical and other professional societies, purchasers of health care services, and management experts as well as with other accrediting organizations, the Joint Commission develops the standards that health care organizations are expected to meet. Besides developing benchmarks and standards of organizational quality, the Joint Commission is credited with promoting improvement in infection control, safety, and patients' rights.

THE JOINT COMMISSION GROWS TO BECOME THE PREEMINENT ACCREDITING BODY. In *The Joint Commission: Over a Century of Quality and Safety* (2015, https://www.jointcommission.org/assets/1/6/TJC_history_timeline_through_2015.pdf), the Joint Commission explains that early efforts to standardize and evaluate care delivered in hospitals began in 1913 by the American College of Surgeons. Thirty-eight years later, in 1951, the Joint Commission on Accreditation of Hospitals (JCAH) was established. In 1966 the JCAH began offering accreditation to long-term-care facilities, and in 1972 the Social Security

Act was amended to require the HHS secretary to validate JCAH findings and include them in the HHS annual report to Congress. In subsequent years the JCAH's mandate was expanded to include a variety of other health care facilities, and in 1987 it was renamed the Joint Commission on Accreditation of Healthcare Organizations. Today, it is known simply as the Joint Commission.

In 1992 the Joint Commission instituted a requirement that accredited hospitals prohibit smoking in the hospital, and in 1993 it began performing random, surprise surveys (unannounced site visits) of 5% of accredited organizations. The Joint Commission also moved to emphasize performance improvement standards by revising its policies on medical errors.

In 1999 the Joint Commission required hospitals to begin collecting and reporting data about the care they provide for five specific diagnoses: acute myocardial infarction (heart attack), congestive heart failure, pneumonia, pregnancy and related medical conditions, and surgical procedures and complications. The Joint Commission calls these diagnoses "core measure data" and uses these data to compare facilities and assess the quality of service delivered. In 2002 the Joint Commission moved to make its recommendations more easily understood by consumers so they can make informed choices about health care providers.

In 2006 the Joint Commission shifted to an unannounced survey program—meaning that organizations receive no advanced notice of their survey date. Before this policy change, the leaders of the nation's more than 4,500 Medicare-participating hospitals had ample notice and time to prepare for Joint Commission visits and inspections. The policy change was intended to shift hospitals' orientation from preparing for the next Joint Commission survey to preparing for the next patient. The policy also required hospitals to conduct an annual periodic performance review using their own internal evaluators to assess their own level of standards compliance and to communicate the results of their audit to the Joint Commission.

This policy change, presumably implemented to improve hospital vigilance about safety, care, and quality, coincided with another, seemingly contradictory Joint Commission policy change, which allowed hospitals to accumulate a higher number of deficiencies (patient care lapses and other violations) before sanctions are imposed on them. The Joint Commission defends this practice by explaining that it would rather identify more problems and have hospitals resolve them than deny hospitals accreditation.

Joint Commission efforts appear to be effective. Stephen P. Schmaltz et al. demonstrate in "Hospital Performance Trends on National Quality Measures and the Association with Joint Commission Accreditation" (*Journal of Hospital Medicine*, vol. 6, no. 8, October 2011) that hospitals accredited by the Joint Commission outperform nonaccredited hospitals on nationally standardized quality measures.

Nonetheless, Mark R. Chassin and Jerod M. Loeb observe in "High-Reliability Health Care: Getting There from Here" (*Milbank Quarterly*, vol. 91, no. 3, September 2013) that despite efforts to improve safety and quality, patients still suffer preventable harm in hospitals. The researchers assert, "No hospitals or health systems have achieved consistent excellence throughout their institutions. High-reliability science is the study of organizations in industries like commercial aviation and nuclear power that operate under hazardous conditions while maintaining safety levels that are far better than those of health care." Chassin and Loeb propose a framework to assist hospitals to improve quality by focusing on leadership, a culture of safety, and robust process improvement—philosophy and tools aimed at improving the outcomes of a process and preparing organizations to accept, implement, and sustain these improved processes.

In *America's Hospitals: Improving Quality and Safety—The Joint Commission's Annual Report 2015* (2016, https://www.jointcommission.org/assets/1/18/TJC _Annual_Report_2015_EMBARGOED_11_9_15.pdf), the Joint Commission names and ranks 1,043 hospitals (31.5% of all Joint Commission–accredited hospitals reporting accountability measure performance data for 2014) distinguished as top performers in the use of evidence-based care processes (approaches and methods based on the results of research), which are closely linked to positive patient outcomes (how patients fare as a result of treatment). Of the 1,043 top performers, 650 earned the distinction for the last two consecutive years, 435 for the last three years, 221 for the last four years, and 117 for the last five years.

**National Committee for Quality Assurance**

The National Committee for Quality Assurance (NCQA) is another well-respected accrediting organization that focuses its attention on the managed care industry. The NCQA began surveying and accrediting managed care organizations (MCOs) in 1991.

NCQA surveys use a set of more than 60 standards, each focusing on a specific aspect of health plan operations, for all types of health plans, such as MCOs, health maintenance organizations (HMOs), and preferred provider organizations (PPOs). The standards address access and service, the qualifications of providers, the organization's commitment to prevention programs and health maintenance, the quality of care delivered to members when they are ill or injured, and the organization's approach to helping members manage chronic diseases such as diabetes, heart disease, and asthma. To ensure fair comparisons between managed health care plans and to track their progress and improvement over time, the NCQA considers many standards, including:

- Management of asthma and effective use of medication

- Controlling hypertension (high blood pressure)

- Effective and appropriate use of antidepressant medications

- Childhood and adult weight and body mass index assessment

- Rates of breast cancer screening

- The frequency and consistency with which beta blockers (drug treatment) are used following heart attack

- Rates of immunization among children and teens

The NCQA combines the Healthcare Effectiveness Data and Information Set with national and regional benchmarks of quality in a national database called the Quality Compass. This national database enables employers and health care consumers to compare health plans to one another and make choices about coverage based on quality and value rather than simply on price and participating providers (physicians, hospitals, and other providers that offer services to the managed care plan members).

The NCQA issues health plan report cards that rate HMOs and MCOs, and health care consumers and other stakeholders can access them at the NCQA website. After the NCQA review, the plans may be granted the NCQA's full accreditation for three years, indicating a level of excellence that exceeds NCQA standards. Those that need some improvement are granted one-year accreditation with recommendations about areas that need improvement, and MCOs that meet some but not all NCQA standards may be denied accreditation or granted provisional accreditation.

Besides certifying and accrediting MCOs, the NCQA publishes health insurance plan ratings for more than 1,300 health insurance plans online (http://healthinsuranceratings.ncqa.org). Consumers can see how their plans rate on a scale of one to five, with five as the highest performance.

The NCQA reports in *The State of Health Care Quality 2015* (2016, http://www.ncqa.org/) that the number of plans that received four- and five-star ratings rose from 40% in 2014 to 45% in 2015. It observes that enrollment in highly rated Medicare plans increased 10% during the same period, which is evidence that health care consumers are using quality ratings and choosing high-performing plans. The NCQA asserts that "what gets measured gets improved" and "what gets included in pay-for-performance can excel," meaning that MCOs' performance improves in the areas they know are monitored and measured and that financial incentives drive quality improvement.

**Accreditation Association for Ambulatory Health Care**

Another accrediting organization, the Accreditation Association for Ambulatory Health Care (AAAHC), was formed in 1979 and focuses exclusively on ambulatory (outpatient) facilities and programs. Outpatient clinics, group practices, student health services, occupational medicine clinics, ambulatory surgery centers, and medical homes (primary care practices that aim to serve as centralized overseers of all the health care needs of individuals) are among the organizations that are evaluated by the AAAHC.

In 2009 the AAAHC established standards for reviewing medical homes. The term *medical home* is a relatively new descriptor of the long-standing practice of having a primary care practitioner (for adults usually an internist or family practitioner and for children a pediatrician) provide and coordinate needed care.

The medical home model of primary care is patient centered, comprehensive, team based, coordinated, and accessible, and emphasizes quality and safety. It is a philosophy of health care delivery that urges providers and care teams to meet patients where they are, from the simplest to the most complex chronic conditions. It endeavors to treat patients with respect, dignity, and compassion and to foster strong and trusting relationships with providers and staff. It is a model for quality primary care excellence that is delivered in the manner that best suits a patient's needs. The AAAHC offers certification and accreditation for medical homes based on the following standards:

- Patient rights and responsibilities

- Organizational governance and administration

- The patient/care team relationship

- Comprehensiveness, continuity, and accessibility of care

- Clinical records and health information

- Quality of care

The AAAHC accreditation process involves a self-assessment by the organization seeking accreditation, peer-review, continuing education, and a survey that is conducted by AAAHC surveyors who are all practicing professionals. The AAAHC grants accreditation for periods ranging from six months to three years. By 2016 the AAAHC (http://www.aaahc.org/about/) was accrediting more than 6,000 organizations.

In 2002 the AAAHC and the Joint Commission signed a collaborative accreditation agreement that permits ambulatory health care organizations to use their

AAAHC accreditation to satisfy the Joint Commission's requirements. That same year the CMS granted the AAAHC authority to review health plans that provide coverage for Medicare beneficiaries. HMOs, PPOs, and ambulatory surgery centers are now considered to be Medicare-certified on their receipt of accreditation from the AAAHC.

### National Quality Forum

In 2006 two other national quality organizations, the National Quality Forum and the National Committee on Quality Health Care, merged to become a new organization, also named the National Quality Forum (NQF; http://www.qualityforum.org). The NQF is a private, nonprofit membership organization created to develop and implement a national strategy for health care quality measurement and reporting. Its mission is to improve health and health care quality in the United States through measurement. In August 2016 the NQF had more than 400 organizational members.

In the press release "NQF, CDC Issue Guidance to Help Hospitals Better Manage Use of Antibiotics" (May 25, 2016, http://www.qualityforum.org/News_And_Resources/Press _Releases/2016/NQF_CDC_Issue_Guidance_to_Help _Hospitals_Better_Manage_Use_of_Antibiotics .aspx), the NQF explains that it worked with the CDC and more than 25 experts to create a guide to help hospitals reduce misuse and overuse of antibiotics. Inappropriate antibiotic use causes antimicrobial resistance, which is responsible for 2 million illnesses and 23,000 deaths per year. The NQF guide emphasizes "the importance of team-wide, systematic approaches to: assessing when patients need antibiotics and when treatment should be adjusted; educating staff, family, and patients about appropriate antibiotic use; and tracking and reporting antibiotic prescribing, use, and resistance."

### PROFESSIONAL SOCIETIES

There are professional and membership organizations and societies for all health professionals, such as physicians, nurses, psychologists, and hospital administrators, as well as for institutional health care providers, such as hospitals, managed care plans, and medical groups. These professional organizations represent the interests and concerns of their members, advocate on their behalf, and frequently compile data and publish information about working conditions, licensing, accreditation, compensation, and scientific advancements of interest to members.

### American Medical Association

The American Medical Association (AMA) is a powerful voice for U.S. physicians' interests. The AMA concerns itself with a wide range of health-related issues, including medical ethics, medical education, physician and patient advocacy, and development of national health policy. The AMA publishes the highly regarded *Journal of the American Medical Association*, as well as nine journals known as the JAMA Network.

Founded in 1847, the AMA has worked to upgrade medical education by expanding medical school curricula and establishing standards for licensing and accreditation of practitioners and postgraduate training programs. Recent activities of the AMA include campaigning to avert a Medicare pay cut for physicians, opposing insurance company mergers that would lessen competition, and supporting efforts to curb the nation's abuse of and addiction to opioids such as heroin, morphine, and prescription pain relievers.

In the press release "AMA Expands Policy on Background Checks, Waiting Period for Gun Buyers" (June 15, 2016, http://www.ama-assn.org/ama/pub/news/news/2016/ 2016-06-15-background-checks-gun-purchasers.page), the AMA calls gun violence in the United States "a public health crisis" and asserts that "uncontrolled ownership and use of firearms, especially handguns, is a serious threat to the public's health inasmuch as the weapons are one of the main causes of intentional and unintentional injuries and deaths." Furthermore, the AMA expands its policy on gun safety to support "waiting periods and background checks for all firearm purchasers." An earlier policy statement advocated waiting periods and background checks for handgun buyers only rather than for all gun purchasers.

### American Nurses Association

The American Nurses Association (ANA; 2016, http:// www.nursingworld.org/FunctionalMenuCategories/About ANA) is a professional organization that represents 3.6 million registered nurses and promotes high standards of nursing practice and education as well as the rights and responsibilities of nurses in the workplace. On behalf of its members, the ANA works to protect patients' rights, lobbies to advocate for health care issues that affect nurses and the public, champions workplace safety, and provides career and continuing education opportunities. The ANA publishes the *American Journal of Nursing* and actively seeks to improve the public image of nurses among health professionals and the community at large.

### American Hospital Association

The American Hospital Association (AHA; 2016, http://www.aha.org/about/index.shtml) represents nearly 5,000 hospitals, health care systems, networks, and other health care providers and 43,000 individual members. Originally established as a membership organization for hospital superintendents in 1898, the AHA eventually expanded its mission to address all facets of hospital care and quality. Besides national advocacy activities and participation in the development of health policy, the

AHA oversees research and pilot programs to improve health service delivery. It also gathers and disseminates hospital and other related health care data, publishes information of interest for its members, and sponsors educational opportunities for health care managers and administrators.

## VOLUNTARY HEALTH ORGANIZATIONS

### American Heart Association

The American Heart Association's mission is to decrease disability and death from cardiovascular disease and stroke. The association's national headquarters is in Dallas, Texas, and seven regional affiliate offices serve the balance of the United States. The American Heart Association explains in "History of the American Heart Association" (January 27, 2015, http://www.heart.org/HEARTORG/General/History-of-the-American-Heart-Association_UCM_308120_Article.jsp#.V6NhsWXMp84) that it was started by a group of physicians and social workers in New York City in 1915. The early efforts of this group, called the Association for the Prevention and Relief of Heart Disease, were to educate physicians and the general public about heart disease. The first fund-raising efforts were launched in 1948 during a radio broadcast, and since then the association has raised millions of dollars to fund research, education, and treatment programs.

Besides research, fund-raising, and generating public awareness about reducing the risk of developing heart disease, the American Heart Association has published many best-selling cookbooks that feature heart-healthy recipes and meal planning ideas. The association is also considered to be one of the world's most trusted authorities about heart health among physicians and scientists. It publishes five print journals, *Circulation, Circulation Research, Stroke, Hypertension,* and *Atherosclerosis, Thrombosis, and Vascular Biology,* also available online, and seven online-only journals.

The American Heart Association supports many initiatives to prevent heart disease and educate the community at large. For example, in the press release "New Initiative Aims to Reduce Repeat Heart Attacks" (August 2, 2016, http://newsroom.heart.org/news/new-initiative-aims-to-reduce-repeat-heart-attacks), the association announces a new educational campaign to help people who have suffered a heart attack prevent another heart attack. The campaign emphasizes the importance of taking medication as directed; timely follow-up appointments with physicians; participation in a cardiac rehabilitation program (education and counseling services to help patients increase physical fitness, improve health, and reduce the risk of future heart problems); effectively manage risk factors such as physical inactivity, high blood pressure, elevated cholesterol, diabetes, smoking, and obesity; and developing a strong social support system.

The American Heart Association also educates consumers about the importance of controlling risk factors for heart disease such as high blood pressure and physical inactivity. For example, in the press release "Midlife Fitness Is Linked to Lower Stroke Risks Later in Life" (June 9, 2016, http://newsroom.heart.org/news/midlife-fitness-is-linked-to-lower-stroke-risks-later-in-life), the association describes research finding that being physically fit in one's 40s is associated with lower risk of stroke after age 65. People with the highest levels of fitness had a 37% lower risk of stroke after age 65, underscoring the importance of fitness independent of other risk factors such as high blood pressure and diabetes.

### American Cancer Society

The American Cancer Society (ACS; April 2015, http://www.cancer.org/aboutus/whoweare/acs-fact-sheet) is headquartered in Atlanta, Georgia, and has local offices throughout the country. The ACS's mission (November 11, 2008, http://www.cancer.org/AboutUs/WhoWeAre/acsmissionstatements) is "eliminating cancer as a major health problem by preventing cancer, saving lives, and diminishing suffering from cancer, through research, education, advocacy, and service."

The ACS is the biggest source of private, nonprofit funding for cancer research—second only to the federal government. The ACS indicates that it has invested more than $4 billion in cancer research at leading centers throughout the United States and has funded 47 Nobel Prize winners early in their careers. It also supports epidemiological research to provide cancer surveillance information about occurrence rates, risk factors, mortality, and availability of treatment services. The ACS publishes an array of patient information brochures and three clinical journals for health professionals: *Cancer, Cancer Cytopathology,* and *CA: A Cancer Journal for Clinicians.* The ACS also maintains a 24-hour consumer telephone line that is staffed by trained cancer information specialists and a website with information for professionals, patients and families, and the media.

Besides education, prevention, and patient services, the ACS advocates for cancer survivors, their families, and every potential cancer patient. Its nonprofit, nonpartisan advocacy affiliate, the American Cancer Society Action Network, seeks to obtain support and passage of laws, policies, and regulations that benefit people who are affected by cancer. It has helped enact policies such as smoke-free laws to help prevent cancer and has educated lawmakers about the importance of quality and affordable cancer screening tests and treatment. The ACS is especially concerned with developing strategies to better serve the poor and people with little formal education, who historically have been disproportionately affected by cancer.

## March of Dimes

The March of Dimes was founded in 1938 by President Franklin D. Roosevelt (1882–1945) to help protect American children from polio. Besides supporting the research that produced the polio vaccine, the nonprofit organization has advocated for birth defects research and the fortification of food supplies with folic acid to prevent neural tube defects. It has also supported increasing access to quality prenatal care and the growth of neonatal intensive care units to help improve the chances of survival for babies born prematurely or with serious medical conditions.

The March of Dimes continues to partner with volunteers, scientific researchers, educators, and community outreach workers to help prevent birth defects. It funds genetic research; investigates the causes and treatment of premature birth; educates pregnant women; and provides health care services for women and children, such as immunizations, checkups, and treatment for childhood illnesses.

In the press release "'This Is the News We've Been Dreading': March of Dimes Reacts to Reports of Local Transmission of Zika Virus in Continental U.S." (July 29, 2016, http://www.marchofdimes.org/news/this-is-the-news-weve-been-dreading-march-of-dimes-reacts-to-reports-of-local-transmission-of-zika-virus-in-continental-us.aspx), the March of Dimes responds to reports of Zika virus transmission in Florida and the health risks for expectant mothers and their babies, which include microcephaly, a severe brain defect. The March of Dimes #ZAPzika campaign advises the public to use U.S. Environmental Protection Agency–registered repellant to keep mosquitoes away, use air conditioning and window screens to prevent mosquitoes from entering, remove still water, wear clothing to prevent bites, and use condoms to prevent sexual transmission of the virus.

# CHAPTER 5
# THE INCREASING COST OF HEALTH CARE

## HOW MUCH DOES HEALTH CARE COST?

American society places a high value on human life and generally wants—and expects—quality medical care. Quality care, however, comes with an increasingly high cost. In 1970 the United States spent 7.2% of its gross domestic product (GDP; the total market value of final goods and services produced within an economy in a given year) on health care. By 2014 health care expenditures reached 17.5% of the GDP. Table 5.1 shows the growth in health care expenditures, the growth in the GDP, and the annual percent change for select years between 1960 and 2014. Table 5.2 shows that the average annual percent change in health expenditures has decreased from a high of 13.1% between 1970 and 1980 to a low of 2.9% from 2012 to 2013 but subsequently increased 5.3% from 2013 to 2014.

For many years the consumer price index (CPI; a measure of the average change in prices paid by consumers) increased at a greater rate for medical care than for any other commodity. In 1990 the average annual increase in the overall CPI was 4.7%, whereas the average annual increase in the medical care index stood at 8.1%. (See Table 5.3.) In 2000 the average annual growth in the medical care index fell to 3.4%, but in 2005 it rose again to 4.4%, outpacing overall inflation, which was 2.5%. In 2012 the increase in the medical care index was 3.7%, still higher than overall inflation of 2.1%, and from June 2015 to June 2016 it was 3.2%. (See Table 5.4.) The medical care index has consistently outpaced the CPI in each decade.

The Centers for Medicare and Medicaid Services (CMS) projects that by 2025 the national health expenditure will be nearly $6 trillion, reaching 20.1% of the GDP, from 18.2% in 2017. (See Table 5.5.) (Because the numbers in Table 5.5 are projections, they may differ from the actual numbers presented in some other tables and figures that appear in this chapter.) In *National Health Expenditure Projections 2015–2025* (2016, https://www.cms.gov/Research-Statistics-Data-and-Systems/Statistics-Trends-and-Reports/NationalHealth ExpendData/Downloads/Proj2015.pdf), the CMS indicates that health spending is anticipated to increase at an average annual rate of 5.8% from 2015 to 2025.

Generally, projections are most accurate for the near future and less accurate for the distant future. For example, predictions for 2030 should be viewed more warily than predictions for 2018 because it is unlikely that the conditions on which the projections are based will remain the same. As a result, the CMS cautions that its projections should not be viewed as predictions for the future. Rather, they are intended to help policy makers evaluate the costs or savings of proposed legislative or regulatory changes.

### Total Health Care Spending

The CMS, along with the Centers for Disease Control and Prevention and the U.S. Government Accountability Office, maintain most of the nation's statistics on health care costs. The CMS projects that the United States will spend $3.5 trillion for health care in 2017, up from $2.8 trillion in 2012. (See Table 5.5.)

CMS forecasts that more than $1.5 trillion of the 2017 health care expenditures will come from private funds, including $364.6 billion in out-of-pocket payments and $1,149 billion in private health insurance), and the balance will be paid with public money. (See Table 5.6.) The 2016 per capita cost for health care (the average cost per individual if spending was divided equally among all people in the country) was $10,345, as reported by Sean P. Keehan et al. of the CMS in "National Health Expenditure Projections, 2015–25: Economy, Prices, and Aging Expected to Shape Spending and Enrollment" (*Health Affairs* vol. 35, no. 8, July 2016).

## WHO PAYS THE BILL?

In general, the public share of health care expenses is growing faster than the portions for which other payers are responsible. In 2016 the public share of the nation's total

**TABLE 5.1**

**Gross domestic product, national health expenditures, per capita amounts, and average annual percentage change, selected years 1960–2014**

[Data are compiled from various sources by the Centers for Medicare & Medicaid Services]

| Gross domestic product and national health expenditures | 1960 | 1970 | 1980 | 1990 | 2000 | 2009 | 2012 | 2013 | 2014 |
|---|---|---|---|---|---|---|---|---|---|
| | | | | | Amount, in billions | | | | |
| Gross domestic product (GDP) | $543 | $1,076 | $2,863 | $5,980 | $10,285 | $14,419 | $16,155 | $16,663 | $17,348 |
| | | | | | Deflator (2009 = 100.0) | | | | |
| Price deflator for GDP[a] | 17.5 | 22.8 | 44.5 | 66.8 | 81.9 | 100.0 | 105.2 | 106.9 | 108.7 |
| | | | | | Amount, in billions | | | | |
| National health expenditures | $27.2 | $74.6 | $255.3 | $721.4 | $1,369.7 | $2,496.4 | $2,799.0 | $2,879.9 | $3,031.3 |
| Health consumption expenditures | 24.7 | 67.0 | 235.5 | 674.1 | 1,286.4 | 2,357.5 | 2,645.8 | 2,727.4 | 2,877.4 |
| Personal health care | 23.3 | 63.1 | 217.0 | 615.3 | 1,162.0 | 2,115.9 | 2,371.8 | 2,441.3 | 2,563.6 |
| Administration and net cost of private health insurance | 1.1 | 2.6 | 12.1 | 38.7 | 81.3 | 167.5 | 197.9 | 209.5 | 234.8 |
| Public health | 0.4 | 1.4 | 6.4 | 20.0 | 43.0 | 74.1 | 76.0 | 76.6 | 79.0 |
| Investment[b] | 2.5 | 7.5 | 19.9 | 47.3 | 83.3 | 139.0 | 153.2 | 152.5 | 153.9 |
| | | | | | Deflator (2009 = 100.0) | | | | |
| Chain-weighted national health expenditure deflator[a] | — | — | — | — | — | 100.0 | 106.9 | 108.3 | 110.2 |
| | | | | | Per capita amount, in dollars | | | | |
| National health expenditures | $146 | $355 | $1,108 | $2,843 | $4,857 | $8,147 | $8,927 | $9,115 | 9,523 |
| Health consumption expenditures | 133 | 319 | 1,022 | 2,657 | 4,562 | 7,693 | 8,438 | 8,632 | 9,040 |
| Personal health care | 125 | 300 | 942 | 2,425 | 4,121 | 6,905 | 7,564 | 7,727 | 8,054 |
| Administration and net cost of private health insurance | 6 | 13 | 52 | 153 | 288 | 546 | 631 | 663 | 738 |
| Public health | 2 | 6 | 28 | 79 | 153 | 242 | 243 | 242 | 248 |
| Investment[b] | 13 | 36 | 86 | 187 | 295 | 453 | 489 | 483 | 483 |
| | | | | | Percent | | | | |
| National health expenditures as percent of GDP | 5.0 | 6.9 | 8.9 | 12.1 | 13.3 | 17.3 | 17.3 | 17.3 | 17.5 |
| | | | | | Percent distribution | | | | |
| National health expenditures | 100.0 | 100.0 | 100.0 | 100.0 | 100.0 | 100.0 | 100.0 | 100.0 | 100.0 |
| Health consumption expenditures | 90.8 | 89.9 | 92.2 | 93.4 | 93.9 | 94.4 | 94.5 | 94.7 | 94.9 |
| Personal health care | 85.5 | 84.6 | 85.0 | 85.3 | 84.8 | 84.8 | 84.7 | 84.8 | 84.6 |
| Administration and net cost of private health insurance | 3.9 | 3.5 | 4.7 | 5.4 | 5.9 | 6.7 | 7.1 | 7.3 | 7.7 |
| Public health | 1.4 | 1.8 | 2.5 | 2.8 | 3.1 | 3.0 | 2.7 | 2.7 | 2.6 |
| Investment[b] | 9.2 | 10.1 | 7.8 | 6.6 | 6.1 | 5.6 | 5.5 | 5.3 | 5.1 |
| | | | | | Average annual percent change from previous year shown | | | | |
| GDP | ... | 7.1 | 10.3 | 7.6 | 5.6 | 3.8 | 3.9 | 3.1 | 4.1 |
| National health expenditures | ... | 10.6 | 13.1 | 10.9 | 6.6 | 6.9 | 3.9 | 2.9 | 5.3 |
| Health consumption expenditures | ... | 10.5 | 13.4 | 11.1 | 6.7 | 7.0 | 3.9 | 3.1 | 5.5 |
| Personal health care | ... | 10.5 | 13.2 | 11.0 | 6.6 | 6.9 | 3.9 | 2.9 | 5.0 |
| Administration and net cost of private health insurance | ... | 9.4 | 16.4 | 12.4 | 7.7 | 8.4 | 5.7 | 5.8 | 12.1 |
| Public health | ... | 13.8 | 16.9 | 12.0 | 8.0 | 6.2 | 0.8 | 0.7 | 3.1 |
| Investment[b] | ... | 11.6 | 10.2 | 9.1 | 5.8 | 5.9 | 3.3 | −0.5 | 0.9 |
| National health expenditures, per capita | ... | 9.3 | 12.1 | 9.9 | 5.5 | 5.9 | 3.1 | 2.1 | 4.5 |
| Health consumption expenditures | ... | 9.1 | 12.3 | 10.0 | 5.6 | 6.0 | 3.1 | 2.3 | 4.7 |
| Personal health care | ... | 9.1 | 12.1 | 9.9 | 5.4 | 5.9 | 3.1 | 2.2 | 4.2 |
| Administration and net cost of private health insurance | ... | 8.0 | 14.9 | 11.4 | 6.5 | 7.4 | 4.9 | 5.1 | 11.3 |
| Public health | ... | 11.6 | 16.7 | 10.9 | 6.8 | 5.2 | 0.1 | −0.4 | 2.5 |
| Investment[b] | ... | 10.7 | 9.1 | 8.1 | 4.7 | 4.9 | 2.6 | −1.2 | 0.0 |

—Data not available.
. . .Category not applicable.
[a]Year 2009 = 100.
[b]Investment consists of research and structures and equipment.
Notes: Dollar amounts shown are in current dollars. Percents are calculated using unrounded data. Estimates may not add to totals because of rounding. Census resident-based population less armed forces overseas and population of outlying areas used to calculate per capita.

SOURCE: "Table 93. Gross Domestic Product, National Health Expenditures, per Capita Amounts, Percent Distribution, and Average Annual Percent Change: United States, Selected Years 1960–2014," in *Health, United States, 2015: With Special Feature on Racial and Ethnic Health Disparities*, U.S. Department of Health and Human Services, Centers for Disease Control and Prevention, National Center for Health Statistics, May 2016, http://www.cdc.gov/nchs/data/hus/hus15.pdf (accessed July 29, 2016)

health care bill was 53.8%, including Medicare (22.5%), Medicaid (18.2%), other health insurance programs (4.1%), and other third-party payers (9%). (See Table 5.7.) It is projected to rise to 55.8% by 2025. In 2016 private health

TABLE 5.2

## National health expenditures, average annual percentage change and percentage distribution by type of expenditure, 1960–2014

[Data are compiled from various sources by the Centers for Medicare & Medicaid Services]

| Type of national health expenditure | 1960 | 1970 | 1980 | 1990 | 2000 | 2012 | 2013 | 2014 |
|---|---|---|---|---|---|---|---|---|
| | Amount, in billions | | | | | | | |
| National health expenditures | $27.2 | $74.6 | $255.3 | $721.4 | $1,369.7 | $2,799.0 | $2,879.9 | $3,031.3 |
| Health consumption expenditures | 24.7 | 67.0 | 235.5 | 674.1 | 1,286.4 | 2,645.8 | 2,727.4 | 2,877.4 |
| Personal health care | 23.3 | 63.1 | 217.0 | 615.3 | 1,162.0 | 2,371.8 | 2,441.3 | 2,563.6 |
| Hospital care | 9.0 | 27.2 | 100.5 | 250.4 | 415.5 | 902.7 | 933.9 | 971.8 |
| Professional services | 7.9 | 19.8 | 64.5 | 207.3 | 387.4 | 749.5 | 767.5 | 801.6 |
| Physician and clinical services | 5.6 | 14.3 | 47.7 | 158.4 | 288.7 | 563.0 | 576.8 | 603.7 |
| Other professional services | 0.4 | 0.7 | 3.5 | 17.3 | 36.6 | 77.6 | 80.3 | 84.4 |
| Dental services | 2.0 | 4.7 | 13.3 | 31.6 | 62.1 | 108.9 | 110.4 | 113.5 |
| Other health, residential, and personal care | 0.4 | 1.3 | 8.4 | 23.8 | 63.9 | 137.9 | 144.5 | 150.4 |
| Home health care[a] | 0.1 | 0.2 | 2.4 | 12.5 | 32.3 | 76.9 | 79.4 | 83.2 |
| Nursing care facilities and continuing care retirement communities[a] | 0.8 | 4.0 | 15.3 | 44.7 | 85.0 | 148.3 | 150.2 | 155.6 |
| Retail outlet sales of medical products | 5.0 | 10.6 | 25.9 | 76.5 | 177.8 | 356.5 | 365.8 | 401.0 |
| Prescription drugs | 2.7 | 5.5 | 12.0 | 40.3 | 121.0 | 259.1 | 265.3 | 297.7 |
| Durable medical equipment | 0.7 | 1.7 | 4.1 | 13.8 | 25.2 | 43.7 | 44.9 | 46.4 |
| Other nondurable medical products | 1.6 | 3.3 | 9.8 | 22.4 | 31.6 | 53.7 | 55.6 | 56.9 |
| Government administration[b] | 0.1 | 0.7 | 2.8 | 7.2 | 17.1 | 33.5 | 36.3 | 40.2 |
| Net cost of health insurance[c] | 1.0 | 1.9 | 9.3 | 31.6 | 64.2 | 164.4 | 173.2 | 194.6 |
| Government public health activities[d] | 0.4 | 1.4 | 6.4 | 20.0 | 43.1 | 76.0 | 76.6 | 79.0 |
| Investment | 2.5 | 7.5 | 19.9 | 47.3 | 83.3 | 153.2 | 152.5 | 153.9 |
| Research[e] | 0.7 | 2.0 | 5.4 | 12.7 | 25.5 | 48.4 | 46.5 | 45.5 |
| Structures and equipment | 1.8 | 5.6 | 14.4 | 34.6 | 57.8 | 104.8 | 106.0 | 108.3 |
| | Average annual percent change from previous year shown | | | | | | | |
| National health expenditures | — | 10.6 | 13.1 | 10.9 | 6.6 | 6.1 | 2.9 | 5.3 |
| Health consumption expenditures | — | 10.5 | 13.4 | 11.1 | 6.7 | 6.2 | 3.1 | 5.5 |
| Personal health care | — | 10.5 | 13.2 | 11.0 | 6.6 | 6.1 | 2.9 | 5.0 |
| Hospital care | — | 11.7 | 14.0 | 9.6 | 5.2 | 6.7 | 3.5 | 4.1 |
| Professional services | — | 9.6 | 12.6 | 12.4 | 6.5 | 5.7 | 2.4 | 4.4 |
| Physician and clinical services | — | 9.9 | 12.8 | 12.7 | 6.2 | 5.7 | 2.5 | 4.6 |
| Other professional services | — | 6.3 | 17.0 | 17.4 | 7.8 | 6.4 | 3.5 | 5.2 |
| Dental services | — | 9.0 | 11.0 | 9.0 | 7.0 | 4.8 | 1.5 | 2.8 |
| Other health, residential, and personal care | — | 11.5 | 20.5 | 11.0 | 10.4 | 6.6 | 4.7 | 4.1 |
| Home health care[a] | — | 14.5 | 26.9 | 18.1 | 9.9 | 7.5 | 3.3 | 4.8 |
| Nursing care facilities and continuing care retirement communities[a] | — | 17.4 | 14.2 | 11.4 | 6.6 | 4.7 | 1.3 | 3.6 |
| Retail outlet sales of medical products | — | 7.7 | 9.4 | 11.4 | 8.8 | 6.0 | 2.6 | 9.6 |
| Prescription drugs | — | 7.5 | 8.2 | 12.8 | 11.6 | 6.5 | 2.4 | 12.2 |
| Durable medical equipment | — | 9.0 | 8.8 | 13.0 | 6.2 | 4.7 | 2.8 | 3.2 |
| Other nondurable medical products | — | 7.4 | 11.4 | 8.6 | 3.5 | 4.5 | 3.5 | 2.4 |
| Government administration[b] | — | 30.0 | 14.1 | 10.0 | 9.0 | 5.8 | 8.5 | 10.7 |
| Net cost of health insurance[c] | — | 6.4 | 17.2 | 13.0 | 7.4 | 8.1 | 5.3 | 12.4 |
| Government public health activities[d] | — | 13.8 | 16.9 | 12.0 | 8.0 | 4.9 | 0.7 | 3.1 |
| Investment | — | 11.6 | 10.2 | 9.1 | 5.8 | 5.2 | −0.5 | 0.9 |
| Research[e] | — | 10.9 | 10.8 | 8.9 | 7.2 | 5.5 | −4.1 | −2.0 |
| Structures and equipment | — | 11.9 | 10.0 | 9.2 | 5.3 | 5.1 | 1.2 | 2.2 |
| | Percent distribution | | | | | | | |
| National health expenditures | 100.0 | 100.0 | 100.0 | 100.0 | 100.0 | 100.0 | 100.0 | 100.0 |
| Health consumption expenditures | 90.8 | 89.9 | 92.2 | 93.4 | 93.9 | 94.5 | 94.7 | 94.9 |
| Personal health care | 85.5 | 84.6 | 85.0 | 85.3 | 84.8 | 84.7 | 84.8 | 84.6 |
| Hospital care | 33.0 | 36.4 | 39.4 | 34.7 | 30.3 | 32.3 | 32.4 | 32.1 |
| Professional services | 29.1 | 26.5 | 25.3 | 28.7 | 28.3 | 26.8 | 26.7 | 26.4 |
| Physician and clinical services | 20.4 | 19.2 | 18.7 | 22.0 | 21.1 | 20.1 | 20.0 | 19.9 |
| Other professional services | 1.4 | 1.0 | 1.4 | 2.4 | 2.7 | 2.8 | 2.8 | 2.8 |
| Dental services | 7.3 | 6.3 | 5.2 | 4.4 | 4.5 | 3.9 | 3.8 | 3.7 |
| Other health, residential, and personal care | 1.6 | 1.7 | 3.3 | 3.3 | 4.7 | 4.9 | 5.0 | 5.0 |
| Home health care[a] | | | | | | | | |
| Nursing care facilities and continuing care | 0.2 | 0.3 | 0.9 | 1.7 | 2.4 | 2.7 | 2.8 | 2.7 |
| retirement communities[a] | 3.0 | 5.4 | 6.0 | 6.2 | 6.2 | 5.3 | 5.2 | 5.1 |
| Retail outlet sales of medical products | 18.5 | 14.2 | 10.1 | 10.6 | 13.0 | 12.7 | 12.7 | 13.2 |
| Prescription drugs | 9.8 | 7.4 | 4.7 | 5.6 | 8.8 | 9.3 | 9.2 | 9.8 |
| Durable medical equipment | 2.7 | 2.3 | 1.6 | 1.9 | 1.8 | 1.6 | 1.6 | 1.5 |
| Other nondurable medical products | 6.0 | 4.5 | 3.8 | 3.1 | 2.3 | 1.9 | 1.9 | 1.9 |
| Government administration[b] | 0.2 | 1.0 | 1.1 | 1.0 | 1.2 | 1.2 | 1.3 | 1.3 |
| Net cost of health insurance[c] | 3.7 | 2.5 | 3.6 | 4.4 | 4.7 | 5.9 | 6.0 | 6.4 |
| Government public health activities[d] | 1.4 | 1.8 | 2.5 | 2.8 | 3.1 | 2.7 | 2.7 | 2.6 |
| Investment | 9.2 | 10.1 | 7.8 | 6.6 | 6.1 | 5.5 | 5.3 | 5.1 |
| Research[e] | 2.6 | 2.6 | 2.1 | 1.8 | 1.9 | 1.7 | 1.6 | 1.5 |
| Structures and equipment | 6.7 | 7.5 | 5.7 | 4.8 | 4.2 | 3.7 | 3.7 | 3.6 |

**TABLE 5.2**

**National health expenditures, average annual percentage change and percentage distribution by type of expenditure, 1960–2014** [CONTINUED]

[Data are compiled from various sources by the Centers for Medicare & Medicaid Services]

| Type of national health expenditure | 1960 | 1970 | 1980 | 1990 | 2000 | 2012 | 2013 | 2014 |
|---|---|---|---|---|---|---|---|---|
| | | | | | Percent distribution | | | |
| Personal health care | 100.0 | 100.0 | 100.0 | 100.0 | 100.0 | 100.0 | 100.0 | 100.0 |
| Hospital care | 38.6 | 43.1 | 46.3 | 40.7 | 35.8 | 38.1 | 38.3 | 37.9 |
| Professional services | 34.1 | 31.3 | 29.7 | 33.7 | 33.3 | 31.6 | 31.4 | 31.3 |
| Physician and clinical services | 23.9 | 22.7 | 22.0 | 25.7 | 24.8 | 23.7 | 23.6 | 23.5 |
| Other professional services | 1.7 | 1.2 | 1.6 | 2.8 | 3.2 | 3.3 | 3.3 | 3.3 |
| Dental services | 8.5 | 7.5 | 6.1 | 5.1 | 5.3 | 4.6 | 4.5 | 4.4 |
| Other health, residential, and personal care | 1.9 | 2.1 | 3.9 | 3.9 | 5.5 | 5.8 | 5.9 | 5.9 |
| Home health care[a] | 0.2 | 0.3 | 1.1 | 2.0 | 2.8 | 3.2 | 3.3 | 3.2 |
| Nursing care facilities and continuing care retirement communities[a] | 3.5 | 6.4 | 7.0 | 7.3 | 7.3 | 6.3 | 6.2 | 6.1 |
| Retail outlet sales of medical products | 21.7 | 16.8 | 11.9 | 12.4 | 15.3 | 15.0 | 15.0 | 15.6 |
| Prescription drugs | 11.5 | 8.7 | 5.6 | 6.5 | 10.4 | 10.9 | 10.9 | 11.6 |
| Durable medical equipment | 3.2 | 2.8 | 1.9 | 2.2 | 2.2 | 1.8 | 1.8 | 1.8 |
| Other nondurable medical products | 7.0 | 5.3 | 4.5 | 3.6 | 2.7 | 2.3 | 2.3 | 2.2 |

—Category not applicable.

[a]Includes expenditures for care in freestanding facilities only. Additional services of this type are provided in hospital-based facilities and are considered hospital care.

[b]Includes all administrative costs (federal and state and local employees' salaries; contracted employees, including fiscal intermediaries; rent and building costs; computer systems and programs; other materials and supplies; and other miscellaneous expenses) associated with insuring individuals enrolled in the following health insurance programs: Medicare, Medicaid, Children's Health Insurance Program, Department of Defense, Department of Veterans Affairs, Indian Health Service, workers' compensation, maternal and child health, vocational rehabilitation, Substance Abuse and Mental Health Services Administration, and other federal programs.

[c]Net cost of health insurance is calculated as the difference between calendar year incurred premiums earned and benefits incurred for private health insurance. This includes administrative costs, and in some cases additions to reserves, rate credits and dividends, premium taxes, and net underwriting gains or losses. Also included in this category is the difference between premiums earned and benefits incurred for the private health insurance companies that insure the enrollees of the following programs: Medicare, Medicaid, Children's Health Insurance Program, and workers' compensation (health portion only).

[d]Includes health care services delivered by government public health agencies.

[e]Research and development expenditures of drug companies and other manufacturers and providers of medical equipment and supplies are excluded. These are included in the expenditure class in which the product falls because such expenditures are covered by the payment received for that product.

Notes: Percents and average annual percent change are calculated using unrounded data.

SOURCE: "Table 94. National Health Expenditures, Average Annual Percent Change, and Percent Distribution, by Type of Expenditure: United States, Selected Years 1960–2014," in *Health, United States, 2015: With Special Feature on Racial and Ethnic Health Disparities*, U.S. Department of Health and Human Services, Centers for Disease Control and Prevention, National Center for Health Statistics, May 2016, http://www.cdc.gov/nchs/data/hus/hus15.pdf (accessed July 29, 2016)

insurance, the major nongovernmental payer of health care costs, paid 33.8% of all health expenditures. The share of health care spending from private, out-of-pocket (paid by the patient) funds declined to 12.4% in 2016 from 13.9% in 2009.

## WHY HAVE HEALTH CARE COSTS AND SPENDING INCREASED?

The increase in the cost of medical care is challenging to analyze because the methods and quality of health care change constantly and as a result are often not comparable. A hospital stay in 1970 did not include the same services offered in 2016, in part because many technologies or therapies were not available at that time. Furthermore, the care received in a physician's office in 2017 is not comparable to that received a generation ago. One contributing factor to the rising cost of health care is the increase in biomedical technology, much of which is now available for use outside of a hospital.

Other factors also contribute to the increase in health care costs. These include population growth, high salaries for physicians and some other health care workers, and the expense of malpractice insurance. Escalating malpractice insurance costs and professional liability premiums have prompted some physicians and

other health care practitioners to refrain from performing high-risk procedures that increase their vulnerability or have caused them to relocate to states where malpractice premiums are lower. Furthermore, to protect themselves from malpractice suits, many health care practitioners routinely order diagnostic tests and prescribe treatments that may not be medically necessary and do not serve to improve their patients' health. This practice is known as defensive medicine, and although its precise contribution to rising health care costs is difficult to gauge, industry observers agree that it is a significant factor.

In *Cracking the Code on Health Care Costs* (January 2014, http://web1.millercenter.org/commissions/healthcare/HealthcareCommission-Report.pdf), Raymond Scheppach et al. attribute high health care costs to nine key factors:

- U.S. physicians, hospitals, facilities and drug costs are the highest in the world.

- Americans make use of more expensive technologies and procedures. For example, magnetic resonance imaging (MRI) is used in the United States twice as often as it is in most other countries.

- Fragmented and uncoordinated care results in duplicative and unnecessary treatment and errors.

TABLE 5.3

**Consumer price index and average annual percentage change for all items, selected items, and medical care costs, selected years 1960–2012**

[Data are based on reporting by samples of providers and other retail outlets]

| Items and medical care components | 1960 | 1970 | 1980 | 1990 | 1995 | 2000 | 2005 | 2011 | 2012 |
|---|---|---|---|---|---|---|---|---|---|
| | | | | Consumer Price Index (CPI) | | | | | |
| All items | 29.6 | 38.8 | 82.4 | 130.7 | 152.4 | 172.2 | 195.3 | 224.9 | 229.6 |
| All items less medical care | 30.2 | 39.2 | 82.8 | 128.8 | 148.6 | 167.3 | 188.7 | 216.3 | 220.6 |
| Services | 24.1 | 35.0 | 77.9 | 139.2 | 168.7 | 195.3 | 230.1 | 265.8 | 271.4 |
| Food | 30.0 | 39.2 | 86.8 | 132.4 | 148.4 | 167.8 | 190.7 | 227.8 | 233.8 |
| Apparel | 45.7 | 59.2 | 90.9 | 124.1 | 132.0 | 129.6 | 119.5 | 122.1 | 126.3 |
| Housing | — | 36.4 | 81.1 | 128.5 | 148.5 | 169.6 | 195.7 | 219.1 | 222.7 |
| Energy | 22.4 | 25.5 | 86.0 | 102.1 | 105.2 | 124.6 | 177.1 | 243.9 | 246.1 |
| Medical care | 22.3 | 34.0 | 74.9 | 162.8 | 220.5 | 260.8 | 323.2 | 400.3 | 414.9 |
| **Components of medical care** | | | | | | | | | |
| Medical care services | 19.5 | 32.3 | 74.8 | 162.7 | 224.2 | 266.0 | 336.7 | 423.8 | 440.3 |
| Professional services | — | 37.0 | 77.9 | 156.1 | 201.0 | 237.7 | 281.7 | 335.7 | 342.0 |
| Physician services | 21.9 | 34.5 | 76.5 | 160.8 | 208.8 | 244.7 | 287.5 | 340.3 | 347.3 |
| Dental services | 27.0 | 39.2 | 78.9 | 155.8 | 206.8 | 258.5 | 324.0 | 408.0 | 417.5 |
| Eyeglasses and eye care[a] | — | — | — | 117.3 | 137.0 | 149.7 | 163.2 | 178.3 | 179.9 |
| Services by other medical professionals[a] | — | — | — | 120.2 | 143.9 | 161.9 | 186.8 | 217.4 | 219.6 |
| Hospital and related services | — | — | 69.2 | 178.0 | 257.8 | 317.3 | 439.9 | 641.5 | 672.1 |
| Hospital services[b] | — | — | — | — | — | 115.9 | 161.6 | 241.2 | 253.6 |
| Inpatient hospital services[b, c] | — | — | — | — | — | 113.8 | 156.6 | 236.6 | 248.8 |
| Outpatient hospital services[a, c] | — | — | — | 138.7 | 204.6 | 263.8 | 373.0 | 546.9 | 574.0 |
| Hospital rooms | 9.3 | 23.6 | 68.0 | 175.4 | 251.2 | — | — | — | — |
| Other inpatient services[a] | — | — | — | 142.7 | 206.8 | — | — | — | — |
| Nursing homes and adult day care[b] | — | — | — | — | — | 117.0 | 145.0 | 182.2 | 188.8 |
| Health insurance[d] | — | — | — | — | — | — | — | 105.5 | 118.3 |
| Medical care commodities | 46.9 | 46.5 | 75.4 | 163.4 | 204.5 | 238.1 | 276.0 | 324.1 | 333.6 |
| Medicinal drugs[e] | — | — | — | — | — | — | — | 105.5 | 108.6 |
| Prescription drugs[f] | 54.0 | 47.4 | 72.5 | 181.7 | 235.0 | 285.4 | 349.0 | 425.0 | 440.1 |
| Nonprescription drugs[e] | — | — | — | — | — | — | — | 98.6 | 99.3 |
| Medical equipment and supplies[e] | — | — | — | — | — | — | — | 99.3 | 100.6 |
| Nonprescription drugs and medical supplies[a, g] | — | — | — | 120.6 | 140.5 | 149.5 | 151.7 | — | — |
| Internal and respiratory over-the-counter drugs[h] | — | 42.3 | 74.9 | 145.9 | 167.0 | 176.9 | 179.7 | — | — |
| Nonprescription medical equipment and supplies[i] | — | — | 79.2 | 138.0 | 166.3 | 178.1 | 180.6 | — | — |
| | | | | Average annual percent change from previous year shown | | | | | |
| All items | ... | 2.7 | 7.8 | 4.7 | 3.1 | 2.5 | 2.5 | 3.2 | 2.1 |
| All items less medical care | ... | 2.6 | 7.8 | 4.5 | 2.9 | 2.4 | 2.4 | 3.2 | 2.0 |
| Services | ... | 3.8 | 8.3 | 6.0 | 3.9 | 3.0 | 3.3 | 1.7 | 2.1 |
| Food | ... | 2.7 | 8.3 | 4.3 | 2.3 | 2.5 | 2.6 | 3.7 | 2.6 |
| Apparel | ... | 2.6 | 4.4 | 3.2 | 1.2 | −0.4 | −1.6 | 2.2 | 3.4 |
| Housing | ... | — | 8.3 | 4.7 | 2.9 | 2.7 | 2.9 | 1.3 | 1.6 |
| Energy | ... | 1.3 | 12.9 | 1.7 | 0.6 | 3.4 | 7.3 | 15.4 | 0.9 |
| Medical care | ... | 4.3 | 8.2 | 8.1 | 6.3 | 3.4 | 4.4 | 3.0 | 3.7 |
| **Components of medical care** | | | | | | | | | |
| Medical care services | ... | 5.2 | 8.8 | 8.1 | 6.6 | 3.5 | 4.8 | 3.1 | 3.9 |
| Professional services | ... | — | 7.7 | 7.2 | 5.2 | 3.4 | 3.5 | 2.3 | 1.9 |
| Physician services | ... | 4.6 | 8.3 | 7.7 | 5.4 | 3.2 | 3.3 | 2.7 | 2.1 |
| Dental services | ... | 3.8 | 7.2 | 7.0 | 5.8 | 4.6 | 4.6 | 2.3 | 2.3 |
| Eyeglasses and eye care[a] | ... | — | — | — | 3.2 | 1.8 | 1.7 | 0.9 | 0.9 |
| Services by other medical professionals[a] | ... | — | — | — | 3.7 | 2.4 | 2.9 | 1.4 | 1.0 |
| Hospital and related services | ... | — | — | 9.9 | 7.7 | 4.2 | 6.8 | 5.6 | 4.8 |
| Hospital services[b] | ... | — | — | — | — | — | 6.9 | 6.2 | 5.1 |
| Inpatient hospital services[b, c] | ... | — | — | — | — | — | 6.6 | 6.8 | 5.2 |
| Outpatient hospital services[a, c] | ... | — | — | — | 8.1 | 5.2 | 7.2 | 5.1 | 5.0 |
| Hospital rooms | ... | 9.8 | 11.2 | 9.9 | 7.4 | — | — | — | — |
| Other inpatient services[a] | ... | — | — | — | 7.7 | — | — | — | — |
| Nursing homes and adult day care[b] | ... | — | — | — | — | — | 4.4 | 2.9 | 3.6 |
| Health insurance[d] | ... | — | — | — | — | — | — | −1.1 | 12.1 |
| Medical care commodities | ... | −0.1 | 5.0 | 8.0 | 4.6 | 3.1 | 3.0 | 3.0 | 2.9 |
| Medicinal drugs[e] | ... | — | — | — | — | — | — | 3.1 | 3.0 |
| Prescription drugs[f] | ... | −1.3 | 4.3 | 9.6 | 5.3 | 4.0 | 4.1 | 4.2 | 3.6 |
| Nonprescription drugs[e] | ... | — | — | — | — | — | — | −1.3 | 0.7 |
| Medical equipment and supplies[e] | ... | — | — | — | — | — | — | 0.3 | 1.2 |
| Nonprescription drugs and medical supplies[a, g] | ... | — | — | — | 3.1 | 1.2 | 0.3 | — | — |
| Internal and respiratory over-the-counter drugs[h] | ... | — | 5.9 | 6.9 | 2.7 | 1.2 | 0.3 | — | — |
| Nonprescription medical equipment and supplies[i] | ... | — | — | 5.7 | 3.8 | 1.4 | 0.3 | — | — |

- Americans mistakenly believe that expensive care is quality care, and they often do not weigh the cost of care when making health care purchases or decisions.

TABLE 5.3

**Consumer price index and average annual percentage change for all items, selected items, and medical care costs, selected years 1960–2012** [CONTINUED]

[Data are based on reporting by samples of providers and other retail outlets]

—Data not available.
. . .Category not applicable.
[a]December 1986 = 100.
[b]December 1996 = 100.
[c]Special index based on a substantially smaller sample.
[d]December 2005 = 100.
[e]December 2009 = 100.
[f]Prior to 2006, this category included medical supplies.
[g]Starting with 2010 updates, this index series will no longer be published.
[h]Starting with 2010 updates, replaced by the series, nonprescription drugs.
[i]Starting with 2010 updates, replaced by the series, Medical equipment and supplies.
Notes: CPI for all urban consumers (CPI-U) U.S. city average, detailed expenditure categories. 1982–1984 = 100, except where noted. Data are not seasonally adjusted. Data for additional years are available.

SOURCE: "Table 113. Consumer Price Index and Average Annual Percent Change for All Items, Selected Items, and Medical Care Components: United States, Selected Years 1960–2012," in *Health, United States, 2013: With Special Feature on Prescription Drugs*, U.S. Department of Health and Human Services, Centers for Disease Control and Prevention, National Center for Health Statistics, May 2014, http://www.cdc.gov/nchs/data/hus/hus13.pdf (accessed August 5, 2016)

---

**TABLE 5.4**

**Average percentage changes in Consumer Price Index for U.S. cities, 2015–16**

| | Seasonally adjusted changes from preceding month | | | | | | | Unadjusted 12-months ended June 2016 |
|---|---|---|---|---|---|---|---|---|
| | Dec. 2015 | Jan. 2016 | Feb. 2016 | Mar. 2016 | Apr. 2016 | May 2016 | June 2016 | |
| **All items** | −0.1 | 0.0 | −0.2 | 0.1 | 0.4 | 0.2 | 0.2 | 1.0 |
| **Food** | −0.2 | 0.0 | 0.2 | −0.2 | 0.2 | −0.2 | −0.1 | 0.3 |
| Food at home | −0.4 | −0.2 | 0.2 | −0.5 | 0.1 | −0.5 | −0.3 | −1.3 |
| Food away from home* | 0.1 | 0.3 | 0.1 | 0.2 | 0.2 | 0.2 | 0.2 | 2.6 |
| **Energy** | −2.8 | −2.8 | −6.0 | 0.9 | 3.4 | 1.2 | 1.3 | −9.4 |
| Energy commodities | −4.8 | −4.8 | −12.5 | 1.9 | 7.8 | 2.4 | 3.3 | −15.3 |
| Gasoline (all types) | −4.8 | −4.8 | −13.0 | 2.2 | 8.1 | 2.3 | 3.3 | −15.4 |
| Fuel oil* | −7.8 | −6.5 | −2.9 | 1.7 | 1.9 | 6.2 | 3.3 | −19.6 |
| **Energy services** | −0.7 | −0.7 | 0.1 | 0.2 | −0.1 | 0.2 | −0.5 | −2.5 |
| Electricity | −0.4 | −0.7 | −0.2 | 0.4 | −0.3 | −0.2 | −0.5 | −1.8 |
| Utility (piped) gas service | −1.9 | −0.6 | 1.0 | −0.7 | 0.6 | 1.7 | −0.4 | −5.0 |
| **All items less food and energy** | 0.2 | 0.3 | 0.3 | 0.1 | 0.2 | 0.2 | 0.2 | 2.3 |
| Commodities less food and energy commodities | −0.1 | 0.2 | 0.3 | −0.2 | −0.1 | −0.2 | −0.2 | −0.6 |
| New vehicles | 0.0 | 0.3 | 0.2 | 0.0 | −0.3 | −0.1 | −0.2 | −0.4 |
| Used cars and trucks | 0.2 | 0.1 | 0.2 | −0.1 | −0.3 | −1.3 | −1.1 | −3.1 |
| Apparel | −0.2 | 0.6 | 1.6 | −1.1 | −0.3 | 0.8 | −0.4 | 0.4 |
| Medical care commodities | 0.1 | 0.4 | 0.6 | 0.3 | 0.5 | −0.2 | 1.1 | 3.2 |
| **Services less energy services** | 0.2 | 0.3 | 0.3 | 0.2 | 0.3 | 0.3 | 0.3 | 3.2 |
| Shelter | 0.2 | 0.3 | 0.3 | 0.2 | 0.3 | 0.4 | 0.3 | 3.5 |
| Transportation services | 0.3 | 0.4 | 0.2 | 0.2 | 0.7 | 0.3 | 0.3 | 3.0 |
| Medical care services | 0.1 | 0.5 | 0.5 | 0.1 | 0.3 | 0.5 | 0.2 | 3.8 |

*Not seasonally adjusted.

SOURCE: "Table A. Percent Change in CPI for All Urban Consumers (CPI-U): U.S. City Average," in *Consumer Price Index–June 2016*, U.S. Bureau of Labor Statistics, July 15, 2016, http://www.bls.gov/news.release/pdf/cpi.pdf (accessed August 5, 2016)

---

- Fee-for-service payment, which reimburses hospitals and physicians for every service they provide, often incentivizes providers to maximize the volume and cost of services.

- Fragmented and unnecessarily complicated insurance and billing processes cost the U.S. health care system billions of dollars each year.

- Unhealthy lifestyles and behaviors cause or contribute to many chronic illnesses (such as heart disease, cancer, and diabetes) that are costly to treat.

- Americans' end-of-life care is expensive, and unnecessary procedures and repeated hospitalizations do not benefit patients or the health care system.

# TABLE 5.5

## National health expenditures and annual percentage change, 2009–25

| Item | 2009 | 2010 | 2011 | 2012 | 2013 | 2014 | 2015 | 2016 | 2017 | 2018 | 2019 | 2020 | 2021 | 2022 | 2023 | 2024 | 2025 |
|---|---|---|---|---|---|---|---|---|---|---|---|---|---|---|---|---|---|
| | | | | | | | | | Projected | | | | | | | | |
| **Amount in billions** | | | | | | | | | | | | | | | | | |
| National health expenditures | $2,496.4 | $2,595.7 | $2,696.6 | $2,799.0 | $2,879.9 | $3,031.3 | $3,197.2 | $3,350.7 | $3,521.6 | $3,731.4 | $3,958.6 | $4,198.3 | $4,457.5 | $4,732.8 | $5,022.0 | $5,321.7 | $5,631.0 |
| Private health insurance—national health expenditures | 832.7 | 863.1 | 902.5 | 934.1 | 949.2 | 991.0 | 1,042.0 | 1,092.7 | 1,149.0 | 1,217.0 | 1,286.3 | 1,350.1 | 1,425.4 | 1,505.1 | 1,587.2 | 1,671.1 | 1,756.2 |
| Private health insurance—personal health care | 734.6 | 754.8 | 790.6 | 822.0 | 834.6 | 868.8 | 913.3 | 957.7 | 1,007.0 | 1,066.7 | 1,127.4 | 1,183.4 | 1,249.3 | 1,319.1 | 1,391.1 | 1,464.7 | 1,539.3 |
| Gross domestic product[a] | 14,418.7 | 14,964.4 | 15,517.9 | 16,155.3 | 16,663.2 | 17,348.1 | 17,947.0 | 18,521.3 | 19,317.7 | 20,292.8 | 21,348.0 | 22,415.4 | 23,513.8 | 24,595.4 | 25,677.6 | 26,807.4 | 27,987.0 |
| Personal income | 12,094.8 | 12,477.1 | 13,254.5 | 13,915.1 | 14,068.4 | 14,694.2 | 15,350.7 | 16,053.1 | 16,795.2 | 17,662.0 | 18,642.3 | 19,622.8 | 20,644.3 | 21,669.5 | 22,709.4 | 23,784.4 | 24,909.8 |
| **Level** | | | | | | | | | | | | | | | | | |
| Gross Domestic Product Implicit Price Deflator, chain weighted 2009 base year | 100.0 | 101.2 | 103.3 | 105.2 | 106.9 | 108.7 | 109.8 | 111.3 | 113.5 | 116.1 | 118.7 | 121.3 | 123.9 | 126.7 | 129.4 | 132.3 | 135.2 |
| Consumer Price Index (CPI-U)—1982–1984 base | 214.5 | 218.1 | 224.9 | 229.6 | 233.0 | 236.7 | 237.0 | 240.1 | 245.6 | 252.0 | 258.6 | 265.3 | 272.2 | 279.3 | 286.5 | 294.0 | 301.6 |
| CMS Personal Health Care Price Index, chain weighted 2009 base year | 100.0 | 102.7 | 104.8 | 106.8 | 108.4 | 109.9 | 110.8 | 112.4 | 114.9 | 117.8 | 120.9 | 124.1 | 127.4 | 130.8 | 134.5 | 138.3 | 142.4 |
| **Millions** | | | | | | | | | | | | | | | | | |
| U.S. population[b] | 306 | 309 | 311 | 314 | 316 | 318 | 321 | 324 | 327 | 330 | 333 | 336 | 339 | 342 | 345 | 348 | 351 |
| Population age 65 years and older | 39 | 40 | 41 | 42 | 44 | 45 | 47 | 48 | 50 | 51 | 53 | 55 | 57 | 58 | 60 | 62 | 64 |
| Population age less than 65 years | 267 | 269 | 271 | 271 | 272 | 273 | 274 | 276 | 277 | 279 | 280 | 281 | 283 | 284 | 285 | 286 | 287 |
| **Average annual percent change from previous year shown** | | | | | | | | | | | | | | | | | |
| National health expenditures | — | 4.0% | 3.9% | 3.8% | 2.9% | 5.3% | 5.5% | 4.8% | 5.1% | 6.0% | 6.1% | 6.1% | 6.2% | 6.2% | 6.1% | 6.0% | 5.8% |
| Private health insurance—national health expenditures | — | 3.6 | 4.6 | 3.5 | 1.6 | 4.4 | 5.1 | 4.9 | 5.1 | 5.9 | 5.7 | 5.0 | 5.6 | 5.6 | 5.5 | 5.3 | 5.1 |
| Private health insurance—personal health care | — | 2.8 | 4.7 | 4.0 | 1.5 | 4.1 | 5.1 | 4.9 | 5.1 | 5.9 | 5.7 | 5.0 | 5.6 | 5.6 | 5.5 | 5.3 | 5.1 |
| Gross domestic product | — | 3.8 | 3.7 | 4.1 | 3.1 | 4.1 | 3.5 | 3.2 | 4.3 | 5.0 | 5.2 | 5.0 | 4.9 | 4.6 | 4.4 | 4.4 | 4.4 |
| Personal income | — | 3.2 | 6.2 | 5.0 | 1.1 | 4.4 | 4.5 | 4.6 | 4.6 | 5.2 | 5.6 | 5.3 | 5.2 | 5.0 | 4.8 | 4.7 | 4.7 |
| Gross Domestic Product Implicit Price Deflator, chain weighted 2009 base year | — | 1.2 | 2.1 | 1.8 | 1.6 | 1.6 | 1.0 | 1.4 | 2.0 | 2.2 | 2.2 | 2.2 | 2.2 | 2.2 | 2.2 | 2.2 | 2.2 |
| Consumer Price Index (CPI-U)—1982–1984 base | — | 1.6 | 3.2 | 2.1 | 1.5 | 1.6 | 0.1 | 1.3 | 2.3 | 2.6 | 2.6 | 2.6 | 2.6 | 2.6 | 2.6 | 2.6 | 2.6 |
| CMS Personal Health Care Price Index | — | 2.7 | 2.1 | 1.8 | 1.5 | 1.4 | 0.8 | 1.5 | 2.2 | 2.6 | 2.6 | 2.6 | 2.7 | 2.7 | 2.8 | 2.9 | 2.9 |
| U.S. Population[a] | — | 0.8 | 0.7 | 0.8 | 0.8 | 0.7 | 0.8 | 0.9 | 0.9 | 0.9 | 0.9 | 0.9 | 0.9 | 0.9 | 0.9 | 0.9 | 0.8 |
| Population age 65 years and older | — | 2.1 | 1.7 | 4.3 | 3.6 | 3.2 | 3.1 | 3.2 | 3.3 | 3.3 | 3.3 | 3.3 | 3.3 | 3.3 | 3.1 | 3.0 | 2.9 |
| Population age less than 65 years | — | 0.6 | 0.6 | 0.2 | 0.3 | 0.4 | 0.5 | 0.5 | 0.5 | 0.5 | 0.5 | 0.5 | 0.5 | 0.4 | 0.4 | 0.4 | 0.4 |
| **Per capita amount** | | | | | | | | | | | | | | | | | |
| National health expenditures | $8,147 | $8,402 | $8,666 | $8,927 | $9,115 | $9,523 | $9,960 | $10,345 | $10,775 | $11,312 | $11,888 | $12,490 | $13,140 | $13,827 | $14,543 | $15,279 | $16,032 |
| Private health insurance—national health expenditures | 2,717 | 2,794 | 2,900 | 2,979 | 3,004 | 3,113 | 3,246 | 3,374 | 3,515 | 3,689 | 3,863 | 4,017 | 4,202 | 4,397 | 4,596 | 4,798 | 5,000 |
| Private health insurance—personal health care | 2,397 | 2,443 | 2,541 | 2,621 | 2,642 | 2,729 | 2,845 | 2,957 | 3,081 | 3,234 | 3,386 | 3,521 | 3,683 | 3,854 | 4,029 | 4,205 | 4,382 |
| Gross domestic product | 47,053 | 48,436 | 49,869 | 51,523 | 52,741 | 54,502 | 55,910 | 57,185 | 59,106 | 61,517 | 64,107 | 66,688 | 69,317 | 71,856 | 74,361 | 76,965 | 79,681 |
| Personal income | 39,470 | 40,385 | 42,595 | 44,378 | 44,528 | 46,165 | 47,822 | 49,565 | 51,388 | 53,542 | 55,982 | 58,380 | 60,858 | 63,308 | 65,765 | 68,286 | 70,920 |
| **Percent change in per capita from previous year shown** | | | | | | | | | | | | | | | | | |
| National health expenditures | — | 3.1% | 3.1% | 3.0% | 2.1% | 4.5% | 4.6% | 3.9% | 4.2% | 5.0% | 5.1% | 5.1% | 5.2% | 5.2% | 5.2% | 5.1% | 4.9% |
| Private health insurance—national health expenditures | — | 2.8 | 3.8 | 2.7 | 0.8 | 3.6 | 4.3 | 3.9 | 4.2 | 4.9 | 4.7 | 4.0 | 4.6 | 4.6 | 4.5 | 4.4 | 4.2 |
| Private health insurance—personal health care | — | 1.9 | 4.0 | 3.2 | 0.8 | 3.3 | 4.2 | 3.9 | 4.2 | 4.9 | 4.7 | 4.0 | 4.6 | 4.6 | 4.5 | 4.4 | 4.2 |
| Gross domestic product | — | 2.9 | 3.0 | 3.3 | 2.4 | 3.3 | 2.6 | 2.3 | 3.4 | 4.1 | 4.2 | 4.0 | 3.9 | 3.7 | 3.5 | 3.5 | 3.5 |
| Personal income | — | 2.3 | 5.5 | 4.2 | 0.3 | 3.7 | 3.6 | 3.6 | 3.7 | 4.2 | 4.6 | 4.3 | 4.2 | 4.0 | 3.9 | 3.8 | 3.9 |
| **Percent** | | | | | | | | | | | | | | | | | |
| National Health Expenditures as a Percent of Gross Domestic Product | 17.3% | 17.3% | 17.4% | 17.3% | 17.3% | 17.5% | 17.8% | 18.1% | 18.2% | 18.4% | 18.5% | 18.7% | 19.0% | 19.2% | 19.6% | 19.9% | 20.1% |

**TABLE 5.5**

**National health expenditures and annual percentage change, 2009–25** [CONTINUED]

aThese projections incorporate estimates of GDP from the U.S. Bureau of Economic Analysis as of May 2016.

bEstimates reflect the U.S. Bureau of Census definition for resident-based population (which includes all persons who usually reside in one of the fifty states or the District of Columbia, but excludes (i) residents living in Puerto Rico and areas under U.S. sovereignty, and (ii) U.S. Armed Forces overseas and U.S. citizens whose usual place of residence is outside of the United States) plus a small (typically less than 0.2% of population) adjustment to reflect Census undercounts. Projected estimates reflect the area population growth assumptions found in the Medicare Trustees Report.

Note: Numbers and percents may not add to totals because of rounding.

SOURCE: "Table 1. National Health Expenditures and Selected Economic Indicators, Levels and Annual Percent Change: Calendar Years 2009–2025," in *National Health Expenditures Projections 2015–2025,* U.S. Department of Health and Human Services, Centers for Medicare and Medicaid Services, July 14, 2016, https://www.cms.gov/research-statistics-data-and-systems/statistics-trends-and-reports/nationalhealthexpenddata/nationalhealthaccountsprojected.html (accessed August 5, 2016)

**TABLE 5.6**

## National health expenditures, by source of funds, 2009–25

| Year | Total | Out-of-pocket payments | Health insurance[a] | | | | | Other third party payers[c] |
|---|---|---|---|---|---|---|---|---|
| | | | Total | Private health insurance | Medicare | Medicaid | Other health insurance programs[b] | |
| **Historical estimates** | | | Amount in billions | | | | | |
| 2009 | $2,496.4 | $294.6 | $1,796.3 | $832.7 | $498.8 | $374.5 | $90.3 | $405.5 |
| 2010 | 2,595.7 | 299.5 | 1,876.3 | 863.1 | 520.5 | 397.2 | 95.6 | 419.9 |
| 2011 | 2,696.6 | 309.7 | 1,955.1 | 902.5 | 546.1 | 406.4 | 100.1 | 431.7 |
| 2012 | 2,799.0 | 318.7 | 2,027.6 | 934.1 | 569.2 | 422.0 | 102.2 | 452.7 |
| 2013 | 2,879.9 | 325.5 | 2,087.9 | 949.2 | 586.3 | 446.7 | 105.6 | 466.5 |
| 2014 | 3,031.3 | 329.8 | 2,216.9 | 991.0 | 618.7 | 495.8 | 111.4 | 484.6 |
| **Projected** | | | | | | | | |
| 2015 | 3,197.2 | 338.4 | 2,353.7 | 1,042.0 | 647.3 | 548.8 | 115.6 | 505.0 |
| 2016 | 3,350.7 | 350.1 | 2,473.7 | 1,092.7 | 681.3 | 577.7 | 122.0 | 526.9 |
| 2017 | 3,521.6 | 364.6 | 2,604.6 | 1,149.0 | 721.1 | 605.7 | 128.9 | 552.5 |
| 2018 | 3,731.4 | 383.2 | 2,765.4 | 1,217.0 | 770.2 | 641.5 | 136.7 | 582.8 |
| 2019 | 3,958.6 | 402.9 | 2,939.8 | 1,286.3 | 827.6 | 680.8 | 145.1 | 615.8 |
| 2020 | 4,198.3 | 427.5 | 3,119.6 | 1,350.1 | 893.1 | 722.0 | 154.4 | 651.2 |
| 2021 | 4,457.5 | 451.3 | 3,317.0 | 1,425.4 | 961.6 | 766.2 | 163.8 | 689.2 |
| 2022 | 4,732.8 | 476.0 | 3,527.5 | 1,505.1 | 1,036.3 | 812.7 | 173.4 | 729.2 |
| 2023 | 5,022.0 | 501.5 | 3,749.8 | 1,587.2 | 1,117.2 | 862.1 | 183.3 | 770.7 |
| 2024 | 5,321.7 | 528.1 | 3,979.6 | 1,671.1 | 1,199.9 | 915.4 | 193.2 | 814.0 |
| 2025 | 5,631.0 | 555.8 | 4,216.1 | 1,756.2 | 1,282.4 | 973.8 | 203.7 | 859.1 |
| **Historical estimates** | | | Per capita amount | | | | | |
| 2009 | $8,147 | $961 | d | d | d | d | d | d |
| 2010 | 8,402 | 969 | d | d | d | d | d | d |
| 2011 | 8,666 | 995 | d | d | d | d | d | d |
| 2012 | 8,927 | 1,016 | d | d | d | d | d | d |
| 2013 | 9,115 | 1,030 | d | d | d | d | d | d |
| 2014 | 9,523 | 1,036 | d | d | d | d | d | d |
| **Projected** | | | | | | | | |
| 2015 | 9,960 | 1,054 | d | d | d | d | d | d |
| 2016 | 10,345 | 1,081 | d | d | d | d | d | d |
| 2017 | 10,775 | 1,116 | d | d | d | d | d | d |
| 2018 | 11,312 | 1,162 | d | d | d | d | d | d |
| 2019 | 11,888 | 1,210 | d | d | d | d | d | d |
| 2020 | 12,490 | 1,272 | d | d | d | d | d | d |
| 2021 | 13,140 | 1,330 | d | d | d | d | d | d |
| 2022 | 13,827 | 1,391 | d | d | d | d | d | d |
| 2023 | 14,543 | 1,452 | d | d | d | d | d | d |
| 2024 | 15,279 | 1,516 | d | d | d | d | d | d |
| 2025 | 16,032 | 1,582 | d | d | d | d | d | d |
| **Historical estimates** | | | Percent distribution | | | | | |
| 2009 | 100.0 | 11.8 | 72.0 | 33.4 | 20.0 | 15.0 | 3.6 | 16.2 |
| 2010 | 100.0 | 11.5 | 72.3 | 33.3 | 20.1 | 15.3 | 3.7 | 16.2 |
| 2011 | 100.0 | 11.5 | 72.5 | 33.5 | 20.3 | 15.1 | 3.7 | 16.0 |
| 2012 | 100.0 | 11.4 | 72.4 | 33.4 | 20.3 | 15.1 | 3.7 | 16.2 |
| 2013 | 100.0 | 11.3 | 72.5 | 33.0 | 20.4 | 15.5 | 3.7 | 16.2 |
| 2014 | 100.0 | 10.9 | 73.1 | 32.7 | 20.4 | 16.4 | 3.7 | 16.0 |
| **Projected** | | | | | | | | |
| 2015 | 100.0 | 10.6 | 73.6 | 32.6 | 20.2 | 17.2 | 3.6 | 15.8 |
| 2016 | 100.0 | 10.4 | 73.8 | 32.6 | 20.3 | 17.2 | 3.6 | 15.7 |
| 2017 | 100.0 | 10.4 | 74.0 | 32.6 | 20.5 | 17.2 | 3.7 | 15.7 |
| 2018 | 100.0 | 10.3 | 74.1 | 32.6 | 20.6 | 17.2 | 3.7 | 15.6 |
| 2019 | 100.0 | 10.2 | 74.3 | 32.5 | 20.9 | 17.2 | 3.7 | 15.6 |
| 2020 | 100.0 | 10.2 | 74.3 | 32.2 | 21.3 | 17.2 | 3.7 | 15.5 |
| 2021 | 100.0 | 10.1 | 74.4 | 32.0 | 21.6 | 17.2 | 3.7 | 15.5 |
| 2022 | 100.0 | 10.1 | 74.5 | 31.8 | 21.9 | 17.2 | 3.7 | 15.4 |
| 2023 | 100.0 | 10.0 | 74.7 | 31.6 | 22.2 | 17.2 | 3.6 | 15.3 |
| 2024 | 100.0 | 9.9 | 74.8 | 31.4 | 22.5 | 17.2 | 3.6 | 15.3 |
| 2025 | 100.0 | 9.9 | 74.9 | 31.2 | 22.8 | 17.3 | 3.6 | 15.3 |
| **Historical estimates** | | | Annual percent change from previous year shown | | | | | |
| 2009 | — | — | — | — | — | — | — | — |
| 2010 | 4.0 | 1.6 | 4.5 | 3.6 | 4.3 | 6.1 | 5.9 | 3.5 |
| 2011 | 3.9 | 3.4 | 4.2 | 4.6 | 4.9 | 2.3 | 4.7 | 2.8 |
| 2012 | 3.8 | 2.9 | 3.7 | 3.5 | 4.2 | 3.8 | 2.2 | 4.9 |
| 2013 | 2.9 | 2.1 | 3.0 | 1.6 | 3.0 | 5.9 | 3.3 | 3.1 |
| 2014 | 5.3 | 1.3 | 6.2 | 4.4 | 5.5 | 11.0 | 5.5 | 3.9 |

**TABLE 5.6**

**National health expenditures, by source of funds, 2009–25** [CONTINUED]

| Year | Total | Out-of-pocket payments | Health insurance[a] | | | | | Other third party payers[c] |
|------|-------|------------------------|---------------------|---|---|---|---|------------------------------|
| | | | Total | Private health insurance | Medicare | Medicaid | Other health insurance programs[b] | |
| **Projected** | | | Annual percent change from previous year shown | | | | | |
| 2015 | 5.5 | 2.6 | 6.2 | 5.1 | 4.6 | 10.7 | 3.7 | 4.2 |
| 2016 | 4.8 | 3.5 | 5.1 | 4.9 | 5.2 | 5.3 | 5.6 | 4.3 |
| 2017 | 5.1 | 4.1 | 5.3 | 5.1 | 5.8 | 4.8 | 5.6 | 4.9 |
| 2018 | 6.0 | 5.1 | 6.2 | 5.9 | 6.8 | 5.9 | 6.1 | 5.5 |
| 2019 | 6.1 | 5.1 | 6.3 | 5.7 | 7.5 | 6.1 | 6.2 | 5.7 |
| 2020 | 6.1 | 6.1 | 6.1 | 5.0 | 7.9 | 6.1 | 6.3 | 5.7 |
| 2021 | 6.2 | 5.6 | 6.3 | 5.6 | 7.7 | 6.1 | 6.1 | 5.8 |
| 2022 | 6.2 | 5.5 | 6.3 | 5.6 | 7.8 | 6.1 | 5.9 | 5.8 |
| 2023 | 6.1 | 5.3 | 6.3 | 5.5 | 7.8 | 6.1 | 5.7 | 5.7 |
| 2024 | 6.0 | 5.3 | 6.1 | 5.3 | 7.4 | 6.2 | 5.4 | 5.6 |
| 2025 | 5.8 | 5.2 | 5.9 | 5.1 | 6.9 | 6.4 | 5.4 | 5.5 |

[a]Includes private health insurance (employer-sponsored insurance and other private insurance, which includes Marketplace plans), Medicare, Medicaid, Children's Health Insurance Program [Titles XIX and XXI], Department of Defense, and Department of Veterans' Affairs.
[b]Children's Health Insurance Program (Titles XIX and XXI), Department of Defense, and Department of Veterans' Affairs.
[c]Includes worksite health care, other private revenues, Indian Health Service, workers' compensation, general assistance, maternal and child health, vocational rehabilitation, other federal programs, Substance Abuse and Mental Health Services Administration, other state and local programs, and school health.
[d]Calculation of per capita estimates is not applicable.
Note: Per capita amounts based on estimates that reflect the U.S. Bureau of Census definition for resident-based population (which includes all persons who usually reside in one of the fifty states or the District of Columbia, but excludes (i) residents living in Puerto Rico and areas under U.S. sovereignty, and (ii) U.S. Armed Forces overseas and U.S. citizens whose usual place of residence is outside of the United States) plus a small (typically less than 0.2% of population) adjustment to reflect Census undercounts. Projected estimates reflect the area population growth assumptions found in the Medicare Trustees Report. Numbers and percents may not add to totals because of rounding.

SOURCE: "Table 3. National Health Expenditures; Aggregate and per Capita Amounts, Percent Distribution and Annual Percent Change by Source of Funds: Calendar Years 2009–2025," in *National Health Expenditures Projections 2015–2025*, U.S. Department of Health and Human Services, Centers for Medicare and Medicaid Services, July 14, 2016, https://www.cms.gov/research-statistics-data-and-systems/statistics-trends-and-reports/nationalhealthexpenddata/nationalhealthaccountsprojected.html (accessed August 5, 2016)

- Mergers and acquisitions among hospitals, health systems, and physician groups are often prompted by the desire to increase market share, and although there may be some economies of scale, consolidation can also act to increase prices.

Other factors for the increase in health care costs include advanced biomedical procedures that require high-technology expertise and equipment, redundant (excessive and unnecessary) technology in hospitals, consumer demand for less restrictive insurance plans (ones that offer more choices, benefits, and coverage, but usually mean higher premiums), and consumer demand for the latest and most comprehensive testing and treatment. The growing number of older adults who use a disproportionate amount of health care services also accelerates health care spending.

As reported in *National Health Expenditure Projections 2015–2025*, the CMS expects government spending on health care to grow 5.8% per year from 2015 through 2025 in response to overall economic growth, continuing implementation of the ACA, and the aging population. Taken together, expansion of coverage and premium subsidies under the ACA and population aging along with changes in economic growth and faster growth in medical prices, are projected to increase the share of federal, state, and local government financing of national health spending to 47% in 2025, an increase of two percentage points from 2014.

During the same period, Medicare spending is expected to grow 7.6%. Beginning in 2016 (following the 12.2% increase in Medicaid spending in 2014 attributable to the ACA expanded coverage), Medicaid spending is expected to grow by 6.1% per year.

Private health insurance spending is projected to grow 5.6% per year from 2017 through 2019 and then slow to about 5% from 2020 through 2025. Out-of-pocket spending is projected to average 5.5% from 2020 through 2025. In response to the ACA, growth in the out-of-pocket share of health spending slowed from 2011 to 2014 but was projected to accelerate each year through 2018 as the impact of the coverage expansions from the ACA subsides, and as the numbers of people covered through high-deductible health plans (plans with lower premiums and higher specified amounts the insured must pay before insurance coverage begins) increase. Nonetheless, out-of-pocket spending as a share of national health expenditures is anticipated to decline and level off from 2015 to 2025. (See Figure 5.1.)

## CONTROLLING HEALTH CARE SPENDING

In an effort to control health expenditures, the nation's health care system underwent some dramatic changes. Beginning in the late 1980s employers began looking for ways to contain health benefit costs for their employees. Many enrolled their employees in managed care programs as alternatives to traditional, fee-for-service insurance.

TABLE 5.7

## Personal health expenditures, by source of funds, 2009–25

| Year | Total | Out-of-pocket payments | Health insurance[a] | | | | | Other third-party payers[c] |
|------|-------|------------------------|---------------------|-------------------------|----------|----------|----------------------------------|------------------------------|
| | | | Total | Private health insurance | Medicare | Medicaid | Other health insurance programs[b] | |
| **Historical estimates** | | | *Amount in billions* | | | | | |
| 2009 | $2,115.9 | $294.6 | $1,636.8 | $734.6 | $470.3 | $346.2 | $85.7 | $184.5 |
| 2010 | 2,194.1 | 299.5 | 1,700.5 | 754.8 | 489.8 | 365.7 | 90.2 | 194.1 |
| 2011 | 2,280.4 | 309.7 | 1,772.1 | 790.6 | 513.4 | 373.6 | 94.6 | 198.6 |
| 2012 | 2,371.8 | 318.7 | 1,841.6 | 822.0 | 534.8 | 387.8 | 97.1 | 211.5 |
| 2013 | 2,441.3 | 325.5 | 1,893.7 | 834.6 | 551.2 | 407.7 | 100.2 | 222.1 |
| 2014 | 2,563.6 | 329.8 | 2,000.3 | 868.8 | 580.7 | 444.9 | 105.9 | 233.5 |
| **Projected** | | | | | | | | |
| 2015 | 2,700.3 | 338.4 | 2,118.6 | 913.3 | 606.0 | 489.7 | 109.6 | 243.3 |
| 2016 | 2,830.4 | 350.1 | 2,225.9 | 957.7 | 636.3 | 516.2 | 115.6 | 254.4 |
| 2017 | 2,975.1 | 364.6 | 2,343.8 | 1,007.0 | 672.4 | 542.4 | 122.0 | 266.7 |
| 2018 | 3,150.8 | 383.2 | 2,487.0 | 1,066.7 | 717.8 | 573.3 | 129.2 | 280.6 |
| 2019 | 3,341.1 | 402.9 | 2,642.3 | 1,127.4 | 770.7 | 607.2 | 136.9 | 295.8 |
| 2020 | 3,543.3 | 427.5 | 2,803.5 | 1,183.4 | 831.9 | 642.8 | 145.4 | 312.3 |
| 2021 | 3,761.0 | 451.3 | 2,979.8 | 1,249.3 | 895.5 | 681.0 | 154.1 | 329.9 |
| 2022 | 3,992.0 | 476.0 | 3,167.7 | 1,319.1 | 964.6 | 721.1 | 162.8 | 348.3 |
| 2023 | 4,234.5 | 501.5 | 3,365.9 | 1,391.1 | 1,039.5 | 763.5 | 171.7 | 367.2 |
| 2024 | 4,485.4 | 528.1 | 3,570.5 | 1,464.7 | 1,116.0 | 809.3 | 180.6 | 386.7 |
| 2025 | 4,743.8 | 555.8 | 3,780.9 | 1,539.3 | 1,192.2 | 859.5 | 189.9 | 407.0 |
| **Historical estimates** | | | *Per capita amount* | | | | | |
| 2009 | $6,905 | $961 | d | d | d | d | d | d |
| 2010 | 7,102 | 969 | d | d | d | d | d | d |
| 2011 | 7,328 | 995 | d | d | d | d | d | d |
| 2012 | 7,564 | 1,016 | d | d | d | d | d | d |
| 2013 | 7,727 | 1,030 | d | d | d | d | d | d |
| 2014 | 8,054 | 1,036 | d | d | d | d | d | d |
| **Projected** | | | | | | | | |
| 2015 | 8,412 | 1,054 | d | d | d | d | d | d |
| 2016 | 8,739 | 1,081 | d | d | d | d | d | d |
| 2017 | 9,103 | 1,116 | d | d | d | d | d | d |
| 2018 | 9,552 | 1,162 | d | d | d | d | d | d |
| 2019 | 10,033 | 1,210 | d | d | d | d | d | d |
| 2020 | 10,542 | 1,272 | d | d | d | d | d | d |
| 2021 | 11,087 | 1,330 | d | d | d | d | d | d |
| 2022 | 11,663 | 1,391 | d | d | d | d | d | d |
| 2023 | 12,263 | 1,452 | d | d | d | d | d | d |
| 2024 | 12,878 | 1,516 | d | d | d | d | d | d |
| 2025 | 13,506 | 1,582 | d | d | d | d | d | d |
| **Historical estimates** | | | *Percent distribution* | | | | | |
| 2009 | 100.0 | 13.9 | 77.4 | 34.7 | 22.2 | 16.4 | 4.0 | 8.7 |
| 2010 | 100.0 | 13.6 | 77.5 | 34.4 | 22.3 | 16.7 | 4.1 | 8.8 |
| 2011 | 100.0 | 13.6 | 77.7 | 34.7 | 22.5 | 16.4 | 4.1 | 8.7 |
| 2012 | 100.0 | 13.4 | 77.6 | 34.7 | 22.5 | 16.3 | 4.1 | 8.9 |
| 2013 | 100.0 | 13.3 | 77.6 | 34.2 | 22.6 | 16.7 | 4.1 | 9.1 |
| 2014 | 100.0 | 12.9 | 78.0 | 33.9 | 22.7 | 17.4 | 4.1 | 9.1 |
| **Projected** | | | | | | | | |
| 2015 | 100.0 | 12.5 | 78.5 | 33.8 | 22.4 | 18.1 | 4.1 | 9.0 |
| 2016 | 100.0 | 12.4 | 78.6 | 33.8 | 22.5 | 18.2 | 4.1 | 9.0 |
| 2017 | 100.0 | 12.3 | 78.8 | 33.8 | 22.6 | 18.2 | 4.1 | 9.0 |
| 2018 | 100.0 | 12.2 | 78.9 | 33.9 | 22.8 | 18.2 | 4.1 | 8.9 |
| 2019 | 100.0 | 12.1 | 79.1 | 33.7 | 23.1 | 18.2 | 4.1 | 8.9 |
| 2020 | 100.0 | 12.1 | 79.1 | 33.4 | 23.5 | 18.1 | 4.1 | 8.8 |
| 2021 | 100.0 | 12.0 | 79.2 | 33.2 | 23.8 | 18.1 | 4.1 | 8.8 |
| 2022 | 100.0 | 11.9 | 79.3 | 33.0 | 24.2 | 18.1 | 4.1 | 8.7 |
| 2023 | 100.0 | 11.8 | 79.5 | 32.9 | 24.5 | 18.0 | 4.1 | 8.7 |
| 2024 | 100.0 | 11.8 | 79.6 | 32.7 | 24.9 | 18.0 | 4.0 | 8.6 |
| 2025 | 100.0 | 11.7 | 79.7 | 32.4 | 25.1 | 18.1 | 4.0 | 8.6 |
| **Historical estimates** | | | *Annual percent change from previous year shown* | | | | | |
| 2009 | — | — | — | — | — | — | — | — |
| 2010 | 3.7 | 1.6 | 3.9 | 2.8 | 4.1 | 5.6 | 5.3 | 5.2 |
| 2011 | 3.9 | 3.4 | 4.2 | 4.7 | 4.8 | 2.2 | 4.9 | 2.3 |
| 2012 | 4.0 | 2.9 | 3.9 | 4.0 | 4.2 | 3.8 | 2.6 | 6.5 |
| 2013 | 2.9 | 2.1 | 2.8 | 1.5 | 3.1 | 5.2 | 3.2 | 5.0 |
| 2014 | 5.0 | 1.3 | 5.6 | 4.1 | 5.4 | 9.1 | 5.6 | 5.1 |

**TABLE 5.7**

**Personal health expenditures, by source of funds, 2009–25** [CONTINUED]

| Year | Total | Out-of-pocket payments | Health insurance[a] | | | | Other health insurance programs[b] | Other third-party payers[c] |
|---|---|---|---|---|---|---|---|---|
| | | | Total | Private health insurance | Medicare | Medicaid | | |
| **Projected** | | | Annual percent change from previous year shown | | | | | |
| 2015 | 5.3 | 2.6 | 5.9 | 5.1 | 4.3 | 10.1 | 3.6 | 4.2 |
| 2016 | 4.8 | 3.5 | 5.1 | 4.9 | 5.0 | 5.4 | 5.5 | 4.6 |
| 2017 | 5.1 | 4.1 | 5.3 | 5.1 | 5.7 | 5.1 | 5.5 | 4.8 |
| 2018 | 5.9 | 5.1 | 6.1 | 5.9 | 6.8 | 5.7 | 5.9 | 5.2 |
| 2019 | 6.0 | 5.1 | 6.2 | 5.7 | 7.4 | 5.9 | 6.0 | 5.4 |
| 2020 | 6.1 | 6.1 | 6.1 | 5.0 | 7.9 | 5.9 | 6.2 | 5.6 |
| 2021 | 6.1 | 5.6 | 6.3 | 5.6 | 7.6 | 5.9 | 6.0 | 5.6 |
| 2022 | 6.1 | 5.5 | 6.3 | 5.6 | 7.7 | 5.9 | 5.7 | 5.6 |
| 2023 | 6.1 | 5.3 | 6.3 | 5.5 | 7.8 | 5.9 | 5.5 | 5.4 |
| 2024 | 5.9 | 5.3 | 6.1 | 5.3 | 7.4 | 6.0 | 5.2 | 5.3 |
| 2025 | 5.8 | 5.2 | 5.9 | 5.1 | 6.8 | 6.2 | 5.2 | 5.2 |

[a]Includes private health insurance (employer-sponsored insurance and other private insurance, which includes Marketplace plans), Medicare, Medicaid, Children's Health Insurance Program (Titles XIX and XXI), Department of Defense, and Department of Veterans' Affairs.
[b]Children's Health Insurance Program (Titles XIX and XXI), Department of Defense, and Department of Veterans' Affairs.
[c]Includes worksite health care, other private revenues, Indian Health Service, workers' compensation, general assistance, maternal and child health, vocational rehabilitation, other federal programs, Substance Abuse and Mental Health Services Administration, other state and local programs, and school health.
[d]Calculation of per capita estimates is not applicable.
Note: Per capita amounts based on estimates that reflect the U.S. Bureau of Census definition for resident-based population (which includes all persons who usually reside in one of the fifty states or the District of Columbia, but excludes (i) residents living in Puerto Rico and areas under U.S. sovereignty, and (ii) U.S. Armed Forces overseas and U.S. citizens whose usual place of residence is outside of the United States) plus a small (typically less than 0.2% of population) adjustment to reflect Census undercounts. Projected estimates reflect the area population growth assumptions found in the Medicare Trustees Report. Numbers and percents may not add to totals because of rounding.

SOURCE: "Table 5. Personal Health Care Expenditures; Aggregate and per Capita Amounts, Percent Distribution and Annual Percent Change by Source of Funds: Calendar Years 2009–2025," in *National Health Expenditures Projections 2015–2025*, U.S. Department of Health and Human Services, Centers for Medicare and Medicaid Services, July 14, 2016, https://www.cms.gov/research-statistics-data-and-systems/statistics-trends-and-reports/nationalhealthexpenddata/nationalhealthaccountsprojected.html (accessed August 5, 2016)

**FIGURE 5.1**

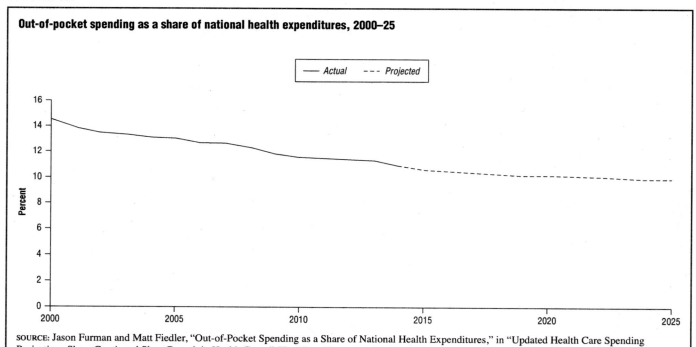

**Out-of-pocket spending as a share of national health expenditures, 2000–25**

SOURCE: Jason Furman and Matt Fiedler, "Out-of-Pocket Spending as a Share of National Health Expenditures," in "Updated Health Care Spending Projections Show Continued Slow Growth in Health Costs," *The White House Briefing Room*, July 13, 2016, https://www.whitehouse.gov/blog/2016/07/14/updated-health-care-spending-projections-show-continued-slow-growth-health-costs (accessed August 6, 2016)

Managed care programs offered lower premiums by keeping a tighter control on costs and utilization and by emphasizing the importance of preventive care. Insurers negotiated discounts with providers (physicians, hospitals, clinical laboratories, and others) in exchange for guaranteed access to employer-insured groups. In 2016 private insurance paid for 33.8% of the nation's health costs. (See Table 5.6.) Public sources covered 53.8% of the nation's costs, and 12.4% of the costs came directly from consumers' pockets.

In "State Options to Control Health Care Costs and Improve Quality" (April 28, 2016, http://healthaffairs .org/blog/2016/04/28/state-options-to-control-health-care-costs-and-improve-quality/), Zeke Emanuel et al. describe state-level actions to control health care costs with the potential to reduce health care expenditures. Examples include making a public commitment to keep health care costs below a set target; publishing a state scorecard to publicly track how much progress is made toward achieving health and cost objectives; giving hospitals global budgets (lump sum payments to cover all care rather than reimbursing them for each individual service); expanding home care services that provide nurse educators and help connect families to health and social services; integrating behavioral health (prevention or intervention in mental illness and substance abuse) and primary care to improve health outcomes; combating addiction to prescription drugs and heroin; improving long-term-care services and encouraging consumers to purchase long-term-care insurance; permitting nurse practitioners a broader scope of practice to relieve provider shortages and improve the productivity of the health care system; expanding the use of telehealth (use of electronic information and telecommunications technologies to support long-distance clinical health care); and reducing unnecessary emergency room use.

## How Has the ACA Influenced Health Care Spending?

Many aspects of the ACA spark fiery debate, but few are as divisive as the question of whether its implementation will ultimately reduce health care costs. Proponents of the legislation claim that it will lower the federal budget deficit over time, whereas critics assert that it will inflate the deficit and national debt. As many key aspects of the ACA take effect, industry observers will assess how new provisions such as permitting the purchase of health insurance across state lines and malpractice reform affect U.S. expenditures for health care.

In "Updated Health Care Spending Projections Show Continued Slow Growth in Health Costs" (July 13, 2016, https://www.whitehouse.gov/blog/2016/07/14/updated-health-care-spending-projections-show-continued-slow-growth-health-costs), Jason Furman and Matt Fiedler of the Council of Economic Advisers report that growth in per-enrollee health care spending remained low in 2015 and 2016. They observe that without the growth in use from expanding insurance coverage, overall health care spending growth would have been close to its lowest point in 2015. (See Figure 5.2.) Furthermore, 2015 was the sixth consecutive year in which per-enrollee Medicare spending grew more slowly than per capita GDP.

National health care spending continued to grow quickly in 2015 because millions of previously uninsured people gained coverage. However, as coverage stabilized at a new, higher level, this driver of health care spending growth was anticipated to subside. Furman and Fiedler opine, "there is reason for optimism that a substantial portion of the recent slow growth in health costs reflects structural changes in the health care system, including reforms in the Affordable Care Act, that may produce sustained downward pressure on health care cost growth in the years ahead."

In "Health Care Costs101: ACA Spurs Modest Growth" (2016, http://www.chcf.org/publications/2016/05/health-care-costs-101), the California Health Care Foundation explains, "After five years of slow growth, national health spending grew by 5.3% in 2014, up from 2.9% in 2013. The faster growth was due in part to coverage expansion under the Patient Protection and Affordable Care Act (also known as the Affordable Care Act [ACA]) and increased spending on prescription drugs." Prescription drug expenditures increased 12.2% ($32.4 billion), much faster than in previous years. More than one-third of the increase ($11.3 billion) was attributable to new drugs to treat hepatitis C (inflammation of the liver). In 2014 federal subsidies for ACA Marketplace premiums and cost sharing totaled $18.5 billion, accounting for 12% of the $151 billion in new health spending. Federal spending on Medicaid increased 18.4% (compared with 0.9% for states), as the federal government fully funded expansion of Medicaid eligibility in participating states. Household spending on the direct purchase of insurance rose 2.2% (more slowly than overall spending at 5.3% and similar to overall household spending at 2%), despite a 19.5% increase in enrollment in directly purchased insurance.

In "Federal Subsidies for Health Insurance Coverage for People under Age 65: 2016 to 2026" (March 2016, https://www.cbo.gov/sites/default/files/114th-congress-2015-2016/reports/51385-HealthInsuranceBaseline.pdf), the Congressional Budget Office (CBO) reports that the projected cost of the ACA provisions from 2016 to 2026 is $1.4 trillion. The CBO notes that tax provisions that increase revenues and reduced Medicare payments to hospitals, other providers of care, and to private insurance plans delivering Medicare benefits are anticipated to reduce budget deficits. Table 5.8 shows the estimated spending and revenue effects of the insurance coverage provisions of the ACA.

The ACA generates revenue because fewer people are covered by employer-sponsored health coverage. As a result, taxable wages in proportion to nontaxable health coverage benefits will increase and generate higher tax revenues. That shift is projected to reduce deficits by a total of $5 billion in 2016 and $248 billion from 2017 to

**FIGURE 5.2**

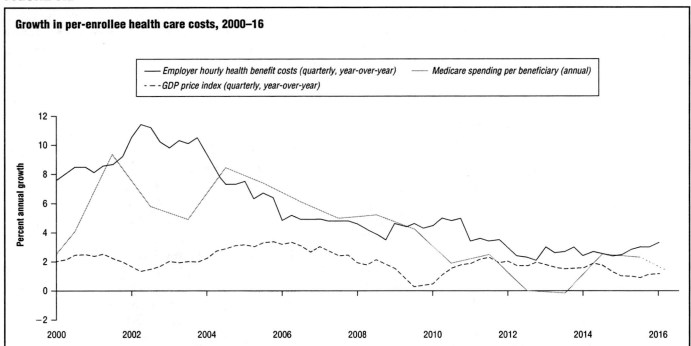

**Growth in per-enrollee health care costs, 2000–16**

*Legend:*
— Employer hourly health benefit costs (quarterly, year-over-year)
- - - GDP price index (quarterly, year-over-year)
···· Medicare spending per beneficiary (annual)

Note: Through 2015, the Medicare series reflects the National Health Expenditure projections. For 2016, the Medicare series reflects Counsel of Economic Advisers (CEA) calculations using Treasury data on Medicare spending and Trustees' projections of Medicare enrollment. The year-to-date growth rate compares the first five months of 2016 to the first five months of 2015. Employment cost index (ECI) and the gross domestic product (GDP) price index through 2016, first quarter.

SOURCE: Jason Furman and Matt Fiedler, "Nominal Growth in Measures of Per-Enrollee Health Care Spending," in "Updated Health Care Spending Projections Show Continued Slow Growth in Health Costs," *The White House Briefing Room*, July 13, 2016, https://www.whitehouse.gov/blog/2016/07/14/updated-health-care-spending-projections-show-continued-slow-growth-health-costs (accessed August 6, 2016)

**TABLE 5.8**

**Spending and revenue effects of the insurance coverage provisions of the Affordable Care Act, 2016–26**

[Billions of dollars, by fiscal year]

| | 2016 | 2017 | 2018 | 2019 | 2020 | 2021 | 2022 | 2023 | 2024 | 2025 | 2026 | Total, 2017–2026 |
|---|---|---|---|---|---|---|---|---|---|---|---|---|
| Subsidies for coverage through marketplaces and related spending and revenues[a] | 43 | 56 | 70 | 78 | 83 | 87 | 91 | 95 | 99 | 102 | 106 | 866 |
| Medicaid and CHIP outlays | 74 | 78 | 81 | 85 | 91 | 100 | 108 | 116 | 125 | 134 | 144 | 1,063 |
| Small-employer tax credits[b] | 1 | 1 | 1 | 1 | 1 | 1 | 1 | 1 | 1 | 1 | 1 | 9 |
| **Gross cost of coverage provisions** | **119** | **134** | **152** | **164** | **174** | **187** | **199** | **212** | **225** | **238** | **252** | **1,938** |
| Penalty payments by uninsured people | −3 | −3 | −3 | −3 | −3 | −4 | −4 | −4 | −4 | −4 | −5 | −38 |
| Penalty payments by employers[b] | 0 | −9 | −16 | −20 | −15 | −16 | −18 | −19 | −20 | −22 | −23 | −178 |
| Excise tax on high-premium insurance plans[b] | 0 | 0 | 0 | 0 | −3 | −7 | −9 | −11 | −13 | −16 | −20 | −79 |
| Other effects on revenues and outlays[c] | −5 | −9 | −13 | −18 | −22 | −24 | −27 | −29 | −31 | −33 | −34 | −239 |
| **Net cost of coverage provisions** | **110** | **113** | **119** | **123** | **130** | **136** | **142** | **150** | **157** | **163** | **170** | **1,403** |
| Memorandum: | | | | | | | | | | | | |
| Increases in mandatory spending | 123 | 137 | 150 | 162 | 172 | 186 | 198 | 210 | 223 | 235 | 248 | 1,920 |
| Increases in revenues | 13 | 24 | 31 | 39 | 42 | 50 | 55 | 60 | 66 | 72 | 78 | 517 |

CHIP = Children's Health Insurance Program.
[a]Includes subsidies for coverage through the Basic Health Program, grants to states for establishing health insurance marketplaces, and net spending and revenues for risk adjustment and reinsurance. The risk corridors program is recorded in the budget as a discretionary program; CBO estimates that payments and collections will offset each other in each year, resulting in no net budgetary effect.
[b]These effects on the deficit include the associated effects of changes in taxable compensation on revenues.
[c]Consists mainly of the effects of changes in taxable compensation on revenues. Congressional Budget Office (CBO) estimates that outlays for Social Security benefits will increase by about $9 billion over the 2017–2026 period and that the coverage provisions will have negligible effects on outlays for other federal programs.
Notes: Estimates exclude effects on the deficit of provisions of the Affordable Care Act that are not related to insurance coverage and effects on discretionary spending of the coverage provisions. Except in the memorandum lines, positive numbers indicate an increase in the deficit, and negative numbers indicate a decrease in the deficit.

SOURCE: "Table 3. Direct Spending and Revenue Effects of the Insurance Coverage Provisions of the Affordable Care Act," in *Federal Subsidies for Health Insurance Coverage for People under Age 65: 2016 to 2026*, Congressional Budget Office, March 2016, https://www.cbo.gov/sites/default/files/114th-congress-2015-2016/reports/51385-HealthInsuranceBaseline_OneCol.pdf (accessed August 6, 2016)

2026, largely by boosting federal tax receipts, but also by reducing outlays from certain refundable tax credits.

Revenues may also be generated by an increase in payroll taxes for individuals and couples with an income between $200,000 and $250,000. High-income taxpayers may be required to pay a 3.8% tax on unearned income over the earning limits. In "About That Cadillac Tax" (HealthAffairs.org, April 25, 2016), Jeff Lemieux and Chad Moutray report that the 40% excise tax (often referred to as a Cadillac tax because it applies to high-cost plans) slated to begin in 2018 on richer, more costly health coverage was postponed by Congress and is anticipated to begin in 2020 unless the ACA is modified or repealed. The ACA also raises the threshold for deducting out-of-pocket unreimbursed medical expenses from 7.5% of a taxpayer's adjusted gross income to 10%.

### Prescription Drug Prices Continue to Rise

One of the fastest-growing components of health care is the market for prescription drugs. In 2016 Americans spent an estimated $342.1 billion on prescription medication. (See Table 5.9.) Private insurers paid $142 billion of the drug costs in 2016, an increase from the $116.1 billion they paid for prescription drugs in 2009. (See Table 5.9.) The health needs and chronic conditions of the aging population have fueled growth in this sector.

In *Observations on Trends in Prescription Drug Spending* (March 8, 2016, https://aspe.hhs.gov/sites/default/files/pdf/187586/Drugspending.pdf), the Office of the Assistant Secretary for Planning and Evaluation (ASPE), a part of the U.S. Department of Health and Human Services (HHS), weighs the factors prompting the rise in prescription drug spending from 2010 to 2014: 10% of spending growth was attributable to population growth, 30% to an increase in prescriptions per person, 30% to overall inflation, and 30% to "either changes in the composition of drugs prescribed toward higher price products or price increases for drugs that together drove average price increases in excess of general inflation." ASPE notes that spending for specialty drugs (drugs that are expensive, manufactured in living systems, difficult to administer, prescribed by specialist physicians, used to treat serious conditions for which few or no alternative therapies are available, administered through specialized pharmacies, or require temperature control or other special handling) seems to be rising more rapidly than expenditures on other drugs.

In "Medicines Use and Spending in the U.S.—A Review of 2015 and Outlook to 2020" (April 2016, http://www.imshealth.com/en/thought-leadership/ims-institute/reports/medicines-use-and-spending-in-the-us-a-review-of-2015-and-outlook-to-2020#form), the QuintilesIMS Institute projects an annual growth rate of 4% to 7% through 2020. Figure 5.3 shows historical and projected prescription drug spending as forecast by CMS and QuintilesIMS.

## HEALTH CARE FOR OLDER ADULTS, PEOPLE WITH DISABILITIES, AND THE POOR

In "Medicines Use and Spending in the U.S.—A Review of 2015 and Outlook to 2020," QuintilesIMS reports that in 2015, prescription drug spending topped $310 billion, up 8.5% from 2014 but still 2% lower than the 2014 peak growth rate.

Despite passage of the groundbreaking ACA, which expands health care coverage, the United States remains one of the few industrialized nations that does not have a government-funded national health care program that provides coverage for all of its citizens. Government-funded health care exists, and it forms a major part of the health care system, but it is available only to specific segments of the U.S. population. In other developed countries government-funded national medical care programs cover almost all their citizens' health-related costs, from prenatal care to long-term care.

In the United States the major government health care entitlement programs are Medicare and Medicaid. They provide financial assistance for people aged 65 years and older, the poor, and people with disabilities. Before the existence of these programs, many older Americans could not afford adequate medical care. For older adults who are beneficiaries, the Medicare program provides reimbursement for hospital and physician care, whereas Medicaid pays for the cost of nursing home care.

### Medicare

The Medicare program, which was enacted under Title XVIII (Health Insurance for the Aged) of the Social Security Act, was approved in 1965. The program consists of four parts:

- Part A provides hospital insurance. Coverage includes physicians' fees, nursing services, meals, semiprivate rooms, special-care units, operating room costs, laboratory tests, and some drugs and supplies. Part A also covers rehabilitation services, limited posthospital care in a skilled nursing facility, home health care, and hospice care for the terminally ill.

- Part B (Supplemental Medical Insurance [SMI]) is elective medical insurance; that is, enrollees must pay premiums to obtain coverage. SMI covers outpatient physicians' services, diagnostic tests, outpatient hospital services, outpatient physical therapy, speech pathology services, home health services, and medical equipment and supplies.

- Part C is the Medicare+Choice program, which was established by the Balanced Budget Act of 1997 to expand beneficiaries' options and allow them to participate in private-sector health plans.

- Part D is also elective and provides voluntary, subsidized access to prescription drug insurance coverage,

## TABLE 5.9

**Prescription drug expenditures, by source of funds, 2009–25**

| Year | Total | Out-of-pocket payments | Health insurance[a] Total | Private health insurance | Medicare | Medicaid | Other health insurance programs[b] | Other third-party payers[c] |
|------|-------|------------------------|------------------|--------------------------|----------|----------|------------------------------------|------------------------------|
| **Historical estimates** | | | | Amount in billions | | | | |
| 2009 | $252.7 | $49.1 | $200.2 | $116.1 | $54.5 | $20.3 | $9.1 | $3.5 |
| 2010 | 253.0 | 45.3 | 204.4 | 116.1 | 58.9 | 20.3 | 9.1 | 3.4 |
| 2011 | 258.7 | 45.5 | 210.4 | 117.2 | 63.2 | 20.6 | 9.4 | 2.9 |
| 2012 | 259.1 | 45.2 | 211.3 | 113.3 | 67.4 | 21.1 | 9.5 | 2.6 |
| 2013 | 265.3 | 43.5 | 219.3 | 114.4 | 73.9 | 22.0 | 9.1 | 2.4 |
| 2014 | 297.7 | 44.7 | 250.9 | 127.3 | 86.4 | 27.3 | 9.9 | 2.0 |
| **Projected** | | | | | | | | |
| 2015 | 321.9 | 46.2 | 273.7 | 134.6 | 96.6 | 32.2 | 10.3 | 2.0 |
| 2016 | 342.1 | 48.3 | 291.8 | 142.0 | 105.2 | 33.8 | 10.8 | 2.0 |
| 2017 | 362.7 | 50.6 | 310.1 | 150.4 | 113.4 | 34.9 | 11.4 | 2.0 |
| 2018 | 393.6 | 54.2 | 337.3 | 163.2 | 124.8 | 37.2 | 12.0 | 2.1 |
| 2019 | 418.6 | 56.8 | 359.6 | 173.2 | 134.3 | 39.5 | 12.6 | 2.2 |
| 2020 | 445.9 | 60.1 | 383.5 | 182.6 | 145.4 | 42.3 | 13.2 | 2.3 |
| 2021 | 474.6 | 63.0 | 409.3 | 193.2 | 157.0 | 45.2 | 13.9 | 2.4 |
| 2022 | 505.1 | 65.8 | 436.9 | 204.1 | 169.8 | 48.3 | 14.7 | 2.5 |
| 2023 | 539.3 | 69.1 | 467.5 | 216.9 | 183.7 | 51.6 | 15.4 | 2.6 |
| 2024 | 575.4 | 72.6 | 500.1 | 230.1 | 198.7 | 55.2 | 16.1 | 2.7 |
| 2025 | 614.5 | 76.5 | 535.2 | 244.2 | 215.0 | 59.1 | 16.9 | 2.8 |
| **Historical estimates** | | | | Per capita amount | | | | |
| 2009 | $825 | $160 | d | d | d | d | d | d |
| 2010 | 819 | 146 | d | d | d | d | d | d |
| 2011 | 831 | 146 | d | d | d | d | d | d |
| 2012 | 826 | 144 | d | d | d | d | d | d |
| 2013 | 840 | 138 | d | d | d | d | d | d |
| 2014 | 935 | 141 | d | d | d | d | d | d |
| **Projected** | | | | | | | | |
| 2015 | 1,003 | 144 | d | d | d | d | d | d |
| 2016 | 1,056 | 149 | d | d | d | d | d | d |
| 2017 | 1,110 | 155 | d | d | d | d | d | d |
| 2018 | 1,193 | 164 | d | d | d | d | d | d |
| 2019 | 1,257 | 170 | d | d | d | d | d | d |
| 2020 | 1,327 | 179 | d | d | d | d | d | d |
| 2021 | 1,399 | 186 | d | d | d | d | d | d |
| 2022 | 1,476 | 192 | d | d | d | d | d | d |
| 2023 | 1,562 | 200 | d | d | d | d | d | d |
| 2024 | 1,652 | 208 | d | d | d | d | d | d |
| 2025 | 1,749 | 218 | d | d | d | d | d | d |
| **Historical estimates** | | | | Percent distribution | | | | |
| 2009 | 100.0 | 19.4 | 79.2 | 46.0 | 21.6 | 8.0 | 3.6 | 1.4 |
| 2010 | 100.0 | 17.9 | 80.8 | 45.9 | 23.3 | 8.0 | 3.6 | 1.3 |
| 2011 | 100.0 | 17.6 | 81.3 | 45.3 | 24.4 | 8.0 | 3.6 | 1.1 |
| 2012 | 100.0 | 17.5 | 81.5 | 43.7 | 26.0 | 8.1 | 3.7 | 1.0 |
| 2013 | 100.0 | 16.4 | 82.7 | 43.1 | 27.8 | 8.3 | 3.4 | 0.9 |
| 2014 | 100.0 | 15.0 | 84.3 | 42.8 | 29.0 | 9.2 | 3.3 | 0.7 |
| **Projected** | | | | | | | | |
| 2015 | 100.0 | 14.4 | 85.0 | 41.8 | 30.0 | 10.0 | 3.2 | 0.6 |
| 2016 | 100.0 | 14.1 | 85.3 | 41.5 | 30.8 | 9.9 | 3.2 | 0.6 |
| 2017 | 100.0 | 13.9 | 85.5 | 41.5 | 31.3 | 9.6 | 3.1 | 0.6 |
| 2018 | 100.0 | 13.8 | 85.7 | 41.5 | 31.7 | 9.5 | 3.0 | 0.5 |
| 2019 | 100.0 | 13.6 | 85.9 | 41.4 | 32.1 | 9.4 | 3.0 | 0.5 |
| 2020 | 100.0 | 13.5 | 86.0 | 41.0 | 32.6 | 9.5 | 3.0 | 0.5 |
| 2021 | 100.0 | 13.3 | 86.2 | 40.7 | 33.1 | 9.5 | 2.9 | 0.5 |
| 2022 | 100.0 | 13.0 | 86.5 | 40.4 | 33.6 | 9.6 | 2.9 | 0.5 |
| 2023 | 100.0 | 12.8 | 86.7 | 40.2 | 34.1 | 9.6 | 2.8 | 0.5 |
| 2024 | 100.0 | 12.6 | 86.9 | 40.0 | 34.5 | 9.6 | 2.8 | 0.5 |
| 2025 | 100.0 | 12.4 | 87.1 | 39.7 | 35.0 | 9.6 | 2.7 | 0.5 |
| **Historical estimates** | | | | Annual percent change from previous year shown | | | | |
| 2009 | — | — | — | — | — | — | — | — |
| 2010 | 0.1 | −7.8 | 2.1 | 0.0 | 8.0 | −0.3 | −0.6 | −3.1 |
| 2011 | 2.2 | 0.4 | 2.9 | 0.9 | 7.3 | 1.6 | 3.6 | −15.5 |
| 2012 | 0.2 | −0.5 | 0.4 | −3.3 | 6.7 | 2.4 | 0.8 | −8.9 |
| 2013 | 2.4 | −3.7 | 3.8 | 1.0 | 9.5 | 4.2 | -4.1 | −7.9 |
| 2014 | 12.2 | 2.7 | 14.4 | 11.3 | 16.9 | 24.3 | 9.2 | −15.0 |

**TABLE 5.9**

**Prescription drug expenditures, by source of funds, 2009–25** [CONTINUED]

| Year | Total | Out-of-pocket payments | Health insurance[a] | | | | | Other third-party payers[c] |
|---|---|---|---|---|---|---|---|---|
| | | | Total | Private health insurance | Medicare | Medicaid | Other health insurance programs[b] | |
| Projected | | | Annual percent change from previous year shown | | | | | |
| 2015 | 8.1 | 3.4 | 9.1 | 5.7 | 11.8 | 17.7 | 4.1 | −2.4 |
| 2016 | 6.3 | 4.5 | 6.6 | 5.5 | 8.9 | 4.9 | 4.9 | 0.3 |
| 2017 | 6.0 | 4.7 | 6.3 | 5.9 | 7.8 | 3.5 | 4.9 | 2.4 |
| 2018 | 8.5 | 7.0 | 8.8 | 8.5 | 10.1 | 6.6 | 5.3 | 3.7 |
| 2019 | 6.4 | 4.8 | 6.6 | 6.1 | 7.6 | 6.2 | 5.2 | 3.8 |
| 2020 | 6.5 | 5.9 | 6.6 | 5.4 | 8.3 | 6.8 | 5.1 | 4.4 |
| 2021 | 6.4 | 4.8 | 6.7 | 5.8 | 8.0 | 6.9 | 5.3 | 4.5 |
| 2022 | 6.4 | 4.5 | 6.7 | 5.7 | 8.2 | 6.9 | 5.3 | 4.4 |
| 2023 | 6.8 | 5.1 | 7.0 | 6.3 | 8.2 | 6.9 | 4.8 | 4.2 |
| 2024 | 6.7 | 5.0 | 7.0 | 6.1 | 8.1 | 7.0 | 4.8 | 4.1 |
| 2025 | 6.8 | 5.3 | 7.0 | 6.1 | 8.2 | 7.1 | 4.8 | 3.9 |

[a]Includes private health insurance (employer-sponsored Insurance and other private insurance, which includes Marketplace plans), Medicare, Medicaid, Children's Health Insurance Program (Titles XIX and XXI), Department of Defense, and Department of Veterans' Affairs.
[b]Children's Health Insurance Program (Titles XIX and XXI), Department of Defense, and Department of Veterans' Affairs.
[c]Includes worksite health care, other private revenues, Indian Health Service, workers' compensation, general assistance, maternal and child health, vocational rehabilitation, other federal programs, Substance Abuse and Mental Health Services Administration, other state and local programs, and school health.
[d]Calculation of per capita estimates is not applicable.
Note: Per capita amounts based on estimates that reflect the U.S. Bureau of Census definition for resident-based population (which includes all persons who usually reside in one of the fifty states or the District of Columbia, but excludes (i) residents living in Puerto Rico and areas under U.S. sovereignty, and (ii) U.S. Armed Forces overseas and U.S. citizens whose usual place of residence is outside of the United States) plus a small (typically less than 0.2% of population) adjustment to reflect Census undercounts. Projected estimates reflect the area population growth assumptions found in the Medicare Trustees Report. Numbers and percents may not add to totals because of rounding.

SOURCE: "Table 11. Prescription Drug Expenditures; Aggregate and per Capita Amounts, Percent Distribution and Annual Percent Change by Source of Funds: Calendar Years 2009–2025," in *National Health Expenditures Projections 2015–2025*, U.S. Department of Health and Human Services, Centers for Medicare and Medicaid Services, July 14, 2016, https://www.cms.gov/research-statistics-data-and-systems/statistics-trends-and-reports/nationalhealthexpenddata/nationalhealthaccountsprojected.html (accessed August 5, 2016)

**FIGURE 5.3**

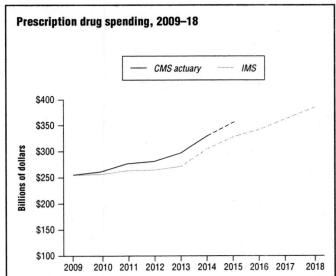

**Prescription drug spending, 2009–18**

CMS = Centers for Medicare and Medicaid Services.
IMS = IMS Health's National Prescription Audit (now a part of QuintilesIMS).

SOURCE: "Figure 1. Historical and Projected Spending on Retail Prescription Drugs in Billions of Nominal Dollars, 2009 to 2018," in "Observations on Trends in Prescription Drug Spending," *ASPE Issue Brief*, U.S. Department of Health and Human Service Office of the Assistant Secretary for Planning and Evaluation, March 8, 2016, https://aspe.hhs.gov/sites/default/files/pdf/187586/Drugspending.pdf (accessed August 7, 2016)

for a premium, to individuals who are entitled to Part A or who are enrolled in Part B. Part D also has provisions (premium and cost-sharing subsidies) for low-income enrollees. Part D coverage began in 2006 and includes most prescription drugs approved by the U.S. Food and Drug Administration (FDA).

In general, Medicare reimburses physicians on a fee-for-service basis (payment for each visit, procedure, or treatment that is delivered), as opposed to per capita or per member per month. In response to the increasing administrative burden of paperwork, reduced compensation, and delays in reimbursements, some physicians opt out of Medicare participation. They do not provide services under the Medicare program and choose not to accept Medicare patients into their practices. Others still provide services to Medicare beneficiaries but do not "accept assignment," meaning that patients must pay out of pocket for services and then seek reimbursement from Medicare.

**Medicare Managed Care Plans Control Costs**

During the 1980s and 1990s, the federal government, employers that provided health coverage for retiring employees, and many states sought to control costs by encouraging Medicare and Medicaid beneficiaries to enroll in HMOs. The federal government paid the health plans fixed fees—a predetermined dollar amount per member per month (PMPM). For these fixed fees, Medicare recipients received a comprehensive array of benefits. PMPM payment provided financial incentives for Medicare-risk HMO physicians to control costs, unlike physicians who were reimbursed on a fee-for-service basis.

Although Medicare recipients were generally pleased with these HMOs (even when enrolling meant they had to change physicians and thereby end long-standing relationships with their family doctors), many of the health plans did not fare well financially. The health plans suffered for various reasons: some had underestimated the service utilization rates of older adults, and some were unable to provide the stipulated range of services as cost effectively as they had believed possible. Other plans found that the PMPM payment was not sufficient to enable them to cover all the clinical services and their administrative overhead.

By the mid-1990s some Medicare-risk plans faced challenges that proved daunting. Their enrollees had aged and required even more health care services than they had previously. For example, a member who had joined as a healthy 65-year-old could now be a frail 75-year-old with multiple chronic health conditions requiring many costly health services. Although the PMPM payment had increased over the years, for some plans it was insufficient to cover their costs. Some Medicare-risk plans, especially those operated by smaller health plans, ended their programs abruptly, leaving thousands of older adults scrambling to join other health plans.

The Balanced Budget Act of 1997 produced another plan for Medicare recipients called Medicare+Choice. This plan offers Medicare beneficiaries a wider range of managed care plan options than just HMOs. Older adults may join preferred provider organizations (PPOs) and provider-sponsored organizations that generally offer greater freedom of choice of providers (physicians and hospitals) than what is available through HMO membership. These plans (as well as those formerly called Medicare-risk plans) are known as Medicare Advantage (MA) plans. MA plans include HMOs, PPOs, private fee-for-service plans, and medical savings account plans (which deposit money from Medicare into an account that can be used to pay medical expenses).

The 2003 Medicare Prescription Drug, Improvement, and Modernization Act renamed the plans, calling them Medicare Advantage Plans. The CMS website, Plan Quality and Performance Ratings (https://www.medicare.gov/find-a-plan/results/planresults/planratings/compare-plan-ratings.aspx?PlanType=MAPD), enables consumers to see ratings for Medicare Advantage Plans and compare their benefits.

## Medicare Faces Challenges

The Medicare program's continuing financial viability is in jeopardy. In 1995, for the first time since 1972, the Medicare trust fund lost money, a sign that the financial condition of Medicare was worse than previously assumed. The CMS did not expect a deficit until 1997; however, income to the trust fund, primarily from payroll taxes, was less than expected, and spending was higher. The deficit was significant because losses were anticipated to grow from year to year.

A NATIONAL BIPARTISAN COMMISSION CONSIDERS THE FUTURE OF MEDICARE. The National Bipartisan Commission on the Future of Medicare was created by Congress in the Balanced Budget Act of 1997. The commission was charged with examining the Medicare program and drafting recommendations to avert a future financial crisis and reinforce the program in anticipation of the retirement of the baby boomers (the large generation of people born between 1946 and 1964 who would begin reaching retirement age in 2011).

The commission observed that much like Social Security, Medicare would suffer because there would be fewer workers per retiree to fund it. Furthermore, it predicted that beneficiaries' out-of-pocket costs would rise and forecast soaring Medicare enrollment.

When the commission disbanded in 1999, it was unable to forward an official recommendation to Congress because its plan fell one vote short of the majority needed to authorize an official recommendation. The plan would have changed Medicare into a premium system, where instead of Medicare directly covering beneficiaries, the beneficiaries would be given a fixed amount of money to purchase private health insurance. The plan would have also raised the age of eligibility from 65 to 67 (as had already been done with Social Security in 1983) and provided prescription drug coverage for low-income beneficiaries, much like the Medicare Prescription Drug, Improvement, and Modernization Act of 2003.

In 2010 President Barack Obama (1961–) established the National Commission on Fiscal Responsibility and Reform to suggest strategies to reduce the federal budget deficit. Among the commission's tasks was to recommend ways to slow the growth in entitlement program spending. The 18-member commission issued its final report in January 2011, which contained a variety of controversial recommendations that were designed to balance the budget by 2015 such as a $200 billion reduction in discretionary spending achieved by reducing defense spending, decreasing the federal workforce by 10%, increasing the payroll tax, and raising the retirement age to 69.

The report was criticized by Republicans and Democrats alike. Republicans were displeased with the increased taxes, and Democrats decried the recommendations that might reduce retiree benefits. President Obama indicated his support for the commission's work but chose not to endorse its recommendations.

**MEDICARE PRESCRIPTION DRUG, IMPROVEMENT, AND MODERNIZATION ACT AIMS TO REFORM MEDICARE.** The Medicare Prescription Drug, Improvement, and Modernization Act of 2003 was a measure intended to introduce private-sector enterprise into a Medicare model in urgent need of reform. Beginning in 2004, Medicare beneficiaries saved 10% to 25% off the cost of most medicines by using a Medicare-approved drug discount card. In 2006, by joining a Medicare-approved plan, beneficiaries were able to reduce their prescription drug costs by at least 50%, in exchange for a monthly premium of about $35. Older adults with low incomes received additional assistance to help pay for their prescription drugs.

The act expanded coverage of preventive medical services, with new beneficiaries receiving a free physical examination along with laboratory tests to screen for heart disease and diabetes. The act also provides employers with subsidies and tax breaks to help offset the costs associated with maintaining retiree health benefits.

**IMPACT OF THE ACA ON MEDICARE.** In "The Affordable Care Act and Medicare: How the Law Is Changing the Program and the Challenges That Remain" (June 2015, http://www.commonwealthfund.org/~/media/files/publications/fund-report/2015/jun/1821_davis_aca_and_medicare_v2.pdf?la=en), Karen Davis, Stuart Guterman, and Farhan Bandeali of the Commonwealth Fund observe that the Medicare provisions in the ACA have served to close gaps in preventive care and prescription drug benefits, strengthen chronic disease management, encourage providers to emphasize high-value care and slow the growth of health care spending. They note that 8 million Medicare beneficiaries saved more than $11.5 billion between 2010 and 2014 from the gradual elimination of the coverage gap called the "donut hole" in Medicare Part D coverage and that projected Medicare spending from 2011 to 2020 is $1 billion less than the CBO originally estimated, in part due to the ACA.

The CMS explains in "The Affordable Care Act & Medicare" (2016, http://www.medicare.gov/about-us/affordable-care-act/affordable-care-act.html) that the ACA ensures the future of Medicare. The viability of the Medicare Trust fund will be extended to at least 2029, which is 12 years longer than originally forecast, by savings resulting from decreases in Medicare costs as well as reductions in waste, fraud, and abuse.

According to the CMS, in "2016 Medicare Costs" (2016, https://www.medicare.gov/Pubs/pdf/11579.pdf), one of the reforms introduced by the act is that older adults with higher incomes face increasing Part B premium costs.

**TABLE 5.10**

**Monthly Medicare premiums, 2016**

| If your yearly income in 2014 was | | | |
|---|---|---|---|
| File individual tax return | File joint tax return | File married & separate tax return | You pay (in 2016) |
| $85,000 or less | $170,000 or less | $85,000 or less | $121.80 |
| above $85,000 up to $107,000 | above $170,000 up to $214,000 | N/A | $170.50 |
| above $107,000 up to $160,000 | above $214,000 up to $320,000 | N/A | $243.60 |
| above $160,000 up to $214,000 | above $320,000 up to $428,000 | above $85,000 up to $129,000 | $316.70 |
| above $214,000 | above $428,000 | above $129,000 | $389.80 |

N/A = not applicable.

SOURCE: "Part B Monthly Premium," in "2016 Medicare Costs," Centers for Medicare and Medicaid Services, CMS Product no. 11579, December 2015, https://www.medicare.gov/Pubs/pdf/11579.pdf (accessed August 7, 2016)

Table 5.10 shows the standard Part B premium of $121.80 per month and monthly premiums for high-income individuals and couples.

### Medicaid

Medicaid was enacted by Congress in 1965 under Title XIX (Grants to States for Medical Assistance Programs) of the Social Security Act. It is a joint federal-state program that provides medical assistance to selected categories of low-income Americans: the aged, people who are blind or disabled, and financially struggling families with dependent children. Medicaid covers hospitalization, physicians' fees, laboratory and radiology fees, and long-term care in nursing homes. It is the largest source of funds for medical and health-related services for the poorest Americans and the second-largest public payer of health care costs, after Medicare.

The Deficit Reduction Act (DRA) was signed into law by President George W. Bush (1946–) in 2006. The act changed many aspects of the Medicaid program. Some of the changes are mandatory provisions that the states must enact, such as proof of citizenship and other criteria that will make it more difficult for people to qualify for or enroll in Medicaid. Other changes are optional; they allow the states to make changes to the Medicaid program through state plan amendments. For example, states can choose to require anyone with a family income more than 150% of the poverty level to pay a premium of as much as 5% of their income. Before the act, the states had to provide a mandatory set of services to Medicaid recipients. Beginning in 2006 the states could modify their Medicaid benefits such that they were comparable to those offered to federal and state employees, the benefits provided by the HMO with the largest non-Medicaid enrollment, or coverage approved by the secretary of HHS.

The ACA expanded coverage by establishing national Medicaid eligibility criteria. People with incomes of 133% of the poverty level and below became eligible for Medicaid coverage. However, because of the calculation method, which disregards 5% of income, the eligibility threshold is effectively 138%. All states expanding Medicaid coverage to individuals with family incomes at or below 138% of the federal poverty level were eligible for increased federal matching funds. Health care costs for newly eligible people through the Medicaid expansion were paid for with 100% federal funds in 2016, 95% in 2017, and will gradually reduce to 90% in 2020.

The ASPE Issue brief "Impacts of the Affordable Care Act's Medicaid Expansion on Insurance Coverage and Access to Care" (June 20, 2016, https://aspe.hhs.gov/sites/default/files/pdf/205141/medicaidexpansion.pdf) reviews the impact of the ACA's Medicaid expansion through 2016. By March 2016, 72.5 million people were enrolled in Medicaid/CHIP (Children's Health Insurance Program covers youth under age 19 whose parents earn too much to qualify for Medicaid but not enough to pay for private insurance), a 26.5% increase (15 million people). The ASPE observes that expansion states had a 49.5% decline in the uninsured rate compared with a 33.8% decline in non-expansion states and notes that the difference between expansion and non-expansion states is actually greater since non-expansion states started with higher uninsured rates.

Medicaid expansion increased access to primary care, expanded use of prescription medications, and increased rates of diagnosis of chronic conditions among new enrollees. It also markedly improved affordability of care: the percentage of low-income adults with problems paying medical bills fell from 34.7% before expansion to 24.2% after expansion, and the percentage reporting unmet medical needs dropped from 55.3% before expansion to 44.8% after expansion. Close to two-thirds of adults covered as a result of Medicaid expansion say they are "better off now than they were before enrolling in Medicaid"; 93% are satisfied with their Medicaid health plans, and 92% are satisfied with their plan physicians.

## LONG-TERM HEALTH CARE

One of the most urgent health care problems facing Americans in the 21st century is the growing need for long-term care. Long-term care refers to health and social services for people with chronic illnesses or mental or physical conditions so disabling that they cannot live independently without assistance; they require care daily. Longer life spans and improved life-sustaining technologies are increasing the likelihood that more people than ever before may eventually require costly long-term care.

### Limited and Expensive Options

Caring for chronically ill or elderly patients presents difficult and expensive choices for Americans: they must either provide long-term care at home or rely on a nursing home. Home health care was the fastest-growing segment of the health care industry during the first half of the 1990s. Although the rate of growth has slowed since that time, the CMS projects that the home health care sector will grow from $97.2 billion in 2017 to $159.5 billion in 2025. (See Table 5.11.)

### High Cost of Long-Term Care

The options for quality, affordable long-term care in the United States are limited but improving. According to the *Genworth 2016 Cost of Care Survey* (2016, https://www.genworth.com/about-us/industry-expertise/cost-of-care.html), nursing home care in 2016 cost an average of $7,698 per month for a private room, or $92,376 per year. Many nursing home residents rely on Medicaid to pay these fees. In 2016 Medicaid covered an estimated 52.4% of nursing home costs for older Americans. (See Table 5.12.) The most common sources of payment at admission were Medicare (which pays only for short-term stays after hospitalization), private insurance, and other private funds. The primary source of payment changes as a stay lengthens. After their funds are exhausted, nursing home residents on Medicare shift to Medicaid.

To be eligible for long-term-care coverage by Medicaid, an individual must have an income that is less than the cost of care in the facility at the Medicaid rate and must meet income and resource limits. Many older adults must "spend down" to deplete their life savings to qualify for Medicaid assistance. This term refers to a provision in Medicaid coverage that provides care for seniors whose income exceeds eligibility requirements. For example, if their monthly income is $100 over the state Medicaid eligibility line, they can spend $100 per month on their medical care, and Medicaid will cover the remainder.

Nursing home care may seem cost-prohibitive, but homemaker and home health care services are costly, and most older adults cannot afford this expense long-term. The *Genworth 2016 Cost of Care Survey* reports that in 2016 the fee for homemaker services ("hands off" care that is limited to household chores rather than patient care) was an average of $3,813 per month, and the cost of home health aide services ("hands on" care that is personal, such as bathing or grooming, but not medical) was an average of $3,861 per month.

In *The Next Four Decades: The Older Population in the United States, 2010 to 2050* (May 2010, http://www.census.gov/prod/2010pubs/p25-1138.pdf), Grayson K. Vincent and Victoria A. Velkoff of the U.S. Census Bureau project that the population over the age of 85 years (those most likely to require long-term care) will nearly

# TABLE 5.11

## National health expenditures, by type of expenditure, 2009–25

| Type of expenditure (billions $) | 2009 | 2010 | 2011 | 2012 | 2013 | 2014 | 2015 | 2016 | Projected 2017 | 2018 | 2019 | 2020 | 2021 | 2022 | 2023 | 2024 | 2025 |
|---|---|---|---|---|---|---|---|---|---|---|---|---|---|---|---|---|---|
| National health expenditures | $2,496.4 | $2,595.7 | $2,696.6 | $2,799.0 | $2,879.9 | $3,031.3 | $3,197.2 | $3,350.7 | $3,521.6 | $3,731.4 | $3,958.6 | $4,198.3 | $4,457.5 | $4,732.8 | $5,022.0 | $5,321.7 | $5,631.0 |
| Health consumption expenditures | 2,357.5 | 2,452.9 | 2,547.1 | 2,645.8 | 2,727.4 | 2,877.4 | 3,037.8 | 3,185.5 | 3,348.9 | 3,549.1 | 3,766.0 | 3,994.7 | 4,242.1 | 4,504.8 | 4,780.9 | 5,066.8 | 5,361.6 |
| Personal health care | 2,115.9 | 2,194.1 | 2,280.4 | 2,371.8 | 2,441.3 | 2,563.6 | 2,700.3 | 2,830.4 | 2,975.1 | 3,150.8 | 3,341.1 | 3,543.3 | 3,761.0 | 3,992.0 | 4,234.5 | 4,485.4 | 4,743.8 |
| Hospital care | 778.1 | 817.6 | 853.2 | 902.7 | 933.9 | 971.8 | 1,019.2 | 1,067.3 | 1,122.1 | 1,185.7 | 1,259.0 | 1,336.0 | 1,420.0 | 1,509.6 | 1,603.6 | 1,700.7 | 1,800.5 |
| Professional services | 669.5 | 691.3 | 721.2 | 749.5 | 767.5 | 801.6 | 844.0 | 881.8 | 924.3 | 975.4 | 1,033.6 | 1,094.5 | 1,160.2 | 1,229.5 | 1,300.9 | 1,373.7 | 1,446.6 |
| Physician and clinical services | 500.5 | 516.4 | 540.9 | 563.0 | 576.8 | 603.7 | 636.3 | 664.9 | 697.3 | 735.8 | 779.9 | 825.1 | 874.7 | 927.3 | 981.8 | 1,037.2 | 1,092.8 |
| Other professional services | 66.6 | 69.9 | 73.3 | 77.6 | 80.3 | 84.4 | 89.1 | 93.3 | 97.9 | 103.6 | 110.0 | 116.8 | 123.9 | 131.5 | 139.3 | 147.4 | 154.9 |
| Dental services | 102.3 | 105.0 | 107.1 | 108.9 | 110.4 | 113.5 | 118.6 | 123.6 | 129.1 | 136.0 | 143.7 | 152.6 | 161.5 | 170.8 | 179.8 | 189.2 | 198.9 |
| Other health, residential, and personal care | 123.3 | 129.0 | 131.8 | 137.9 | 144.5 | 150.4 | 158.1 | 166.0 | 174.2 | 183.3 | 193.2 | 203.6 | 214.8 | 226.5 | 238.6 | 251.3 | 264.5 |
| Home health care | 67.4 | 71.1 | 73.6 | 76.9 | 79.4 | 83.2 | 88.2 | 92.2 | 97.2 | 102.8 | 109.2 | 116.3 | 123.9 | 132.1 | 140.7 | 149.9 | 159.5 |
| Nursing care facilities and continuing care retirement communities | 136.9 | 140.9 | 146.8 | 148.3 | 150.2 | 155.6 | 161.6 | 169.5 | 178.3 | 187.7 | 198.2 | 209.7 | 221.8 | 234.7 | 248.0 | 262.0 | 276.4 |
| Retail outlet sales of medical products | 340.9 | 344.2 | 353.8 | 356.5 | 365.8 | 401.0 | 429.2 | 453.6 | 479.1 | 515.9 | 547.8 | 583.1 | 620.4 | 659.7 | 702.7 | 747.9 | 796.2 |
| Prescription drugs | 252.7 | 253.0 | 258.7 | 259.1 | 265.3 | 297.7 | 321.9 | 342.1 | 362.7 | 393.6 | 418.6 | 445.9 | 474.6 | 505.1 | 539.3 | 575.4 | 614.5 |
| Other medical products | 88.1 | 91.2 | 95.1 | 97.4 | 100.5 | 103.3 | 107.3 | 111.5 | 116.3 | 122.3 | 129.3 | 137.2 | 145.7 | 154.6 | 163.4 | 172.5 | 181.7 |
| Durable medical equipment | 37.8 | 39.9 | 42.3 | 43.7 | 44.9 | 46.4 | 48.4 | 50.4 | 52.8 | 55.6 | 58.9 | 62.9 | 67.2 | 71.8 | 76.2 | 80.8 | 85.5 |
| Other non-durable medical products | 50.3 | 51.2 | 52.8 | 53.7 | 55.6 | 56.9 | 59.0 | 61.1 | 63.6 | 66.8 | 70.3 | 74.3 | 78.5 | 82.8 | 87.2 | 91.7 | 96.3 |
| Government administration | 29.6 | 30.2 | 32.4 | 33.5 | 36.3 | 40.2 | 44.4 | 47.3 | 50.5 | 53.8 | 57.7 | 61.7 | 66.1 | 70.8 | 75.8 | 81.3 | 87.3 |
| Net cost of private health insurance | 137.9 | 153.2 | 160.3 | 164.4 | 173.2 | 194.6 | 209.7 | 220.4 | 231.3 | 247.0 | 263.7 | 279.8 | 298.2 | 318.0 | 338.8 | 360.5 | 382.6 |
| Government public health activities | 74.1 | 75.4 | 74.0 | 76.0 | 76.6 | 79.0 | 83.3 | 87.4 | 92.0 | 97.5 | 103.5 | 109.9 | 116.7 | 124.0 | 131.7 | 139.6 | 147.8 |
| Investment | 139.0 | 142.7 | 149.5 | 153.2 | 152.5 | 153.9 | 159.4 | 165.2 | 172.7 | 182.3 | 192.6 | 203.6 | 215.4 | 228.0 | 241.1 | 254.9 | 269.4 |
| Research* | 45.4 | 49.2 | 49.6 | 48.4 | 46.5 | 45.5 | 46.2 | 47.3 | 49.1 | 51.3 | 53.8 | 56.4 | 59.2 | 62.1 | 65.1 | 68.2 | 71.4 |
| Structures & equipment | 93.6 | 93.5 | 99.8 | 104.8 | 106.0 | 108.3 | 113.3 | 117.8 | 123.6 | 130.9 | 138.9 | 147.2 | 156.3 | 165.9 | 176.0 | 186.7 | 198.0 |

### Annual percent change by type of expenditure (%)

| Type of expenditure | 2009 | 2010 | 2011 | 2012 | 2013 | 2014 | 2015 | 2016 | Projected 2017 | 2018 | 2019 | 2020 | 2021 | 2022 | 2023 | 2024 | 2025 |
|---|---|---|---|---|---|---|---|---|---|---|---|---|---|---|---|---|---|
| National health expenditures | — | 4.0% | 3.9% | 3.8% | 2.9% | 5.3% | 5.5% | 4.8% | 5.1% | 6.0% | 6.1% | 6.1% | 6.2% | 6.2% | 6.1% | 6.0% | 5.8% |
| Health consumption expenditures | — | 4.0 | 3.8 | 3.9 | 3.1 | 5.5 | 5.6 | 4.9 | 5.1 | 6.0 | 6.1 | 6.1 | 6.2 | 6.2 | 6.1 | 6.0 | 5.8 |
| Personal health care | — | 3.7 | 3.9 | 4.0 | 2.9 | 5.0 | 5.3 | 4.8 | 5.1 | 5.9 | 6.0 | 6.1 | 6.1 | 6.1 | 6.1 | 5.9 | 5.8 |
| Hospital care | — | 5.1 | 4.3 | 5.8 | 3.5 | 4.1 | 4.9 | 4.7 | 5.1 | 5.7 | 6.2 | 6.1 | 6.3 | 6.3 | 6.2 | 6.1 | 5.9 |
| Professional services | — | 3.3 | 4.3 | 3.9 | 2.4 | 4.4 | 5.3 | 4.5 | 4.8 | 5.5 | 6.0 | 5.9 | 6.0 | 6.0 | 5.8 | 5.6 | 5.3 |
| Physician and clinical services | — | 3.2 | 4.7 | 4.1 | 2.5 | 4.6 | 5.4 | 4.5 | 4.9 | 5.5 | 6.0 | 5.8 | 6.0 | 6.0 | 5.9 | 5.6 | 5.4 |
| Other professional services | — | 4.9 | 4.8 | 5.9 | 3.5 | 5.2 | 5.6 | 4.7 | 5.0 | 5.8 | 6.2 | 6.2 | 6.1 | 6.1 | 6.0 | 5.8 | 5.1 |
| Dental services | — | 2.7 | 2.0 | 1.6 | 1.5 | 2.8 | 4.4 | 4.2 | 4.5 | 5.3 | 5.7 | 6.1 | 5.9 | 5.7 | 5.3 | 5.2 | 5.1 |
| Other health, residential, and personal care | — | 4.6 | 2.2 | 4.6 | 4.7 | 4.1 | 5.2 | 4.9 | 5.0 | 5.2 | 5.4 | 5.4 | 5.5 | 5.4 | 5.3 | 5.3 | 5.3 |
| Home health care | — | 5.5 | 3.6 | 4.4 | 3.3 | 4.8 | 6.0 | 4.5 | 5.4 | 5.8 | 6.2 | 6.5 | 6.5 | 6.6 | 6.6 | 6.5 | 6.4 |
| Nursing care facilities and continuing care retirement communities | — | 2.9 | 4.2 | 1.0 | 1.3 | 3.6 | 3.9 | 4.9 | 5.2 | 5.3 | 5.6 | 5.8 | 5.8 | 5.8 | 5.7 | 5.6 | 5.5 |
| Retail outlet sales of medical products | — | 1.0 | 2.8 | 0.8 | 2.6 | 9.6 | 7.0 | 5.7 | 5.6 | 7.7 | 6.2 | 6.4 | 6.4 | 6.3 | 6.5 | 6.4 | 6.5 |
| Prescription drugs | — | 0.1 | 2.2 | 0.2 | 2.4 | 12.2 | 8.1 | 6.3 | 6.0 | 8.5 | 6.4 | 6.5 | 6.4 | 6.4 | 6.8 | 6.7 | 6.8 |
| Other medical products | — | 3.4 | 4.3 | 2.4 | 3.2 | 2.8 | 3.9 | 3.9 | 4.4 | 5.2 | 5.6 | 5.6 | 6.2 | 6.1 | 5.7 | 5.5 | 5.4 |
| Durable medical equipment | — | 5.6 | 5.8 | 3.4 | 2.8 | 3.2 | 4.3 | 4.2 | 4.7 | 5.3 | 6.1 | 6.7 | 6.9 | 6.7 | 6.3 | 6.0 | 5.8 |
| Other non-durable medical products | — | 1.8 | 3.1 | 1.7 | 3.5 | 2.4 | 3.6 | 3.6 | 4.1 | 5.0 | 5.3 | 5.7 | 5.6 | 5.5 | 5.3 | 5.2 | 5.0 |
| Government administration | — | 2.2 | 7.2 | 3.3 | 8.5 | 10.7 | 10.5 | 6.6 | 6.7 | 6.5 | 7.2 | 7.0 | 7.1 | 7.1 | 7.1 | 7.3 | 7.4 |
| Net cost of private health insurance | — | 11.1 | 4.6 | 2.6 | 5.3 | 12.4 | 7.8 | 5.1 | 5.0 | 6.8 | 6.7 | 6.1 | 6.6 | 6.6 | 6.6 | 6.4 | 6.1 |
| Government public health activities | — | 1.8 | -1.8 | 2.7 | 0.7 | 3.1 | 5.4 | 4.9 | 5.2 | 6.0 | 6.1 | 6.2 | 6.3 | 6.3 | 6.2 | 6.0 | 5.9 |
| Investment | — | 2.7 | 4.7 | 2.5 | -0.5 | 0.9 | 3.6 | 3.6 | 4.6 | 5.5 | 5.7 | 5.7 | 5.8 | 5.8 | 5.8 | 5.7 | 5.7 |
| Research* | — | 8.5 | 0.9 | -2.4 | -4.1 | -2.0 | 1.4 | 2.6 | 3.8 | 4.5 | 4.7 | 4.9 | 4.9 | 4.9 | 4.9 | 4.8 | 4.7 |
| Structures & equipment | — | -0.1 | 6.7 | 5.0 | 1.2 | 2.2 | 4.6 | 4.0 | 4.9 | 5.9 | 6.1 | 6.0 | 6.2 | 6.2 | 6.1 | 6.1 | 6.0 |

**TABLE 5.11**

**National health expenditures, by type of expenditure, 2009–25** [CONTINUED]

*Research and development expenditures of drug companies and other manufacturers and providers of medical equipment and supplies are excluded from research expenditures. These research expenditures are implicitly included in the expenditure class in which the product falls, in that they are covered by the payment received for that product.
Note: Numbers may not add to totals because of rounding.

SOURCE: "Table 2. National Health Expenditures Amounts and Annual Percent Change by Type of Expenditure," in *National Health Expenditures Projections 2015–2025*, U.S. Department of Health and Human Services, Centers for Medicare and Medicaid Services, July 14, 2016, https://www.cms.gov/research-statistics-data-and-systems/statistics-trends-and-reports/nationalhealthexpenddata/nationalhealthaccountsprojected.html (accessed August 5, 2016)

**TABLE 5.12**

**Nursing home and continuing care expenditures, by source of funds, 2009–25**

| Year | Total | Out-of-pocket payments | Health insurance[a] Total | Private health insurance | Medicare | Medicaid | Other health insurance programs[b] | Other third-party payers[c] |
|---|---|---|---|---|---|---|---|---|
| **Historical estimates** | | | | Amount in billions | | | | |
| 2009 | $136.9 | $38.2 | $89.7 | $10.2 | $30.1 | $45.5 | $3.9 | $9.0 |
| 2010 | 140.9 | 37.7 | 93.5 | 10.8 | 32.4 | 46.3 | 4.1 | 9.7 |
| 2011 | 146.8 | 37.9 | 99.1 | 11.2 | 35.9 | 47.7 | 4.3 | 9.8 |
| 2012 | 148.3 | 40.1 | 97.9 | 11.9 | 34.0 | 47.6 | 4.4 | 10.3 |
| 2013 | 150.2 | 40.8 | 98.9 | 12.1 | 34.3 | 48.1 | 4.5 | 10.5 |
| 2014 | 155.6 | 41.2 | 103.1 | 13.1 | 35.7 | 49.6 | 4.7 | 11.3 |
| **Projected** | | | | | | | | |
| 2015 | 161.6 | 42.8 | 107.1 | 14.2 | 37.3 | 50.8 | 4.7 | 11.7 |
| 2016 | 169.5 | 44.9 | 112.3 | 15.4 | 39.7 | 52.4 | 4.9 | 12.3 |
| 2017 | 178.3 | 47.4 | 118.0 | 16.4 | 42.5 | 54.0 | 5.0 | 12.9 |
| 2018 | 187.7 | 50.2 | 123.9 | 17.6 | 45.1 | 56.0 | 5.3 | 13.6 |
| 2019 | 198.2 | 53.3 | 130.6 | 18.6 | 48.4 | 58.0 | 5.5 | 14.4 |
| 2020 | 209.7 | 56.5 | 138.1 | 19.7 | 52.3 | 60.2 | 5.8 | 15.1 |
| 2021 | 221.8 | 60.1 | 145.9 | 20.7 | 56.6 | 62.4 | 6.1 | 15.9 |
| 2022 | 234.7 | 63.9 | 154.1 | 21.8 | 61.3 | 64.5 | 6.4 | 16.7 |
| 2023 | 248.0 | 67.9 | 162.6 | 22.9 | 66.5 | 66.5 | 6.7 | 17.5 |
| 2024 | 262.0 | 72.3 | 171.3 | 24.0 | 71.9 | 68.5 | 6.9 | 18.4 |
| 2025 | 276.4 | 77.0 | 180.2 | 25.2 | 77.4 | 70.5 | 7.1 | 19.3 |
| **Historical estimates** | | | | Per capita amount | | | | |
| 2009 | $447 | $125 | d | d | d | d | d | d |
| 2010 | 456 | 122 | d | d | d | d | d | d |
| 2011 | 472 | 122 | d | d | d | d | d | d |
| 2012 | 473 | 128 | d | d | d | d | d | d |
| 2013 | 475 | 129 | d | d | d | d | d | d |
| 2014 | 489 | 129 | d | d | d | d | d | d |
| **Projected** | | | | | | | | |
| 2015 | 503 | 133 | d | d | d | d | d | d |
| 2016 | 523 | 139 | d | d | d | d | d | d |
| 2017 | 546 | 145 | d | d | d | d | d | d |
| 2018 | 569 | 152 | d | d | d | d | d | d |
| 2019 | 595 | 160 | d | d | d | d | d | d |
| 2020 | 624 | 168 | d | d | d | d | d | d |
| 2021 | 654 | 177 | d | d | d | d | d | d |
| 2022 | 686 | 187 | d | d | d | d | d | d |
| 2023 | 718 | 197 | d | d | d | d | d | d |
| 2024 | 752 | 207 | d | d | d | d | d | d |
| 2025 | 787 | 219 | d | d | d | d | d | d |
| **Historical estimates** | | | | Percent distribution | | | | |
| 2009 | 100.0 | 27.9 | 65.5 | 7.4 | 22.0 | 33.2 | 2.9 | 6.6 |
| 2010 | 100.0 | 26.8 | 66.4 | 7.7 | 23.0 | 32.9 | 2.9 | 6.9 |
| 2011 | 100.0 | 25.8 | 67.5 | 7.7 | 24.4 | 32.5 | 2.9 | 6.7 |
| 2012 | 100.0 | 27.1 | 66.0 | 8.0 | 22.9 | 32.1 | 3.0 | 6.9 |
| 2013 | 100.0 | 27.2 | 65.9 | 8.0 | 22.8 | 32.0 | 3.0 | 7.0 |
| 2014 | 100.0 | 26.5 | 66.3 | 8.4 | 22.9 | 31.9 | 3.0 | 7.3 |
| **Projected** | | | | | | | | |
| 2015 | 100.0 | 26.5 | 66.3 | 8.8 | 23.1 | 31.5 | 2.9 | 7.2 |
| 2016 | 100.0 | 26.5 | 66.2 | 9.1 | 23.4 | 30.9 | 2.9 | 7.3 |
| 2017 | 100.0 | 26.6 | 66.2 | 9.2 | 23.8 | 30.3 | 2.8 | 7.3 |
| 2018 | 100.0 | 26.8 | 66.0 | 9.4 | 24.0 | 29.8 | 2.8 | 7.3 |
| 2019 | 100.0 | 26.9 | 65.9 | 9.4 | 24.4 | 29.3 | 2.8 | 7.3 |
| 2020 | 100.0 | 27.0 | 65.8 | 9.4 | 25.0 | 28.7 | 2.8 | 7.2 |
| 2021 | 100.0 | 27.1 | 65.8 | 9.3 | 25.5 | 28.1 | 2.8 | 7.2 |
| 2022 | 100.0 | 27.2 | 65.7 | 9.3 | 26.1 | 27.5 | 2.7 | 7.1 |
| 2023 | 100.0 | 27.4 | 65.6 | 9.2 | 26.8 | 26.8 | 2.7 | 7.1 |
| 2024 | 100.0 | 27.6 | 65.4 | 9.2 | 27.5 | 26.1 | 2.6 | 7.0 |
| 2025 | 100.0 | 27.8 | 65.2 | 9.1 | 28.0 | 25.5 | 2.6 | 7.0 |
| **Historical estimates** | | | | Annual percent change from previous year shown | | | | |
| 2009 | — | — | — | — | — | — | — | — |
| 2010 | 2.9 | −1.1 | 4.2 | 6.0 | 7.3 | 1.8 | 3.7 | 7.4 |
| 2011 | 4.2 | 0.4 | 6.0 | 4.1 | 10.8 | 3.0 | 6.5 | 1.2 |
| 2012 | 1.0 | 5.9 | −1.2 | 5.5 | −5.2 | −0.1 | 2.0 | 5.3 |
| 2013 | 1.3 | 1.6 | 1.1 | 1.7 | 0.9 | 1.0 | 2.3 | 2.0 |
| 2014 | 3.6 | 0.9 | 4.2 | 8.5 | 4.1 | 3.1 | 5.3 | 7.7 |

TABLE 5.12

**Nursing home and continuing care expenditures, by source of funds, 2009–25** [CONTINUED]

| | | | Health insurance[a] | | | | Other health insurance programs[b] | Other third-party payers[c] |
|---|---|---|---|---|---|---|---|---|
| Year | Total | Out-of-pocket payments | Total | Private health insurance | Medicare | Medicaid | | |
| Projected | | | Annual percent change from previous year shown | | | | | |
| 2015 | 3.9 | 4.0 | 3.8 | 8.5 | 4.5 | 2.5 | −0.7 | 3.5 |
| 2016 | 4.9 | 4.9 | 4.9 | 8.2 | 6.5 | 3.0 | 3.1 | 5.2 |
| 2017 | 5.2 | 5.4 | 5.1 | 7.1 | 6.9 | 3.2 | 4.0 | 5.0 |
| 2018 | 5.3 | 6.1 | 5.0 | 6.7 | 6.1 | 3.5 | 4.5 | 5.5 |
| 2019 | 5.6 | 6.1 | 5.4 | 6.0 | 7.3 | 3.7 | 5.0 | 5.5 |
| 2020 | 5.8 | 6.1 | 5.8 | 5.6 | 8.3 | 3.7 | 5.5 | 5.0 |
| 2021 | 5.8 | 6.3 | 5.6 | 5.4 | 8.1 | 3.6 | 5.1 | 5.1 |
| 2022 | 5.8 | 6.4 | 5.6 | 5.2 | 8.3 | 3.4 | 4.5 | 5.1 |
| 2023 | 5.7 | 6.2 | 5.5 | 4.9 | 8.4 | 3.1 | 4.1 | 4.9 |
| 2024 | 5.6 | 6.4 | 5.4 | 5.0 | 8.2 | 3.0 | 3.4 | 5.0 |
| 2025 | 5.5 | 6.5 | 5.1 | 4.9 | 7.6 | 2.9 | 3.5 | 5.0 |

[a]Includes private health insurance (employer-sponsored insurance and other private insurance, which includes Marketplace plans), Medicare, Medicaid, Children's Health Insurance Program (Titles XIX and XXI), Department of Defense, and Department of Veterans' Affairs.
[b]Children's Health Insurance Program (Titles XIX and XXI), Department of Defense, and Department of Veterans' Affairs.
[c]Includes worksite health care, other private revenues, Indian Health Service, workers' compensation, general assistance, maternal and child health, vocational rehabilitation, other federal programs, Substance Abuse and Mental Health Services Administration, other state and local programs, and school health.
[d]Calculation of per capita estimates is not applicable.
Note: Per capita amounts based on estimates that reflect the U.S. Bureau of Census definition for resident-based population (which includes all persons who usually reside in one of the fifty states or the District of Columbia, but excludes (i) residents living in Puerto Rico and areas under U.S. sovereignty, and (ii) U.S. Armed Forces overseas and U.S. citizens whose usual place of residence is outside of the United States) plus a small (typically less than 0.2% of population) adjustment to reflect Census undercounts. Projected estimates reflect the area population growth assumptions found in the Medicare Trustees Report. Numbers and percents may not add to totals because of rounding.

SOURCE: "Table 13. Nursing Care Facilities and Continuing Care Retirement Communities; Aggregate and per Capita Amounts, Percent Distribution and Annual Percent Change by Source of Funds: Calendar Years 2009–2025," in *National Health Expenditures Projections 2015–2025*, U.S. Department of Health and Human Services, Centers for Medicare and Medicaid Services, July 14, 2016, https://www.cms.gov/research-statistics-data-and-systems/statistics-trends-and-reports/nationalhealthexpenddata/nationalhealthaccountsprojected.html (accessed August 5, 2016)

quadruple by 2050. Although disability rates among older adults have declined in recent years, reducing somewhat the need for long-term care, the CBO anticipates that the growing population of people likely to require long-term care will no doubt increase spending commensurate with this growth.

## MENTAL HEALTH SPENDING

In *Projections of National Expenditures for Treatment of Mental and Substance Use Disorders, 2010–2020* (2014, http://store.samhsa.gov/shin/content/SMA14-4883/SMA14-4883.pdf), the Substance Abuse and Mental Health Services Administration (SAMHSA) predicts that spending for mental health and substance use (alcohol and chemical dependency) treatment in the United States will reach $280.5 billion in 2014, up from $171.7 billion in 2009. Treatment spending is projected to grow at an average annual rate of 4.6%, less than the 5.8% increase forecast for total health care spending. This is in part because many prescription drugs used in treatment will lose their patent protection in 2020, and lower-cost generic drugs will slow spending growth. State psychiatric hospital closures also contribute to slower spending growth. Mental health and substance abuse treatment, as a share of all health spending, is anticipated to decrease to 6.5% in 2020. Figure 5.4 shows how mental health spending will account for a smaller share of total health care spending through 2020.

Health care industry observers attribute the decrease in mental health inpatient services to an increased emphasis on drug treatment of mental health disorders, the growing frequency of outpatient treatment, and the cost containment efforts of managed care. Despite the higher spending for psychoactive prescription drugs, some industry observers believe the increased availability of effective drug therapy actually serves to contain mental health spending by enabling providers to offer drug therapy instead of costlier inpatient treatment.

In "Seizing Opportunities under the Affordable Care Act for Transforming the Mental and Behavioral Health System" (*Health Affairs*, vol. 31, no. 2, February 2012), David Mechanic of Rutgers University explains that new forms of reimbursement for mental health services such as fixed payments per client per period and single payment for a package of services incentivize providers to improve the coordination and continuity of care. For example, the ACA encourages state Medicaid programs to offer health homes for people with mental illness that are supported by matching federal funds for the first two years. Funds may be used to pay a "patient-designated health home provider who provides care management, makes necessary referrals, provides individual and family support, and uses health information technology to monitor and coordinate the various service providers involved."

FIGURE 5.4

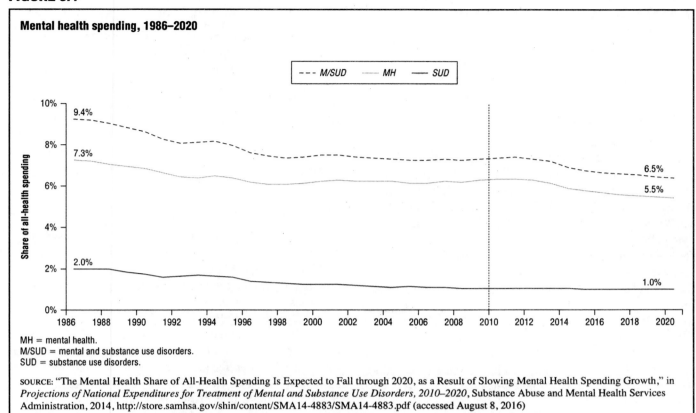

**Mental health spending, 1986–2020**

MH = mental health.
M/SUD = mental and substance use disorders.
SUD = substance use disorders.

SOURCE: "The Mental Health Share of All-Health Spending Is Expected to Fall through 2020, as a Result of Slowing Mental Health Spending Growth," in *Projections of National Expenditures for Treatment of Mental and Substance Use Disorders, 2010–2020*, Substance Abuse and Mental Health Services Administration, 2014, http://store.samhsa.gov/shin/content/SMA14-4883/SMA14-4883.pdf (accessed August 8, 2016)

## SAMHSA Spending

According to the HHS, in *HHS Budget in Brief, Fiscal Year 2017* (2016, http://www.hhs.gov/sites/default/files/fy2017-budget-in-brief.pdf), the fiscal year (FY) 2017 budget for SAMHSA was $4.3 billion, $590 million more than the FY 2016 budget. The funds were used to continue to improve access to mental health services, to support families of people with mental health and substance abuse disorders, build stronger communities, and prevent costly behavioral health problems.

## State Mental Health Agency Expenditures

Court rulings during the 1970s and an evolution in professional thinking prompted the release of many people with serious mental illness from institutions to community treatment programs. The census (the number of patients or occupants, which is frequently referred to as a rate) of public mental hospitals sharply declined, and increasing pressure was put on the states to deliver community-based treatment.

State mental health agencies (SMHAs) operate the public mental health system that acts as a safety net for poor, uninsured, and otherwise indigent people suffering from mental illness. In *Mental Health Financing in the United States: A Primer* (April 2011, http://www.kff.org/medicaid/upload/8182.pdf), the Kaiser Commission on Medicaid and the Uninsured explains that these public mental health systems are heavily dependent on Medicaid, and "in many states, the two are jointly budgeted, with states attributing their matching funds for Medicaid to the budget of state mental health agencies." The SMHAs vary from state to state. Some state agencies purchase, regulate, administer, manage, and provide care and treatment, whereas others simply purchase care using public funds that include general state revenues and federal funds. Medicaid is also the fastest-growing component of SMHA spending; however, the share of Medicaid mental health spending that is controlled by the SMHAs varies widely by state.

Increased Medicaid financing of the SMHAs has had several beneficial effects on state systems. For example, it increased the amount of funds that are available for mental health services, catalyzed the shift to community-based treatment over institutional care, and improved access to insurance coverage and treatment for low-income people with mental health needs. Similar to the movement of privately insured people into managed care, during the 1990s state Medicaid programs turned to managed care organizations (MCOs) and behavioral health services in an effort to contain costs.

The SMHAs manage funds from the SAMHSA Mental Health Block Grant program. The program was created in 1982, and its flexible funding enables states to innovate, develop, and expand successful community-based programs. Block grants (lump sums of money) are awarded based on a formula that considers each state's population, service costs, income, and taxable resources, and the funds enable the states to finance community mental health treatment programs.

## HIGH COSTS OF RESEARCH

Medical and pharmaceutical research, disease prevention research, and the work to develop and conduct clinical trials of new drugs are expensive. The National Institutes of Health (NIH) reports in "Estimates of Funding for Various Research, Condition, and Disease Categories" (February 10, 2016, https://report.nih.gov/categorical_spending.aspx) that its FY 2017 budget allocated an estimated $699 million for breast cancer research, compared with $28 million to investigate child abuse and neglect. Pharmaceutical manufacturers also spend billions of dollars every year researching and developing new medicines. For example, according to the Pharmaceutical Research and Manufacturers of America (PhRMA; 2016 http://www.phrma.org/about/phrma), U.S. pharmaceutical companies spent $58.8 billion in 2015 and more than half a trillion dollars since 2000. By contrast, the entire NIH budget for FY 2011 was $30.4 billion.

Decisions about how much is spent to research a particular disease are not based solely on how many people develop the disease or die from it. Rightly or wrongly, economists base the societal value of an individual on his or her earning potential and productivity (the ability to contribute to society as a worker). The bulk of the people who die from heart disease, stroke, and cancer are older adults. Many have retired from the workforce, and their potential economic productivity is usually low or nonexistent. (This is not an observation about how society values older adults; instead, it is simply an economic measure of present and future financial productivity.)

In contrast, AIDS patients are often much younger, and without treatment may die within three years of diagnosis. Until they develop AIDS, their potential productivity, measured in economic terms, is high. The number of work years lost when they die is considerable. Using this economic equation to determine how disease research should be funded, it may be considered economically wise to invest more money to research AIDS because the losses, which are measured in potential work years rather than in lives, are so much greater.

Once a new drug receives FDA approval, its manufacturer is ordinarily allowed to hold the patent on the drug to recoup its investment. During the life of the patent the drug is priced much higher than if other manufacturers were allowed to compete by producing generic versions of the same drug. After the patent expires, competition between pharmaceutical manufacturers generally lowers the price.

In *PhRMA 2016 Profile* (2016, http://phrma.org/sites/default/files/pdf/biopharmaceutical-industry-profile.pdf), PhRMA explains that the pharmaceutical manufacturer must cover the cost of research and development for the approximately 12% drugs that succeed in clinical trials and are approved by FDA. PhRMA observes that manufacturers spend about $2.6 billion to bring a brand-name drug from discovery to FDA approval, including the expense of 10 to 15 years of product development and the costs associated with failures.

### High Cost of Prescription Drugs

Spending for prescription drugs is the fastest-growing component of health care spending. According to the CMS, in 2016 prescription drug expenditures were an estimated $342.1 billion and were projected to rise to $614.5 billion by 2025. (See Table 5.9.) In "Decoding Big Pharma's Secret Drug Pricing Practices" (Bloomberg.com, June 29, 2015), Robert Langreth, Michael Keller, and Christopher Cannon report that cost analyses of 39 prescription drugs found that 30 had price increases that were more than twice the rate of inflation from 2009 to 2015. Langreth, Keller, and Cannon note that of the drugs analyzed, 27 had discounted prices that rose 25% or more over the six-year period, which was much higher than the CPI, which rose 9.5% during the same period.

To control prescription drug expenditures, many hospitals, health plans, employers, and other group purchasers have attempted to obtain discounts and rebates for bulk purchases from pharmaceutical companies. Some have developed programs to encourage health care practitioners and consumers to use less-expensive generic drugs, and others have limited, reduced, or even eliminated prescription drug coverage.

In "The Affordable Care Act and the U.S. Economy: A Five-Year Perspective" (February 2016, http://www.commonwealthfund.org/~/media/files/publications/fund-report/2016/feb/1860_schoen_aca_and_us_economy_v2.pdf), Cathy Schoen of the Commonwealth Fund, cautions that while the patent expiration for several costly drugs and a hiatus in development of new, breakthrough drugs slowed drug spending in recent years, there are indications that this slowdown is ending as evidenced by rapidly increasing prices for even generic drugs and the launch of new cancer drugs and a new drug for hepatitis C that costs $82,000. Schoen also observes that private insurers as well as consumers are contending with the rising costs of prescription drugs.

### Generic Drugs Promise Cost Savings

When patents expire on popular brand-name drugs, the entry of generic versions of these drugs to the market promises cost savings for consumers and payers. Generic drugs usually cost 10% to 30% less when they first enter the market and even less once additional generic manufacturers join in the competition. In "Blockbuster Drugs Facing Patent Expiration in 2016" (PharmacyTimes.com, January 27, 2016), Allison Gilchrist reports that several widely used, brand-name drugs lost their patent protection in 2016, including Crestor (rosuvastatin calcium), AstraZeneca's cholesterol and triglyceride lowering drug that is intended to reduce the risk of heart attack and stroke; Benicar (olmesartan medoxomil), Daiichi Sankyo's drug used to treat high blood pressure in adults and children; and Zetia (ezetimibe), Merck's cholesterol-lowering drug. Gilchrist notes that these three drugs generate $11.6 billion in annual revenue. Popular brand-name drugs that lose their patent protection in 2017 include Merck's Vytorin (ezetimibe and simvastatin), used to lower blood cholesterol to reduce the risk of heart attack and stroke; Lilly's Strattera (atomoxetine), used to treat attention deficit/hyperactivity disorder (ADHD; a chronic condition characterized by persistent problems, such as difficulty sustaining attention and controlling behavior); and Tamiflu (oseltamivir phosphate), Roche's antiviral medication that blocks the actions of influenza virus types A and B to reduce the severity and duration of flu symptoms.

### How Will the ACA Affect Drug Costs?

Because it mandates prescription drugs as one of 10 essential health benefits that insurance plans must offer, the ACA makes drug coverage a core part of coverage, effectively prohibiting insurers from adding on a prescription drug benefit plan to health coverage at an additional cost. In addition, prescription drug costs count toward out-of-pocket caps on medical expenses (about $6,400 for individuals and $12,800 for families).

The ACA also authorizes the FDA to approve generic versions of biosimilars (drugs derived from living organisms that are used to prevent, diagnose, or treat diseases) and grant biologics manufacturers 12 years of exclusive use before generics can be developed. In "Medicines Use and Spending in the U.S.—A Review of 2015 and Outlook to 2020," the QuintilesIMS Institute reports, "The outlook for medicine spending through 2020 is for mid-single-digit growth driven by further clusters of innovative treatments, offset by a rising impact from brands facing generic or biosimilar competition."

## RATIONING HEALTH CARE

When health care rationing (allocating medical resources) is defined as "all care that is expected to be beneficial is not always available to all patients," most health care practitioners, policy makers, and consumers accept that rationing has been, and will continue to be, a feature of the U.S. health care system. Most American opinion leaders and industry observers accept that even a country as wealthy as the United States cannot afford all the care that is likely to benefit its citizens. The practical considerations of allocating health care resources involve establishing priorities and determining how these resources should be rationed.

### Opponents of Rationing

There is widespread agreement among Americans that rationing according to patients' ability to pay for health care services or insurance is unfair. Ideally, health care should be equitably allocated on the basis of need and the potential benefit derived from the care. Those who argue against rationing fear that society's most vulnerable populations (older adults, the poor, and people with chronic illnesses) suffer most from the rationing of health care.

Many observers believe improving the efficiency of the U.S. health care system will save enough money to supply basic health care services to all Americans. They suggest that because expenditures for the same medical procedures vary greatly in different areas of the country, standardizing fees and costs could realize great savings. They also believe money could be saved if greater emphasis is placed on preventive care and on effective strategies to prevent or reduce behaviors that increase health risks such as smoking, alcohol and drug abuse, and unsafe sexual practices. Furthermore, they insist that the high cost of administering the U.S. health care system could be streamlined with a single payer for health care as in the Canadian system.

### Supporters of Rationing

Those who endorse rationing argue that the spiraling cost of the U.S. health care system stems from more than simple inefficiency. They attribute escalating costs to the aging population, rapid technological innovation, and the increasing costs of labor and supplies.

Not everyone who supports rationing thinks the U.S. health care system is working well. Some rationing supporters believe that the nation's health care system charges too much for the services it delivers and that it fails altogether to deliver to the millions of the uninsured. In fact, they point out that the United States already rations health care by not covering the uninsured. Other health care–rationing advocates argue that the problem is one of basic cultural assumptions, not the economics of the health care industry. Americans value human life, believe in the promise of health and quality health care for all, and insist that diseases can be cured. They contend the issue is not whether health care should be rationed but how care is rationed. They believe the United States spends too much on health compared with other societal needs, too much on the old rather than on the young, more on curing and not enough on caring, and too much on extending the length of life and not enough on enhancing the quality of life. Supporters of rationing argue instead for a system that guarantees a minimally acceptable level of health care for all, while reining in the expensive excesses of the current system, which often acts to prolong life at any cost.

### The Oregon Health Plan: An Experiment in Rationing

In 1987 Oregon designed a new, universal health care plan that would simultaneously expand coverage and contain costs by limiting services. Unlike other states, which trimmed budgets by eliminating people from Medicaid eligibility, Oregon chose to eliminate low-priority services. Michael Janofsky reports in "Oregon Starts to Extend Health Care" (*New York Times*, February 19, 1994) that the Oregon Health Plan, which was approved in August 1993, aimed to provide Medicaid to 120,000 additional residents living below the federal poverty level. The plan also established a high-risk insurance pool for people who were refused health insurance coverage because of preexisting medical conditions, offered more insurance options for small businesses, and improved employees' abilities to retain their health insurance benefits when they changed jobs. A gradual increase in the state cigarette tax was expected to provide $45 million annually, to help fund the additional estimated $200 million needed over the next several years.

Oregon developed a table of health care services and performed a cost-benefit analysis to rank them. It was decided that Oregon Medicaid would cover the top 565 services on a list of 696 medical procedures. Janofsky notes that services that fell below the cutoff point were "not deemed to be serious enough to require treatment, like common colds, flu, mild food poisoning, sprains, cosmetic procedures and experimental treatments for diseases in advanced stages."

As the Oregon Health Services Commission (HSC) prepared to establish the priorities, it decided that disease prevention and quality of well-being (QWB) were the factors that most influenced the ranking of the treatments. QWB drew fire from those who believed that such judgments could not be decided subjectively. Active medical or surgical treatment of terminally ill patients also ranked low on the QWB scale, whereas comfort and hospice care ranked high. The HSC emphasized that its QWB judgments were not based on an individual's quality of life at a given time; such judgments were considered ethically questionable. Instead, it focused on the potential for change in an individual's life, posing questions such as: "After treatment, how much better or worse off would the patient be?"

Critics countered that the plan obtained its funding by reducing services that were currently offered to Medicaid recipients (often poor women and children) rather than by emphasizing cost control. Others objected to the ranking and the ethical questions raised by choosing to support some treatments over others.

According to Jonathan Oberlander of the University of North Carolina, Chapel Hill, in "Health Reform Interrupted: The Unraveling of the Oregon Health Plan" (*Health Affairs*, vol. 26, no. 1, January 2007), the Oregon Health Plan initially did serve to reduce the percentage of uninsured Oregonians from 18% in 1992 to 11% in 1996, but its early success proved difficult to sustain. By 2003 the Oregon plan was not even close to achieving its goal of having no uninsured people in the state. In fact, the ranks of the uninsured were growing, so much so that by 2003 they reached 17%. An economic downturn in the state and the state's strategy of explicit rationing are cited by Oberlander as reasons for the ambitious plan's failure to achieve its goals.

The Oregon HSC continued to modify the plan's covered benefits. In 2002 the HSC began refining the list of covered services. The HSC sought to reduce the overall costs of the plan by eliminating less effective treatments and determining if any covered medical conditions could be more effectively treated using standardized clinical practice guidelines (step-by-step instructions for diagnosis and treatment of specific illnesses or disorders) while preserving basic coverage. The benefit review process is ongoing with the HSC submitting a new prioritized list of benefits on July 1 of each even-numbered year for review by the legislative assembly.

In 2012 legislation was enacted creating coordinated care organizations (CCOs), local entities responsible for providing and integrating physical, behavioral, and dental health care to Medicaid beneficiaries. These community-based organizations largely replaced Medicaid managed-care plans and are responsible for the care and medical outcomes for their Medicaid beneficiaries and for keeping their spending within preset targets. The global budgets of CCOs combine the previous patchwork of funding for medical, dental, and behavioral health care. They organize and pay providers to deliver care using a patient-centered, team-based approach, and they are held accountable for quality and costs against benchmarks established by the state government, which works with CCOs to help them improve their performance.

In accordance with the ACA option of expanding Medicaid, in 2014 the Oregon Health Plan coverage was extended to more low-income adults who in the past did not qualify for the plan. Prior to 2014, to be eligible people had to be at or below 100% of the federal poverty level. In 2014 coverage was offered to people who earned up to 138% of the federal poverty level, which at that time was about $16,100 per year for a single person or $32,900 a year for a family of four. In the first three months of the year, more than 200,000 Oregonians signed up for coverage, as reported by the Oregon Health Authority.

In "5 Years Later: How the Affordable Care Act Is Working for Oregon" (November 2, 2015, http://www.hhs.gov/healthcare/facts-and-features/state-by-state/how-aca-is-working-for-oregon/index.html), the HHS assistant secretary for Public Affairs reports that the uninsured rate in Oregon was 11.7% in 2014, down from 19.4% in 2013. By January 2015, 409,834 Oregonians had gained Medicaid or CHIP coverage and nearly 50,000 Oregonians with private insurance received refunds from insurance companies because of the provisions of the ACA.

## Rationing by HMOs

Managed care programs have sought to control costs by limiting coverage for experimental, duplicative, and unnecessary treatments. Before physicians can perform experimental procedures or prescribe new treatment plans, they must obtain prior authorization (approval from the patient's managed care plan) to ensure that the expenses will be covered.

Increasingly, patients and physicians are battling HMOs for approval to use and receive reimbursement for new technology and experimental treatments. Judges and juries, moved by the desperate situations of patients, have frequently decided cases against HMOs, regardless of whether the new treatment has been shown to be effective.

**"SILENT RATIONING."** Physicians and health care consumers are concerned that limiting coverage for new, high-cost technology will discourage research and development for new treatments before they have even been developed. This is called "silent rationing" because patients will never know what they have missed.

In an effort to control costs, some HMOs have discouraged physicians from informing patients about certain treatment options, including those that are extremely expensive or not covered by the HMO. This has proved to be a highly controversial issue, both politically and ethically. In December 1996 the HHS ruled that HMOs and other health plans cannot prevent physicians from telling Medicare patients about all available treatment options.

**RATIONING BY PHYSICIANS.** The results of a survey to assess physicians' attitudes about and behaviors around rationing were reported in "Self-Reported Rationing Behavior among US Physicians: A National Survey" (*Journal of General Internal Medicine*, July 19, 2016). Robert D. Sheeler et al. find that more than one half of the survey respondents engaged in behaviors consistent with rationing, "refraining from offering specific clinical services that would have provided the best patient care, because of health system cost."

Sheeler et al. find that the most commonly rationed health care were prescription drugs (48.3%) and MRI (44.5%). Primary care physicians were more likely than surgeons and other specialists who perform procedures to

report rationing, and physicians in medical school settings were less likely to ration care than those in small or solo practices. Physicians who characterized their political views as somewhat or very liberal were less likely to report rationing than those who described themselves as somewhat or very conservative.

## Could Less Health Care Be Better Than More?

Although health care providers and consumers fear that rationing sharply limits access to medical care and will ultimately result in poorer health among affected Americans, researchers are also concerned about the effects of too much care on the health of the nation. Several studies suggest that an oversupply of medical care may be as harmful as an undersupply.

In the landmark study *Geography and the Debate over Medicare Reform* (February 13, 2002, http://content.healthaffairs.org/cgi/reprint/hlthaff.w2.96v1), John E. Wennberg, Elliott S. Fisher, and Jonathan S. Skinner of Dartmouth Medical School find tremendous regional variation in both the utilization and the cost of health care that they believe is explained, at least in part, by the distribution of health care providers. Variations in physicians' practice styles—whether they favor outpatient treatment over hospitalization for specific procedures such as biopsies (surgical procedures to examine tissue to detect cancer cells)—greatly affect demand for hospital care.

Variation in demand for health care services in turn produces variation in health care expenditures. Wennberg, Fisher, and Skinner report wide geographic variation in Medicare spending. Medicare paid more than twice as much to care for a 65-year-old in Miami, Florida, where the supply of health care providers is overabundant, than it spent on care for a 65-year-old in Minneapolis, Minnesota, a city with an average supply of health care providers. To be certain that the differences were not simply higher fees in Miami, the researchers also compared rates of utilization. They find that older adults in Miami visited physicians and hospitals much more often than their counterparts in Minneapolis did.

Wennberg, Fisher, and Skinner also wanted to be sure that the differences were not caused by the severity of illness, so they compared care during the last six months of life to control for any underlying regional differences in the health of the population. Remarkably, the widest variations were observed in care during the last six months of life, when older adults in Miami saw physician specialists six times as often as those in Minneapolis. The researchers assert that higher expenditures, particularly at the end of life, do not purchase better care. Instead, they finance generally futile interventions that are intended to prolong life rather than to improve the quality of patients' lives. Wennberg, Fisher, and Skinner conclude that areas with more medical care, higher utilization, and higher costs fared no better in terms of life expectancy, morbidity (illness), or mortality (death), and that the care that people received was no different in quality from care received by people in areas with average supplies of health care providers.

In *The Care of Patients with Severe Chronic Illness: An Online Report on the Medicare Program by the Dartmouth Atlas Project* (2006, http://www.dartmouthatlas .org/downloads/atlases/2006_Chronic_Care_Atlas.pdf), John E. Wennberg et al. detail differences in the management of Medicare patients with severe chronic illnesses. The researchers find that average utilization and health care spending varied by state, region, and even by hospital in the same region. Expenditures were not linked with rates of illness in different parts of the country; instead, they reflected how intensively selected resources (e.g., acute care hospital beds, specialist physician visits, tests, and other services) were used to care for patients who were very ill but could not be cured. Because other research demonstrates that, for these chronically ill Americans, receiving more services does not result in improved health outcomes, and because most Americans say they prefer to avoid excessively high-tech end-of-life care, the researchers conclude that Medicare spending for the care of the chronically ill could be reduced by as much as 30%, while improving quality, patient satisfaction, and outcomes. The research by Wennberg et al. and similar studies pose two important and as yet unanswered questions: How much health care is needed to deliver the best health to a population? Are Americans getting the best value for the dollars spent on health care?

In "Competing with the Conventional Wisdom: Newspaper Framing of Medical Overtreatment" (*Health Communication*, vol. 29, no. 2, 2014), Kim Walsh-Childers and Jennifer Braddock observe that although overtreatment likely accounts for as much as 30% of all U.S. health care spending, a review of 98 newspaper articles about it published from January 2007 through December 2010 finds that few stories emphasized the financial burden of overtreatment. Instead, the articles focused more on legal issues and uncertainty, specifically about cancer testing and treatment as a driver of overutilization.

In "Primary Care Clinicians' Perspectives on Reducing Low-Value Care in an Integrated Delivery System" (*Permanente Journal*, vol. 20, no. 1, Winter 2016), Diana S. M. Buist et al. report the results of a survey of salaried primary care physicians and physician assistants to explore perceptions about the use of low-value care (medical tests and procedures that may be unnecessary and/or harmful) and their responsibility for reducing low value care. Buist et al. find that more than 90% of the practitioners surveyed think cost is important, and that it is reasonable to ask clinicians to be cost conscious. About the same percentage (88%) said they were comfortable discussing low-value

care with their patients, but 80% said they would order tests or procedures when patients were insistent. Survey respondents identified the barriers to reducing low-value care as time constraints (45%), overcoming patient preferences/values (44%), community standards (43%), fear of patient dissatisfaction (41%), patients' knowledge about the harms of low-value care (38%), and availability of tools to support shared decision making (37%).

## Economic Impact of Repealing the ACA

There have been several proposals to repeal the ACA, and with the 2016 election of Donald J. Trump (1946–) to the presidency, it is likely that repeal or reform of the law will be undertaken by the Republican-controlled Congress in 2017. The CBO and the staff of the Joint Committee on Taxation analyzed the budgetary and economic consequences that would result from repealing the law and reported their findings in *Budgetary and Economic Effects of Repealing the Affordable Care Act* (June 19, 2015, https://www.cbo.gov/sites/default/files/ 114th-congress-2015-2016/reports/50252-Effects_of_ACA _Repeal.pdf). The CBO and Joint Committee on Taxation predict that repealing the ACA would likely increase the federal deficit by $137 billion from 2016 to 2025. The CBO forecasts that a repeal would reduce deficits during the first half of the decade but would markedly increase them from 2021 through 2025.

Repealing the ACA would increase federal budget deficits by growing amounts after 2025 because the net savings attributable to a repeal of ACA insurance coverage provisions would grow more slowly than would the estimated costs of repealing other ACA provisions—most notably, the provisions that reduce federal outlays for Medicare. The CBO estimates that repealing all of the provisions would increase expenditures over the decade by $879 billion.

The ACA also includes provisions other than those related to insurance coverage that are anticipated to increase federal revenues. Provisions with the greatest budgetary impact are the increased Hospital Insurance payroll tax rate for high-income taxpayers, the surtax on those taxpayers' net investment income, and annual fees for health insurers. Repealing these provisions would slash revenues by $631 billion from 2016 through 2025.

All told, the CBO predicts that repealing the ACA would increase the federal budget deficit by $9 billion in 2021 and $98 billion in 2025. (See Figure 5.5.)

It is also anticipated that by enabling workers to seek new job opportunities without the fear of losing their employer-sponsored health care coverage, the legislation may stimulate business growth; however, the full impact of this provision is not yet known. In "Obamacare: What Went Right and What Went Wrong?" (USNews.com, February 4, 2016), Kimberly Leonard and Lindsey Cook observe that job growth in the private sector and falling

**FIGURE 5.5**

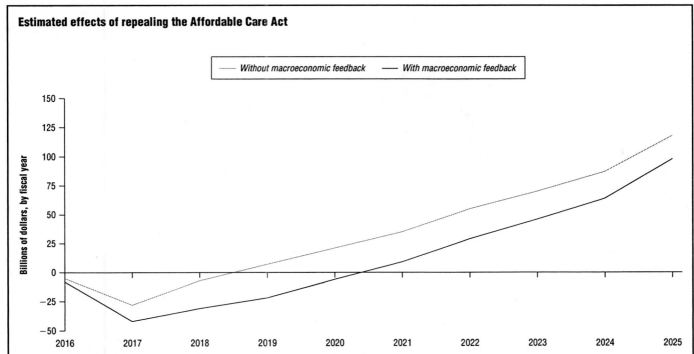

**Estimated effects of repealing the Affordable Care Act**

Note: The term "macroeconomic feedback" refers to the estimated effects on the federal budget that would arise from changes in economic output or other macroeconomic variables—such as changes in the number of hours that people work and in their aggregate compensation, which would change revenues, or changes in interest rates, which would change interest payments.

SOURCE: "Figure 1. Estimated Effects on Deficits of Repealing the Affordable Care Act," in *Budgetary and Economic Effects of Repealing the Affordable Care Act*, Congressional Budget Office, June 2015, https://www.cbo.gov/sites/default/files/114th-congress-2015-2016/reports/50252-Effects_of_ACA_Repeal.pdf (accessed August 9, 2016)

unemployment rates since enactment of the ACA support the positive economic impact of the law, but these favorable economic indicators may not be entirely attributable to the law.

In "United States Health Care Reform Progress to Date and Next Steps" (*Journal of the American Medical Association*, vol. 316, no. 5, August 2, 2016), President Obama affirmed the positive economic impact of the ACA stating, "While the Great Recession and other factors played a role in recent trends, the Council of Economic Advisers has found evidence that the reforms introduced by the ACA helped both slow health care cost growth and drive improvements in the quality of care." In "Five Years Old, Going on Ten: The Future of the Affordable Care Act" (March 27, 2016, https://www.brookings.edu/blog/health360/2015/03/27/five-years-old-going-on-ten-the-future-of-the-affordable-care-act/), Henry J. Aaron of the Brookings Institution wrote that "despite having reached the age of five, the ACA continues to live on a precipice. Nonetheless, I think the law will survive. More than twenty-five million people already enjoy insurance coverage as a result of the ACA. Even more will be covered by January 2017 when the next president takes office. All major elements of the health care system—insurers, hospitals, doctors, drug and device manufacturers—have an interest in continuation of the ACA. This alignment of forces suggests that Obamacare will survive current threats."

# CHAPTER 6

# INSURANCE: THOSE WITH AND THOSE WITHOUT

In 1798 Congress established the U.S. Marine Hospital Services for seamen. It was the first time an employer offered health insurance in the United States. Payments for hospital services were deducted from the sailors' salary.

In the 21st century many factors affected the availability of health insurance, including the economy, employment, income, personal health status, and age. Implementation of the Patient Protection and Affordable Care Act (also known as the Affordable Care Act [ACA]) reduced the impact of these factors on access to health insurance coverage, extending coverage to millions of Americans who were previously unable to obtain it. By February 2016, the close of the ACA's third open enrollment period, about 20 million people who were previously uninsured had obtained coverage since the enactment of the ACA, as reported by Namrata Uberoi, Kenneth Finegold, and Emily Gee of the Office of the Assistant Secretary for Planning and Evaluation of the U.S. Department of Health and Human Services (HHS) (March 3, 2016, https://aspe.hhs .gov/sites/default/files/pdf/187551/ACA2010-2016.pdf). However, the overall future of the ACA was uncertain as of November 2016. With the election of Donald J. Trump (1946–) to the presidency, it appeared likely that at least some degree of reform of the law would be undertaken by the Republican-controlled Congress in 2017.

Jessica C. Smith and Carla Medalia of the U.S. Census Bureau report in *Health Insurance Coverage in the United States: 2014* (September 2015, http://www.census.gov/ content/dam/Census/library/publications/2015/demo/p60- 253.pdf) that in 2014, 66% of Americans were covered by private health insurance during all or part of the year, and 55.4% were covered by employment-based health insurance. (See Figure 6.1.) The researchers note that the percentage of Americans covered by private health insurance increased from 2013 to 2014 as did the percentage of people covered by government health

insurance. Medicare (a federal health insurance program for people aged 65 years and older and people with disabilities) covered 16% of Americans in 2014, and Medicaid (a state and federal health insurance program for low-income people) covered 19.5%. Another 10.4% of Americans were without health coverage. Smith and Medalia indicate that the percentage of the U.S. population without health coverage in 2014 decreased from its peak in 2010 and dropped 2.9 percentage points from 2013 to 2014. (See Figure 6.2.)

According to Robin A. Cohen, Michael E. Martinez, and Emily P. Zammitti of the National Center for Health Statistics, in *Health Insurance Coverage: Early Release of Estimates from the National Health Interview Survey, 2015* (May 2016, https://www.cdc.gov/nchs/data/nhis/earlyre lease/insur201605.pdf), the percentage of adults aged 18 to 64 years without health care coverage at the time of the survey interview was 12.8% in 2015, down from its peak of 22.3% in 2010. (See Figure 1.1 in Chapter 1.) In 2015 there were 28.6 million (9.1%) people of all ages who were uninsured for at least part of the 12 months preceding the interview, 7.4 million fewer people than in 2014.

The overwhelming majority of the uninsured were adults aged 18 to 64 years. Figure 6.3 shows the percentages of adults aged 18 to 65 years that were uninsured at the time of the interview, by age group. In 2015 more adults in the 25–34 age group were uninsured than were uninsured in younger or older age groups.

## WHO WAS UNINSURED IN 2015?

Not surprisingly, in 2015 poverty status was associated with a lack of health insurance coverage. Among people of all ages, the poor or near poor were more likely than those who were not poor to be uninsured. (The Census Bureau defines "poor" people as those below the poverty threshold, which, in 2016 was $24,300 for a family of four. "Near poor" people have incomes of 100% to less than 200% of

**FIGURE 6.1**

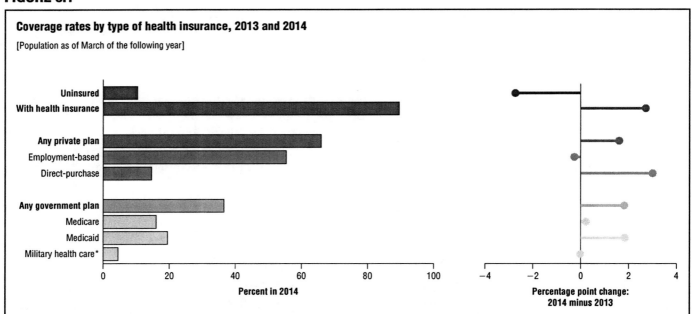

Coverage rates by type of health insurance, 2013 and 2014

[Population as of March of the following year]

*Military health care includes TRICARE and CHAMPVA (Civilian Health and Medical Program of the Department of Veterans Affairs), as well as care provided by the Department of Veterans Affairs and the military.
Note: Between 2013 and 2014, there was not a statistically significant change in the percentage of people covered by employment-based health insurance or military health care.

SOURCE: Jessica C. Smith and Carla Medalia, "Figure 2. Percentage of People by Type of Health Insurance Coverage and Change from Last Year: 2014," in *Health Insurance Coverage in the United States: 2014*, U.S. Census Bureau, September 2015, http://www.census.gov/content/dam/Census/library/publications/2015/demo/p60-253.pdf (accessed August 9, 2016)

**FIGURE 6.2**

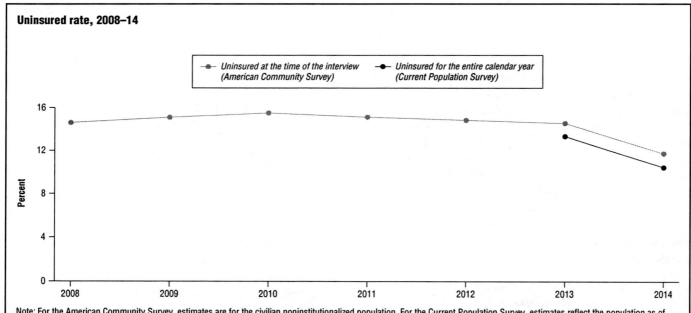

Uninsured rate, 2008–14

Note: For the American Community Survey, estimates are for the civilian noninstitutionalized population. For the Current Population Survey, estimates reflect the population as of March of the following year.

SOURCE: Jessica C. Smith and Carla Medalia, "Figure 1. Uninsured Rate: 2008 to 2014," in *Health Insurance Coverage in the United States: 2014*, U.S. Census Bureau, September 2015, http://www.census.gov/content/dam/Census/library/publications/2015/demo/p60-253.pdf (accessed August 9, 2016)

the poverty threshold; and "not poor" people have incomes equal to or greater than 200% of the poverty threshold.) For example, among people aged 18 to 64 years, 25.2% of those who were poor and 24.1% of those who were near poor were uninsured at the time of the interview, compared with 7.6% of those who were not poor in 2015. (See Figure 6.4.)

**FIGURE 6.3**

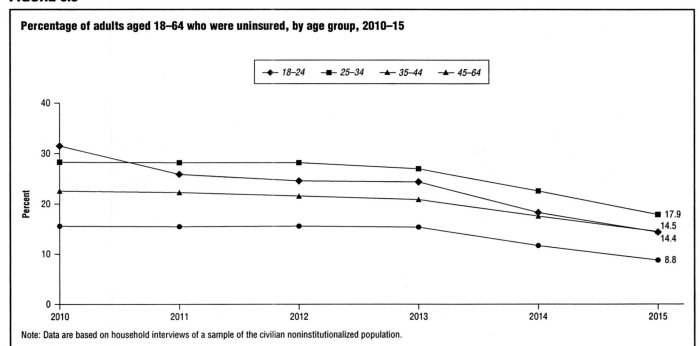

Percentage of adults aged 18–64 who were uninsured, by age group, 2010–15

Note: Data are based on household interviews of a sample of the civilian noninstitutionalized population.

SOURCE: Robin A. Cohen, Michael E. Martinez, and Emily P. Zammitti, "Figure 3. Percentage of Adults Aged 18–64 Who Were Uninsured at the Time of Interview, by Age Group, United States, 2010–2015," in *Health Insurance Coverage: Early Release of Estimates from the National Health Interview Survey, 2015*, National Center for Health Statistics, May 2016, http://www.cdc.gov/nchs/data/nhis/earlyrelease/insur201605.pdf (accessed July 25, 2016)

The proportion of people who did not have health insurance in 2015 at the time of the interview varied by geography. It was greatest in the South (17.3%) and West (11.8%), and less in the Midwest (10%) and Northeast (8.1%). (See Table 6.1.) Hispanics (27.7%), non-Hispanic African Americans (14.4%) and people who identified as other races or multiple races (16.1%) were more likely than Asian Americans (7.9%) and non-Hispanic whites (8.7%) to be uninsured in 2015.

**The Uninsured by Age and Sex**

Among people under the age of 65 years in 2015, the percentage of people without insurance at the time of the interview was highest among adults aged 25 to 34 years (17.9%) and lowest among those aged zero to 17 years (4.5%). (See Table 6.2.) Among adults of all ages, men were more likely than women to be uninsured.

**The Uninsured by Type of State Health Insurance Marketplace and Medicaid Expansion Status**

Under provisions of the ACA, states had the option of expanding Medicaid coverage to cover more low-income Americans. As expected residents of states that opted to expand Medicaid were less likely than residents of states that had not expanded Medicaid to be uninsured. (See Table 6.3.)

The ACA also created online health insurance marketplaces (also known as health exchanges) in each state where people can compare and purchase government-regulated and standardized plans. The online marketplaces also provide information about programs that help people with low to moderate incomes pay for coverage. In some states, the marketplace is run by the state; in others the federal government runs it. Enrollment via the online marketplaces began in October 2013.

In 2015 adults aged 18 to 64 years in states with federally operated marketplaces were more likely to be uninsured than were residents of the same age in states with state-based marketplaces or in states with partnership marketplaces (hybrid marketplaces in which the state runs certain functions and makes key decisions, including tailoring the marketplace to meet local needs and market conditions, but which is operated by the federal government). (See Table 6.4.)

**ACA Rollout and Enrollment Projections**

The ACA rollout in October 2013 was plagued with problems. HealthCare.gov, the website enrollment system that was intended to make shopping for and purchasing coverage easy, was plagued by problems. At first the website was slow, erratic, and unreliable. Many users were unable to log in or complete their applications, and the site crashed often or was inaccessible. Some of the website problems occurred because multiple contractors were involved with its development, resulting in various components being incompatible.

**FIGURE 6.4**

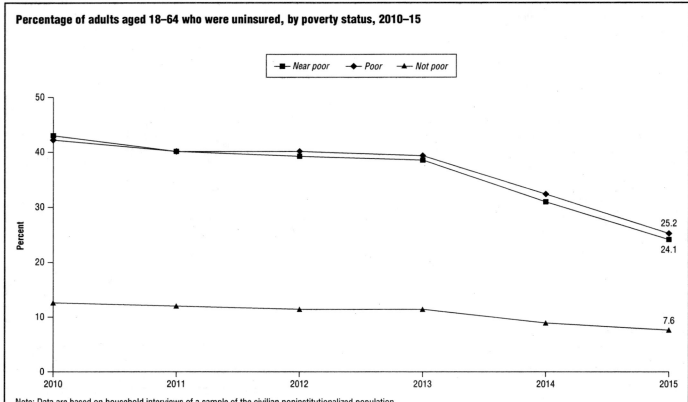

**Percentage of adults aged 18–64 who were uninsured, by poverty status, 2010–15**

Note: Data are based on household interviews of a sample of the civilian noninstitutionalized population.

SOURCE: Robin A. Cohen, Michael E. Martinez, and Emily P. Zammitti, "Figure 4. Percentage of Adults Aged 18–64 Who Were Uninsured at the Time of Interview, by Poverty Status: United States, 2010–2015," in *Health Insurance Coverage: Early Release of Estimates from the National Health Interview Survey, 2015*, National Center for Health Statistics, May 2016, http://www.cdc.gov/nchs/data/nhis/earlyrelease/insur201605.pdf (accessed July 25, 2016)

Many state exchange websites were similarly unsuccessful, leaving consumers frustrated and angry. In "How the iPod President Crashed" (Businessweek.com, October 31, 2013), Ezra Klein asserted that "the disastrous launch of healthcare.gov ... dealt a devastating blow to Obama's vision" of health care reform. Along with the flawed website, the president's promise that all Americans could keep their existing insurance policies if they so wished proved to be untrue, as insurers stopped offering plans that did not meet ACA requirements. Despite the ill-fated launch, Klein opined that the ACA could "emerge from a troubled launch to become a wildly successful program." By December 2013 the website problems were resolving, and enrollments picked up.

Lena H. Sun reports in "More Than 11.3 Million Americans Signed Up for Obamacare, HHS Says" (WashingtonPost.com, January 7, 2016) that by January 2016, 8.6 million Americans in 38 states had signed up for private health insurance via the HealthCare.gov and 2.7 million had signed up in 13 state insurance exchanges. Sun notes that, "Enrollment is well ahead of the figures announced in late 2014, when more than 7.1 million people had signed up for 2015 health plans—6.5 million via HealthCare.gov and 633,000 in the 14 states that were then running their own marketplaces."

## HEALTH CONSEQUENCES OF BEING UNINSURED

The Institute of Medicine observes in *America's Uninsured Crisis: Consequences for Health and Health Care* (February 2009, http://books.nap.edu/openbook .php?record_id=12511) that the economic downturn of 2007–09 exacerbated Americans' health problems because more Americans became uninsured when they lost employment-based health insurance. The institute explains that in such a situation "fewer people have access to coverage at work, more people find the costs of private coverage too expensive, and others lose public coverage because of changed personal circumstances, administrative barriers, and program cutbacks." The institute also notes that rigorous research confirms that being uninsured has a profound negative effect on the health and mortality of adults and children.

Families USA, a national nonprofit, nonpartisan organization dedicated to helping all Americans obtain quality health care, finds that having health insurance is literally a matter of life or death for some Americans. In *Dying for*

TABLE 6.1

**Percentages of adults aged 18–64 who were uninsured, had public health plan coverage, and had private health insurance at the time of interview, by selected demographic characteristics, 2015**

| Selected characteristic | Uninsured[a] at the time of interview | Public health plan coverage[b] | Private health insurance coverage[c] |
|---|---|---|---|
| **Race and ethnicity** | | | |
| Hispanic or Latino | 27.7 | 23.0 | 50.0 |
| Non-Hispanic: | | | |
|     White, single race | 8.7 | 15.7 | 77.3 |
|     Black, single race | 14.4 | 29.7 | 57.8 |
|     Asian, single race | 7.9 | 15.5 | 77.2 |
|     Other races and multiple races | 16.1 | 29.0 | 56.9 |
| **Region** | | | |
| Northeast | 8.1 | 20.1 | 73.3 |
| Midwest | 10.0 | 17.7 | 73.7 |
| South | 17.3 | 16.6 | 67.8 |
| West | 11.8 | 22.9 | 66.4 |
| **Education** | | | |
| Less than high school | 30.2 | 35.0 | 36.3 |
| High school diploma or GED[d] | 17.1 | 24.7 | 60.0 |
| More than high school | 7.7 | 13.5 | 80.2 |
| **Employment status** | | | |
| Employed | 11.9 | 10.5 | 78.4 |
| Unemployed | 30.3 | 36.4 | 34.1 |
| Not in workforce | 12.1 | 42.7 | 49.0 |
| **Poverty status[e]** | | | |
| <100% FPL | 25.2 | 51.7 | 24.3 |
| ≥100% and ≤138% FPL | 25.0 | 42.4 | 35.0 |
| >138% and ≤250% FPL | 20.9 | 24.2 | 56.8 |
| >250% and ≤400% FPL | 11.3 | 11.8 | 78.6 |
| >400% FPL | 3.6 | 5.6 | 92.1 |
| Unknown | 12.3 | 17.4 | 71.4 |
| **Marital status** | | | |
| Married | 9.5 | 13.7 | 78.4 |
| Widowed | 12.9 | 34.6 | 56.1 |
| Divorced or separated | 15.4 | 28.3 | 58.2 |
| Living with partner | 21.6 | 23.3 | 56.0 |
| Never married | 15.9 | 23.8 | 61.6 |

[a]A person was defined as uninsured if he or she did not have any private health insurance, Medicare, Medicaid, Children's Health Insurance Program (CHIP), state-sponsored or other government-sponsored health plan, or military plan. A person was also defined as uninsured if he or she had only Indian Health Service coverage or had only a private plan that paid for one type of service, such as accidents or dental care.

[b]Includes Medicaid, CHIP, state-sponsored or other government-sponsored health plan, Medicare, and military plans. A small number of persons were covered by both public and private plans and were included in both categories.

[c]Includes any comprehensive private insurance plan (including health maintenance and preferred provider organizations). These plans include those obtained through an employer, purchased directly, purchased through local or community programs, or purchased through the Health Insurance Marketplace or a state-based exchange. Private coverage excludes plans that pay for only one type of service, such as accidents or dental care. A small number of persons were covered by both public and private plans and were included in both categories.

[d]GED is General Educational Development high school equivalency diploma.

[e]FPL is federal poverty level, based on family income and family size, using the U.S. Census Bureau's poverty thresholds. The percentage of respondents with "Unknown" poverty status for this five-level categorization is 9.6%. This value is greater than the corresponding value for the three-level poverty categorization because of greater uncertainty when assigning individuals to more detailed poverty groups. For more information on poverty status, see Technical Notes. Estimates may differ from estimates that are based on both reported and imputed income.

Note: Data are based on household interviews of a sample of the civilian noninstitutionalized population.

SOURCE: Adapted from Robin A. Cohen, Michael E. Martinez, and Emily P. Zammitti, "Table X. Percentages (and Standard Errors) of Adults Aged 18–64 Who Lacked Health Insurance Coverage, Had Public Health Plan Coverage, and Had Private Health Insurance Coverage at the Time of Interview, by Selected Demographics: United States, 2015," in *Health Insurance Coverage: Early Release of Estimates from the National Health Interview Survey, 2015*, National Center for Health Statistics, May 2016, http://www.cdc.gov/nchs/data/nhis/earlyrelease/insur201605.pdf (accessed July 25, 2016)

*Coverage: The Deadly Consequences of Being Uninsured* (June 2012, http://familiesusa.org/sites/default/files/product_documents/Dying-for-Coverage.pdf), Kim Bailey of Families USA reports that 26,100 people aged 25 to 64 years "died prematurely due to a lack of health coverage in 2010." Between 2005 and 2010, 134,120 deaths were attributable to the lack of health insurance.

In "Monitoring the Impact of Health Reform on Americans Ages 50–64: Access to Health Care Improved during Early ACA Marketplace Implementation" (October 2015, http://www.aarp.org/content/dam/aarp/ppi/2015/aarp-impact-of-health-reform-insight.pdf), Laura Skopec et al. observe that uninsured people with chronic conditions such as hypertension and diabetes are more likely to have their conditions underdiagnosed or poorly controlled and are more likely to suffer poor outcomes than people with insurance. The uninsured also are less likely to have a usual source of care and less likely to receive preventive services such as cancer screenings and flu shots.

TABLE 6.2

**Percentages of persons who were uninsured, had public health plan coverage, and had private health insurance at the time of interview, by age group and sex, 2015**

| Age group and sex | Uninsured[a] at the time of interview | Public health plan coverage[b] | Private health insurance coverage[c] |
|---|---|---|---|
| Age group (years) | | | |
| All ages | 9.1 | 35.6 | 63.2 |
| Under age 65 | 10.5 | 25.3 | 65.6 |
| 0–17 | 4.5 | 42.2 | 54.7 |
| 18–64 | 12.8 | 18.9 | 69.7 |
| 18–24 | 14.4 | 21.6 | 65.1 |
| 25–34 | 17.9 | 17.8 | 65.2 |
| 35–44 | 14.5 | 16.1 | 69.9 |
| 45–64 | 8.8 | 19.9 | 73.6 |
| 65 and over | 0.6 | 95.1 | 49.4 |
| 19–25 | 15.8 | 19.5 | 65.7 |
| Sex | | | |
| Male: | | | |
| All ages | 10.4 | 33.5 | 63.3 |
| Under age 65 | 11.9 | 24.1 | 65.5 |
| 0–17 | 4.3 | 42.9 | 54.3 |
| 18–64 | 14.9 | 16.6 | 69.9 |
| 18–24 | 16.4 | 18.3 | 66.2 |
| 25–34 | 21.7 | 13.6 | 65.7 |
| 35–44 | 16.8 | 13.3 | 70.3 |
| 45–64 | 9.8 | 19.2 | 73.3 |
| 65 and over | 0.6 | 94.4 | 49.3 |
| 19–25 | 18.0 | 16.0 | 66.9 |
| Female: | | | |
| All ages | 7.8 | 37.6 | 63.1 |
| Under age 65 | 9.2 | 26.5 | 65.7 |
| 0–17 | 4.7 | 41.4 | 55.2 |
| 18–64 | 10.8 | 21.2 | 69.6 |
| 18–24 | 12.3 | 24.8 | 63.9 |
| 25–34 | 14.2 | 21.9 | 64.7 |
| 35–44 | 12.2 | 18.9 | 69.6 |
| 45–64 | 7.9 | 20.6 | 74.0 |
| 65 and over | 0.6 | 95.6 | 49.6 |
| 19–25 | 13.6 | 23.0 | 64.4 |

[a]A person was defined as uninsured if he or she did not have any private health insurance, Medicare, Medicaid, Children's Health Insurance Program (CHIP), state-sponsored or other government-sponsored health plan, or military plan at the time of interview. A person was also defined as uninsured if he or she had only Indian Health Service coverage or had only a private plan that paid for one type of service, such as accidents or dental care.
[b]Includes Medicaid, CHIP, state-sponsored or other government-sponsored health plan, Medicare, and military plans. A small number of persons were covered by both public and private plans and were included in both categories.
[c]Includes any comprehensive private insurance plan (including health maintenance and preferred provider organizations). These plans include those obtained through an employer, purchased directly, purchased through local or community programs, or purchased through the Health Insurance Marketplace or a state-based exchange. Private coverage excludes plans that pay for only one type of service, such as accidents or dental care. A small number of persons were covered by both public and private plans and were included in both categories.
Note: Data are based on household interviews of a sample of the civilian noninstitutionalized population.

SOURCE: Adapted from Robin A. Cohen, Michael E. Martinez, and Emily P. Zammitti, "Table VII. Percentages (and Standard Errors) of Persons Who Lacked Health Insurance Coverage, Had Public Health Plan Coverage, and Had Private Health Insurance Coverage at the Time of Interview, by Age Group and Sex: United States, 2015," in *Health Insurance Coverage: Early Release of Estimates from the National Health Interview Survey, 2015*, National Center for Health Statistics, May 2016, http://www.cdc.gov/nchs/data/nhis/earlyrelease/insur201605.pdf (accessed July 25, 2016).

## SOURCES OF HEALTH INSURANCE

### People under the Age of 65 Years

For people under the age of 65 years there are two principal sources of health insurance coverage: private insurance (from employer or private policies) and Medicaid. The ACA created new designations for health plans and providers. Qualified health plans are private health plans that are approved for sale in the health insurance marketplace (they may, for example, be offered by insurance exchanges). As reported in the 2015 National Health Interview Survey, between January 2010 and December 2015 the proportion of those covered by both private and public health insurance at the time of the interview increased. (See Table 6.5.)

The Employee Benefit Research Institute observes in "Fewer Small Employers Offering Health Coverage; Large Employers Holding Steady" (*Notes*, vol. 37, no. 8, July 2016) that among larger employers, the percentage offering health coverage to their workers did not change between 2008 and 2015. About 99% of employers with 1,000 or more employees, and 92.5% to 95.1% of employers with 100 to 999 employees offer health insurance coverage. By contrast, the rates among smaller employers have been falling since 2009. Among employers with

**TABLE 6.3**

**Percentage with and without health insurance, by state Medicaid expansion status, 2010–15**

| Age group, state Medicaid expansion status, and year | Uninsured[a] at the time of interview | Public health plan coverage[b] | Private health insurance coverage[c] |
|---|---|---|---|
| **Under 65 years** | | | |
| **Medicaid expansion states[d]:** | | | |
| 2010 | 16.4 | 21.8 | 63.1 |
| 2011 | 15.3 | 23.1 | 62.9 |
| 2012 | 15.0 | 23.1 | 63.3 |
| 2013 | 14.9 | 24.1 | 62.3 |
| 2014 | 10.9 | 25.6 | 64.9 |
| 2015 | 8.2 | 26.7 | 66.4 |
| **Non-Medicaid expansion states[e]:** | | | |
| 2010 | 20.3 | 22.1 | 59.0 |
| 2011 | 19.6 | 22.7 | 59.1 |
| 2012 | 19.2 | 24.0 | 58.3 |
| 2013 | 18.4 | 23.4 | 59.6 |
| 2014 | 16.0 | 23.2 | 62.1 |
| 2015 | 14.0 | 23.2 | 64.4 |
| **0–17 years** | | | |
| **Medicaid expansion states[d]:** | | | |
| 2010 | 6.7 | 38.2 | 56.5 |
| 2011 | 5.9 | 40.2 | 55.4 |
| 2012 | 5.3 | 40.4 | 55.9 |
| 2013 | 5.6 | 41.3 | 54.5 |
| 2014 | 4.3 | 41.0 | 56.2 |
| 2015 | 3.8 | 41.1 | 56.7 |
| **Non-Medicaid expansion states[e]:** | | | |
| 2010 | 9.0 | 41.7 | 50.7 |
| 2011 | 8.3 | 42.0 | 50.9 |
| 2012 | 8.0 | 43.9 | 49.4 |
| 2013 | 7.5 | 43.1 | 50.5 |
| 2014 | 6.7 | 43.5 | 51.0 |
| 2015 | 5.5 | 43.7 | 52.0 |
| **18–64 years** | | | |
| **Medicaid expansion states[d]:** | | | |
| 2010 | 20.1 | 15.5 | 65.6 |
| 2011 | 18.9 | 16.6 | 65.8 |
| 2012 | 18.5 | 16.7 | 66.0 |
| 2013 | 18.4 | 17.7 | 65.2 |
| 2014 | 13.3 | 19.9 | 68.1 |
| 2015 | 9.8 | 21.5 | 70.0 |
| **Non-Medicaid expansion states[e]:** | | | |
| 2010 | 24.8 | 14.4 | 62.2 |
| 2011 | 24.1 | 15.1 | 62.3 |
| 2012 | 23.7 | 16.1 | 61.8 |
| 2013 | 22.7 | 15.6 | 63.2 |
| 2014 | 19.6 | 15.3 | 66.5 |
| 2015 | 17.5 | 14.9 | 69.4 |

[a]A person was defined as uninsured if he or she did not have any private health insurance, Medicare, Medicaid, Children's Health Insurance Program (CHIP), state-sponsored or other government-sponsored health plan, or military plan. A person was also defined as uninsured if he or she had only Indian Health Service coverage or had only a private plan that paid for one type of service, such as accidents or dental care.

[b]Includes Medicaid, CHIP, state-sponsored or other government-sponsored health plan, Medicare, and military plans. A small number of persons were covered by both public and private plans and were included in both categories.

[c]Includes any comprehensive private insurance plan (including health maintenance and preferred provider organizations). These plans include those obtained through an employer, purchased directly, purchased through local or community programs, or purchased through the Health Insurance Marketplace or a state-based exchange. Private coverage excludes plans that pay for only one type of service, such as accidents or dental care. A small number of persons were covered by both public and private plans and were included in both categories.

[d]For 2010 through 2014, states moving forward with Medicaid expansion include AZ, AR, CA, CO, CT, DE, DC, HI, IL, IA, KY, MD, MA, MI, MN, NV, NJ, NM, NY, ND, OH, OR, RI, VT, WA, and WV (as of October 31, 2013). Beginning with 2015, three additional states are included as expansion states: IN, NH, and PA.

[e]For 2010 through 2014, states not moving forward with Medicaid expansion include AL, AK, FL, GA, ID, IN, KS, LA, ME, MS, MO, MT, NE, NH, NC, OK, PA, SC, SD, TN, TX, UT, VA, WI, and WY (as of October 31, 2013). Beginning with 2015, three states have been removed from this grouping: IN, NH, and PA.

Note: Data are based on household interviews of a sample of the civilian noninstitutionalized population.

SOURCE: Adapted from Robin A. Cohen, Michael E. Martinez, and Emily P. Zammitti, "Table XIII Percentages (and Standard Errors) of Persons under Age 65 Who Lacked Health Insurance Coverage, Had Public Health Plan Coverage, and Had Private Health Insurance Coverage at the Time of Interview, by Age Group and State Medicaid Expansion Status: United States, 2010–2015," in *Health Insurance Coverage: Early Release of Estimates from the National Health Interview Survey, 2015*, National Center for Health Statistics, May 2016, http://www.cdc.gov/nchs/data/nhis/earlyrelease/insur201605.pdf (accessed July 25, 2016)

TABLE 6.4

**Percentages of adults aged 18–64 who were uninsured or had public or private health insurance by state Health Insurance Marketplace type and year, 2010–15**

| Age group, state Health Insurance Marketplace type, and year | Uninsured[a] at the time of interview | Public health plan coverage[b] | Private health insurance coverage[c] |
|---|---|---|---|
| **Under 65 years** | | | |
| **State-based Marketplace states[d]:** | | | |
| 2010 | 16.3 | 21.6 | 63.2 |
| 2011 | 15.9 | 23.6 | 61.8 |
| 2012 | 15.2 | 24.2 | 61.8 |
| 2013 | 15.2 | 25.0 | 61.0 |
| 2014 | 11.1 | 26.4 | 63.7 |
| 2015 | 7.7 | 28.1 | 65.4 |
| **Partnership Marketplace states[e]:** | | | |
| 2010 | 14.7 | 22.5 | 64.8 |
| 2011 | 14.3 | 22.7 | 64.5 |
| 2012 | 14.1 | 20.8 | 66.7 |
| 2013 | 14.2 | 21.8 | 65.6 |
| 2014 | 10.2 | 24.4 | 67.2 |
| 2015 | 8.0 | 26.1 | 67.7 |
| **Federally Facilitated Marketplace states[f]:** | | | |
| 2010 | 20.1 | 22.1 | 59.1 |
| 2011 | 18.8 | 22.6 | 60.0 |
| 2012 | 18.6 | 23.6 | 59.3 |
| 2013 | 17.9 | 23.3 | 60.2 |
| 2014 | 15.3 | 23.3 | 62.8 |
| 2015 | 12.8 | 23.4 | 65.3 |
| **0–17 years** | | | |
| **State-based Marketplace states[d]:** | | | |
| 2010 | 6.7 | 38.0 | 56.4 |
| 2011 | 6.4 | 40.9 | 54.2 |
| 2012 | 5.4 | 42.2 | 53.9 |
| 2013 | 5.7 | 42.8 | 52.6 |
| 2014 | 4.2 | 42.0 | 54.9 |
| 2015 | 3.1 | 42.4 | 55.8 |
| **Partnership Marketplace states[e]:** | | | |
| 2010 | 4.1 | 40.7 | 57.9 |
| 2011 | 4.2 | 39.6 | 58.0 |
| 2012 | 3.6 | 38.5 | 59.9 |
| 2013 | 4.2 | 38.4 | 59.2 |
| 2014 | 3.2 | 40.8 | 58.4 |
| 2015 | 4.3 | 40.3 | 57.5 |
| **Federally Facilitated Marketplace states[f]:** | | | |
| 2010 | 9.2 | 40.7 | 51.3 |
| 2011 | 8.0 | 41.4 | 51.8 |
| 2012 | 7.9 | 42.7 | 50.8 |
| 2013 | 7.5 | 42.6 | 51.3 |
| 2014 | 6.6 | 42.6 | 52.0 |
| 2015 | 5.3 | 42.4 | 53.6 |
| **18–64 years** | | | |
| **State-based Marketplace states[d]:** | | | |
| 2010 | 19.9 | 15.3 | 65.9 |
| 2011 | 19.5 | 17.1 | 64.7 |
| 2012 | 18.8 | 17.7 | 64.7 |
| 2013 | 18.7 | 18.4 | 64.1 |
| 2014 | 13.6 | 20.6 | 67.0 |
| 2015 | 9.4 | 22.9 | 68.9 |
| **Partnership Marketplace states[e]:** | | | |
| 2010 | 18.9 | 15.3 | 67.6 |
| 2011 | 18.4 | 15.9 | 67.1 |
| 2012 | 18.1 | 13.9 | 69.3 |
| 2013 | 17.9 | 15.7 | 68.0 |
| 2014 | 12.8 | 18.2 | 70.5 |
| 2015 | 9.4 | 20.8 | 71.5 |

fewer than 10 employees, 35.6% offered insurance in 2008 compared with 22.7% in 2015. Among employers with 10 to 24 employees, 66.1% offered insurance in 2008, compared with 48.9% in 2015. Among employers with 25 to 99 employees, 81.3% offered insurance in 2008, compared with 73.5% in 2015.

TABLE 6.4

**Percentages of adults aged 18–64 who were uninsured or had public or private health insurance by state Health Insurance Marketplace type and year, 2010–15** [CONTINUED]

| Age group, state Health Insurance Marketplace type, and year | Uninsured[a] at the time of interview | Public health plan coverage[b] | Private health insurance coverage[c] |
|---|---|---|---|
| **Federally Facilitated Marketplace states[f]:** | | | |
| 2010 | 24.5 | 14.7 | 62.2 |
| 2011 | 23.0 | 15.1 | 63.3 |
| 2012 | 22.8 | 16.1 | 62.7 |
| 2013 | 22.0 | 15.9 | 63.6 |
| 2014 | 18.6 | 15.8 | 66.9 |
| 2015 | 15.7 | 16.0 | 69.9 |

[a]A person was defined as uninsured if he or she did not have any private health insurance, Medicare, Medicaid, Children's Health Insurance Program (CHIP), state-sponsored or other government-sponsored health plan, or military plan. A person was also defined as uninsured if he or she had only Indian Health Service coverage or had only a private plan that paid for one type of service, such as accidents or dental care.
[b]Includes Medicaid, CHIP, state-sponsored or other government-sponsored health plan, Medicare, and military plans. A small number of persons were covered by both public and private plans and were included in both categories.
[c]Includes any comprehensive private insurance plan (including health maintenance and preferred provider organizations). These plans include those obtained through an employer, purchased directly, purchased through local or community programs, or purchased through the Health Insurance Marketplace or a state-based exchange. Private coverage excludes plans that pay for only one type of service, such as accidents or dental care. A small number of persons were covered by both public and private plans and were included in both categories.
[d]State-based Marketplace states are CA, CO, CT, DC, HI, ID, KY, MD, MA, MN, NV, NM, NY, OR, RI, VT, and WA (as of October 31, 2013).
[e]Partnership Marketplace states are AR, DE, IL, IA, MI, NH, and WV (as of October 31, 2013).
[f]Federally Facilitated Marketplace states are AL, AK, AZ, FL, GA, IN, KS, LA, ME, MS, MO, MT, NE, NJ, NC, ND, OH, OK, PA, SC, SD, TN, TX, UT, VA, WI, and WY (as of October 31, 2013).
Note: Data are based on household interviews of a sample of the civilian noninstitutionalized population.

SOURCE: Adapted from Robin A. Cohen, Michael E. Martinez, and Emily P. Zammitti, "Table XIV. Percentages (and Standard Errors) of Persons under Age 65 Who Lacked Health Insurance Coverage, Had Public Health Plan Coverage, and Had Private Health Insurance Coverage at the Time of Interview, by Age, and State Health Insurance Marketplace Type, and Year: United States, 2010–2015," in *Health Insurance Coverage: Early Release of Estimates from the National Health Interview Survey, 2015*, National Center for Health Statistics, May 2016, http://www.cdc.gov/nchs/data/nhis/earlyrelease/insur201605.pdf (accessed July 25, 2016)

Many industry observers predict that the percentage of employers offering health benefits will continue to decrease over time. In the book *Reinventing American Health Care* (2014), Ezekiel Emanuel, a physician, medical ethicist, and academic, predicts that under the ACA this decrease will likely accelerate. He asserts that employers will choose instead to raise salaries or offer large, defined contributions to workers. Emanuel believes that the exchanges will offer consumers many choices, and most will purchase their coverage through the exchanges. Because government-subsidized insurance is available to people earning less than 400% of the federal poverty limit, some employers may opt to save money by relying on the government to subsidize their workers' health insurance rather than doing so themselves. Emanuel predicts that by 2025 fewer than 20% of private-sector workers will have employer-sponsored health coverage.

### People Aged 65 Years and Older

There are three sources of health insurance for people aged 65 years and older: private insurance, Medicare, and Medicaid. Medicare is the federal government's health program for people with disabilities and people who are aged 65 years and older. Medicaid is the federal health program for the poor. Cohen, Martinez, and Zammitti report in *Health Insurance Coverage* that in 2015 a scant 0.6% of adults aged 65 years and older were without health insurance at the time of the interview. (See Table 6.2.)

Older adults may be covered by a combination of private health insurance and Medicare, or Medicare and Medicaid, depending on their income and level of disability. Nearly all adults over age 65 are covered by Medicare. In *Health, United States, 2015: With Special Feature on Racial and Ethnic Disparities* (May 2016, http://www.cdc.gov/nchs/data/hus/hus15.pdf), the National Center for Health Statistics reports that in 2013, 27.4% of older adults were covered by an employer-sponsored plan, 31.2% were covered by a Medicare Advantage plan, 18.7% had Medigap insurance to supplement their Medicare coverage, 14.6% used Medicare to obtain care on a fee-for-service basis, and 8.2% were covered by Medicaid.

### MEDICARE ADVANTAGE

Medicare Advantage plans (also known as Part C) are offered by private insurance companies that contract with Medicare to provide Part A (hospital coverage) and Part B (physician and other outpatient services) benefits. Medicare Advantage plans may be health maintenance organizations (HMOs; HMO members must use physicians and other providers in the plan's network and need a referral from a primary care physician to see a specialist), preferred provider organizations (PPOs; PPO members pay less when they use network providers and more if they use providers outside the network), or traditional private fee-for-service plans.

Medicare Savings Account (MSA) plans combine a high-deductible health plan with a bank account. Medicare deposits money into the account (usually less than the deductible) and members can use the money to pay

**TABLE 6.5**

**Adults under age 65 who were uninsured or had public or private health insurance, by year and quarter, January 2010–December 2015**

| Year and quarter | Uninsured[a] | Private health insurance coverage[c] | Exchange-based private health insurance coverage[c] | Public health plan coverage[b] |
|---|---|---|---|---|
| **2010 full year** | **18.2** | **61.2** | **—** | **22.0** |
| Quarter 1 | 17.5 | 62.6 | — | 21.2 |
| Quarter 2 | 19.2 | 60.9 | — | 21.2 |
| Quarter 3 | 18.8 | 60.6 | — | 22.0 |
| Quarter 4 | 17.2 | 60.6 | — | 23.5 |
| **2011 full year** | **17.3** | **61.2** | **—** | **23.0** |
| Quarter 1 | 17.4 | 61.3 | — | 22.7 |
| Quarter 2 | 17.4 | 61.4 | — | 22.5 |
| Quarter 3 | 17.3 | 60.8 | — | 23.3 |
| Quarter 4 | 16.9 | 61.1 | — | 23.3 |
| **2012 full year** | **16.9** | **61.0** | **—** | **23.5** |
| Quarter 1 | 17.6 | 60.2 | — | 23.5 |
| Quarter 2 | 16.0 | 63.0 | — | 22.6 |
| Quarter 3 | 17.0 | 60.3 | — | 24.2 |
| Quarter 4 | 17.2 | 60.3 | — | 23.8 |
| **2013 full year** | **16.6** | **61.0** | **—** | **23.8** |
| Quarter 1 | 17.1 | 60.3 | — | 23.9 |
| Quarter 2 | 16.4 | 62.1 | — | 22.9 |
| Quarter 3 | 16.5 | 61.2 | — | 23.7 |
| Quarter 4 | 16.2 | 60.5 | — | 24.5 |
| **2014 full year** | **13.3** | **63.6** | **2.2** | **24.5** |
| Quarter 1 | 15.2 | 61.8 | 1.4 | 24.2 |
| Quarter 2 | 12.9 | 63.8 | 2.4 | 24.7 |
| Quarter 3 | 13.2 | 64.0 | 2.5 | 24.0 |
| Quarter 4 | 12.1 | 64.4 | 2.5 | 25.0 |
| **2015 full year** | **10.5** | **65.6** | **3.8** | **25.3** |
| Quarter 1 | 10.7 | 66.5 | 3.6 | 24.2 |
| Quarter 2 | 10.3 | 66.7 | 4.0 | 24.6 |
| Quarter 3 | 10.8 | 64.5 | 4.2 | 26.1 |
| Quarter 4 | 10.3 | 64.7 | 3.4 | 26.3 |

—Category not applicable.

[a]A person was defined as uninsured if he or she did not have any private health insurance, Medicare, Medicaid, Children's Health Insurance Program (CHIP), state-sponsored or other government-sponsored health plan, or military plan. A person was also defined as uninsured if he or she had only Indian Health Service coverage or had only a private plan that paid for one type of service, such as accidents or dental care.

[b]Includes any comprehensive private insurance plan (including health maintenance and preferred provider organizations). These plans include those obtained through an employer, purchased directly, purchased through local or community programs, or purchased through the Health Insurance Marketplace or a state-based exchange. Private coverage excludes plans that pay for only one type of service, such as accidents or dental care. A small number of persons were covered by both public and private plans and were included in both categories.

[c]Includes persons who have purchased a private health insurance plan through the Health Insurance Marketplace or state-based exchanges that were established as part of the Affordable Care Act of 2010 (P.L. 111–148, P.L. 111–152). All persons who have exchange-based coverage are considered to have private health insurance and have also been included in the estimate for "private health insurance coverage."

[d]Includes Medicaid, Children's Health Insurance Program (CHIP), state-sponsored or other government-sponsored health plan, Medicare, and military plans. A small number of persons were covered by both public and private plans and were included in both categories.

Notes: These health insurance estimates are being released prior to final data editing and final weighting to provide access to the most recent information from the National Health Interview Survey. The resulting estimates for persons without health insurance are generally 0.1–0.3 percentage points lower than those based on the editing procedures used for the final data files. Occasionally, due to decisions made for the final data editing and weighting, estimates based on preliminary editing procedures may differ by more than 0.3 percentage points from estimates based on final files. The estimates are based on a sample of the population and therefore are subject to sampling error. Data are based on household interviews of a sample of the civilian noninstitutionalized population.

SOURCE: Adapted from "Table 1. Percentages (and Standard Errors) of Persons under Age 65 Who Were Uninsured, Had Private Health Insurance overage, and Had Public Health Plan Coverage at the Time of Interview, by Year and Quarter: United States, January 2010–December 2015," in *National Health Interview Survey Early Release Program*, National Center for Health Statistics, May 2016, https://www.cdc.gov/nchs/data/nhis/earlyrelease/quarterly_estimates_2010_2015_q1234.pdf (accessed August 10, 2016)

for health care services during the year. Unlike most Medicare Advantage Plans, which include Medicare prescription drug coverage (Part D), MSAs do not provide drug coverage.

In "Medicare Advantage" (May 11, 2016, http://kff.org/medicare/fact-sheet/medicare-advantage/), the Henry J. Kaiser Family Foundation (KFF) reports that in 2016 Medicare Advantage plans covered an estimated 17.6 million older adults or 31% of Medicare beneficiaries. The average out-of-pocket limit increased to $5,223 in 2016 from $5,041 in 2014, and about half (52%) of plans had out-of-pocket limits of $5,000 or more. According to the Centers for Medicare and Medicaid Services (CMS), average plan premiums in 2016 were about $33 per month.

## CHANGING MEDICARE REIMBURSEMENT

Medicare reimbursement varies in different parts of the country, although everyone pays the same amount to

Medicare through taxes. As a result, older adults in some geographic regions have access to a more comprehensive range of services (e.g., coverage for nursing home care and eyeglasses) than older adults in other regions.

Describing this practice as unfair and outdated, legislators have repeatedly called for more equitable reimbursement formulas. For example, since 2002 the MediFair Act (previously called the Medicare Fairness in Reimbursement Act) aimed to improve the provision of items and services provided to Medicare beneficiaries residing in rural areas in part by improving reimbursement) has repeatedly failed to pass. The Medicare Improvements for Patients and Providers Act of 2008 aimed to stem declining reimbursement by postponing a provision to reduce some Medicare reimbursement rates. The bill became law in July 2008.

The ACA aims to make health care financing more transparent. According to the CMS, in the press release "Medicare Provider Utilization and Payment Data: Physician and Other Supplier" (May 5, 2016, http:// https://www .cms.gov/research-statistics-data-and-systems/statistics-trends-and-reports/medicare-provider-charge-data/physician-and-other-supplier.html), in 2016 the CMS continued to release physician and other health care provider charge data, enabling Medicare beneficiaries to compare charges for common inpatient and outpatient services across the country. The CMS releases comparable data for hospitals, enabling comparisons by specialty, location, the types of medical service and procedures delivered, and Medicare payment.

### Medicare Prescription Drug, Improvement, and Modernization Act

In December 2003 President George W. Bush (1946–) signed the Medicare Prescription Drug, Improvement, and Modernization Act into law. Heralded as landmark legislation, the act provides older adults and people with disabilities with a prescription drug benefit, more choices, and improved benefits under Medicare. On June 1, 2004, older adults and people with disabilities began using their Medicare-approved drug discount cards to obtain savings on prescription medicines. Low-income beneficiaries qualified for a $600 credit to help pay for their prescriptions. Besides providing coverage for prescription drugs, this legislation gave seniors the opportunity to choose the coverage that best meets their needs. For example, some older adults opted for traditional Medicare coverage along with the new prescription benefit. Others obtained dental or eyeglass coverage or enrolled in plans that reduced their out-of-pocket costs.

The legislation stipulated that as of 2005 all newly enrolled Medicare beneficiaries would be covered for a complete physical examination and other preventive services, such as blood tests to screen for diabetes. The law also aimed to assist Americans to pay out-of-pocket

health costs by enabling the creation of health savings accounts, which allow Americans to set aside up to $4,500 per year, tax free, to save for medical expenses.

Nonetheless, concerns about the solvency of the Medicare program and its capacity to meet the health care needs of growing numbers of Americans aging into eligibility have been increasing in recent years. The media have reported the ill effects of coverage gaps, with multiple stories of older adults opting to forgo prescription medication because they were unable to afford it. The ACA not only extends the program's solvency but closes the coverage gap (known as the donut hole) in prescription drug coverage by 2020. The coverage gap closes by maintaining the 50% discount drug manufacturers offer and increasing what Medicare drug plans cover. For example, in 2015 Medicare paid 35% of the price for generic drugs during the coverage gap and beneficiaries paid the remaining 65% of that price. The percentage beneficiaries pay for generic drugs during the coverage gap decreases each year until it reaches 25% in 2020.

### CHILDREN

In 2015 nearly 5% of children aged zero to 17 years were uninsured, according to the National Health Interview Survey. (See Table 6.6.) Approximately 7.7% had been uninsured for part of the year preceding the interview, and 2.3% had been uninsured for more than a year. Cohen, Martinez and Zammitti report in *Health Insurance Coverage: Early Release of Estimates from the National Health Interview Survey, 2015* that in 2015 poor children (4.4%) and near-poor children (6.7%) were much more likely to be uninsured at the time of the interview than children who were not poor (3.3%). (See Figure 6.5.) Figure 6.5 shows that between 2013 and 2015 the percentage of poor and near-poor children who lacked health insurance coverage decreased.

Some industry analysts attribute the declining proportion of uninsured children and the increasing proportion of children covered by Medicaid during the late 1990s to expansion of the Children's Health Insurance Program (CHIP), which targeted children from low-income families and was instituted during the late 1990s. Medicaid enrollment growth peaked during the recession and then slowed as the economy started to recover.

The ACA increased health coverage, improves benefits, and provides insurance protections for children. It eliminated preexisting coverage exclusions for children and improves health insurance for children by expanding coverage through Medicaid and CHIP. It requires children's health insurance to provide coverage for basic dental and vision care and guarantees children access to affordable health insurance policies, regardless of whether their parents change or leave their jobs, relocate, or become ill or disabled.

TABLE 6.6

**Percentages of persons who were uninsured at the time of interview, for at least part of the past year or for more than a year, by age group, 2010–15**

| Age group and year | Uninsured[a] at the time of interview | Uninsured[a] for at least part of the past year[b] | Uninsured[a] for more than a year[b] |
|---|---|---|---|
| **All ages** | | | |
| 2010 | 16.0 | 19.8 | 11.7 |
| 2011 | 15.1 | 19.2 | 11.2 |
| 2012 | 14.7 | 18.6 | 11.1 |
| 2013 | 14.4 | 17.8 | 10.7 |
| 2014 | 11.5 | 16.5 | 8.4 |
| 2015 | 9.1 | 13.2 | 6.2 |
| **Under 65 years** | | | |
| 2010 | 18.2 | 22.5 | 13.3 |
| 2011 | 17.3 | 21.8 | 12.7 |
| 2012 | 16.9 | 21.3 | 12.7 |
| 2013 | 16.6 | 20.4 | 12.4 |
| 2014 | 13.3 | 19.0 | 9.7 |
| 2015 | 10.5 | 15.3 | 7.2 |
| **0–17 years** | | | |
| 2010 | 7.8 | 11.6 | 4.5 |
| 2011 | 7.0 | 10.9 | 3.7 |
| 2012 | 6.6 | 10.4 | 3.7 |
| 2013 | 6.5 | 10.0 | 3.6 |
| 2014 | 5.5 | 9.4 | 3.0 |
| 2015 | 4.5 | 7.7 | 2.3 |
| **18–64 years** | | | |
| 2010 | 22.3 | 26.7 | 16.8 |
| 2011 | 21.3 | 26.0 | 16.3 |
| 2012 | 20.9 | 25.5 | 16.2 |
| 2013 | 20.4 | 24.4 | 15.7 |
| 2014 | 16.3 | 22.6 | 12.3 |
| 2015 | 12.8 | 18.1 | 9.1 |
| **19–25 years** | | | |
| 2010 | 33.9 | 41.7 | 24.1 |
| 2011 | 27.9 | 36.1 | 20.1 |
| 2012 | 26.4 | 33.0 | 19.6 |
| 2013 | 26.5 | 31.3 | 19.8 |
| 2014 | 20.0 | 26.9 | 14.2 |
| 2015 | 15.8 | 22.2 | 10.2 |

[a]A person was defined as uninsured if he or she did not have any private health insurance, Medicare, Medicaid, Children's Health Insurance Program (CHIP), state-sponsored or other government-sponsored health plan, or military plan. A person was also defined as uninsured if he or she had only Indian Health Service coverage or had only a private plan that paid for one type of service, such as accidents or dental care.
[b]In references to "part of the past year" and "more than a year," a year is defined as the 12 months prior to interview.
Note: Data are based on household interviews of a sample of the civilian noninstitutionalized population.

SOURCE: Adapted from Robin A. Cohen, Michael E. Martinez, and Emily P. Zammitti, "Table I. Percentages (and Standard Errors) of Persons Who Lacked Health Insurance Coverage at the Time of the Interview, for at Least Part of the Past Year, and for More Than a Year, by Age Group and Year: United States, 2010–2015," in *Health Insurance Coverage: Early Release of Estimates from the National Health Interview Survey, 2015*, National Center for Health Statistics, May 2016, http://www.cdc.gov/nchs/data/nhis/earlyrelease/insur201605.pdf (accessed July 25, 2016)

According to the CMS, in "Medicaid and CHIP Application, Eligibility Determination, and Enrollment Data" (May 2016, https://www.medicaid.gov/medicaid-chip-program-information/program-information/medicaid-and-chip-enrollment-data/medicaid-and-chip-application-eligibility-determination-and-enrollment-data.html), from October 2013 through May 2016, enrollment in Medicaid and CHIP grew by 15.1 million. These enrollment counts are in addition to the enrollment increases from the nearly 950,000 individuals who gained coverage as a result of the ACA before open enrollment began. Enrollment in states that expanded Medicaid coverage increased 35.3% compared with 11.8% in states that did not expand Medicaid.

## HEALTH INSURANCE PORTABILITY AND ACCOUNTABILITY ACT

In August 1996 President Bill Clinton (1946–) signed the Health Insurance Portability and Accountability Act (HIPAA). This legislation aimed to provide better portability (transfer) of employer-sponsored insurance from one job to another. HIPAA ensured that people who had employer-sponsored health coverage would be able to maintain their health insurance even if they lost their job or moved to a different company. They would, of course, have to continue to pay for their insurance. However, they no longer had to fear that they would be denied coverage because of preexisting medical conditions or be forced to go without health insurance for prolonged waiting periods.

Industry observers and policy makers viewed HIPAA as an important first step in the federal initiative to significantly reduce the number of uninsured people in the United States. Besides its portability provisions, HIPAA changed tax laws to make it easier for Americans to pay for medical care and initiated a pilot program of MSAs that would grow into a significant new initiative in paying for health care.

In 2013 HHS released final regulations that reflect legislative changes made to the HIPAA's privacy and data security rules. The new regulations prohibit the sale of protected health information and the use of such information for marketing or fund-raising.

## HEALTH SAVINGS ACCOUNTS

HIPAA also authorized a five-year demonstration project designed to test the concept of MSAs, which are similar to individual retirement accounts. Beginning on January 1, 1997, approximately 750,000 people with high-deductible health plans (high-deductible plans were defined as those that carried a deductible of $1,600 to $2,400 for an individual or $3,200 to $4,800 for families) could make tax-deductible contributions into interest-bearing savings accounts. The funds deposited into these accounts could be used to purchase health insurance policies and pay co-payments and deductibles. People using MSAs could also deduct any employer contributions into the accounts as tax-deductible income. Any unspent money remaining in the MSA at the end of the year was carried over to the next year, thereby allowing the account to grow.

To be eligible to create an MSA, individuals had to be younger than 65 years old, self-employed, and

FIGURE 6.5

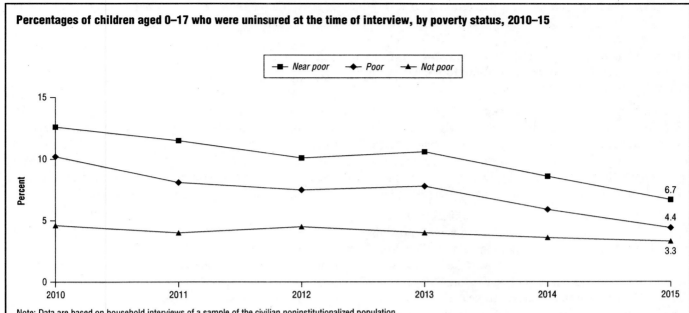

**Percentages of children aged 0–17 who were uninsured at the time of interview, by poverty status, 2010–15**

Note: Data are based on household interviews of a sample of the civilian noninstitutionalized population.

SOURCE: Robin A. Cohen, Michael E. Martinez, and Emily P. Zammitti, "Figure 5. Percentages of Children Aged 0–17 Who Were Uninsured at the Time of the Interview, by Poverty Status United States, 2010–2015," in *Health Insurance Coverage: Early Release of Estimates from the National Health Interview Survey, 2015*, National Center for Health Statistics, May 2016, http://www.cdc.gov/nchs/data/nhis/earlyrelease/insur201605.pdf (accessed July 25, 2016)

uninsured or had to work in firms with 50 or fewer employees that did not offer health care coverage. Withdrawals to cover out-of-pocket medical expenses were tax free, and the money invested grew on a tax-deferred basis. Using MSA funds for any purpose unrelated to medical care or disability resulted in a 15% penalty. However, when MSA users reached age 65, the money could be withdrawn for any purpose and was taxed at the same rate as ordinary income.

Supporters of MSAs believed consumers would be less likely to seek unnecessary medical care if they knew they could keep the money that was left in their accounts for themselves at the end of the year. Experience demonstrated that MSAs could simultaneously help contain health care costs, allow consumers greater control and freedom of choice of health care providers, enable consumers to save for future medical and long-term-care expenses, and improve access to medical care.

In February 2001 President Bush advocated more liberal rules governing MSAs and proposed making them permanently available to all eligible Americans. Congress reviewed the president's proposed reforms and during its 2001–02 session lowered the minimum annual deductible to increase the number of eligible Americans, allowed annual MSA contributions up to 65% of the maximum deductible for individuals and 75% for families, and extended the availability of MSAs through December 31, 2003.

The Medicare Modernization Act of 2003 included provisions to establish health savings accounts (HSAs) for the general population. Like the MSA program it replaced, HSAs offer a variety of benefits, including more choice, greater control, and individual ownership. Specific features of HSAs include:

- Permanence and portability
- Availability to all individuals with a qualified high-deductible health plan
- Minimum deductible of $1,000 per individual plan and $2,000 per family plan
- Allowing annual contributions to equal 100% of the deductible
- Allowing both employer and employee contributions
- Not placing a cap on taxpayer participation
- Allowing tax-free rollover of up to $500 in unspent flexible spending accounts

For 2017, HSAs enabled individuals to deposit up to $3,400 ($6,750 for families) per year in the accounts tax free, and the funds were rolled over from one year to the next. Also, funds could be withdrawn to pay for medical bills or saved for future needs, including retirement.

**Pros and Cons of HSAs**

Brent Hunsberger explains in "HSAs: The Pros and Cons of Health Savings Accounts" (OregonLive.com,

May 18, 2013) that the timing of contributions to an HSA is flexible (funds accrue and roll over from year to year, and contributions may be made up to the filing date of that year's tax return). For example, for 2015, contributions could be made until April 15, 2016. Others (parents, spouses or even friends) can contribute to the HSA, and its owner still takes the tax deduction for it.

Hunsberger also notes the potential pitfalls. Many HSAs have monthly maintenance and withdrawal fees, receipts and records must be kept documenting qualified health expenses, and HSA owners must be covered by a high-deductible health plan. They cannot, for example, be covered on a parent's or spouse's low-deductible plan.

Nonetheless, America's Health Insurance Plans, a national association that represents companies providing health insurance coverage to more than 200 million Americans, reports in "New Census Survey Shows Continued Growth in HSA Enrollment" (Clare Krusing, November 11, 2015, https://ahip.org/new-census-survey-shows-continued-growth-in-hsa-enrollment/) that as of January 2015, 19.7 million people had an HSA, up from 17.4 million in January 2014. HSA plan enrollment varied by geography, with the highest numbers in Texas (1,533,416 enrollees), Illinois (1,280,655 enrollees), Pennsylvania (843,182 enrollees), Ohio (841,970 enrollees), and Minnesota (834,594 enrollees).

Advocates of HSAs believe that by having consumers assume a portion escalating medical care costs, HSAs will stimulate both comparison shopping for health care providers and competition that will ultimately reduce the rate at which costs are rising. In "Employer and Worker Contributions to Health Reimbursement Arrangements and Health Savings Accounts, 2006–2013" (*EBRI Notes*, vol. 35, no. 2, February 2014), Paul Fronstin of the Employee Benefit Research Institute finds a relationship between health engagement and contributions to an HSA. Consumers engaged in their health care were more likely to check whether their plans covered their care or medication and checked the cost of a visit, medication, or other service before receiving care. They also checked quality ratings of providers before seeking care, talked to their doctors about prescription costs and were more likely to use online cost-tracking tools to manage health expenses. Engaged consumers also contributed higher amounts to their HSAs than those with no engagement.

## HEALTH INSURANCE COSTS
## CONTINUE TO SKYROCKET

According to the KFF, in *Employer Health Benefits: 2015 Annual Survey* (September 22, 2015, http://kff.org/report-section/ehbs-2015-section-one-cost-of-health-insurance/), health insurance premiums increased modestly but still outpaced inflation (1.1%), with the average family premium increasing 4% between 2014 and 2015. Premiums averaged $6,251 for individual coverage and $17,545 for family coverage. Workers paid an average of 18% of the premium for individual coverage and 29% of the premium for family coverage.

The KFF explains that the percentage of workers with deductibles for individual coverage of $1,000 or more increased, as did the average co-payments for primary or specialty physician office visits. The average annual deductible for individual coverage was $1,318 up from $917 in 2010. The majority (68%) of covered workers incurred co-payments for office visits and prescription drugs. Cost sharing for prescription drugs generally varies depending on the type of drug (generic, brand-name, or specialty drug) and whether the drug is on the plan's formulary (the list of prescription drugs covered by the health insurance plan).

The KFF finds that 57% of employers offered health benefits in 2015, essentially unchanged from the previous year. More than half (53%) of large employers (200 or more workers) that offer health insurance coverage say that they "conducted an analysis to determine if any of their plans would exceed the Cadillac tax thresholds" (the ACA's excise tax on high-cost health plans), and 19% of this group report that their plan with the largest enrollment will exceed the threshold amount. Thirteen percent of large firms that offer health insurance coverage indicated that they have modified their plans to avoid reaching the excise tax thresholds, and 8% switched to lower-cost health plans.

## HEALTH INSURERS HAVE
## HEIGHTENED OVERSIGHT

The ACA established the Office of Consumer Information and Insurance Oversight (2016, https://www.cms.gov/CCIIO/Resources/About-Us/index.html) to provide "national leadership in setting and enforcing standards for health insurance that promote fair and reasonable practices to ensure affordable, quality health care coverage is available to all Americans." Renamed the Center for Consumer Information and Insurance Oversight (CCIIO), it is a part of the CMS.

The CCIIO has ongoing responsibility for "implementing, monitoring compliance with, and enforcing the new rules governing the insurance market and the new rules regarding the Medical Loss Ratio" (the requirement that insurance companies spend at least 80% or 85% of premium dollars on medical care). It is also responsible for "rate review at the federal level and for assisting states in cracking down on unreasonable rate increases."

### Impact of the ACA on Health Insurers

In *Report to Congress on the Impact on Premiums for Individuals and Families with Employer-Sponsored Health Insurance from the Guaranteed Issue, Guaranteed Renewal and Fair Health Insurance Premiums Provisions of the*

*Affordable Care Act* (February 21, 2014, http://www.cms.gov/Research-Statistics-Data-and-Systems/Research/ActuarialStudies/Downloads/ACA-Employer-Premium-Impact.pdf), the CMS Office of the Actuary notes that health insurance companies can only vary their premiums based on consumers' age, tobacco use, geographical location, family size, and the value of the plan. The oldest consumers cannot be charged more than three times as much as the youngest adults, and smokers may be charged no more than 1.5 times the premium for nonsmokers.

Before provisions of the ACA took effect in 2014, insurers could offer lower premiums to small employers with younger and healthier employees who presumably would have fewer health care needs, and much higher rates to small employers with older and sicker employees with more health care needs. As a result, firms with older employees paid higher premiums. The sex distribution of workers also influenced premiums. Before 2014, employers with more women of childbearing age were frequently charged higher premiums.

In "Insurer Obamacare Losses Reach Billions of Dollars after Two Years" (Forbes.com, February 7, 2016), Bruce Japsen reports that after two years of offering uninsured Americans subsidized health plans on insurance exchanges, many health plans are reporting significant losses. United Health Group lost over $720 million on its public exchange business in 2015 and Anthem, which operates Blue Cross and Blue Shield plans in 14 states, attributed its 64% plunge in profits in the fourth quarter of 2015 to the ACA. Insurers suffered these losses because of costs associated with care for the influx of new enrollees, many of whom were previously uninsured; these costs were not offset by the premiums paid by healthy enrollees. Despite these losses, most major insurers, with the exception of United Health Group (which announced plans to exit most of the states where it offers plans on ACA insurance exchanges), hope to recover from losses generated by caring for their previously uninsured enrollees.

## MENTAL HEALTH PARITY

In terms of mental health care, parity refers to the premise that the same range and scope of insurance benefits available for other illnesses should be provided for people with mental illness. Historically, private health insurance plans have provided less coverage for mental illness than for other medical conditions. Coverage for mental health was more restricted and often involved more cost sharing (higher co-payments and deductibles) than coverage for medical care. As a result, many patients with severe mental illness, who frequently required hospitalizations and other treatment, quickly depleted their mental health coverage.

During the 1990s there was growing interest in parity of mental health with other health services. The Mental Health Parity Act of 1996 sought to bring mental health benefits closer to other health benefits. The act amended the 1944 Public Health Service Act and the 1974 Employee Retirement Income Security Act by requiring parity for annual and lifetime dollar limits but did not place restrictions on other plan features such as hospital and office visit limits. It also imposed federal standards on the mental health coverage offered by employers through group health plans. The National Council of State Legislatures, in *State Laws Mandating or Regulating Mental Health Benefits* (December 30, 2015, http://www.ncsl.org/research/health/mental-health-benefits-state-mandates.aspx), observes that by 2015, all states had laws governing mental health parity.

### Legislation Establishes Mental Health Parity

The Paul Wellstone and Pete Domenici Mental Health Parity and Addiction Equity Act (MHPAEA) of 2008 expanded the Mental Health Parity Act by prohibiting group health plans and group health insurance companies from imposing treatment limitations or financial requirements for coverage of mental health that are different from those used for medical and surgical benefits. In "New Rules Promise Better Mental Health Coverage" (NYTimes.com, January 29, 2010), Robert Pear explains that eliminating disparities between physical health care and mental health care makes it easier for people to obtain care for conditions ranging from depression and anxiety to eating disorders and substance abuse. The Obama administration predicted that the parity requirement would benefit "111 million people in 446,400 group health plans offered by private employers, and 29 million people in 20,000 plans sponsored by state and local governments." The act was projected to increase insurance premiums 0.4%, which translates into $25.6 billion between 2010 and 2019.

### Effects of the ACA on Mental Health Parity

According to the National Council of State Legislatures, in *State Laws Mandating or Regulating Mental Health Benefits*, the ACA contains two main provisions that are aimed at improving mental health parity: expanding "the reach of the applicability of the federal mental health parity requirements" and establishing "a mandated benefit for the coverage of certain mental health and substance abuse disorder services." Furthermore, the legislation expands the reach of federal mental health parity requirements to qualified health plans as established by the ACA, to Medicaid nonmanaged care plans, and to plans offered to individuals.

In 2016 all qualified health plans offered through health insurance exchanges were required to include coverage for mental and/or substance use disorders as one of the 10 categories of essential health benefits, and this coverage must comply with the federal parity requirements set forth in the MHPAEA.

In March 2016 the Office of the Assistant Secretary for Planning and Evaluation published a report, "Benefits of Medicaid Expansion for Behavioral Health" (March 28, 2016, https://aspe.hhs.gov/pdf-report/benefits-medicaid-expansion-behavioral-health) averring that improved access to mental health and substance abuse treatment is one more reason why states should expand Medicaid to cover low-income adults under the age of 65 years.

### Parity May Not Solve All Access Problems

According to Susan Brink, in "Mental Health Now Covered under ACA, but Not for Everyone" (USNews.com, April 29, 2014), parity alone will not eliminate all obstacles to gaining access to mental health care. Brink explains that although the ACA permits young adults to remain on their parents' health plans to age 26 and prevents insurance companies from denying coverage to people with preexisting mental health disorders, such as schizophrenia, depression, or drug or alcohol dependence, shortages of mental health providers and gaps in coverage may still compromise access to care.

Some states (Colorado, Massachusetts, Minnesota, New Jersey, Oregon, and Vermont) have taken steps to improve mental health care using novel delivery systems. Accountable care organizations, patient-centered medical homes, and community care organizations use teams of health professionals to coordinate and provide mental health care. Medicaid programs in states such as Oregon also incentivize providers to keep people healthy and out of the hospital by paying a fixed amount per patient.

Brink, however, observes that mental health patients may not fare as well in the states that have not opted to expand Medicaid coverage. Joel Miller, executive director of the American Mental Health Counselors Association, asserts, "Nearly 4 million uninsured people with mental health conditions will be locked out of the health insurance system, and therefore lack access to timely, quality mental health services and a consistent source of care."

## FINANCING THE ACA

The ACA is financed by a combination of health care savings resulting from programs that improve efficiency and accountability, incentivize quality and cost-effective care, and reduce waste, fraud, and inefficiencies. It also contains provisions to raise revenue such as the excise tax on high-premium insurance plans (the Cadillac tax), annual fees paid by health insurers and manufacturers and importers of prescription drugs along with taxes on indoor tanning services and medical devices.

The excise tax on the high-premium plans is expected to generate $18 billion between 2017 and 2026, the individual mandate penalty $38 billion, the tax on health insurance providers $156 billion, and the employer responsibility penalty $228 billion.

In *Federal Subsidies for Health Insurance Coverage for People under Age 65: 2016 to 2026* (March 24, 2016, https://www.cbo.gov/publication/51385), the CBO anticipates that the health insurance coverage provisions of the ACA will cost the federal government $1.4 trillion from 2017 to 2026. (See Table 5.8 in Chapter 5.) The federal government subsidy for health insurance coverage for people under the age of 65 years was an estimated $660 billion (3.6% of the GDP) in 2016 and $8.9 trillion from 2017 through 2026. The cost of subsidies will be offset by an estimated $517 billion from taxes and penalties.

The CBO estimate of the cost of coverage for the 2017 to 2026 period was higher than the previous year's estimate because Medicaid and employer coverage were significantly higher than was previously expected. The CBO also projects that throughout the next decade earnings for lower-income workers will increase more slowly than the previous projection anticipated, making even more people eligible for Medicaid and subsidies.

Nonetheless, the projected cost of the ACA is still markedly less than originally forecast. In 2010 the ACA coverage provisions were an estimated $623 billion from 2016 to 2019. In 2016 they were projected to cost $466 billion. The dramatic reduction is attributable to slower than expected growth of subsidized coverage, reduced health care inflation, and other considerations, such as the Supreme Court decision allowing states to choose whether to expand Medicaid.

# CHAPTER 7
# INTERNATIONAL COMPARISONS OF HEALTH CARE

International comparisons are often difficult to interpret because the definitions of terms, the reliability of data, the cultures, and the values differ. What is important in one society may be unimportant or even nonexistent in another. A political or human right that is important in one nation may be meaningless in a neighboring nation. Evaluating the quality of health care systems is an example of the difficulties involved in comparing one culture to another.

Even within the United States there are cultural and regional variations in health care delivery. A visit to a busy urban urgent care center might begin with the patient completing a brief medical history, followed by five minutes with a nurse who measures and records the patient's vital signs (pulse, respiration, and temperature), and conclude with a 15-minute visit with a physician assistant or nurse practitioner, who diagnoses the problem and prescribes treatment. In contrast, on the islands of Hawaii a visit with a healer may last several hours and culminate with a prayer, a song, or an embrace. Hawaiian healers, called kahunas, are unhurried and offer an array of herbal remedies and bodywork (massage, touch, and manipulative therapies), along with counseling and guidance because they believe that the healing quality of the encounter, independent of any treatment offered, improves health and well-being.

Although comparing the performance of health care systems and health outcomes (how people fare as a result of receiving health care services) is of benefit to health care planners, administrators, and policy makers, the subjective nature of such assessments should be duly considered.

## A COMPARISON OF HEALTH CARE SPENDING, RESOURCES, AND UTILIZATION

The Organisation for Economic Co-operation and Development (OECD) provides information about 35 member countries that are governed democratically and participate in the global market economy. It collects and publishes data about a wide range of economic and social issues including health and health care policy. The OECD member nations are generally considered to be the wealthier, more developed nations in the world. As of 2016 the OECD member countries were Australia, Austria, Belgium, Canada, Chile, the Czech Republic, Denmark, Estonia, Finland, France, Germany, Greece, Hungary, Iceland, Ireland, Israel, Italy, Japan, Latvia, Luxembourg, Mexico, the Netherlands, New Zealand, Norway, Poland, Portugal, the Slovak Republic, Slovenia, South Korea, Spain, Sweden, Switzerland, Turkey, the United Kingdom, and the United States.

## Percentage of Gross Domestic Product Spent on Health Care

Although health has always been a concern for Americans, the growth in the health care industry since the mid-1970s has made it a major factor in the U.S. economy. For many years the United States has spent a larger proportion of its gross domestic product (GDP; the total market value of final goods and services produced within an economy in a given year) on health care than have other nations with similar economic development. According to the OECD, the United States spent 16.9% of its GDP on health care in 2015. (See Figure 7.1.) The next highest country was Switzerland, with 11.5%. Other nations that spent large percentages of their GDP on health care in 2015 included Japan (11.2%), Germany (11.1%), Sweden (11.1%), France (11%), the Netherlands (10.8%), Denmark (10.6%), Austria (10.3%), Belgium (10.4%), and Canada (10.2%). The OECD member nations that spent low percentages of GDP on health care in 2015 were Turkey (5.2%), Latvia (5.6%), Mexico (5.9%), Estonia (6.3%), and Poland (6.3%).

## Per Capita Spending on Health Care

According to the OECD, in *Health at a Glance 2015: OECD Indicators* (November 4, 2015, http://www.oecd.org/els/health-systems/health-at-a-glance-19991312.htm),

FIGURE 7.1

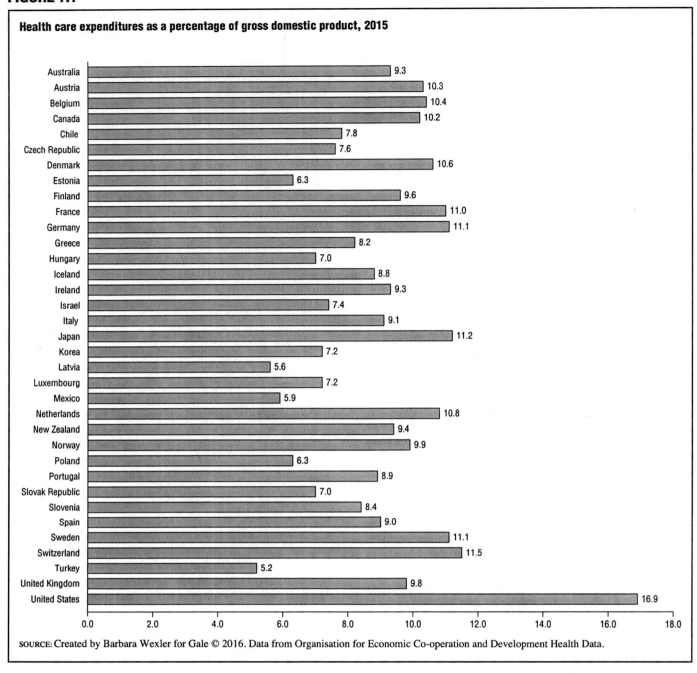

**Health care expenditures as a percentage of gross domestic product, 2015**

SOURCE: Created by Barbara Wexler for Gale © 2016. Data from Organisation for Economic Co-operation and Development Health Data.

the United States also had the highest per capita spending for health care services in 2013, spending an average of $8,713 per citizen. No other country came close to spending this amount per capita: Switzerland spent $6,325 per citizen; Norway spent $5,862; the Netherlands, $5,131; Sweden, $4,904; Germany, $4,819; Denmark, $4,553; Austria, $4,553; Luxembourg, $4,371; Canada, $4,351; Belgium, $4,256; France, $4,124; and Australia, $3,866. Of the countries tracked by the OECD in *Health at a Glance 2015*, India ($215; not an OECD country) spent the least per capita on health care in 2013, followed by Indonesia ($293; not an OECD country), China ($649; not an OECD member), Colombia ($864;

not an OECD country), Turkey ($941), and Mexico ($1,048).

**Who Pays for Health Care?**

Public expenditures for health care services as a percentage of GDP vary widely among the OECD member countries. In *Health at a Glance 2015*, the OECD notes that public spending (general government and social security) on health accounted for an average of 75% of spending for medical services across OECD member countries in 2013 and that, on average, 19% of spending was paid by private sources, mainly private insurance and individuals. In the United States public funding accounted for about 48% of spending for medical services. By contrast, public sources in the Netherlands accounted for 88%, in Norway for 86%, and in Denmark, the Czech Republic, and Sweden for 84% of spending. Other nations with above-average contributions of public funding to medical service expenditures included Japan, Luxembourg, and the United Kingdom with 83%, Iceland (81%), New Zealand (80%), France (79%), Turkey and Estonia (78%), Belgium, Germany, and Italy (77%), and Austria (76%). Among the OECD nations, public expenditures on medical services per capita were lowest in Chile (46%), the United States (50%), and Mexico (51%).

In terms of out-of-pocket payments as a share of total household expenditures in 2013, the United States, at 2.6%, was below the OECD average of 2.8%. In Turkey and the Netherlands out-of-pocket payments as a share of total household expenditures were low, at 1.2% and 1.3%, respectively. In contrast, out-of-pocket spending as a share of total household spending was highest in South Korea (4.7%), Switzerland (4.5%) and Greece (4.1%).

Because the United States does not currently have a government-funded national health care program that provides coverage for all of its citizens, U.S. private insurance expenditures cover the costs generally assumed by government programs that finance health care delivery in comparable OECD member nations. The Patient Protection and Affordable Care Act (also known as the Affordable Care Act [ACA]) aims to not only provide health insurance coverage for the overwhelming majority of Americans but also change the ways in which Americans purchase and pay for health care. As previously uninsured Americans are covered by either subsidized private plans or Medicaid expansion, the mix of payment sources (public, private, and out of pocket) is shifting. For example, expanded Medicaid eligibility has increased the share of public expenditures, and limits on maximum health plan deductibles may reduce out-of-pocket expenditures.

### Spending on Pharmaceutical Drugs

The OECD indicates in *Health at a Glance 2015* that in 2013 the United States spent more per capita ($1,026) on pharmaceutical drugs than any other OECD member country. The OECD average pharmaceutical spending was $515 per capita. Per capita pharmaceutical spending was also high in Japan ($752), Greece ($721), Canada ($713), Germany ($678), and Switzerland ($666). In contrast, Denmark spent $240 per capita on pharmaceuticals; Estonia, $273; Israel, $287; and Poland, $326.

### Hospital Utilization Statistics

The number of hospital beds is a broad measure of resource availability. However, it is important to remember that it does not reflect capacity to provide emergency or outpatient hospital care. In general, it also does not measure the number of beds that are devoted to nonacute or other long-term care, although it is known that in Japan many of the beds designated as acute care are actually used for long-term care. Of the OECD member countries reporting acute care hospital beds per 1,000 population in 2013, Japan (13.3) and South Korea (11) had the highest numbers. The United States at 2.9 beds per 1,000 population was well below the OECD average of 4.8, trailed by Ireland, New Zealand, and the United Kingdom (2.8), Canada and Turkey (2.7), Sweden (2.6), Brazil and South Africa (2.3; not OECD countries), Chile (2.2), Mexico (1.6), Colombia (1.5; not an OECD country), Indonesia (1; not an OECD country) and India (0.5; not an OECD country).

Hospital lengths of stay have consistently declined since 1960, in part because increasing numbers of illnesses can be treated as effectively in outpatient settings and because many countries have reduced inpatient hospitalization rates and the average length of stay to control health care costs. In 2013 Japan (17.2 days) had the longest average length of stay of the OECD member nations, followed by South Korea (16.5), Finland (10.8 days), France (10.1 days), Hungary (9.5 days), Germany (9.1 days), and Luxembourg (8.9). The shortest hospital stays among OECD countries in 2013 were in Turkey (3.9 days), Mexico (4 days), and Denmark (4.3 days).

Medical practice, particularly the types and frequency of procedures performed, also varies from one country to another. The OECD looks at rates of cesarean section (delivery of a baby through an incision in the abdomen as opposed to vaginal delivery) per 1,000 live births and found both growth in the rates of cesarean section (as a percentage of all births) and considerable variation in the rates for this surgical procedure. In 2013 the highest rates for cesarean sections per 100 live births were reported in Turkey (50.4), Mexico (45.2), and Chile (44.7) and the lowest were in Iceland (15.2), Israel (15.4) and the Netherlands (15.6). The U.S. rate was 32.5. In "Cesarean Section—Desired Rate versus Actual Need" (*Archives of Medical and Biomedical Research*, vol. 3, no. 1, March 2016), Smriti Agnihotri, Okezie I. Aruoma and Arun K. Agnihotri report that the cesarean section rate is rising globally, especially in high- and middle-income countries. The researchers assert that 10% to 15% is the ideal rate to reduce maternal and infant mortality, and higher rates do not improve health outcomes.

Table 7.1 shows the dramatic rise in cesarean sections between 1989 and 2014 in the United States. Because cesarean section is performed in the hospital and involves at least an overnight stay, the frequency with which it and other surgical procedures are performed contributes to hospitalization rates and expenditures.

TABLE 7.1

**Births, by delivery method and race and Hispanic origin of mother, 1989–2014**

| | | Vaginal | | | | Cesarean | | | | | | | |
| | | Number | | | | Number | | | | Rate[a] | | | |
| Year | All births | Total[b] | Non-Hispanic white[c] | Non-Hispanic black[c] | Hispanic[d] | Total[b] | Non-Hispanic white[c] | Non-Hispanic black[c] | Hispanic[d] | Total[b] | Non-Hispanic white[c] | Non-Hispanic black[c] | Hispanic[d] |
|---|---|---|---|---|---|---|---|---|---|---|---|---|---|
| 2014 | 3,988,076 | 2,699,951 | 1,473,298 | 379,055 | 622,033 | 1,284,551 | 674,254 | 209,361 | 291,520 | 32.2 | 31.4 | 35.6 | 31.9 |
| 2013 | 3,932,181 | 2,642,892 | 1,446,270 | 374,054 | 610,196 | 1,284,339 | 680,521 | 209,015 | 290,016 | 32.7 | 32.0 | 35.8 | 32.2 |
| 2012 | 3,952,841 | 2,650,744 | 1,441,894 | 374,035 | 615,095 | 1,296,070 | 688,932 | 208,562 | 291,697 | 32.8 | 32.3 | 35.8 | 32.2 |
| 2011 | 3,953,590 | 2,651,428 | 1,447,969 | 374,978 | 623,010 | 1,293,267 | 693,591 | 206,009 | 293,816 | 32.8 | 32.4 | 35.5 | 32.0 |
| 2010 | 3,999,386 | 2,680,947 | 1,454,861 | 379,617 | 643,682 | 1,309,182 | 702,548 | 208,520 | 300,138 | 32.8 | 32.6 | 35.5 | 31.8 |
| 2009 | 4,130,665 | 2,764,285 | 1,481,660 | 392,715 | 682,512 | 1,353,572 | 723,687 | 214,810 | 315,025 | 32.9 | 32.8 | 35.4 | 31.6 |
| 2008 | 4,247,694 | 2,864,343 | 1,527,340 | 406,379 | 716,811 | 1,369,273 | 732,641 | 214,416 | 321,859 | 32.3 | 32.4 | 34.5 | 31.0 |
| 2007 | 4,316,233 | 2,933,056 | 1,565,555 | 413,088 | 737,478 | 1,367,340 | 735,744 | 211,615 | 322,554 | 31.8 | 32.0 | 33.9 | 30.4 |
| 2006 | 4,265,555 | 2,929,590 | 1,580,794 | 411,097 | 728,854 | 1,321,054 | 718,960 | 203,723 | 307,981 | 31.1 | 31.3 | 33.1 | 29.7 |
| 2005 | 4,138,349 | 2,873,918 | 1,579,613 | 392,064 | 698,089 | 1,248,815 | 690,260 | 189,287 | 285,376 | 30.3 | 30.4 | 32.6 | 29.0 |
| 2004 | 4,112,052 | 2,903,341 | 1,617,994 | 397,877 | 679,118 | 1,190,210 | 667,836 | 178,461 | 263,454 | 29.1 | 29.2 | 31.0 | 28.0 |
| 2003 | 4,089,950 | 2,949,853 | 1,671,414 | 405,671 | 667,656 | 1,119,388 | 637,482 | 167,506 | 241,159 | 27.5 | 27.6 | 29.2 | 26.5 |
| 2002 | 4,021,726 | 2,958,423 | 1,687,144 | 416,516 | 653,516 | 1,043,846 | 598,682 | 159,297 | 219,777 | 26.1 | 26.2 | 27.7 | 25.2 |
| 2001 | 4,025,933 | 3,027,993 | 1,746,551 | 435,455 | 648,821 | 978,411 | 567,488 | 151,908 | 199,874 | 24.4 | 24.5 | 25.9 | 23.6 |
| 2000 | 4,058,814 | 3,108,188 | 1,804,550 | 454,736 | 633,220 | 923,991 | 540,794 | 146,042 | 179,583 | 22.9 | 23.1 | 24.3 | 22.1 |
| 1999 | 3,959,417 | 3,063,870 | 1,810,682 | 449,580 | 599,118 | 862,086 | 514,051 | 135,508 | 161,035 | 22.0 | 22.1 | 23.2 | 21.2 |
| 1998 | 3,941,553 | 3,078,537 | 1,842,420 | 457,186 | 580,143 | 825,870 | 495,550 | 131,999 | 150,317 | 21.2 | 21.2 | 22.4 | 20.6 |
| 1997 | 3,880,894 | 3,046,621 | 1,829,213 | 451,744 | 563,114 | 799,033 | 481,982 | 126,138 | 142,907 | 20.8 | 20.9 | 21.8 | 20.2 |
| 1996 | 3,891,494 | 3,061,092 | 1,851,058 | 449,544 | 558,105 | 797,119 | 485,530 | 124,836 | 139,554 | 20.7 | 20.8 | 21.7 | 20.0 |
| 1995 | 3,899,589 | 3,063,724 | 1,867,024 | 457,104 | 539,731 | 806,722 | 496,103 | 127,171 | 136,640 | 20.8 | 21.0 | 21.8 | 20.2 |
| 1994 | 3,952,767 | 3,087,576 | 1,896,609 | 480,551 | 525,928 | 830,517 | 518,021 | 134,526 | 135,569 | 21.2 | 21.5 | 21.9 | 20.5 |
| 1993 | 4,000,240 | 3,098,796 | 1,902,433 | 496,333 | 514,493 | 861,987 | 542,013 | 139,702 | 136,279 | 21.8 | 22.2 | 22.0 | 20.9 |
| 1992[e] | 4,065,014 | 3,100,710 | 1,916,414 | 502,669 | 494,338 | 888,622 | 566,788 | 143,153 | 133,369 | 22.3 | 22.8 | 22.2 | 21.2 |
| 1991[e] | 4,110,907 | 3,100,891 | 1,941,726 | 507,522 | 472,126 | 905,077 | 587,802 | 142,417 | 129,752 | 22.6 | 23.2 | 21.9 | 21.6 |
| 1990[f] | 4,110,563 | 3,111,421 | 1,972,754 | 503,720 | 458,242 | 914,096 | 603,467 | 142,838 | 122,969 | 22.7 | 23.4 | 22.1 | 21.2 |
| 1989[g] | 3,798,734 | 2,793,463 | 1,806,753 | 440,310 | 385,462 | 826,955 | 556,585 | 125,290 | 105,268 | 22.8 | 23.6 | 22.2 | 21.5 |

[a]Percentage of all live births by cesarean delivery.

[b]Includes races other than white and black and origin not stated.

[c]Race and Hispanic origin are reported separately on birth certificates. Persons of Hispanic origin may be of any race. Race categories are consistent with 1977 Office of Management and Budget standards. Forty-nine states and the District of Columbia reported multiple-race data for 2014 that were bridged to single-race categories for comparability with other states. Multiple-race reporting areas vary for 2003–2014.

[d]Includes all persons of Hispanic origin of any race.

[e]Excludes data for New Hampshire, which did not report Hispanic origin.

[f]Excludes data for New Hampshire and Oklahoma, which did not report data by Hispanic origin. Oklahoma did not report method of delivery.

[g]Excludes data for Louisiana, Maryland, Nebraska, Nevada, and Oklahoma, which did not report method of delivery on the birth certificate; data by Hispanic origin also excludes New Hampshire, which did not report Hispanic origin.

SOURCE: Brady E. Hamilton et al., "Table 21. Births, by Method of Delivery and Race and Hispanic Origin of Mother: United States, 1989–2014," in "Births: Final Data for 2014," in *National Vital Statistics Reports*, vol. 64, no. 12, December 23, 2015, http://www.cdc.gov/nchs/data/nvsr/nvsr64/nvsr64_12.pdf (accessed August 11, 2016)

## Physicians' Numbers Are Increasing

Since 1960 the OECD member nations have all enjoyed growing physician populations. In *Health at a Glance 2015*, the OECD reports that in 2013 Greece reported the highest ratio of practicing physicians, 6.3 per 1,000 population, with most countries ranging between 2 and 4 physicians per 1,000 population. Non-OECD countries had the fewest practicing physicians, including Indonesia (0.3 per 1,000 population), India (0.7), South Africa (0.8), China (1.7), Brazil (1.8), and Colombia (1.8). Turkey (1.8 per 1,000 population) had the lowest ratio of practicing physicians to population among OECD members, followed by Chile (1.9). At 2.6 physicians per 1,000 population, the United States was also below the OECD average of 3.3.

The ratio of physicians to population is a limited measure of health care quality, because many other factors, such as the availability of other health care providers as well as the accessibility and affordability of health care services, also influence the quality of health care systems. Furthermore, since the early 1990s research has shown that more medical care, in terms of numbers and concentration of health care providers, is not necessarily linked to better health status for the population. For example, the Dartmouth Institute for Health Policy and Clinical Practice indicates in "The Physician Workforce" (2014, http://www.dartmouthatlas.org/keyissues/issue.aspx?con=2940) that increasing the physician population will make the U.S. health care system worse rather than better. The institute contends that "first, unfettered growth is likely to exacerbate regional inequities in supply and spending; our research has shown that physicians generally do not choose to practice where the need is greatest. Second, expansion of graduate medical education would most likely further undermine primary care and reinforce trends toward a fragmented, specialist-oriented health care system."

# OVERVIEWS OF SELECTED HEALTH CARE SYSTEMS

Chloe Anderson of the Commonwealth Fund presents data from the OECD and other agencies to compare health care systems in industrialized countries in *Multinational Comparisons of Health Systems Data, 2014* (November 2014, http://www.commonwealthfund.org/~/media/files/publications/chartbook/2014/nov/pdf_1788_anderson_multinational_comparisons_2014_oecd_chartpack_v2.pdf). This section also presents data from a report edited by Elias Mossialos and Martin Wenzl of the London School of Economics and Political Science and Robin Osborn and Dana Sarnak of the Commonwealth Fund, *2015 International Profiles of Health Care Systems* (January 2016, http://www.commonwealthfund.org/~/media/files/publications/fund-report/2016/jan/1857_mossialos_intl_profiles_2015_v7.pdf).

Anderson looks at OECD data for 13 industrialized countries: Australia, Canada, Denmark, France, Germany, Japan, the Netherlands, New Zealand, Norway, Sweden, Switzerland, the United Kingdom, and the United States. She finds that the United States outspends other industrialized countries. However, the quality of U.S. health care, in terms of measures such as flu immunization, breast cancer survival rates, and the percentage of the population that smokes, is not significantly superior to other less costly health care systems.

Another significant difference between the United States and other OECD countries is the lack of universal health insurance coverage. This gap in coverage explains why Americans go without needed health care more often than people in other OECD countries and why, in comparison with the other industrialized countries, the United States does not fare well in measures of access to care and equity in health care between high- and low-income populations. As the provisions of the ACA take effect, and the majority of Americans obtain health care coverage, these disparities will likely diminish, but not disappear entirely.

According to the Henry J. Kaiser Family Foundation (KFF), in "Key Facts about the Uninsured Population" (October 5, 2016, http://kff.org/uninsured/fact-sheet/key-facts-about-the-uninsured-population/), even with full implementation of the ACA millions of Americans will still lack health coverage, and 28.5 million people in the United States remained uninsured in 2015. The high cost of insurance is the most commonly cited reason for remaining uninsured. Some people do not have access to coverage through an employer, and others, particularly low-income adults in states that did not expand Medicaid, do not meet eligibility requirements for public coverage. In addition, undocumented immigrants are not eligible for Medicaid and cannot purchase coverage through the exchanges.

## United States

The ACA established the U.S. health care financing system as a "shared responsibility" model—the government, employers and individuals ensure access to health care services. Employer-based health insurance is tax subsidized; that is, health insurance premiums are a tax-deductible business expense and are not generally taxed as employee compensation. Premiums for individual policies purchased by self-employed Americans became fully tax deductible in 2003. In 2014 state and federally administered health insurance exchanges were established to improve access and offer premium subsidies for low-and middle-income Americans. Nonetheless, there are still gaps in insured rates throughout the nation, and benefits, premiums, and provider reimbursement methods differ among private insurance plans and among public programs.

Most physicians who provide both ambulatory care (hospital outpatient service and office visits) and inpatient hospital care are reimbursed on either a fee-for-service or capitation basis (literally, per head, but in managed care frequently per member per month), and payment rates vary among insurers. Increasing numbers of physicians are salaried. They are employees of the government, hospital, and health care delivery systems, universities, and private industry.

The nation's hospitals are paid on the basis of charges, costs, negotiated rates, diagnosis-related groups (fixed payments for a specific diagnosis), or bundled payments, which may place the hospital at risk for readmissions and other services, depending on the insurer. There are no overall global budgets or expenditure limits. Managed care (oversight to verify the medical necessity of treatments and to control the cost of health care) has assumed an expanding role. Managed care plans and payers (government and private health insurance) now exert greater control over the practices of individual health care providers in an effort to control costs. To the extent that they govern reimbursement, managed care organizations are viewed by many industry observers as dictating the methods, terms, and quality of health care delivery.

**IS THE UNITED STATES SPENDING MORE AND GETTING LESS?** A primary indicator of the quality of health care delivery in any nation is the health status of its people. Many factors affect the health of individuals and populations: heredity, race and ethnicity, gender, income, education, geography, violent crime, environmental agents, and exposure to infectious diseases, as well as access to and availability of health care services.

Still, in the nation that spends the most on the health of its citizens, it seems reasonable to expect to see tangible benefits of expenditures for health care; that is, measurable gains in health status. This section considers three health outcomes (measures used to assess the health of a population)—life expectancy at birth, infant mortality (death), and health care costs—and selected aspects of health care delivery such as access and quality to determine the extent to which U.S. citizens derive health benefits from record-high outlays for medical care.

Overall, life expectancy at birth consistently has increased in all the OECD member countries since 1960; however, historically, U.S. life expectancy has remained slightly below the OECD average. For example, Figure 7.2 shows that in 2013 U.S. life expectancy for women (81.2 years) was surpassed by all OECD

member countries except the Slovak Republic (80.9 years), Turkey (80.7 years; not shown in Figure 7.2), Hungary (79.1), Mexico (77.4 years). Infant mortality also declined sharply during this period, but the United States fared far worse than most OECD member countries—in 2012 the United States ranked number 25 with an infant mortality rate of 6 deaths per 1,000 live births. (See Table 7.2.)

Compared with the systems of other industrialized countries, the U.S. health care system is not only costlier

**FIGURE 7.2**

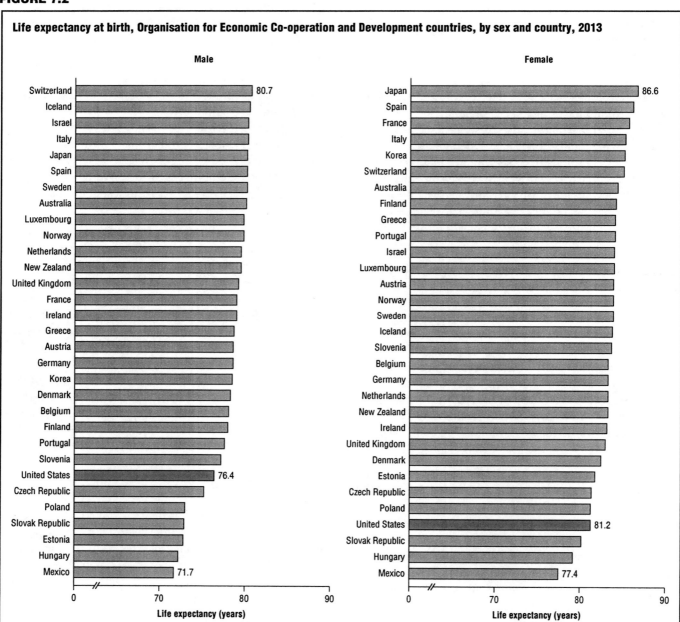

Life expectancy at birth, Organisation for Economic Co-operation and Development countries, by sex and country, 2013

Notes: Countries with estimated life expectancies or series breaks for 2013 are not presented. Differences in life expectancy may reflect differences in reporting methods, which can vary by country, in addition to actual differences in mortality rates.

SOURCE: "Figure 1. Life Expectancy at Birth, by Sex and Country: Organisation for Economic Co-operation and Development (OECD) Countries, 2013," in *Health, United States, 2015: With Special Feature on Racial and Ethnic Health Disparities*, U.S. Department of Health and Human Services, Centers for Disease Control and Prevention, National Center for Health Statistics, May 2016, http://www.cdc.gov/nchs/data/hus/hus15.pdf (accessed July 29, 2016)

TABLE 7.2

**Infant mortality and international rankings, Organisation for Economic Co-operation and Development countries, selected years 1960–2012**

[Data are based on reporting by OECD countries]

| Country[b] | 1960 | 1970 | 1980 | 1990 | 2000 | 2010 | 2011 | 2012 | International rankings[a] 1960 | International rankings[a] 2012 |
|---|---|---|---|---|---|---|---|---|---|---|
| | | | | | Infant[c] deaths per 1,000 live births | | | | | |
| Australia | 20.2 | 17.9 | 10.7 | 8.2 | 5.2 | 4.1 | 3.8 | 3.3 | 5 | 11 |
| Austria | 37.5 | 25.9 | 14.3 | 7.8 | 4.8 | 3.9 | 3.6 | 3.2 | 19 | 10 |
| Belgium | 31.4 | 21.1 | 12.1 | 8.0 | 4.8 | 3.6 | 3.4 | 3.8 | 17 | 20 |
| Canada | 27.3 | 18.8 | 10.4 | 6.8 | 5.3 | 5.0 | 4.8 | — | 12 | — |
| Chile | 120.3 | 79.3 | 33.0 | 16.0 | 8.9 | 7.4 | 7.7 | 7.4 | 27 | 26 |
| Czech Republic[d] | 20.0 | 20.2 | 16.9 | 10.8 | 4.1 | 2.7 | 2.7 | 2.6 | 4 | 4 |
| Denmark | 21.5 | 14.2 | 8.4 | 7.5 | 5.3 | 3.4 | 3.5 | 3.4 | 8 | 13 |
| Finland | 21.0 | 13.2 | 7.6 | 5.6 | 3.8 | 2.3 | 2.4 | 2.4 | 6 | 2 |
| France | 27.7 | 18.2 | 10.0 | 7.3 | 4.5 | 3.6 | 3.5 | 3.5 | 13 | 15 |
| Germany[e] | 35.0 | 22.5 | 12.4 | 7.0 | 4.4 | 3.4 | 3.6 | 3.3 | 18 | 11 |
| Greece | 40.1 | 29.6 | 17.9 | 9.7 | 5.9 | 3.8 | 3.4 | 2.9 | 20 | 6 |
| Hungary | 47.6 | 35.9 | 23.2 | 14.8 | 9.2 | 5.3 | 4.9 | 4.9 | 23 | 23 |
| Ireland | 29.3 | 19.5 | 11.1 | 8.2 | 6.2 | 3.6 | 3.5 | 3.5 | 15 | 15 |
| Israel[f] | — | 24.2 | 15.6 | 9.9 | 5.5 | 3.7 | 3.5 | 3.6 | — | 17 |
| Italy | 43.9 | 29.6 | 14.6 | 8.1 | 4.3 | 3.2 | 2.9 | 2.9 | 22 | 6 |
| Japan | 30.7 | 13.1 | 7.5 | 4.6 | 3.2 | 2.3 | 2.3 | 2.2 | 16 | 1 |
| Korea | — | 45.0 | — | — | — | 3.2 | 3.0 | 2.9 | — | 6 |
| Mexico | 92.3 | — | 52.6 | 32.5 | 20.8 | 14.1 | 13.7 | 13.3 | 26 | 28 |
| Netherlands | 16.5 | 12.7 | 8.6 | 7.1 | 5.1 | 3.8 | 3.6 | 3.7 | 2 | 19 |
| New Zealand | 22.6 | 16.7 | 13.0 | 8.4 | 6.3 | 5.5 | 5.2 | — | 10 | — |
| Norway | 16.0 | 11.3 | 8.1 | 6.9 | 3.8 | 2.8 | 2.4 | 2.5 | 1 | 3 |
| Poland | 56.1 | 36.4 | 25.4 | 19.4 | 8.1 | 5.0 | 4.7 | 4.6 | 24 | 22 |
| Portugal | 77.5 | 55.5 | 24.3 | 10.9 | 5.5 | 2.5 | 3.1 | 3.4 | 25 | 13 |
| Slovak Republic[d] | 28.6 | 25.7 | 20.9 | 12.0 | 8.6 | 5.7 | 4.9 | 5.8 | 14 | 24 |
| Spain | 43.7 | 28.1 | 12.3† | 7.6 | 4.4 | 3.2 | 3.1 | 3.1 | 21 | 9 |
| Sweden | 16.6 | 11.0 | 6.9 | 6.0 | 3.4 | 2.5 | 2.1 | 2.6 | 3 | 4 |
| Switzerland | 21.1 | 15.1 | 9.1 | 6.8 | 4.9 | 3.8 | 3.8 | 3.6 | 7 | 17 |
| Turkey | — | — | — | — | 28.9 | 12.2 | 11.7 | 11.6 | — | 27 |
| United Kingdom | 22.5 | 18.5 | 12.1 | 7.9 | 5.6 | 4.2 | 4.2 | 4.1 | 9 | 21 |
| United States | 26.0 | 20.0 | 12.6 | 9.2 | 6.9 | 6.1 | 6.1 | 6.0 | 11 | 25 |

—Data not available.
OECD = Organisation for Economic Co-operation and Development.
†Break in series.
[a]Rankings are from lowest to highest infant mortality rates (IMR). Countries with the same IMR receive the same rank. The country with the next highest IMR is assigned the rank it would have received had the lower-ranked countries not been tied, i.e., skip a rank. The latest year's international rankings are based on 2012 data because that is the most current data year for which most countries have reported their final data to OECD. Countries without an estimate in the OECD database are omitted from this table. Relative rankings for individual countries may be affected if not all countries have reported data to OECD.
[b]Refers to countries, territories, cities, or geographic areas with at least 2.5 million population in 2000 and with complete counts of live births and infant deaths according to the United Nations Demographic Yearbook.
[c]The infant mortality rate is defined as the number of deaths of children under one year of age, expressed per 1,000 live births. Some of the international variation in infant mortality rates is due to variations among countries in registering practices for premature infants.
[d]In 1993, Czechoslovakia was divided into two nations, the Czech Republic and Slovakia. Data for years prior to 1993 are from the Czech and Slovak regions of Czechoslovakia.
[e]Until 1990, estimates refer to the Federal Republic of Germany; from 1995 onward data refer to Germany after reunification.
[f]Statistical data for Israel are supplied by, and under the responsibility of, the relevant Israeli authorities. The use of such data by the OECD is without prejudice to the status of the Golan Heights, East Jerusalem, and Israeli settlements in the West Bank under the terms of international law.

SOURCE: "Table 13. Infant Mortality Rates and International Rankings: Organisation for Economic Co-operation and Development (OECD) Countries, Selected Years 1960–2012," in *Health, United States, 2015: With Special Feature on Racial and Ethnic Health Disparities*, U.S. Department of Health and Human Services, Centers for Disease Control and Prevention, National Center for Health Statistics, May 2016, http://www.cdc.gov/nchs/data/hus/hus15.pdf (accessed July 29, 2016)

but also less affordable and accessible. In "Understanding What Makes Americans Dissatisfied with Their Health Care System: An International Comparison" (*Health Affairs*, vol. 35, no. 3, March 2016), Joachim O. Hero et al. compared how people in the United States and 17 high-income countries assess satisfaction with their health care systems. Hero et al. compared three measures of satisfaction—access to care, satisfaction with the last health care experience, and confidence that when seriously ill, one will receive the best treatment available and be seen by the doctor of one's choice, which the researchers termed, "access to most preferred care." They found that slightly more than half of U.S. survey respondents said they were satisfied with the country's health care system. Just three countries, Japan, Portugal, and the Slovak Republic had lower satisfaction levels.

The United States received higher marks on other measures. For example, the researchers note that 63% of Americans felt they had access to most preferred care, a higher proportion than in most other countries. Interestingly, this measure was a stronger driver of overall satisfaction in the United States than in other countries. By contrast, satisfaction with recent health care experiences was the most important determinant of satisfaction in other countries and mattered less in the United States.

Hero et al. explain that Americans' insurance status strongly influenced their perceptions of access to most preferred care, with Medicare beneficiaries reporting the most confidence about access to preferred care. The researchers conclude, "Changes in insurance that threaten to widen the gaps in access to and perceived quality of care between more and less privileged Americans may serve to increase the number of people who feel that their health care preferences are out of reach."

## Germany

The German health care system is based on the social insurance model. Sickness funds and private insurance cover the entire population. In "The German Health Care System, 2015" in *2015 International Profiles of Health Care Systems*, Miriam Blümel and Reinhard Busse of the Berlin University of Technology state that mandatory health insurance for all citizens and permanent residents is provided by competing, nonprofit, nongovernmental health insurance funds in the statutory health insurance scheme or by voluntary private health insurance.

The OECD notes in *Health at a Glance 2015* that by 2013 Germany ranked sixth in health expenditures per capita. Public funds, a combination of social insurance and general government funds, paid for about three-quarters (73%) of total expenditures for health care in 2013, which was nearly the OECD average of 75%.

Ambulatory (outpatient) and inpatient care operate separately in the German health care system. German hospitals are public and private, operate for profit and not for profit, and generally do not have outpatient departments. About half of all hospital beds are not for profit, but the number of private, for-profit hospitals has increased in recent years and accounts for about one-sixth of all beds. Since 2004 inpatient care has been paid for via diagnosis-related groups based on 1,187 categories. Ambulatory care physicians are paid on the basis of fee schedules that are negotiated between the organizations of sickness funds and the organizations of physicians. A separate fee schedule for private patients uses a similar scale.

In 1993 Germany's Health Care Reform Law went into effect. It tied increases in physician, dental, and hospital expenditures to the income growth rate of members of the sickness funds. It also limited the licensing of new ambulatory care physicians (based on the number of physicians already in an area) and set a cap for overall pharmaceutical outlays. Still, according to the OECD,

Germany boasted 4 practicing physicians per 1,000 population in 2014, a ratio that was higher than the OECD average of 3.3.

The health care reforms were not, however, successful at containing health care costs. Growth in health care spending was attributed to the comparatively high level of health care activity and resources, along with rising pharmaceutical expenditures and efforts to meet the health care needs of an aging population.

To incentivize coordinated care, primary care physicians receive a fixed annual bonus for patients enrolled in disease management programs, in which they provide patient education and document patient care and outcomes. Prescription drug costs are controlled by establishing maximum reimbursement for different classes of drugs, which cannot be exceeded unless the drugs demonstrate novel medical benefits. Pharmaceutical companies are required to produce scientific evidence of the medical benefits of new drugs, and the Federal Association of Sickness Funds negotiates drug prices with the companies. In 2016 more than $380 million was allocated to an Innovation Fund aimed at improving coordination of care and reducing health care disparities.

In "The Strengths and Limitations of the German Health Care System" (*European Heart Journal*, vol. 34, 2013), Georg Ertl and Till Neumann enumerate the strengths and weaknesses of the German health care system in terms of promoting heart health. Ertl and Neumann praise the system's comprehensive coverage of health care costs for nearly 100% of the population, rapid adoption of medical innovation, and support for medical research but note that economic incentives favor performing procedures rather than comprehensive patient care.

## Canada

The Canadian system is characterized as a provincial government health insurance model, in which each of the provinces operates its own health system under general federal rules and with a fixed federal contribution. All provinces are required to offer insurance coverage for all medically necessary services, including hospital care and physician services. However, additional services and benefits may be offered at the discretion of each province. Most cover preventive services, routine dental care for children, and outpatient drugs for older adults (with a co-payment) and the poor.

Canadian citizens have equal access to medical care, regardless of their ability to pay. Entitlement to benefits is linked to residency, and the system is financed through general taxation. Private insurance is prohibited from covering the same benefits that are covered by the public system, yet a majority of Canadians are covered by private supplemental insurance policies. These policies generally cover services such as adult dental care, cosmetic surgery, and private or semiprivate hospital rooms. The OECD reports in *Health at a Glance 2015* that Canada's total health expenditures accounted for 10.9% of the GDP in 2013.

The delivery system consists mostly of community hospitals and self-employed physicians. Nearly all of Canadian hospital beds are public; private hospitals do not participate in the public insurance program. Most hospitals are nonprofit and are funded on the basis of global institution-specific or regional budgets. (A global institution-specific budget allocates a lump sum of money to a large department or area; then all the groups in that department or area must negotiate to see how much of the total money each group receives.) Physicians in both inpatient and outpatient settings are paid on a negotiated, fee-for-service basis. Sara Allin and David Rudoler of the University of Toronto report in "The Canadian Health Care System, 2015" (*International Profiles of Health Care Systems, 2015*) that 70.7% of total health expenditures were publicly funded in 2015, and the balance of health expenditures were from private sources (private insurance, 12%, and out-of-pocket payments, 14.2%). Many Canadians obtain supplementary private insurance coverage through their employers. These supplemental plans cover services such as vision and dental care, prescription drugs, rehabilitation services, home care, and hospice care.

CONTROLLING COSTS. According to Allin and Rudoler, cost containment is achieved through single-payer purchasing power and that increases in health care expenditures generally occur in response to government investment decisions. Actions to control costs include "mandatory global budgets for hospitals and regional health authorities, negotiated fee schedules for providers, drug formularies, and resource restrictions." The federal Patented Medicine Prices Review Board, an independent body, regulates the prices of newly patented prescription medications. It guarantees that patented drug prices are not "'excessive,' on the basis of their 'degree of innovation,'" and compares the prices of existing prescription drugs in Canada with the prices of these drugs in other countries, including the United States and United Kingdom.

Allin and Rudoler report that cost-containment efforts include negotiations to reduce the prices of drugs and a national technology assessment that aims to control the costs of new technologies. In 2015 a publicly funded program, Choosing Wisely Canada, was launched to advise governments, health care providers and consumers about how to reduce the use of low-value care (practices, procedures and technologies that provide no or very little health gain for their cost).

In "The Determinants of Efficiency in the Canadian Health Care System" (*Health Economics, Policy and Law*, vol. 11, no. 1, January 2016), Sara Allin, Michael Grignon, and Li Wang report their assessment of the efficiency of the Canadian health system. The researchers identified large inefficiencies in the Canadian health care system that they attribute to three types of problems—management issues such as excessive hospital readmissions, public health issues such as the prevalence of obesity and smoking, and environmental issues such as income.

According to A. Scott Carson, in "Managing a Canadian Healthcare Strategy: An Introduction" (2016, http://www .queensu.ca/sps/sites/webpublish.queensu.ca.spswww/ files/files/Research/2015_QHPCC_Whitepaper.pdf), Canadians continue to experience "inequities in access, availability, and costs to patients between provinces; discrepant performance metrics across jurisdictions; and few of the efficiencies that could be achieved by working together." Carson asserts that learning from other countries could benefit Canadian efforts to create change at the national, provincial, and territorial levels.

### England

England employs the National Health Service (NHS) to finance and deliver health care. The entire population is covered under a system that is financed primarily from general taxation. There is minimal cost sharing. In 2013, 83.3% of all health spending was from public funds. Ruth Thorlby and Sandeepa Arora of the Nuffield Trust in London explains in "The English Health Care System, 2015" (*International Profiles of Health Care Systems, 2015*) that the NHS "provides or pays for: preventive services, including screening, immunization, and vaccination programs; inpatient and outpatient hospital care; physician services; inpatient and outpatient drugs; clinically necessary dental care; some eye care; mental health care, including some care for those with learning disabilities; palliative care; some long-term care; rehabilitation, including physiotherapy (e.g., after-stroke care); and home visits by community-based nurses."

England's hospital beds are public and generally owned by the NHS. The OECD reports in "OECD Health Statistics 2016—Frequently Requested Data" that in 2014 there were 2.7 beds per 1,000 population, which was comparable to the United States (2.9 beds in 2013), but fewer than other European nations, such as France (6.2) and Germany (6.2).

Parliament and the Department of Health share the responsibility for health legislation and policy matters. Health services are organized and managed by regional and local public authorities. General practitioners serve as primary care physicians and are reimbursed on the basis of a combination of capitation payments (payments for each person served), fee for service, and other allowances. Hospitals receive overall budget allotments from district health authorities, and hospital-based physicians are salaried. Harrison notes that private insurance reimburses both physicians and hospitals on a fee-for-service basis. Approximately 11% of the population had private health insurance in 2012.

Most general practitioners, who are the front line of health care delivery, are either self-employed or salaried hospital-based physicians. According to Thorlby and Arora, the structure of general practices is changing—moving away from "corner shops" and toward larger multispecialty groups that include teams of physicians, pharmacists, and social workers.

Michael Ybarra notes in "Healthcare around the World" (*American Academy of Emergency Medicine*, vol. 16, no. 6, 2009) that the NHS pioneered many cost-containment measures that are used by the United States and other countries seeking to slow health care expenditures. These approaches include:

- Cost-effective analysis—calculated as a ratio, and often expressed as the cost per year per life saved, the cost-effectiveness analysis of a drug or procedure relates the cost of the drug or procedure to the health benefits it produces. This analysis enables delivery of clinically efficient, cost-effective care.

- Cost-minimization analysis—primarily applied to the pharmaceutical industry, this technique identifies the lowest cost among pharmaceutical alternatives that provide clinically comparable health outcomes.

- Cost-utility analysis—this measures the costs of therapy or treatment. Economists use the term *utility* to describe the amount of satisfaction a consumer receives from a given product or service. This analysis measures outcomes in terms of patient preference and is generally expressed as quality-adjusted life years. For example, an analysis of cancer chemotherapy drugs considers the various adverse side effects of these drugs because some patients may prefer a shorter duration of symptom-free survival rather than a longer life span marked by pain, suffering, and dependence on others for care.

Thorlby and Arora report cost-containment strategies include freezing staff pay increases, increased use of generic drugs, reducing payments to hospitals, and reducing administrative costs. The NHS budget rose a scant 0.6% to 0.9% from 2010 through 2015 and did not keep pace with growing demand for services. Although the NHS realized cost savings during this period, there also were some quality of care issues, most notably, longer waiting time to receive care.

Although the Commonwealth Fund has repeatedly ranked the NHS as one of the best health care systems, scoring highest on quality, access, and efficiency and known for its coordinated, patient-centered care, England's health care system also faces access challenges and disparities in health outcomes. For example, in "Over the

Rainbow: Delivering on the Promise of England's New Public Health System" (*Journal of Epidemiology and Community Health*, vol. 68, no.1, 2014), David Conrad of Public Health England cites the gap in life expectancy between the general population and residents of "deprived areas" as a glaring example of persistent health inequality. Conrad hopes that England's new public health system, which began in 2014, will be able to effectively address these kinds of inequalities. Thorlby and Arora report that the NHS is working to ensure that "local areas receive adequate resources to tackle inequalities and that the outcomes for at-risk groups are routinely monitored."

### France

The French health care system is based on the social insurance, or Bismarck, model. Virtually the entire population is covered by a legislated, compulsory health insurance plan that is financed by the social security system. The system is funded through employer and employee payroll taxes (64%), a national income tax (16%), revenue from taxes on tobacco, alcohol, the pharmaceutical industry, and voluntary health companies (12%), state subsidies (2%), and funds from other branches of social security (6%). The OECD estimates in *OECD Health Statistics 2016* (http://www.oecd.org/health/health-data.htm) that the total expenditure for health in France was 11% of the GDP in 2015.

According to the OECD, the public share of total health spending in 2013 was 76%, and 8.8% of expenditures represented direct, out-of-pocket payments. Physicians practicing in municipal health centers and public hospitals are salaried, but physicians in private hospitals and ambulatory care settings are typically paid on a negotiated, fee-for-service basis. The government establishes the reimbursement schedule for physicians and for other health care goods and services including pharmaceutical drugs. Public hospitals are granted lump-sum budgets, and private hospitals are paid on the basis of negotiated per diem payment rates. The OECD reports that there were eight hospital beds per 1,000 population in 2014.

Isabelle Durand-Zaleski of Assistance Publique, Hôpitaux de Paris, explains in "The French Health Care System, 2015" (*International Profiles of Health Care Systems, 2015*) that in 2004 health financing reform laws introduced a gatekeeping system for adults. Although the system is voluntary, strong financial incentives, such as higher co-payments for visits and prescriptions without referral from the gatekeeper, encourage participation. Patients who refuse generic drugs also have higher co-payments.

In "5 Essential Pros and Cons of the French Healthcare System" (September 11, 2015, http://nlcatp.org/5-essential-pros-and-cons-of-the-french-healthcare-system/), Crystal R. Lombardo writes that the French health care system boasts accessibility and availability of care and quality of care as well as strong preventive services. Lombardo cites the cost of the system, which is largely financed by taxes, as a shortcoming and observes that the current health care workforce may not be sufficient to meet future demand for care.

Strategies intended to reduce "low-value" care include efforts to reduce prescription of benzodiazepines for older adults; reductions in avoidable hospital admissions for patients with heart failure; early release from the hospital after orthopedic surgery and normal childbirth; information on the absence of the benefit of prostate cancer screening; using financial incentives to shift surgical patients to outpatient surgery; strengthening controls for the prescription of expensive new drugs; and using taxicabs, instead of ambulances, to transport chronically ill patients.

The French health care system, like systems in other countries, has problems with access and inequalities. In "Disparities in Access to Health Care in Three French Regions" (*Health Policy*, vol. 114, no 1, January 2014), Michael K. Gusmano et al. compare access to primary and specialty care in three metropolitan regions of France and identify the factors that contribute to disparities in access to care in these regions. Not surprisingly, the researchers find that residents in low-income areas and patients treated in public hospitals had poorer access to primary and specialty care. Gusmano et al. conclude, "Even within a national health insurance system that minimizes the financial barriers to health care and has one of the highest rates of spending on health care in Europe, the challenge of minimizing these disparities remains."

Durand-Zaleski notes that efforts to reduce disparities in access to care include incentives for physicians practicing in underserved areas and the use of telemedicine to coordinate care and social services for selected populations such as infants, prisoners and people with disabilities.

## Japan

Japan's health care financing is based on the social insurance model. According to the OECD, in *Health at a Glance 2015*, 83% of health expenditures were from public funds in 2013. Ryozo Matsuda of Ritsumeikan University notes in "The Japanese Health Care System, 2015" (*International Profiles of Health Care Systems, 2015*) that the universal public health insurance system involves coverage from more than 3,400 insurers.

The OECD indicates that the health care system, which cost 10.2% of Japan's GDP in 2013, is financed through employer and employee income-related premiums. Limited private insurance exists for supplemental coverage and is purchased by about one-third of the population. In 2012 out-of-pocket expenses accounted for 14% of health expenditures.

Physicians and hospitals are paid on the basis of national, negotiated fee schedules. Japan manages with fewer physicians per capita than most OECD member countries—just 2.3 physicians per 1,000 population in 2013. Physicians practicing in public hospitals are salaried, whereas those practicing in physician-owned clinics and private hospitals are reimbursed on a fee-for-service basis, with financial incentives for taking better care of patients with chronic diseases. Physicians not only diagnose, treat, and manage illnesses but also prescribe and dispense pharmaceuticals.

According to Matsuda, most of Japan's hospitals are nonprofit and privately operated; just 14% are government owned or operated. Although hospital admissions are less frequent, hospital stays in Japan are typically far longer than in the United States or in any other OECD member nation, allowing hospitals and physicians to overcome the limitations of the fee schedules. The number of hospital beds is regulated according to national guidelines as is medical school capacity, which has been increasing since 2007 to address physician shortages.

The health status of the Japanese is one of the best in the world. Japanese men and women are among the longest living in all of the OECD member countries. In 2013 life expectancy at birth for females was 86.6 years. (See Figure 7.2.) The Japanese infant mortality rate in 2012, at 2.2 deaths per 1,000 live births, was the lowest of the OECD countries. (See Table 7.2.) These two statistics are usually considered to be reliable indicators of a successful health care system. It should be noted, however, that Japan does not have a large impoverished class, as the United States does, and its diet is considered to be among the most healthful in the world.

Although Japan's health care system produces excellent health for its population, it has some limitations. Universal health coverage does not include preventive care, and financial incentives prompt overuse of diagnostic tests. Other problems are the high cost of prescription drugs and long hospital stays for older patients because there are too few long-term-care facilities.

The government acts to control health care costs by promoting healthy behavior, reducing hospital lengths of stay by making effective use of care coordination and home care, and increasing the frequency of generic drug dispensing. Financial incentives, education, and training are used to encourage cost-effective practices among physicians. Peer review committees monitor claims and may deny payment for services considered unnecessary or otherwise inappropriate. In addition, some pharmaceuticals with questionable medical effectiveness are not covered by the public health insurance system. A cost-effectiveness evaluation for coverage of selected pharmaceuticals and medical devices was initiated in 2016.

# CHAPTER 8
# CHANGE, CHALLENGES, AND INNOVATION
# IN HEALTH CARE DELIVERY

Since the 1970s the U.S. health care system has experienced rapid and unprecedented change. The sites where health care is delivered have shifted from acute inpatient hospitals to outpatient settings, such as ambulatory care and surgical centers, clinics, physicians' offices, and long-term care and rehabilitation facilities. Patterns of disease have changed from acute infectious diseases that require episodic care to chronic conditions that require ongoing care. Even threats to U.S. public health have changed. For example, epidemics of infectious diseases have largely been replaced by epidemics of chronic conditions such as obesity, diabetes, and mental illness. In 2009 the nation mobilized to mitigate the effects of the H1N1 pandemic influenza; and in 2010 the government took historic action by passing the Patient Protection and Affordable Care Act (also known as the Affordable Care Act [ACA]), which aims to provide health care coverage to nearly all of the nation's people. In 2014 the health care system organized a response to the Ebola virus outbreak in West Africa and treated cases of the disease that were diagnosed in the United States, and in 2016 it prepared for Zika, a virus spread primarily by infected mosquitoes.

There are new health care providers, including mid-level practitioners (advanced practice nurses, certified nurse midwives, physician assistants, and medical technologists), and new modes of diagnosis such as genetic testing. Furthermore, the rise of managed care, the explosion of biotechnology, and the availability of information on the Internet have dramatically changed how health care is delivered.

The ACA emphasizes the use of health information technology (IT), especially the adoption of electronic health records (EHRs). The act promotes the use of EHRs and other IT not only to help achieve the objectives of health care reform, including intensifying efforts to assess, monitor, and improve patient safety and quality of service delivery, but also to simplify the administration of health services, ensure cost-effective health service delivery, and reduce the growth of health care expenditures.

The use of EHRs also has given rise to a new health-related job, the medical scribe, who is hired to enter information into the EHR under clinician supervision. According to George A. Gellert, Ricardo Ramirez, and S. Luke Webster, in "The Rise of the Medical Scribe Industry: Implications for the Advancement of Medical Records" (*Journal of the American Medical Association*, vol. 313, no.13, April 7, 2015), scribes enable physicians to "see more patients; generate more revenue; and improve productivity, efficiency, accuracy of clinical documentation and billing, and patient satisfaction."

In "The Affordable Care Act at 5 Years" (*New England Journal of Medicine*, vol. 373, no. 16, October 2015), David Blumenthal, Melinda Abrams, and Rachel Nuzum describe the ACA as "one of the most aggressive efforts in the history of the nation to address the problems of the delivery system." They observe that the law is ambitious and has already begun to make changes in the way the government pays for health care, the organization of health care delivery, workforce policy, and changes aimed at making the government better able to pursue future health care reforms. Blumenthal, Abrams, and Nuzum assert that even after five years, it is premature to assess the full effects of ACA apart from improving access to care. Although the rate of health care spending has slowed and some measures of quality such as hospital acquired conditions and readmissions have improved, these strides are not necessarily attributable to the ACA.

Some health care industry observers suggest the speed at which these changes have occurred has further harmed an already complicated and uncoordinated health care system. There is concern that the current health care system cannot keep pace with scientific and technological advances. Many worry that the health care system is already unable to deliver quality care to all Americans and that it is so disorganized that it will be unable to meet the needs of the growing population of older Americans and the millions of Americans who gained health insurance under the ACA, or to respond to the threat of a pandemic or an act of bioterrorism.

This chapter considers several of the most pressing challenges and opportunities faced by the U.S. health care system, including:

- Safety—ensuring safety by protecting patients from harm or injury inflicted by the health care system (e.g., preventing medical errors, reducing hospital-acquired infections, and safeguarding consumers from medical fraud). Besides actions to reduce problems caused by the health care system, safety and quality may be ensured by providers' use of clinical practice guidelines (standardized plans for diagnosis and treatment of disease and the effective application of technology to information and communication systems).

- Information management—IT, including the Internet, can provide health care providers and consumers with timely access to medical data, patient information, and the clinical expertise of specialists. Many studies evaluating the effectiveness of IT to improve health outcomes are underway. For example, in "Improving Rates of Influenza Vaccination through Electronic Health Record Portal Messages, Interactive Voice Recognition Calls and Patient-Enabled Electronic Health Record Updates: Protocol for a Randomized Controlled Trial" (*JMIR Research Protocols*, vol. 11, July 7, 2016), Sarah L. Cutrona et al. are investigating whether computerized reminders for providers and patients improves rates of influenza vaccination.

## SAFETY

Patient safety is a critical component of health care quality. Although the United States is generally viewed as providing quality health care services to its citizens, the Institute of Medicine (IOM) estimates in the landmark report *To Err Is Human: Building a Safer Health System* (1999, http://www.nap.edu/books/0309068371/html) that as many as 98,000 deaths per year in the United States are the result of preventable medical errors. More than 7,000 of these deaths are estimated to be due to preventable medication errors.

Martin A. Makary and Michael Daniel, researchers at Johns Hopkins University School of Medicine, report in "Medical Error—The Third Leading Cause of Death in the US" (*BMJ*, May 3, 2016) that more than 250,000 deaths per year are attributable to medical errors, making medical errors the third-leading cause of death in the United States. In an interview with Ariana Eunjung Cha in "Researchers: Medical Errors Now Third Leading

Cause of Death in United States" (WashingtonPost.com, May 3, 2016), Makary asserts that in addition to bad doctors, communication breakdowns cause medical errors resulting in patient deaths "from the care that they receive rather than the disease for which they are seeking care."

In the same article, Kenneth Sands, who directs health care quality at a hospital affiliate of Harvard Medical School expressed surprise that the number of medical errors, with the exception of hospital-acquired infections, had not changed since the IOM report. Sands attributes the problem to the diversity and complexity of the U.S. health care system. He asserts, "There has just been a higher degree of tolerance for variability in practice than you would see in other industries." Using an analogy from Sands, reporter Cha explains, "When passengers get on a plane, there's a standard way attendants move around, talk to them and prepare them for flight . . . yet such standardization isn't seen at hospitals. That makes it tricky to figure out where errors are occurring and how to fix them."

### Assessing Hospital Safety

In an April 5, 2016, media release, "Healthgrades Releases Its 2016 Outstanding Patient Experience Award and 2016 Patient Safety Excellence Award Recipients" (April 5, 2016, https://www.healthgrades.com/about/press-room/healthgrades-releases-its-2016-outstanding-patient-experience-award-and-2016-patient-safety-excellence-award-recipients), Healthgrades Operating Company, Inc., an independent health care quality research organization that evaluates hospitals and provides hospital ratings to health plans and other payers, reports that three-quarters of all patient safety issues are attributable to four types of problems—collapsed lung, infections, bedsores, and accidental cut, puncture, or hemorrhage. Healthgrades estimates that "270,457 patient safety events could have been avoided if all hospitals, as a group from 2012 to 2014, performed similarly to hospitals performing better than expected on each of 13 patient safety indicators evaluated."

### AHRQ Patient Safety Indicators

The Agency for Healthcare Research and Quality (AHRQ), a part of the U.S. Department of Health and Human Services (HHS), has identified qualities and characteristics of organizational culture that contribute to or detract from patient safety in hospitals. Figure 8.1 lists the 12 composites that are used to assess the safety culture in hospitals.

In *Hospital Survey on Patient Safety Culture: 2016 User Comparative Database Report* (March 2016, http://www.ahrq.gov/sites/default/files/wysiwyg/professionals/quality-patient-safety/patientsafetyculture/hospital/2016/2016_hospitalsops_report_pt1.pdf), Theresa Famolaro et al. report the results of a survey of 680 hospitals with a total of 447,584 hospital staff respondents that was conducted between 2010 and 2014. The composite scores,

**FIGURE 8.1**

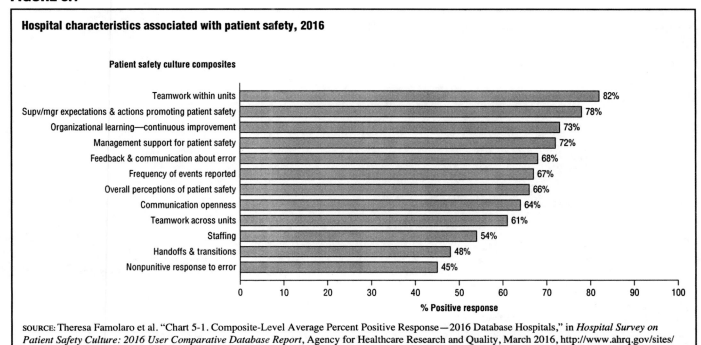

**Hospital characteristics associated with patient safety, 2016**

Patient safety culture composites

| Characteristic | % Positive response |
|---|---|
| Teamwork within units | 82% |
| Supv/mgr expectations & actions promoting patient safety | 78% |
| Organizational learning—continuous improvement | 73% |
| Management support for patient safety | 72% |
| Feedback & communication about error | 68% |
| Frequency of events reported | 67% |
| Overall perceptions of patient safety | 66% |
| Communication openness | 64% |
| Teamwork across units | 61% |
| Staffing | 54% |
| Handoffs & transitions | 48% |
| Nonpunitive response to error | 45% |

% Positive response

SOURCE: Theresa Famolaro et al. "Chart 5-1. Composite-Level Average Percent Positive Response—2016 Database Hospitals," in *Hospital Survey on Patient Safety Culture: 2016 User Comparative Database Report*, Agency for Healthcare Research and Quality, March 2016, http://www.ahrq.gov/sites/default/files/wysiwyg/professionals/quality-patient-safety/patientsafetyculture/hospital/2016/2016_hospitalsops_report_pt1.pdf (accessed August 21, 2016)

which give each hospital equal weight rather than favoring larger hospitals with more survey respondents, show how hospitals fared on these indicators in 2016. The survey items with the highest average percent positive response (82%) were from the patient safety culture characteristic Teamwork within Units: "Staff support one another in this unit, treat each other with respect, and work together as a team." The item with the lowest average percent positive response (37%) was from the patient safety culture characteristic Nonpunitive Response to Error: "Staff worry that mistakes they make are kept in their personnel file."

Figure 8.2 shows how survey respondents view their hospital work area or unit in terms of its overall patient safety. On average, most respondents were positive, with three-quarters (76%) awarding their work area or unit a patient safety grade of A (34%) or B (42%). More than half (53%) of the survey respondents said the number of events reported during the past 12 months had not changed. (See Figure 8.3.) About a quarter (26%) of hospitals reported a 5% or greater increase in the number of events reported. The frequency of patient safety event reporting was deemed an area for improvement for most hospitals because the underreporting of events suggests that potential patient safety problems may go undetected and, as a result, may not be addressed.

**Strengthening Safety Measures**

In response to a request from HHS, the IOM's Committee on Data Standards for Patient Safety created a detailed plan to develop standards for the collection, coding, and classification of patient safety information. The 550-page plan, *Patient Safety: Achieving a New Standard for Care* (2004), called on HHS to assume the lead in establishing a national health information infrastructure that would provide immediate access to complete patient information and decision-support tools, such as clinical practice guidelines, and capture patient safety data for use in designing constantly improving and safer health care delivery systems.

The IOM plan exhorted all health care settings to develop and implement comprehensive patient safety programs and recommended that the federal government launch patient safety research initiatives aimed at increasing knowledge, developing tools, and disseminating results to maximize the effectiveness of patient safety systems. The plan also advised the designation of a standardized format and terminology for identifying and reporting data related to medical errors.

In July 2005 President George W. Bush (1946–) signed into law the Patient Safety and Quality Improvement Act. Angela S. Mattie and Rosalyn Ben-Chitrit surmise in "Patient Safety Legislation: A Look at Health Policy Development" (*Policy, Politics, and Nursing Practice*, vol. 8, no. 4, November 2007) that the IOM call for action to improve patient safety in *To Err Is Human* prompted Congress to pass legislation.

**ACA Initiatives Improve Patient Safety**

In 2011 HHS formed the Partnership for Patients Initiative, a public-private partnership funded by the ACA

**FIGURE 8.2**

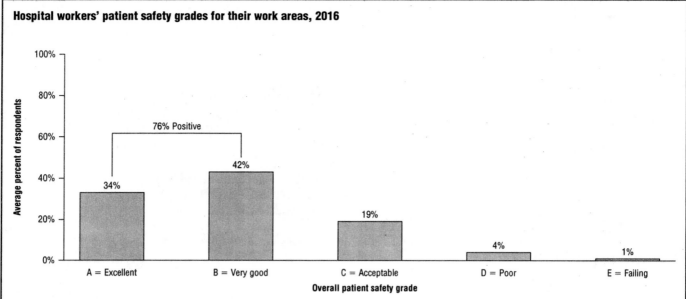

Hospital workers' patient safety grades for their work areas, 2016

Notes: Percentages may not add to 100 due to rounding.

SOURCE: Theresa Famolaro et al. "Chart 5-3. Average Percentage of 2016 Database Respondents Giving Their Work Area/Unit a Patient Safety Grade," in *Hospital Survey on Patient Safety Culture: 2016 User Comparative Database Report*, Agency for Healthcare Research and Quality, March 2016, http://www.ahrq.gov/sites/default/files/wysiwyg/professionals/quality-patient-safety/patientsafetyculture/hospital/2016/2016_hospitalsops_report_pt1.pdf (accessed August 21, 2016)

with the goal of reducing hospital-acquired conditions. In *Saving Lives and Saving Money: Hospital-Acquired Conditions Update*, (December 2015, http://www.ahrq.gov/professionals/quality-patient-safety/pfp/interimhacrate2014.html), the AHRQ reports a 17% decrease in hospital-acquired conditions (HACs) from 2010 to 2014. A total of 2.1 million fewer HACs occurred in 2011 through 2014 relative to the number that would have occurred if rates had remained steady at the 2010 level. About 87,000 fewer patients died in the hospital as a result of this decrease, and an estimated $19.8 billion in health care costs were saved over the same period. (See Figure 8.4.)

Although it is impossible to attribute the decrease in HACs to any one program, the AHRQ posits that along with its own efforts, and ACA-sponsored quality improvement initiatives, other public and private programs to improve health care quality and patient safety were implemented during these years including the use of EHRs, and together these initiatives improved hospital patient safety.

The ACA also supports patient safety organizations. In "Common Formats" (2016, http://www.pso.ahrq.gov/common), the AHRQ explains that patient safety organizations collect information about three kinds of safety events: incidents (safety events that reached the patient, independent of whether they caused harm), near misses (safety events that did not reach the patient), and unsafe

**FIGURE 8.3**

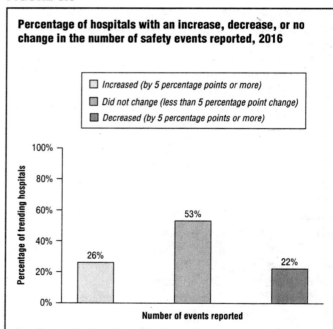

Percentage of hospitals with an increase, decrease, or no change in the number of safety events reported, 2016

Note: Based on data from 326 trending hospitals that responded to this item.

SOURCE: Theresa Famolaro et al. "Chart 7-3. Trending: Percentage of 2016 Hospitals That Increased, Decreased, or Did Not Change on Number of Events Reported as Equal to One or More Events Reported," in *Hospital Survey on Patient Safety Culture: 2016 User Comparative Database Report*, Agency for Healthcare Research and Quality, March 2016, http://www.ahrq.gov/sites/default/files/wysiwyg/professionals/quality-patient-safety/patientsafetyculture/hospital/2016/2016_hospitalsops_report_pt1.pdf (accessed August 21, 2016)

FIGURE 8.4

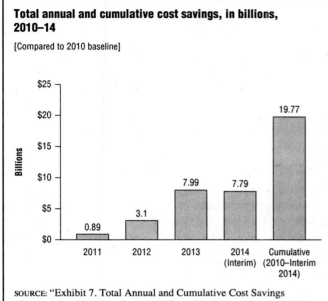

**Total annual and cumulative cost savings, in billions, 2010–14**

[Compared to 2010 baseline]

SOURCE: "Exhibit 7. Total Annual and Cumulative Cost Savings (Compared to 2010 Baseline), in Billions," in *Saving Lives and Saving Money: Hospital-Acquired Conditions Update*, Agency for Healthcare Research and Quality, December 2015, http://www.ahrq.gov/professionals/quality-patient-safety/pfp/interimhacrate2014.html (accessed August 22, 2016).

conditions (situations that increase the likelihood of a patient safety event).

### Who Is Responsible for Patient Safety?

Many federal, state, and private-sector organizations work together to reduce medical errors and improve patient safety. The Centers for Disease Control and Prevention (CDC) and the U.S. Food and Drug Administration are the leading federal agencies that conduct surveillance and collect information about adverse events resulting from treatment or the use of medical devices, drugs, or other products.

The U.S. Departments of Defense and Veterans Affairs (VA), which are responsible for health care services for U.S. military personnel, their families, and veterans, have instituted computerized systems that have reduced medical errors. The VA established the Patient Safety Centers of Inquiry, and its hospitals also use bar-code technology and computerized medical records to prevent medical errors.

Safe medical care is also a top priority of the states and the private sector. In 2000 some of the nation's largest corporations, including General Motors and General Electric, joined together to address health care safety and efficacy (the ability of an intervention to produce the intended diagnostic or therapeutic effect in optimal circumstances) and to help direct their workers to health care providers (hospitals and physicians) with the best performance records. Called the Leapfrog Group (http://www.leapfroggroup.org), this business coalition was founded by the Business Roundtable, a national association of Fortune 500 chief executive officers, to leverage employer purchasing power that initiates innovation and improves the safety of health care.

The Leapfrog Group publishes hospital quality and safety data to assist consumers in making informed hospital choices. Hospitals provide information to the Leapfrog Group through a voluntary survey that requests information about hospital performance across four quality and safety practices with the potential to reduce preventable medical mistakes and improve health care quality. In the media release "President and CEO Leah Binder Shares Statement Supporting CMS' 5-Star Ratings for Hospitals " (July 28, 2016, http://www.leapfroggroup.org/news-events/president-and-ceo-leah-binder-shares-statement-supporting-cms'-5-star-ratings-hospitals), the Leapfrog Group commended the Centers for Medicare and Medicaid Services (CMS) release of consumer-friendly five-star hospital quality ratings. In July 2016 the CMS updated the star ratings on the Hospital Compare website (https://www.medicare.gov/hospitalcompare/search.html) which enables consumers to compare facilities.

The Leapfrog Group issues its own hospital ratings. Hospital safety scores are available to the public online at http://hospitalsafetyscore.org. Website visitors can search for hospital scores for free. The site also offers information on how patients can protect themselves during a hospital stay.

**PREVENTING MEDICAL ERRORS AND IMPROVING PATIENT SAFETY.** TeamSTEPPS (http://teamstepps.ahrq.gov/abouttoolsmaterials.htm), a program developed jointly by the U.S. Department of Defense and the AHRQ, aims to optimize patient outcomes by improving communication and other teamwork skills among health care professionals. TeamSTEPPS applies team training principles that were developed in military aviation and private industry to health care delivery. Figure 8.5 shows the four competency areas that lead to improved team performance, attitude, and knowledge. TeamSTEPPS helps improve team performance by teaching:

- Leadership—how to direct, coordinate, assign tasks, motivate team members, and facilitate optimal performance

- Situation monitoring—how to develop common understandings of team environment, apply strategies to monitor teammate performance, and maintain a shared mental model

- Mutual support—how to anticipate other team members' needs through accurate knowledge and shift workload to achieve balance during periods of high workload or stress

- Communication—how to effectively exchange information among team members, regardless of how it is communicated

## FIGURE 8.5

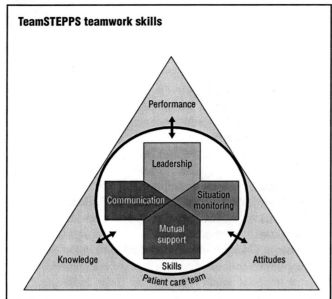

**TeamSTEPPS teamwork skills**

**Leadership:**
• Holds a teamwork system together.
• Ensures a plan is conveyed, reviewed, and updated.
• Facilitated through communication, continuous monitoring of the situation, and fostering of an environment of mutual support.

SOURCE: "Slide 4. TeamSTEPPS Teamwork Skills," in *TeamSTEPPS Fundamentals Course: Module 4. Leading Teams*, Agency for Healthcare Research and Quality, March 2014, http://www.ahrq.gov/professionals/education/curriculum-tools/teamstepps/instructor/fundamentals/module4/slleadership.html#im1 (accessed August 23, 2016)

Studies of the effectiveness of TeamSTEPPS report improvements in teamwork and patient safety. For example, in "Virtual TeamSTEPPS Simulations Produce Teamwork Attitude Changes among Health Professions Students" (*Journal of Nursing Education*, vol. 55, no. 1, January 2016), Linda I. Sweigart et al. report that participants showed significant attitude changes in the areas of leadership, mutual support, situation monitoring, and communication. In "MP16-01 Team Strategies and Tools to Enhance Performance and Patient Safety (TeamSTEPPS) Improves Operating Room Efficiency" (*Journal of Urology*, vol. 193, no. 4, April 2015), Matthew Stringer et al. find that "TeamSTEPPS improves operating room efficiency by decreasing operating room time and increasing on-time first-start rates."

Professional societies are also concerned with patient safety. Based in Illinois, the Joint Commission (https://www.jointcommission.org/) is a nonprofit organization that accredits and certifies hospitals and other health care organizations in the United States. Over half of its hospital standards pertain to patient safety. Since 2002 hospitals seeking accreditation from the Joint Commission have been required to adhere to stringent patient safety standards to prevent medical errors. The Joint Commission standards also require hospitals and individual health

care providers to inform patients when they have been harmed in the course of treatment. The goal of these standards is to prevent medical errors by identifying actions and systems that are likely to produce problems before they occur. An example of this type of preventive measure, which is called prospective review, is close scrutiny of hospital pharmacies to be certain that the ordering, preparation, and dispensing of medications is accurate. Similar standards have been developed for Joint Commission–accredited nursing homes, outpatient clinics, laboratories, and managed care organizations.

In 2004 the Joint Commission began surveying and evaluating health care organizations using new medication management standards. The revised standards placed greater emphasis on medication safety by increasing the pharmacists' role in managing safe, appropriate medication use and strengthening their authority to implement organization-wide improvements in medication safety.

In "2016 National Patient Safety Goals" (2016, https://www.jointcommission.org/assets/1/6/2016_NPSG_HAP_ER.pdf), the Joint Commission describes new national patient safety goals. For example, hospitals will be expected to improve communication among caregivers and ensure the accuracy of patient identification by using at least two patient identifiers when providing care.

## CLINICAL PRACTICE GUIDELINES

Clinical practice guidelines (CPGs) are evidence-based protocols—documents that advise health care providers about how to diagnose and treat specific medical conditions and diseases. CPGs offer physicians, nurses, other health care practitioners, health plans, and institutions objective, detailed, and condition- or disease-specific action plans.

Widespread dissemination and use of CPGs began during the 1990s in an effort to improve the quality of health care delivery by giving health care professionals access to current scientific information on which to base clinical decisions. The use of guidelines also aimed to enhance quality by standardizing care and treatment throughout a health care delivery system such as a managed care plan or hospital and throughout the nation.

Early attempts to encourage physicians and other health professionals to use CPGs was met with resistance because many physicians rejected CPGs as formulaic "cookbook medicine" and believed they interfered with physician-patient relationships. Over time, however, physicians were educated about the quality problems that resulted from variations in medical practice, and opinions about CPGs gradually changed. Physician willingness to use CPGs increased when they learned that adherence to CPGs offered some protection from medical malpractice and other liability. Nurses and other health professionals more readily adopted CPGs, presumably because their training and practice was oriented more toward following instructions than physicians' practices had been.

The National Guideline Clearinghouse (http://www.guideline.gov) is a database of CPGs that have been produced by the AHRQ in conjunction with the American Medical Association (AMA) and the American Association of Health Plans. The clearinghouse offers guideline summaries and comparisons of guidelines covering the same disease or condition prepared by different sources and serves as a resource for the exchange of guidelines between practitioners and health care organizations.

CPGs vary depending on their source. All recovery and treatment plans, however, are intended to generate the most favorable health outcomes. Federal agencies such as the U.S. Public Health Service and the CDC, as well as professional societies, managed care plans, hospitals, academic medical centers, and health care consulting firms, have produced their own versions of CPGs.

Practically all guidelines assume that treatment and healing will occur without complications. Because CPGs represent an optimistic approach to treatment, they are not used as the sole resource for development or evaluation of treatment plans for specific patients. CPGs are intended for use in conjunction with evaluation by qualified health professionals able to determine the applicability of a specific CPG to the specific circumstances involved. Modification of the CPGs is often required and advisable to meet specific, organizational objectives of health care providers and payers.

It is unrealistic to expect that all patients will obtain ideal health outcomes as a result of health care providers' use of CPGs. Guidelines may have greater utility as quality indicators. Evaluating health care delivery against CPGs enables providers, payers, and policy makers to identify and evaluate care that deviates from CPGs as part of a concerted program of continuous improvement of health care quality.

A 2016 white paper by Helen Hoesing of the Joint Commission International, "Clinical Practice Guidelines: Closing the Gap between Theory and Practice" (https://www.elsevier.com/__data/assets/pdf_file/0007/190177/JCI-Whitepaper_cpgs-closing-the-gap.pdf), asserts that use of CPGs "have contributed to the continuous improvements in safety and patient care seen across the globe." Hoesing cites many examples of the impact of CPGs including the observation that if U.S. clinicians adhered to six heart failure guidelines, an estimated 68,000 deaths could be prevented each year.

## COMMUNICATION AND INFORMATION MANAGEMENT TECHNOLOGIES

The explosion of communication and information management technologies has already revolutionized health care delivery and holds great promise for the future. Health care data can be easily and securely collected, shared, stored, and used to promote research and development over great geographic distances. Online distance learning programs for health professionals and the widespread availability of reliable consumer health information on the Internet have increased understanding and awareness of the causes and treatment of illness. This section describes recent applications of technology to the health care system.

### Telemedicine and Telehealth

The terms *telemedicine* (healing at a distance) and *telehealth* (the remote exchange of data between a patient and a clinician as part of health care management) describe a variety of technology-enhanced interactions that occur by way of telephone lines, videoconferencing, iPads, and smartphone applications. Telemedicine may be as simple and commonplace as a phone conversation between a patient and a health professional in the same town or as sophisticated as surgery directed via satellite and video technology from one continent to another.

Advocates of telemedicine opine that it can effectively address health care workforce shortages; save patients time, money, and travel; reduce unnecessary emergency department and hospital visits; and improve the management of chronic conditions. However, widespread adoption of telemedicine faces ongoing challenges. Physicians must be licensed in each state where they treat patients, even when treating them remotely. Most health care professionals have not been trained in telemedicine, and concerns about security of sensitive health-related information persist.

Annette M. Totten et al. reviewed the large volume of research reported about telehealth interventions in *Telehealth: Mapping the Evidence for Patient Outcomes from Systematic Reviews* (June 2016, https://www.effective healthcare.ahrq.gov/ehc/products/624/2254/telehealth-report-160630.pdf). The researchers find that there is sufficient evidence to support its effectiveness for:

- Remote monitoring for patients with chronic conditions
- Communication and counseling for patients with chronic conditions
- Psychotherapy as part of behavioral health

An example of using telehealth for behavioral health is its ability to help school-aged children and their parents gain access to psychiatric treatment. Alison Knopf notes in "School-Based Telehealth Brings Psychiatry to Rural

Georgia" (*Behavioral Healthcare*, vol. 33, no. 1, January–February 2013) that telemedicine makes psychiatry available to children who otherwise would have no access to care from child and adolescent psychiatrists. Knopf observes that a school-based telemedicine program reduced emergency department utilization, resulting in savings of more than $350,000 in one year.

Totten et al. recommend that further research be conducted to assess the utility of telehealth to triage for urgent care and improve outcomes in maternal and child health and about how to promote broader use of telehealth interventions and how to address barriers to its widespread use. They also encourage research to consider the use and impact of telehealth in new health care organizational and payment models.

In an issue brief, "An Examination of Private Payer Reimbursements to Primary Care Providers for Health-care Services Using Telehealth, United States 2009–2013" (Health Care Cost Institute, National Academy for State Policy, 2016, http://www.healthcostinstitute .org/files/HCCI-Issue-Brief-Examination-of-Private-Payer-Reimbursements.pdf), Fernando A. Wilson et al. report that despite growing numbers of telehealth-related policies, an analysis of private-payer reimbursements to primary care providers for telehealth services remained low from 2009 to 2013. The researchers note that although there is interest in expanding telehealth availability, just seven states (Arkansas, Delaware, Hawaii, Minnesota, Mississippi, Tennessee, and Virginia) have passed statutes making reimbursement for telehealth services comparable to those for non-telehealth (in-person) services. Twenty-one states require coverage for live video transmission, and four states require coverage for remote patient monitoring. Mississippi was the only state to require some coverage for all three of these technologies. Many state Medicaid programs reimburse for telehealth services, but policies vary.

Joseph Kvedar, Molly Joel Coye, and Wendy Everett emphasize in "Connected Health: A Review of Technologies and Strategies to Improve Patient Care with Telemedicine and Telehealth" (*Health Affairs*, vol. 33, no. 2, February 2014) that despite its limited uptake from 2009 to 2013, telemedicine is one of the keys to achieving the ACA goal of expanded access to health care for millions of Americans. The researchers assert, "When properly implemented, the broad adoption of connected health has the potential to extend care across populations of both acute and chronically ill patients and help achieve the important policy goals of improving access to high-quality and efficient health care." Kvedar, Coye, and Everett explain that health care can be more effective and efficient when clinicians are electronically connected to other clinicians, patients to clinicians, and patients to other patients. They opine that these technologies will be even more useful as "devices become smaller; are powered by longer-lasting sources of energy; and are connected more effectively to other devices and to re-positories of data, such as electronic health records."

## Online Patient-Physician Consultations and Communication

Physician use of health IT and online communication is growing. In "Where Are We on the Diffusion Curve? Trends and Drivers of Primary Care Physicians' Use of Health Information Technology" (*Health Services Research*, vol. 49, no. 1, February 2014), Anne-Marie J. Audet, David Squires, and Michelle M. Doty compare physician use of technology in 2009 and 2012. The researchers find that primary care physicians' use of health IT significantly increased since 2009. For example, 40% of physicians prescribed medication electronically in 2009, compared with 64% in 2012, and adoption of EHRs rose to 69% from 46% during the same period. In 2012, 30% of primary care practices allowed patients to request appointments online, 34% of patients could e-mail physicians, and 36% of patients could request prescription refills online. Wilson et al. found that from 2009 to 2013, one in eight primary care providers used the Internet or e-mail for some patient consultations during a given week.

Brett Keller et al. surveyed public health professionals to find out about their use of social media, including blogs, Facebook, Twitter, and YouTube, and reported their findings in "Mind the Gap: Social Media Engagement by Public Health Researchers" (*Journal of the Medical Internet Research*, vol. 16, no. 1, January 2014). The researchers note that despite the public health professionals' belief that social media has the potential to advance public health objectives, only a small minority of them use it professionally. The majority of respondents were either disinterested or actively opposed to professional engagement in the social media space, opining that it is too time consuming or that an activity such as blogging might compromise their academic credibility.

In "Patient Use of Email, Facebook, and Physician Websites to Communicate with Physicians: A National Online Survey of Retail Pharmacy Users" (*Journal of General Internal Medicine*, vol. 31, no. 1, January 2016), Joy L. Lee et al. find that among consumers who use retail pharmacies, there is strong interest in communicating with physicians via e-mail and Facebook. A survey of more than 2,000 CVS customers found that more than one-third (37%) of survey respondents had contacted their physicians via e-mail in the six months prior to the survey, and nearly one in five (18%) had contacted their physicians via Facebook. Not surprisingly, Lee et al. find that people younger than age 45 were more likely than older adults to use the web to contact their physicians. The researchers conclude, "Given the importance that patients place on having access to their physicians,

physicians and their institutions should consider how best to permit and reinforce the use of these channels."

## Disseminating Health Information via Twitter

Ranit Mishori et al. describe the growing use of Twitter in medicine in "Mapping Physician Twitter Networks: Describing How They Work as a First Step in Understanding Connectivity, Information Flow, and Message Diffusion" (*Journal of Medical Internet Research*, vol. 16, no. 4, April 2014). The researchers list the characteristics of four medical networks—the AMA, the American Academy of Family Physicians (AAFP), the American Academy of Pediatrics (AAP), and the American College of Physicians (ACP)—and analyze their dissemination potential and their actual dissemination of health and medical information. For each network, tweets sent between July 1, 2012, and September 12, 2012, were counted, along with the number of retweets and the details of their dissemination.

Mishori et al. find that "the AMA had the largest number of followers—and thus, information diffusion potential—and was trailed by the AAP, AAFP, and ACP, respectively." The researchers conclude that although having a large number of followers promotes dissemination, small networks can achieve high levels of dissemination if they have a community that actively retweets. They also counsel that "the content of the messages is of course of utmost importance. Even with strong channels for dissemination, tweets must be timely and engaging in order to provide the hook for followers to retweet and begin to reach the vast potential audience."

In "Let's Have a Tweetup: The Case for Using Twitter Professionally" (*Archives of Pathology & Laboratory Medicine*, May 16, 2016), Maren Y. Fuller and Timothy Craig Allen assert that "professional use of Twitter is ideal for physicians interested in both networking and education.... Live-tweeting (posting real-time reactions to events) at professional meetings is also a popular and highly successful use of Twitter. Physicians report patient privacy as the top concern preventing use of social media for professional reasons, and although generally social media use is safe, it is essential to understand how to protect patient confidentiality."

TECHNOLOGY MAY HELP EDUCATE MORE NURSES. One key factor limiting the supply of nurses is a shortage of nursing faculty, which restricts class size and ultimately the numbers of nurses graduating each year. According to the American Association of Colleges of Nursing, in "Nursing Faculty Shortage Fact Sheet" (March 6, 2015, http://www.aacn.nche.edu/media-relations/FacultyShortage FS.pdf), in 2014–15 approximately 68,938 qualified applicants were turned away from nursing schools because of a lack of faculty. One way to remedy this situation may be to offer some nursing courses online. In "Student Perceptions

of Group Experience in Online RN-to-BSN Research Course" (*Journal of Nursing Education and Practice*, vol. 60, no. 9, April 2016), Yeoun Soo Kim-Godwin and Michael Martinez report that in 2015 there 676 RN-to-BSN programs in the United States, and more than 400 of them offered programs that were at least partially online.

MORE STAFF, RATHER THAN TECHNOLOGY, IS KEY TO IMPROVING PATIENT SAFETY AND QUALITY OF CARE. Despite rapid advances in technology, many industry observers maintain that it is not sufficient to solve the looming nursing shortage projected by the U.S. Bureau of Labor Statistics (BLS) in "Employment Projections—2012–22" (December 19, 2013, http://www.bls.gov/news.release/ecopro.t08.htm). The BLS estimates that the United States will require about 1.1 million additional registered nurses by 2022.

In "Unmet Nursing Care Linked to Rehospitalization among Older Black AMI Patients: A Cross-Sectional Study of U.S. Hospitals" (*Medical Care*, vol. 54, no. 5, May 2016), J. Margo Brooks-Carthon et al. observe that "nurses may be unable to complete all aspects of necessary care due to a lack of time." They note that the likelihood of hospital readmission decreases when there are higher levels of nurse staffing. Inadequate staffing and higher nurse workloads are associated with medication errors, falls, infections, readmissions and decreased patient satisfaction.

According to Kathleen J. H. Sparbel et al., who presented "Interprofessional Education: Building Collaborations in Didactic and Clinical Nurse Practitioner Education for Improved Patient Outcomes" (April 5, 2014, https://nonpf.confex.com/nonpf/2014co/webprogram/Session3794 .html) at the National Organization of Nurse Practitioner Faculties' 40th annual meeting, collaboration of diverse and varied disciplines—nursing, physical therapy, social services, pharmacy, and others—is necessary to decrease health care errors, improve patient safety, and enhance patient outcomes. Collaboration is enhanced by education and communication and practiced in the classroom and clinical settings.

## Promise of Robotics

One technological advance that promises to reduce hospital operating costs and enable hospital workers to spend more time caring for patients is the use of robots. Once relegated to the realm of science fiction, automated machines such as self-guided robots to perform many routine hospital functions have been introduced in the 21st century.

In "Robots Get to Work" (*Modern Healthcare*, vol. 43, no. 21, May 2013), Rachel Landen and Jaimy Lee describe the growing use of robotics in hospitals: robots that deliver linens and lab results and dispense medication; that enable physicians to perform remote, real-time consultations and communicate with patients at a distance;

and that monitor critically ill patients in the intensive care unit. Robots in hospitals either replace tasks formerly performed by employees such as packaging drugs or delivering surgical tools or enhance those that use telemedicine to connect clinicians and patients. Many academic medical centers have invested in robotic technology, but the cost (often more than $1 million) has impeded adoption by smaller hospitals. Landen and Lee note that although robotic automation can improve safety by reducing errors and "help reduce costs, make operations more efficient and serve as a marketing tool to position hospitals as early adopters of cutting-edge technology," it is still not yet known whether this costly technology delivers on its promise.

Landen and Lee describe novel uses of robotic technology, including a system that "replicates a person in a distant location" by using a camera, microphones, and video display. The system enables the remote user to "travel" throughout a facility and may be used by family members to "virtually visit" hospital and nursing home patients. Also in development is a system that uses robotics, radio frequency identification technology, and computer vision to locate, sort, deliver, and sterilize surgical tools.

Some robots are involved in more than simply routine, menial tasks. Ada T. Ng and P. C. Tam assert in "Current Status of Robot-Assisted Surgery" (*Hong Kong Medical Journal*, vol. 20, no. 3, June 2014) that "the introduction of robot-assisted surgery, and specifically the da Vinci Surgical System, is one of the biggest breakthroughs in surgery since the introduction of anaesthesia, and represents the most significant advancement in minimally invasive surgery of this decade." The researchers observe that although robotics was first used in orthopedics, neurosurgery, and cardiac surgery, its use in urology, especially prostate surgery, led to its widespread adoption. They also note that studies show that robotic surgery patients fare as well as those who receive unassisted surgery. However, additional research is needed to fully determine the clinical value and cost-effectiveness of robots in surgical procedures.

Some surgical robots are miniature versions that can be inserted through a laparoscope, whereas others may be small enough to be inserted without incisions through the body's naturally occurring openings, such as the mouth, vagina, or rectum. Apollon Zygomalas et al. describe in "Miniature Surgical Robots in the Era of NOTES and LESS: Dream or Reality?" (*Surgical Innovations*, May 14, 2014) the potential application of inserting micro-robots through natural orifices to perform specific tasks in the abdomen, including minimally invasive surgery.

However, some researchers believe robotic surgery has been adopted without the necessary evaluation of its clinical utility and cost-effectiveness. For example, in "Localised Prostate Cancer: Clinical and Cost-Effectiveness of New and Emerging Technologies" (*Journal of Clinical Urology*, vol. 7, no. 4, July 2014), Yiannis Philippou et al. assert that implementation of techniques such as robotic prostatectomy may be driven by economic incentives rather than by rigorous clinical evidence. The researchers state, "Treatment decisions should be driven by cancer risk and patient preference rather than by financial incentives or availability of technology."

Other applications of robotic surgery have demonstrated cost-effectiveness. J. Kenneth Byrd et al. report in "Transoral Robotic Surgery and the Unknown Primary: A Cost-Effectiveness Analysis" (*Otorhinolaryngology—Head and Neck Surgery*, vol. 150, no. 6, March 11, 2014) the results of a study of the cost-effectiveness of transoral robotic surgery for the diagnosis and treatment of head and neck cancer. The researchers find that this type surgery is cost-effective when compared with traditional examination under anesthesia.

Similarly, an economic assessment of robot-assisted surgical training finds that it is cost-effective. In "Simulation-Based Robot-Assisted Surgical Training: A Health Economic Evaluation" (*International Journal of Surgery*, vol. 11, no. 9, November 2013), Shabnam Rehman et al. note that robotic simulation is a useful and efficient way to teach technical skills.

In "Seeing Is Comforting: Effects of Teleoperator Visibility in Robot-Mediated Health Care" (The 11th ACM/IEEE International Conference, 2016), Kory Kraft and William D. Smart note that robots can be used to provide medical care to patients in infectious disease outbreaks, allowing workers to be in dangerous infectious zones only as long as absolutely necessary. Kraft and Smart tested three hypotheses related to patients' comfort and trust of operators and robots in a sham treatment setting. The investigators find that patients trust the robot more when they can see the teleoperator (the person operating the robot).

## INNOVATION SUPPORTS QUALITY HEALTH CARE DELIVERY

The health care industry is awash in wave after wave of new technologies, models of service delivery, reimbursement formulae, legislative and regulatory changes, and increasingly specialized personnel ranks. Creating change in hospitals and in other health care organizations requires an understanding of diffusion (the process and channels by which new ideas are communicated, spread, and adopted throughout institutions and organizations). Diffusion of technology involves all the stakeholders in the health care system: policy makers and regulatory agencies establish safety and efficacy, government and private payers determine reimbursement, vendors of the technology are compared and one is selected, hospitals and health professionals adopt the technology and are trained in its use, and consumers are informed about the benefits of the new technology.

The decision to adopt new technology involves a five-stage process beginning with knowledge about the innovation. The second stage is persuasion, the period when decision makers form opinions based on experience and knowledge. Decision is the third phase, when commitment is made to a trial or pilot program, and is followed by implementation, the stage during which the new technology is put in place. The process concludes with the confirmation stage, the period during which the decision makers seek reinforcement for their decision to adopt and implement the new technology.

## Communicating Quality

Industry observers hope that as time goes on consumers armed with data about comparative costs and quality will be better able to make informed health care purchases—choosing providers that offer quality care and competitive fees. Gregory A. Freeman asserts in "How Real Is Healthcare Consumerism?" (*Health Leaders Media*, August 11, 2016) that the ACA has accelerated the trend of consumers viewing health care as a commodity, and actively assessing the quality and cost of health care services in part because higher deductibles prompt them to seek the most cost-effective care.

Freeman observes that consumers have access to more quality ratings and health care provider rankings than ever before. For example, they can find out how much experience a physician has performing a particular procedure or a hospital's complication, mortality, and readmission rates. Despite this wealth of information, health care consumers still have to make decisions based on which physicians and hospitals work together and are covered by their insurance plans.

Interestingly, consumers and physicians both believe that a physician's experience is important, especially for complex conditions and procedures. For routine medical care, consumers are more likely to value patient satisfaction scores. Increasingly, consumers expect transparency, and they are more likely to trust hospitals, health systems, health plans and providers that make their data available. It is also important the data are understandable. Freeman quotes a hospital administrator, "This team works to translate all the healthcare gobbledygook about healthcare costs, quality, and outcomes into the way two women at the hairdresser would talk about it, or two guys over a beer and a football game."

In "Evidence-Based Health Information from the Users' Perspective—A Qualitative Analysis" (*BMC Health Services Research*, vol. 13, October 10, 2013), Irene Hirschberg et al. look at how consumers understand and respond to evidence-based health care, which consists of unbiased and reliable information based on the current state of medical knowledge and encompasses a range of actions, including use of medical practice guidelines, shared decision making, comparative effectiveness research, and transparency of cost and quality information. Consumer attitudes, assumptions, and beliefs about evidence-based health care are of increasing importance because the ACA emphasizes its use.

Hirschberg et al. find that many consumers are unused to understanding and interpreting evidence-based health information. The researchers observe that there is a broad range of reactions to evidence-based health information and that health literacy (the ability to process and understand health information needed to make appropriate health decisions) varies widely among consumers. Because there are gaps in knowledge about the characteristics of quality care, considerable consumer education will likely be required before consumers can become fully engaged in evidence-based decision making. Hirschberg et al. recommend involving consumers in the development of evidence-based health information messages to identify effective ways to convey the information. The researchers conclude that "a clearer presentation of the basis of scientific research, e.g. on data acquisition and study quality, as well as the limits and possibilities, may help improve consumers' understanding."

MAKING THE GRADE: HEALTH CARE REPORT CARDS. The publication of medical outcomes report cards and disease- and procedure-specific morbidity rates (the degree of disability caused by disease) and mortality rates (the number of deaths caused by disease) has attracted widespread media attention and sparked controversy. Advocates for the public release of clinical outcomes and other performance measures contend that despite some essential limitations, these studies offer consumers, employers, and payers the means for comparing health care providers.

Some skeptics question the clinical credibility of scales such as surgical mortality, which they claim are incomplete indicators of quality. Others cite problems with data collection or speculate that data are readily manipulated by providers to enhance marketing opportunities sufficient to compromise the utility and validity of published reports. Long term, the effects of published comparative evaluations of health care providers on network establishment, contracting, and exclusion from existing health plans are uncertain and in many instances may be punitive (damaging). Hospitals and medical groups may be forced to compete for network inclusion on the basis of standardized performance measures.

The number of websites that rate physicians and hospitals continues to grow, with Angie's List and Vitals.com joining more established sites such as Health.org and Healthgrades.com and the CMS's Hospital Compare and Physician Compare websites, which compare hospital and physician costs, outcomes, and patient satisfaction data. The sites describe physicians' training, experience, certification, and any disciplinary actions taken against them, as well as patient ratings. They also encourage physicians to respond to patient comments. Some industry observers contend that the sites, especially those that use anonymous ratings, have the potential to further erode patient-physician relationships by prompting physicians to behave defensively.

Aleksandra Zgierska, David Rabago, and Michael M. Miller assess in "Impact of Patient Satisfaction Ratings on Physicians and Clinical Care" (*Patient Preference and Adherence*, no. 8, April 2014) physicians' perceptions about the impact of patient surveys on their job satisfaction and clinical practice. Not unexpectedly, the researchers find that if physicians view patient satisfaction survey data as potentially punitive, then the data are more likely to have an extremely unfavorable impact on physician satisfaction. Some physicians even reported that the use of patient satisfaction surveys prompted them to consider leaving medical practice. More concerning, however, is the finding that "the use of patient satisfaction surveys may promote, at least among some clinicians and under certain circumstances, a culture of care that can be partially driven by satisfaction score rather than evidence based; this can potentially compromise health-care outcomes as well as violate clinicians' sense of professional integrity, contributing, in turn, to job dissatisfaction." Physicians were concerned that aiming to score well on such surveys might promote inappropriate treatment, such as prescribing unnecessary antibiotics or ordering unnecessary tests.

Zgierska, Rabago, and Miller conclude that their findings are troubling, especially in view of "the widespread and progressive utilization of patient satisfaction ratings as an integral metric of quality-of-care assessment, and call for a more rigorous evaluation of the use of patient satisfaction surveys and the linkage of data from such surveys to other variables (such as physician compensation, job retention, or job promotion)."

Despite legitimate concern about the objectivity, reliability, validity, and potential for manipulating data, there is consensus that scrutiny and dissemination of quality data will escalate. Business groups and employers continue to request physician, hospital, and health plan data to design their health benefit programs. When choosing between health plans involving the same group of participating hospitals and physicians, employers request plan-specific information to guide their decisions. Companies and employer-driven health care coalitions seeking to assemble their own provider networks rely on physician- and hospital-specific data, such as the quality data provided by Healthgrades, during the selection process.

The most beneficial use of the data is to inspire providers to improve health care delivery systematically. When evidence of quality problems is identified, health plans and providers must be prepared to launch a variety of interventions to address and promptly resolve issues.

## CHAPTER 9
# PUBLIC OPINION ABOUT THE HEALTH CARE SYSTEM

As with many other social issues, public opinion about health care systems, providers, plans, coverage, and benefits varies in response to a variety of personal, political, and economic forces. Personal experience and the experience of friends, family, and community opinion leaders (trusted sources of information such as clergy, prominent physicians, and local business and civic leaders) exert powerful influences on public opinion. Health care marketing executives have known for years that the most potent advertising any hospital, medical group, or managed care plan can have is not a prominently placed billboard or prime-time television advertising campaign. It is positive word-of-mouth publicity.

The influence of the news media, advertising, and other attempts to sway health care consumers' attitudes and purchasing behaviors cannot be overlooked. A single story about a miraculous medical breakthrough or life-saving procedure can reflect favorably on an entire hospital or health care delivery system. Similarly, a lone mistake, an adverse reaction to a drug, or a misstep by a single health care practitioner can impugn (attack as lacking integrity) a hospital, managed care plan, or pharmaceutical company for months or even years, prompting intense media scrutiny of every action taken by the practitioner, facility, or organization.

Political events, the economy, and pending legislation can focus public attention on a particular health care concern, supplant one health-related issue with another, or eclipse health care from public view altogether. For example, during 2015 and 2016 there was media and public scrutiny of exorbitant drug prices for certain prescription medications.

In "High Drug Prices Prompt Demands for Transparency" (March 7, 2016, http://www.pewtrusts.org/en/research-and-analysis/blogs/stateline/2016/03/07/high-drug-prices-prompt-demands-for-transparency), Michael Ollove of the Pew Charitable Trusts reports that in 2016 at least

11 states introduced legislation that would require pharmaceutical companies to publicly disclose their spending for research, manufacturing, and marketing in order to justify the prices they charge. These calls for transparency arose in response to several startling price tags, including the $95,000 per year for new drugs to treat hepatitis C, and a move by Martin Shkreli (1983–), the chief executive officer of Turing Pharmaceuticals, to increase the price of a drug used by people with AIDS from $13.50 per tablet to $750 per tablet. Clare Krusing of America's Health Insurance Plans favors this legislation. As quoted by Ollove, she explains, "Health plans have to make rates public and they are scrutinized by consumers and regulators so it's clear where every dollar of premium is going. We don't have that with drug pricing."

Besides prescription drug prices, government funding of entitlement programs, and other public policy issues that are frequently divisive, some industry observers believe health care providers, policy makers, biomedical technology and research firms, and academic medical centers have fanned the flames of consumer dissatisfaction with the U.S. health care system by overselling the promise and the progress of modern medicine. They fear that the overzealous promotion of every scientific discovery with a potential clinical application has created unrealistic expectations of modern medicine. Health care consumers who believe there should be "one pill for every ill" or think all technology should be made widely available even before its efficacy (the ability of an intervention to produce the intended diagnostic or therapeutic effect in optimal circumstances) has been demonstrated are more likely to be dissatisfied with the current health care system.

## AMERICANS' OPINIONS ABOUT THE HEALTH CARE SYSTEM

Most Americans think the U.S. health care system is working. In *Ratings of U.S. Healthcare Quality No Better*

**FIGURE 9.1**

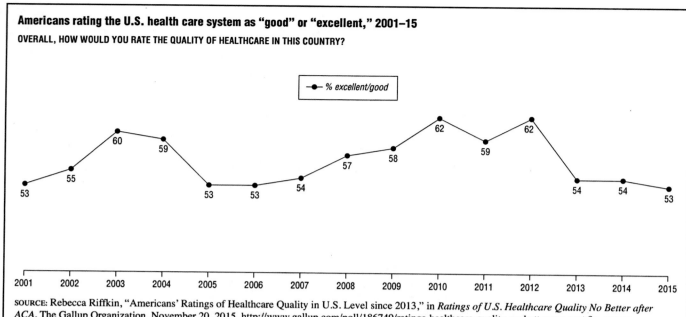

**Americans rating the U.S. health care system as "good" or "excellent," 2001–15**

OVERALL, HOW WOULD YOU RATE THE QUALITY OF HEALTHCARE IN THIS COUNTRY?

— % excellent/good

SOURCE: Rebecca Riffkin, "Americans' Ratings of Healthcare Quality in U.S. Level since 2013," in *Ratings of U.S. Healthcare Quality No Better after ACA*, The Gallup Organization, November 20, 2015, http://www.gallup.com/poll/186749/ratings-healthcare-quality-no-better-aca.aspx?g_source= CATEGORY_HEALTHCARE&g_medium=topic&g_campaign=tiles (accessed August 26, 2016). Copyright © 2016 Gallup, Inc. All rights reserved. The content is used with permission; however, Gallup retains all rights of republication.

*after ACA* (November 20, 2015, http://www.gallup.com/poll/186749/ratings-healthcare-quality-no-better-aca.aspx), Rebecca Rifkin of the Gallup Organization reports that Americans' ratings of health care quality did not change significantly from 2001 through 2015, with the exception of a slight increase in positive ratings from 2010 to 2012, following passage of the Patient Protection and Affordable Care Act (also known as the Affordable Care Act [ACA]). More than half (53%) of Americans in 2015 rated the quality of health care as "good" or "excellent." (See Figure 9.1.)

Americans are not as positive about health care coverage as they are about quality. Although the percentage of Americans rating health care coverage as "good" or "excellent" rose from 26% in 2008 to 38% in 2009, it has varied very little since then. In 2015 about one-third of Americans rated U.S. health care coverage as "good" or "excellent." (See Figure 9.2.)

Even fewer are satisfied with U.S. health care costs. Just one in five (21%) Americans in 2015 were satisfied with health care costs, down from 28% in 2001. Rifkin notes that in 2009 the percentage satisfied with health care costs rose to 26%, perhaps indicating optimism about the prospect of health care reform. This spike, however, was short-lived, and by 2011 the percentage of Americans satisfied with costs had dropped 6%. (See Figure 9.3.) In *Healthcare Costs Top U.S. Families' Financial Concerns* (April 27, 2016, http://www.gallup.com/poll/191126/healthcare-costs-top-families-financial-concerns.aspx), Zac Auter reports on an April 2016 Gallup poll in which 15% of Americans said health care

costs were their top financial concern and the most important financial problem they face.

Although many Americans are dispirited about health care costs, health care insecurity (being unable to afford needed medical care or medication during the 12 months preceding the interview) is at a record low. Jeffrey M. Jones and Nader Nekvasil report in *In U.S. Healthcare Insecurity at Record Low* (June 20, 2016, http://www.gallup.com/poll/192914/healthcare-insecurity-record-low.aspx) that the percentage of health care insecure adults fell nearly 4% from the fourth quarter of 2013 to 2016 as reported in interviews conducted by Gallup and Healthways Well-Being. (See Figure 9.4.) This decrease in health care insecurity corresponds with the decline in the percentage of uninsured Americans, which fell from 17.1% in the fourth quarter of 2013 to 11% in the first quarter of 2016.

## CHANGING VIEWS OF HEALTH CARE REFORM

Art Swift of the Gallup Organization observes in *Americans Slowly Embracing Affordable Care Act More* (May 13, 2016, http://www.gallup.com/poll/191486/americans-slowly-embracing-affordable-care-act.aspx) that in 2016, six years after the ACA was passed, Americans remain nearly evenly divided about the Act, with 47% of poll respondents saying they approve of it, and 49% saying they disapprove. Figure 9.5 shows that in 2016 approval of the ACA was at its highest since 2012. (See Figure 9.5.)

The percentage of Americans who say the ACA has helped them and their families has grown steadily. Swift reports that 22% of poll respondents in 2016 said the law

**FIGURE 9.2**

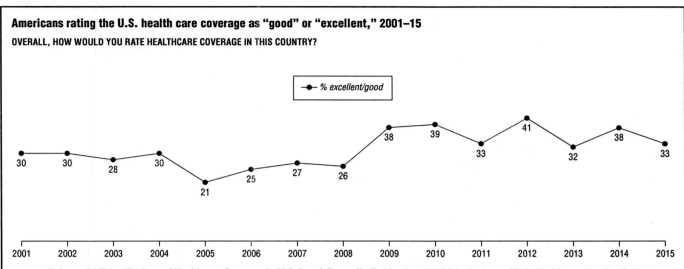

**Americans rating the U.S. health care coverage as "good" or "excellent," 2001–15**

OVERALL, HOW WOULD YOU RATE HEALTHCARE COVERAGE IN THIS COUNTRY?

SOURCE: Rebecca Riffkin, "Ratings of Healthcare Coverage in U.S. Level Generally Stable since 2009," in *Ratings of U.S. Healthcare Quality No Better after ACA*, The Gallup Organization, November 20, 2015, http://www.gallup.com/poll/186749/ratings-healthcare-quality-no-better-aca.aspx?g_source=CATEGORY_HEALTHCARE&g_medium=topic&g_campaign=tiles (accessed August 26, 2016). Copyright © 2016 Gallup, Inc. All rights reserved. The content is used with permission; however, Gallup retains all rights of republication.

**FIGURE 9.3**

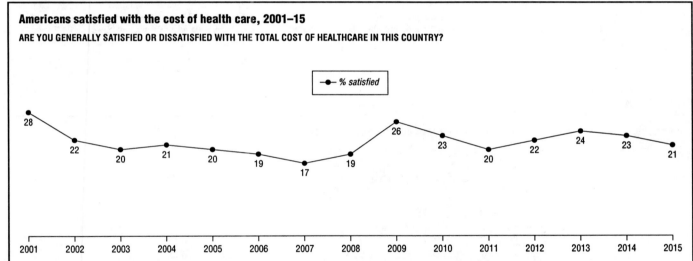

**Americans satisfied with the cost of health care, 2001–15**

ARE YOU GENERALLY SATISFIED OR DISSATISFIED WITH THE TOTAL COST OF HEALTHCARE IN THIS COUNTRY?

SOURCE: Rebecca Riffkin, "Fewer Than One in Four Satisfied with the Cost of Healthcare in the U.S.," in *Ratings of U.S. Healthcare Quality No Better after ACA*, The Gallup Organization, November 20, 2015, http://www.gallup.com/poll/186749/ratings-healthcare-quality-no-better-aca.aspx?g_source=CATEGORY_HEALTHCARE&g_medium=topic&g_campaign=tiles (accessed August 26, 2016). Copyright © 2016 Gallup, Inc. All rights reserved. The content is used with permission; however, Gallup retains all rights of republication.

had helped them or their families, and 26% said it had hurt them. (See Figure 9.6.) Although half (50%) continue to say the law has had no effect on them, the percentage claiming they have been unaffected has fallen 20% since 2012. Figure 9.7 shows fluctuations in Americans' views about the long-term impact of the ACA. Swift reports that in 2016, the same proportions predicted that the law would improve health care nationwide (40%) and worsen U.S. health care (41%); 16% expected it will make no difference.

### Political Affiliation Predicts ACA Support

Ashley Kirzinger, Elise Sugarman, and Mollyann Brodie of the Kaiser Family Foundation (KFF) concur with Gallup poll findings in "Kaiser Health Tracking Poll: June 2016" (June 30, 2016, http://kff.org/global-health-policy/poll-finding/kaiser-health-tracking-poll-june-2016/), reporting that 44% of Americans hold unfavorable opinions about the ACA and 42% favor the law. The KFF researchers note that although the attitudes of Republicans have remained relatively unchanged, support for the ACA

**FIGURE 9.4**

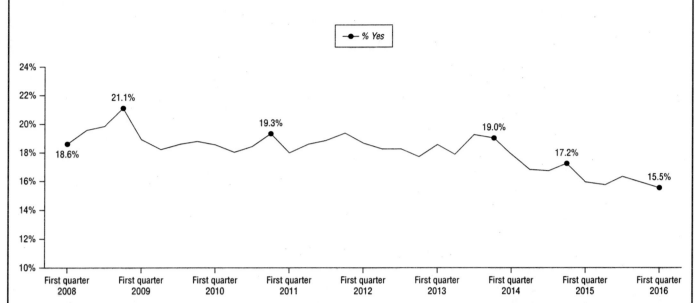

**Percentage of Americans unable to afford needed health care or medicine in preceding 12 months, 2008–16**

HAVE THERE BEEN TIMES IN THE PAST 12 MONTHS WHEN YOU DID NOT HAVE ENOUGH MONEY TO PAY FOR HEALTHCARE AND/OR MEDICINES THAT YOU OR YOUR FAMILY NEEDED?

SOURCE: Jeffrey M. Jones and Nader Nekvasil, "Have There Been Times in the Past 12 Months When You Did Not Have Enough Money to Pay for Healthcare and/or Medicines That You and Your Family Needed?" in *In U.S., Healthcare Insecurity at Record Low*, The Gallup Organization, June 20, 2016, http://www.gallup.com/poll/192914/healthcare-insecurity-record-low.aspx?g_source=CATEGORY_HEALTHCARE&g_medium=topic&g_campaign=tiles (accessed August 26, 2016). Copyright © 2016 Gallup, Inc. All rights reserved. The content is used with permission; however, Gallup retains all rights of republication.

**FIGURE 9.5**

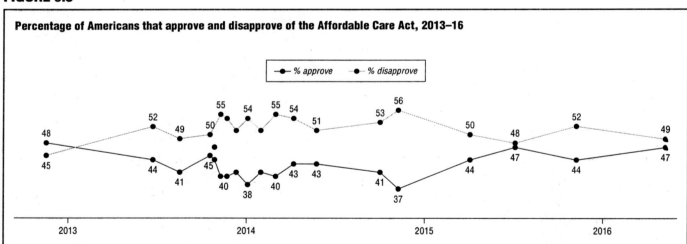

**Percentage of Americans that approve and disapprove of the Affordable Care Act, 2013–16**

SOURCE: Art Swift, "Do You Generally Approve or Disapprove of the 2010 Affordable Care Act, Signed into Law by President Obama That Restructured the U.S. Healthcare System?" in *Americans Slowly Embracing Affordable Care Act More*, The Gallup Organization, May 13, 2016, http://www.gallup.com/poll/191486/americans-slowly-embracing-affordable-care-act.aspx?g_source=CATEGORY_HEALTHCARE&g_medium=topic&g_campaign=tiles (accessed August 26, 2016). Copyright © 2016 Gallup, Inc. All rights reserved. The content is used with permission; however, Gallup retains all rights of republication.

has grown among Democrats. In April 2016 nearly two-thirds (63%) of Democrats held favorable opinions about the ACA, and by June 2016 the percentage of favorable opinions rose to 71%.

Kirzinger, Sugarman, and Brodie find that increasing numbers of Republicans favor repealing the ACA. In 2010 roughly half of Republicans (51%) said they would like to see Congress repeal the law. By 2016, two-thirds

**FIGURE 9.6**

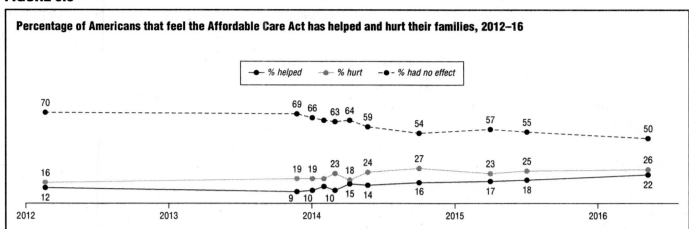

Percentage of Americans that feel the Affordable Care Act has helped and hurt their families, 2012–16

SOURCE: Art Swift, "The Affordable Care Act's Effect on Families," in *Americans Slowly Embracing Affordable Care Act More*, The Gallup Organization, May 13, 2016, http://www.gallup.com/poll/191486/americans-slowly-embracing-affordable-care-act.aspx?g_source=CATEGORY_HEALTHCARE&g_medium=topic&g_campaign=tiles (accessed August 26, 2016). Copyright © 2016 Gallup, Inc. All rights reserved. The content is used with permission; however, Gallup retains all rights of republication.

**FIGURE 9.7**

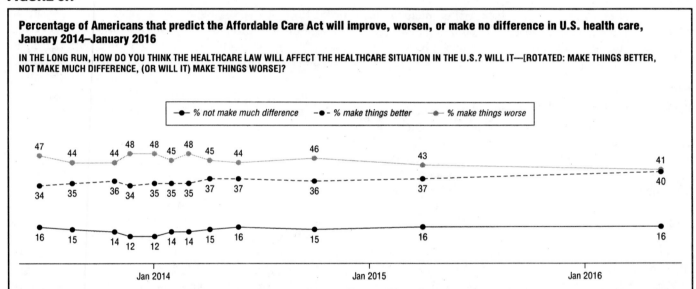

Percentage of Americans that predict the Affordable Care Act will improve, worsen, or make no difference in U.S. health care, January 2014–January 2016

IN THE LONG RUN, HOW DO YOU THINK THE HEALTHCARE LAW WILL AFFECT THE HEALTHCARE SITUATION IN THE U.S.? WILL IT—[ROTATED: MAKE THINGS BETTER, NOT MAKE MUCH DIFFERENCE, (OR WILL IT) MAKE THINGS WORSE]?

SOURCE: Art Swift, "Americans' Views of the Long-Term National Impact of the Healthcare Law," in *Americans Slowly Embracing Affordable Care Act More*, The Gallup Organization, May 13, 2016, http://www.gallup.com/poll/191486/americans-slowly-embracing-affordable-care-act.aspx?g_source=CATEGORY_HEALTHCARE&g_medium=topic&g_campaign=tiles (accessed August 26, 2016). Copyright © 2016 Gallup, Inc. All rights reserved. The content is used with permission; however, Gallup retains all rights of republication.

of Republicans (66%) wanted to repeal the entire law. By contrast, in 2016 about half (48%) of Democrats said they would like to see Congress expand the law.

## MARKETPLACE CUSTOMERS' SATISFACTION WITH COVERAGE

In February and March 2016, the KFF conducted a survey of people who purchase their own health insurance and found that those who purchased through the marketplace (also known as exchanges, services that help people shop for

and enroll in health insurance) were largely satisfied with their coverage. In "Survey Finds Most Enrollees Like Their Coverage, though Satisfaction with Premiums and Deductibles Has Declined since 2014" (May 20, 2016, http://kff.org/health-reform/press-release/survey-finds-most-marketplace-enrollees-like-their-coverage-though-satisfaction-with-premiums-and-deductibles-has-declined-since-2014/), the KFF finds that about two-thirds (68%) of marketplace customers say their coverage is "good" or "excellent." Roughly three-quarters were satisfied with their choice of hospitals (75%) and primary care physicians (74%), and more than half (59%) of respondents were satisfied with their specialists and health insurance premiums.

The KFF survey finds that marketplace enrollees were generally satisfied with their experience shopping for their plans. About three-quarters of consumers said it was easy to compare premiums (74%), cost-sharing (69%), and provider networks (61%), and to find plans that met their needs (59%). Fewer enrollees reported difficulties setting up accounts in 2016 than in 2014.

Satisfaction with plan premiums and deductibles declined since 2014, and as a result, people enrolled through the marketplace are divided about the value of their chosen plans. Nearly half (48%) rate their plans' value as "good" or "excellent," whereas 51% give their plans "fair" or "poor" ratings.

Although this survey examined the experiences and satisfaction of people who purchase their own health insurance, the KFF reports, "Similar trends are affecting people with employer coverage, a group that is generally better off economically. An annual survey of employer health benefits finds workers face rising deductibles, while other Kaiser polls reveal those with employer coverage are somewhat less satisfied than in the past."

## CONSUMER SATISFACTION WITH HEALTH CARE FACILITIES

Despite the problems that continue to plague hospitals, such as shortages of nurses and other key personnel, diminished reimbursement, shorter inpatient lengths of stay, sicker patients, and excessively long waiting times for patients in emergency and other hospital departments, consumer satisfaction with many aspects of hospital service has remained relatively high.

For example, in "Patient Survey—National" (2016, https://data.medicare.gov/Hospital-Compare/Patient-survey-HCAHPS-National/99ue-w85f), the Centers for Medicare and Medicaid Services (CMS) provides data from the Hospital Consumer Assessment of Healthcare Providers and Systems (HCAHPS). The HCAHPS assesses eight dimensions: Nurse Communication, Doctor Communication, Hospital Staff Responsiveness, Pain Management, Medicine Communication, Discharge Information, Hospital Cleanliness and Quietness, and Overall Hospital Rating, of which the last two dimensions each have two measures (cleanliness and quietness) for a total of 10 distinct measures. These data find high levels of patient satisfaction with communication with nurses (80% said nurses always communicated well) and physicians (82% said doctors always communicated well). They also indicate high levels of patient satisfaction with pain control (71%), room cleanliness (74%), and information given to them about what to do during their recovery at home (87%).

In "Patient Complaints in Healthcare Systems: A Systematic Review and Coding Taxonomy" (*BMJ Quality and Safety*, vol. 23, 2014), Tom W. Reader, Alex Gillespie, and Jane Roberts of the London School of Economics review 59 studies describing more than 88,000 patient complaints and analyze the issues underlying the complaints. The most common issues that triggered patient complaints concerned how they were treated (15.6%) and communication (13.7%).

Lise M. Verhoef et al. observe in "Social Media and Rating Sites as Tools to Understanding Quality of Care: A Scoping Review" (*Journal of Medical Internet Research*, vol. 16, no. 2, February 20, 2014) that increasing numbers of consumers share health care experiences online, at social networking sites, or at sites where they rate the quality of their health care providers. The researchers looked at research considering the relationship between the information shared on social media and the quality of care. They assert that social media could foster transparency in the quality of health care from the consumer's perspective. They also note that hospital ratings on online sites such as Yelp (a commercial rating website) correlate well with more traditional ratings, such as the HCAHPS scores at government websites. However, Verhoef et al. caution that people using social media are not representative of the population because, for example, older adults and ethnic minorities may be underrepresented. Nonetheless, they conclude that "social media, and especially rating sites, could be a fast and efficient way to gather information about quality of care" and "might make expensive, traditional measures of patient experiences unnecessary in the future."

In "Demographic Factors and Hospital Size Predict Patient Satisfaction Variance—Implications for Hospital Value-Based Purchasing" (*Journal of Hospital Medicine*, vol. 10, no. 8, August 2016), Daniel C. McFarland, Katherine Ornstein, and Randall F. Holcombe note that the ACA ties government payment to hospitals to the quality of health care delivered, which includes objective measures of hospital performance and the HCAHPS as a measure of patient satisfaction. The researchers observe that while low levels of patient satisfaction have, historically, been associated with poor quality of care, other factors influence patient satisfaction ratings. McFarland, Ornstein, and Holcombe find that education, ethnicity, primary language, and number of hospital beds predict patient satisfaction scores. They assert, "Hospitals that treat a disproportionate percentage of non-English speaking, non-White, non-educated patients in large facilities are not meeting patient satisfaction standards. This inequity is not ameliorated by the adjustments currently performed by CMS and has financial consequences for those hospitals that are not meeting national standards in patient satisfaction." These hospitals, many of which are academic medical centers in urban centers, may be unfairly penalized under the existing reimbursement model.

## Patient Satisfaction Survey Data

Industry observers attribute some of the improvement in inpatient hospital care satisfaction to the fact that the federal government posts the results of the HCAHPS survey on the Hospital Compare website (http://www.hospitalcompare.hhs.gov), which enables consumers to compare up to three hospitals. The website is a public-private venture led by organizations that represent the hospital industry, providers, and consumers, with coordination and oversight from government agencies.

Hospital Compare aims to help consumers choose the best hospital for selected surgical procedures by detailing how often hospitals give recommended treatments that are known to get the best results for patients with certain medical conditions. It includes mortality rates and hospital readmission rates for each hospital as well as other information such as whether the hospital uses electronic health records and the waiting times for selected emergency departments. It also provides information about a hospital's quality of care, as measured by patient satisfaction surveys.

In "Association between Medicare Summary Star Ratings for Patient Experience and Clinical Outcomes in U.S. Hospitals" (*Journal of Patient Experience*, vol. 3, no. 1, March 2016), Stephen Trzeciak et al. consider the association between the CMS patient experience (patient satisfaction) star ratings and clinical outcomes. Analyzing data from more than 3,000 hospitals, the researchers find statistically significant associations between the number of stars for patient experience and certain clinical outcomes such as the rates of hospital complications and readmission. Higher patient satisfaction ratings were associated with lower rates of complications. Trzeciak et al. offer several possible explanations for these findings including:

- Health care providers who work hard to provide excellent patient experience may be similarly hardworking and attentive to all elements of patient care.

- Patients, even those without medical training, may be able to identify quality care, and excellent patient experience scores may reflect patients' perceptions of the quality of care provided.

- The quality and effectiveness of patient care may depend on the quality of provider-patient communication, which is a major component of patient experience surveys.

- Excellent patient experience can inspire patient confidence in, and adherence to prescribed treatment in the hospital and upon discharge.

In "Finding Order in Chaos: A Review of Hospital Ratings" *American Journal of Medical Quality*, vol. 31, no. 2, March/April 2016), Wenke Hwang et al. express concern that because hospital rating systems vary in scope, methods, and transparency as well as how they present their results, consumers may find them confusing rather than helpful for clinical decision making.

For example, Max Masnick et al. looked at whether patients were able to accurately interpret hospital-acquired infection data on the Hospital Compare website in "Lack of Patient Understanding of Hospital-Acquired Infection Data Published on the Centers for Medicare and Medicaid Services Hospital Compare Website" (*Infection Control & Hospital Epidemiology*, vol. 37, no. 2, February 2016). Presented with simple data, consumers were able to accurately gauge hospital performance 72% of the time. Nonetheless, as the complexity of data increased, accurate interpretation of the data occurred just 35% of the time. Masnick et al. conclude, "this study found that the current tabular methods are inadequate for presenting hospital-acquired infection (HAI) data to the general public as used by CMS Hospital Compare and other hospital comparison websites. ... Further research is necessary to identify methods for improving the way these data are presented."

## ACCESSING ONLINE HEALTH INFORMATION

Although public trust in hospitals and personal physicians remains relatively high, and many people seek and receive health education from physicians, nurses, and other health professionals, a growing number of Americans are seeking health information online. Internet access and use have grown rapidly, and health information technology available via the Internet is considered an important way to encourage personal health management. The most frequently used health information technologies are searching for information online, mobile health technologies, and personal health records. The key issues that have not yet been completely resolved are confidentiality, privacy and security concerns, and ensuring that consumers have access to accurate and reliable health information

Brian Kennedy and Cary Funk of the Pew Research Center note in "Public Interest in Science and Health Linked to Gender, Age and Personality" (December 11, 2015, http://www.pewinternet.org/files/2015/12/PI_2015-12-11_Science-and-Health_FINAL.pdf) that 37% of adults who go online say "health and medicine" is among the topics they find most interesting. Women and older adults (ages 50–64) are more likely than men and younger adults (ages 18–29) to express interest in health and medical topics. About half of women who go online (52%) say health and medicine is one of the top three topics of interest to them, compared with less than one-quarter (22%) of men.

In "Sixth Annual 'Pulse of Online Search' Survey Finds Consumers Weighing Trust, Ease-of-Use When Seeking Health Guidance" (PRNewswire.com, March 10, 2016), Makovsky Integrated Communications reports the results of a survey of 1,035 American adults aged 18 years and older about health care information use. The survey finds that consumers are actively seeking health information online, especially about treatment options, to supplement their conversations with health care providers.

Alexandra Peterson of Makovsky Health explains, "Consumer actions to prepare for and then validate conversations with physicians via online search illustrate the balance between patient empowerment and desire for professional guidance. Combined with the fact that the majority of patients are likely to ask their doctor for a prescription by name, survey results show that patients are walking into the doctor's office armed with more information than ever, eager to have a more active role in the treatment discussion and decision."

Although survey respondents consider government websites trustworthy and credible, they prefer sites that are easy to use. For example, the popular and widely used websites WebMD and Wikipedia were deemed trustworthy by only 39% and 26% of survey respondents respectively, but were rated as easy to use by 56% and 55% respectively. Health system websites such as the Mayo Clinic were considered trustworthy by 53% and easy to use by 41%.

In "Teens, Health and Technology: A National Survey" (*Media and Communication*, vol. 4, no. 3, June 16, 2016), Ellen Wartella et al. examines the sources young people aged 13 to 18 years used to obtain health information online. About half of teens use search engines such as Google to direct them to health information (49%) or visit medical websites (31%). Some use social media platforms to find health information. For example, one in five (20%) found health information on YouTube, 9% on Facebook, and 4% on Twitter. Younger teens (ages 13–15) were more likely than older teens to obtain health information from YouTube (28% vs. 21%) and to have visited a website specifically for teens (12% vs. 7% of older teens). Hispanic teens were more likely than others to have used Yahoo to search for health information (23% vs. 10% of white and 8% of African American teens); and girls were more likely than boys to go to medical websites (42% vs. 32%).

## Finding Reliable Health Information Online

Reliable public sources of consumer and provider health information on the Internet include the National Institutes of Health, the Centers for Disease Control and Prevention, and MEDLINE, as well as websites that are produced by medical professional organizations such as the American Medical Association, the American Heart Association, and the American Cancer Society. Health

plans, hospitals, and other providers also post accurate, reliable information online. The "Pulse of Online Search" Survey respondents rated websites from advocacy and professional societies as the most trustworthy (59%) but visited them the least (16%). There is, however, also an abundance of unreliable information, from companies marketing "cures" for medical problems to health-related user-generated content that contains incorrect or misleading information. All but the savviest of consumers may have trouble distinguishing accurate, credible sources of health information from those that are not trustworthy.

Kenneth Lee et al. assert in "Interventions to Assist Health Consumers to Find Reliable Online Health Information: A Comprehensive Review" (*PLoS ONE*, vol. 9, no. 4, 2014) that "there appears to be a need for initiatives to assist health consumers to develop their capacity to find reliable health information on the Internet." They evaluate a variety of interventions, including face-to-face, online, and other types of instruction, designed to help consumers find reliable online information about chronic health conditions. Lee et al. note that various student-centered educational approaches help consumers learn to find credible information online and observe that a contributing factor to the positive results reported by workshop-based training may be due to engagement between the trainers and the participants.

## Using Social Media to Communicate Health Information

Social media sites have the potential to serve as an important platform for health education, information, and intervention. Examples of social media use in health care include provision of health education, disseminating prevention and wellness messages, and providing peer-support forums for groups of patients. In "Effectiveness of Social Media in Reducing Risk Factors for Noncommunicable Diseases: A Systematic Review and Meta-analysis of Randomized Controlled Trials" (*Nutrition Reviews*, vol. 74, no. 4, April 2016), George Mita, Cliona Ni Mhurchu, and Andrew Jull review 16 studies to find out if social media is an effective way to help reduce risk factors for disease such as obesity, physical inactivity, and low fruit and vegetable intake. The researchers find that interventions with social media components appear to be effective but caution that social media use has some risks, including varying degrees of accuracy of information and privacy issues. Social media enables people to share their opinions and feelings directly with one another, and there are opportunities for misuse of the personal information available on social media websites.

Heather J. Hether, Sheila T. Murphy, and Thomas W. Valente report in "It's Better to Give Than to Receive: The Role of Social Support, Trust, and Participation on

Health-Related Social Networking Sites" (*Journal of Health Communication: International Perspectives*, April 25, 2014) that Internet users are no longer just consumers of online health content; many produce online health content as well. Social networking sites and peer-to-peer support communities are increasingly used as venues for the exchange of health-related information and advice. The positive impacts of social support on health outcomes have been observed in both offline, face-to-face encounters and online interactions.

Hether, Murphy, and Valente surveyed more than 100 pregnant members of popular pregnancy-related sites. They find that time spent at the sites was less likely to predict health-related outcomes, such as having a positive attitude toward living healthfully while pregnant and following recommendations posted on the sites, than users' assessments of qualities such as trust in the sites. The perception of providing, rather than receiving, social support from the sites was associated with the most positive outcomes, including seeking more information from additional sources and following recommendations posted on the sites. The researchers explain, "This suggests that highly supportive community members may act as information bridges, seeking information from other sources and relaying it back to the online community."

### Physician Use of Digital Media and Communication

Physician use of e-mail, patient portals, and texting to communicate with patients is growing, but Alicia Ault reports in "Survey: Physicians behind the Curve on Digital Communications" (Medscape.com, November 4, 2015) that a survey of 626 physicians finds that they are "behind the curve when it comes to offering patients a wide variety of ways to communicate by smartphone or online." Just one in five physicians (21%) offered online appointment scheduling, and only 15% use e-mail to communicate with their patients.

Kaye Rolls et al. looked at how professionals use social networks in "How Health Care Professionals Use Social Media to Create Virtual Communities: An Integrative Review" (*Journal of Medical Internet Research*, vol. 18, no. 6, June 2016). Rolls et al. reviewed 72 studies describing social media use by health professionals and find that some health professionals use social media to "develop virtual communities that facilitate professional networking, knowledge sharing, and evidence-informed practice," and appear to prefer to use social media to communicate within their own clinical specialties.

### MARKETING PRESCRIPTION DRUGS TO CONSUMERS

Although health care consumers continue to receive much of their information from health professionals and the Internet, many also learn about health care services and products from reports in the news media and from advertising. Media advertising (the promotion of hospitals, health insurance, managed care plans, medical groups, and related health services and products) has been a mainstay of health care marketing efforts since the 1970s. During the early 1990s pharmaceutical companies made their first forays into advertising of prescription drugs directly to consumers. Before the 1990s pharmaceutical companies' promotion efforts had focused almost exclusively on physicians, the health professionals who prescribe their products.

Since the mid-1990s spending on prescription drugs has escalated. In 1997 the U.S. Food and Drug Administration (FDA) released guidelines governing direct-to-consumer (DTC) advertising and seemingly opened a floodgate of print, radio, and television advertisements promoting prescription drugs. Some industry observers maintain that this upsurge in DTC advertising has resulted in more, and possibly inappropriate, prescribing and higher costs.

### AMA POSITION ON DIRECT-TO-CONSUMER ADVERTISING

In the media release "AMA Calls for Ban on Direct to Consumer Advertising of Prescription Drugs and Medical Devices" (November 17, 2015, http://www.ama-assn.org/ama/pub/news/news/2015/2015-11-17-ban-consumer-prescription-drug-advertising.page), Patrice A. Harris, AMA board chair-elect, called for a complete ban on DTC advertising of prescription drugs and medical devices. The AMA asserts that direct-to-consumer advertising increases demand for more expensive treatments when less expensive alternatives provide the same clinical efficacy. Harris explains that the recommended ban is aimed at making prescription drugs more affordable, saying, "Today's vote in support of an advertising ban reflects concerns among physicians about the negative impact of commercially-driven promotions, and the role that marketing costs play in fueling escalating drug prices."

The pharmaceutical industry opposes the ban as reported in a follow-up story by Lindsey Tanner of the Associated Press (BigStory.ap.org, November 18, 2015). She quotes Tina Stow of the Pharmaceutical Research and Manufacturers of America, who asserts that DTC advertising delivers "scientifically accurate information to patients so that they are better informed about their health care and treatment options."

### Spending on Direct-to-Consumer Advertising

Pharmaceutical companies must be receiving significant returns on their DTC advertising investments to justify increasing budgets for consumer advertising, but it is difficult to measure the precise impact of consumer advertising on drug sales. In the press release "U.S. Measured Ad Expenditures Declined 3.9% in Q3 2015 to $36 Billion"

(December 16, 2015, http://www.kantarmedia.com/us/
newsroom/press-releases/us-measured-ad-expenditures-
declined-3-9-q3-2015-36-billion), Kantar Media reports
that pharmaceutical spending for advertising rose 18% in
the third quarter of 2015 to $1,343 million. Nearly three-
quarters (71%) of spending was for cable and broadcast
television advertising. After falling to a low of $3.9 billion
in 2012, pharmaceutical spending resurged to $5.6 billion
in 2015, a record high. An increase in new brand launches
was in part responsible for the uptick in spending.

## Advertising Prescription Drugs through Social Media

According to David Christopher DeAndrea and
Megan Ashley Vendemia, in "How Affiliation Disclosure
and Control over User-Generated Comments Affects
Consumer Health Knowledge and Behavior: A Randomized Controlled Experiment of Pharmaceutical Direct-to-
Consumer Advertising on Social Media" (*Journal of Medical
Internet Research*, vol. 18, no. 7, July 2016), pharmaceutical
companies are increasingly marketing through interactive
websites and social media. Some industry observers are concerned that pharmaceutical companies may market their
drugs on social media indirectly through seemingly neutral
third-party sources such as health organizations that are, in
fact, controlled by the pharmaceutical companies. DeAndrea
and Vendemia examined how disclosing an affiliation with a
pharmaceutical company affected how people respond to
drug information provided by health organizations and online
commenters, and how knowledge that health organizations
control the display of user-generated comments affects consumers' behavior.

Not surprisingly, DeAndrea and Vendemia find that
disclosing a pharmaceutical affiliation diminished trust in
the organization that posted information about a drug as
well as trust in comments posted by other site users. It also
decreased the likelihood that site visitors would recommend the drug to family or friends and decreased the likelihood that they would spread the drug message further via
their online social networks. DeAndrea and Vendemia note
that in the past, some pharmaceutical companies have tried
to minimize or blur their affiliations with social media sites
and assert that some sites make it easy to mask the identity
of an information source and difficult to determine whether
companies are removing user comments. The researchers
indicate that their findings underscore "the need for future
FDA guidelines to mandate that pharmaceutical companies
clearly disclose connections within messages posted to any
website or social media platform that they directly fund,
control, or support in some manner."

## FDA Scrutiny of Direct-to-Consumer Advertising

The FDA Office of Prescription Drug Promotion
(OPDP; http://www.fda.gov/AboutFDA/CentersOffices/
OfficeofMedicalProductsandTobacco/CDER/ucm090276
.htm#research) scrutinizes issues related to DTC and
professional promotional prescription drug materials.
Among other research, the OPDP conducts surveys to
gauge consumer understanding of DTC advertising. For
example, in 2015 the OPDP completed a research study
to find out whether consumers understood composite
scores, which are scores based on a combination of multiple
aspects of drug efficacy measurement. For example, nasal
congestion is measured by measuring individual symptoms
such as runny nose, itchiness, and sneezing and then com-
puting an overall score. If, for example, an allergy medicine
has a significantly better overall score than the comparison
group, then it may be approved by the FDA and marketed
for nasal congestion. The drug may be better overall than
other drugs but may not be significantly better on a particular symptom, like itchiness. Health professionals understand the difference between composite scores and individual measures but most consumers do not.

In "Communicating Efficacy Information Based on
Composite Scores in Direct-to-Consumer Prescription
Drug Advertising" (*Patient Education & Counseling*, vol.
99, no. 4, April 2016), Pamela A. Williams et al. describe
the results of the study, which showed 1,967 allergy suffer-
ers mock print advertisements that varied in terms of the
information offered. Some of the print ads defined composite scores and others did not. The researchers find that ads
that included a definition of a composite score improved
the consumers' understanding of composite scores and led
to lower confidence in the drug's benefits and lower perception of risks associated with the drug.

Another study completed in 2015 sought to determine whether consumers think that DTC advertisements
offer enough information about the risks and benefits of
prescription drugs. The OPDP analyzed data from 3,959
survey respondents collected by the National Cancer
Institute and find that more than half of consumers surveyed (52%) said that DTC advertisements do not contain enough information about drug risks; 46% of survey
respondents said that DTC ads do not provide enough
information about drug benefits.

As of 2016 DTC pharmaceutical advertising was the
subject of numerous research studies. One such study was
considering the effect of promotional offers such as free
trial offers and coupons on consumer perception of the risks
and benefits of the drug or product. Another project was
examining the use of animation in DTC prescription drug
advertising and whether animation improved consumer
comprehension and recall of drug risks and benefits. Other
researchers were assessing the ability of consumers and
health professionals to identify deceptive drug advertising
and the influence of deceptive advertising on their attitudes
toward and impressions of the advertised drug. The results
of these and other research endeavors were expected to
improve understanding of the economic and medical
impacts of DTC advertising on health consumers.

# IMPORTANT NAMES
## AND ADDRESSES

**Accreditation Association for Ambulatory Health Care**
5250 Old Orchard Rd., Ste. 200
Skokie, IL 60077
(847) 853-6060
FAX: (847) 853-9028
E-mail: info@aaahc.org
URL: http://www.aaahc.org/

**Administration for Community Living**
330 C St. SW
Washington, DC 20201
(202) 401-4634
E-mail: aclinfo@acl.hhs.gov
URL: http://www.acl.gov/

**Agency for Healthcare Research and Quality**
**Office of Communications and Knowledge Transfer**
5600 Fishers Ln., Seventh Floor
Rockville, MD 20857
(301) 427-1364
URL: http://www.ahrq.gov/

**American Academy of Child and Adolescent Psychiatry**
3615 Wisconsin Ave. NW
Washington, DC 20016-3007
(202) 966-7300
FAX: (202) 464-0131
URL: http://www.aacap.org/

**American Academy of Family Physicians**
11400 Tomahawk Creek Pkwy.
Leawood, KS 66211-2680
(913) 906-6000
1-800-274-2237
FAX: (913) 906-6075
URL: http://www.aafp.org/

**American Academy of Physician Assistants**
2318 Mill Rd., Ste. 1300
Alexandria, VA 22314
(703) 836-2272

E-mail: aapa@aapa.org
URL: http://www.aapa.org/

**American Association for Geriatric Psychiatry**
6728 Old McLean Village Dr.
McLean, VA 22101
(703) 556-9222
FAX: (703) 556-8729
URL: http://www.aagponline.org/

**American Association for Marriage and Family Therapy**
112 S. Alfred St.
Alexandria, VA 22314-3061
(703) 838-9808
FAX: (703) 838-9805
URL: http://www.aamft.org/

**American Association of Pastoral Counselors**
PO Box 3030
Oakton, VA 22124
(703) 385-6967
FAX: (703) 352-7725
E-mail: info@aapc.org
URL: http://www.aapc.org/

**American Cancer Society**
250 Williams St. NW
Atlanta, GA 30303
1-800-227-2345
URL: http://www.cancer.org/

**American Chiropractic Association**
1701 Clarendon Blvd., Ste. 200
Arlington, VA 22209
(703) 276-8800
FAX: (703) 243-2593
E-mail: memberinfo@acatoday.org
URL: http://www.acatoday.org/

**American College of Nurse Practitioners**
225 Reinekers Ln., Ste. 525
Alexandria, VA 22314

(703) 740-2529
FAX: (703) 740-2533
URL: https://acnp.enpnetwork.com/

**American Counseling Association**
6101 Stevenson Ave.
Alexandria, VA 22304
(703) 823-9800
1-800-347-6647
FAX: (703) 823-0252
URL: http://www.counseling.org/

**American Dental Association**
211 E. Chicago Ave.
Chicago, IL 60611-2678
(312) 440-2500
URL: http://www.ada.org/

**American Diabetes Association**
2451 Crystal Dr., Ste. 900
Alexandria, VA 22202
1-800-342-2383
URL: http://www.diabetes.org/

**American Geriatrics Society**
40 Fulton St., 18th Floor
New York, NY 10038
(212) 308-1414
FAX: (212) 832-8646
E-mail: info.amger@americangeriatrics.org
URL: http://www.americangeriatrics.org/

**American Heart Association**
7272 Greenville Ave.
Dallas, TX 75231
(214) 570-5978
1-800-242-8721
URL: http://www.americanheart.org/

**American Hospital Association**
155 N. Wacker Dr.
Chicago, IL 60606
(312) 422-3000
URL: http://www.aha.org/

**American Medical Association**
AMA Plaza
330 N. Wabash Ave., Ste. 39300
Chicago, IL 60611-5885
1-800-262-3211
URL: http://www.ama-assn.org/

**American Osteopathic Association**
142 E. Ontario St.
Chicago, IL 60611-2864
(312) 202-8000
1-800-621-1773
FAX: (312) 202-8200
URL: http://www.osteopathic.org/

**American Pharmacists Association**
2215 Constitution Ave. NW
Washington, DC 20037
(202) 628-4410
1-800-237-2742
FAX: (202) 783-2351
URL: http://www.pharmacist.com/

**American Physical Therapy Association**
1111 N. Fairfax St.
Alexandria, VA 22314-1488
(703) 684-2782
1-800-999-2782
FAX: (703) 684-7343
URL: http://www.apta.org/

**American Psychiatric Association**
1000 Wilson Blvd., Ste. 1825
Arlington, VA 22209-3901
(703) 907-7300
1-888-357-7924
E-mail: apa@psych.org
URL: http://www.psych.org/

**American Psychiatric Nurses Association**
3141 Fairview Park Dr., Ste. 625
Falls Church, VA 22042
(571) 533-1919
1-855-863-2762
FAX: 1-855-883-2762
URL: http://www.apna.org/

**American Psychological Association**
750 First St. NE
Washington, DC 20002-4242
(202) 336-5500
1-800-374-2721
URL: http://www.apa.org/

**America's Essential Hospitals**
401 Ninth St. NW, Ste. 900
Washington, DC 20004-2145
(202) 585-0100
FAX: (202) 585-0101
E-mail: info@essentialhospitals.org
URL: http://essentialhospitals.org/

**Association of American Medical Colleges**
655 K St. NW, Ste. 100
Washington, DC 20001-2399
(202) 828-0400
URL: http://www.aamc.org/

**Association for Psychological Science**
1800 Massachusetts Ave. NW, Ste. 402
Washington, DC 20036-1218
(202) 293-9300
FAX: (202) 293-9350
URL: http://www.psychologicalscience.org/

**Center for Mental Health Services**
**Substance Abuse and Mental Health**
**Services Administration**
5600 Fishers Ln.
Rockville, MD 20857
(240) 276-1310
FAX: (301) 480-8491
URL: http://www.samhsa.gov/about-us/
who-we-are/offices-centers/cmhs

**Centers for Disease Control and**
**Prevention**
1600 Clifton Rd.
Atlanta, GA 30329-4027
1-800-232-4636
URL: http://www.cdc.gov/

**Centers for Medicare and Medicaid**
**Services**
7500 Security Blvd.
Baltimore, MD 21244
(410) 786-3000
1-877-267-2323
URL: http://www.cms.gov/

**Children's Defense Fund**
25 E St. NW
Washington, DC 20001
1-800-233-1200
E-mail: cdfinfo@childrensdefense.org
URL: http://www.childrensdefense.org/

**Families USA**
1225 New York Ave. NW, Ste. 800
Washington, DC 20005
(202) 628-3030
FAX: (202) 347-2417
E-mail: info@familiesusa.org
URL: http://www.familiesusa.org/

**Health Coalition on Liability and Access**
PO Box 78096
Washington, DC 20013-8096
E-mail: info@protectpatientsnow.org
URL: http://www.hcla.org/

**Health Resources and Services**
**Administration**
**U.S. Department of Health and Human**
**Services**
5600 Fishers Ln.
Rockville, MD 20857
1-800-221-9393
URL: http://www.hrsa.gov/index.html

**Hospice Association of America**
228 Seventh St. SE
Washington, DC 20003
(202) 546-4759
FAX: (202) 547-9559
URL: http://www.nahc.org/HAA/

**The Joint Commission**
One Renaissance Blvd.
Oakbrook Terrace, IL 60181
(630) 792-5800
FAX: (630) 792-5005
URL: http://www.jointcommission.org/

**March of Dimes Birth Defects Foundation**
1275 Mamaroneck Ave.
White Plains, NY 10605
(914) 997-4488
URL: http://www.marchofdimes.com/

**Mathematica Policy Research**
1100 First St. NE, 12th Floor
Washington,, DC 20002-4221
(202) 484-9220
FAX: (202) 863-1763
URL: https://www.mathematica-mpr.com/

**Medical Group Management Association**
104 Inverness Terrace East
Englewood, CO 80112-5306
(303) 799-1111
1-877-275-6462
E-mail: support@mgma.org
URL: http://www.mgma.com/

**Mental Health America**
500 Montgomery St., Ste. 820
Alexandria, VA 22314
(703) 684-7722
1-800-969-6642
FAX: (703) 684-5968
URL: http://www.mentalhealthamerica.net/

**National Association of Community**
**Health Centers**
7501 Wisconsin Ave., Ste. 1100W
Bethesda, MD 20814
(301) 347-0400
URL: http://www.nachc.com/

**National Association of School**
**Psychologists**
4340 East West Hwy., Ste. 402
Bethesda, MD 20814
(301) 657-0270
1-866-331-6277
FAX: (301) 657-0275
URL: http://www.nasponline.org/

**National Association of Social**
**Workers**
750 First St. NE, Ste. 800
Washington, DC 20002
(202) 408-8600
URL: http://www.socialworkers.org/

**National Center for Health Statistics**
**U.S. Department of Health and Human**
**Services**
3311 Toledo Rd.
Hyattsville, MD 20782-2064
1-800-232-4636
URL: http://www.cdc.gov/nchs/

**National Committee for Quality Assurance**
1100 13th St. NW, Ste. 1000
Washington, DC 20005
(202) 955-3500
1-888-275-7585
FAX: (202) 955-3599
URL: http://www.ncqa.org/

**National Institute of Mental Health**
Science Writing, Press, and Dissemination
Branch
6001 Executive Blvd.
Rm. 6200, MSC 9663
Bethesda, MD 20892-9663
1-866-615-6464

FAX: (301) 443-4279
E-mail: nimhinfo@nih.gov
URL: http://www.nimh.nih.gov/

**National Institutes of Health**
9000 Rockville Pike
Bethesda, MD 20892
(301) 496-4000
E-mail: NIHinfo@od.nih.gov
URL: https://www.nih.gov/

**United Network for Organ Sharing**
700 N. Fourth St.
Richmond, VA 23219
(804) 782-4800
1-888-894-6361

FAX: (804) 782-4817
URL: http://www.unos.org/

**U.S. Census Bureau**
4600 Silver Hill Rd.
Washington, DC 20233
(301) 763-4636
1-800-923-8282
URL: http://www.census.gov/en.html

**World Health Organization**
Avenue Appia 20
Geneva 27, 1211Switzerland
(011-41-22) 791-2111
FAX: (011-41-22) 791-3111
URL: http://www.who.int/

# RESOURCES

Agencies of the U.S. Department of Health and Human Services collect, analyze, and publish a wide variety of health statistics that describe and measure the operation and effectiveness of the U.S. health care system. The Centers for Disease Control and Prevention tracks nationwide health trends and reports its findings in several periodicals, especially its *Advance Data* series, the National Ambulatory Medical Care Survey, the *HIV Surveillance Reports*, and the *Morbidity and Mortality Weekly Reports*. The National Center for Health Statistics provides a complete statistical overview of the nation's health in its annual *Health, United States*.

The National Institutes of Health provides definitions, epidemiological data, and research findings about a comprehensive range of medical and public health subjects. The Centers for Medicare and Medicaid Services monitors the nation's health spending. The agency's quarterly *Health Care Financing Review* and annual *Data Compendium* provide complete information on health care spending, particularly on allocations for Medicare and Medicaid. The Administration for Community Living provides information about the health, welfare, and services available for older Americans.

The Agency for Healthcare Research and Quality researches and documents access to health care, quality of care, and efforts to control health care costs. It also examines the safety of health care services and ways to prevent medical errors. The Joint Commission and the National Committee for Quality Assurance are accrediting organizations that focus attention on institutional health care providers, including the managed care industry.

The U.S. Census Bureau, in its *Current Population Reports* series, details the status of insurance among selected U.S. households.

Medical, public health, and nursing journals offer a wealth of health care system information and research findings. The studies cited in this edition are drawn from a range of professional publications, including *American Academy of Emergency Medicine*, *American Journal of Medical Quality*, *American Journal of Nursing*, *American Journal of Respiratory and Critical Care Medicine*, *Annals of Emergency Medicine*, *BMC Health Services Research*, *BMJ*, *Health Affairs*, *Health Economics, Policy and Law*, *Health Policy*, *Health Services Research*, *International Journal of Health Economics and Management*, *Journal of the American Medical Association*, *Journal of Epidemiology and Community Health*, *Journal of Hospital Medicine*, *Journal of Medical Internet Research*, *Journal of Nursing Education and Practice*, *Medical Care*, *Medicinal Chemistry*, *Medicine, Health Care and Philosophy*, *Pediatrics*, *PLoS ONE*, and *Policy, Politics, and Nursing Practice*.

Gale, Cengage Learning thanks the Gallup Organization for the use of its public opinion research about health care costs, quality, and concerns. It would also like to thank the many professional associations, voluntary medical organizations, and foundations dedicated to research, education, and advocacy about the efforts to reform and improve the health care system that were included in this edition.

# INDEX

CPSIA information can be obtained
at www.ICGtesting.com
Printed in the USA
FFOW04n1655100517
35499FF